NEEDLEWORK & SEWING
TECHNIQUES

NEEDLEWORK & SEWING
TECHNIQUES

JG PRESS

A QUANTUM BOOK

Published in the USA 1997 by JG Press.
Distributed by World Publications Inc.

The JG Press imprint is a trademark of
JG Press Inc.
455 Somerset Avenue
North Dighton, MA 02764

This edition produced for sale in the USA, its
territories and dependencies only.

ISBN 1-57215-229-X

QUMNOT

This book was produced by
Quantum Books Ltd
6 Blundell Street
London N7 9BH

Design Director: Peter Bridgewater
Art Director: Ian Hunt
Designers: Stuart Walden, Nicki Simmonds
Editors: Amanda O'Neill, Belinda Giles
Illustrator: Lorraine Harrison
Needlework for jacket and chapter openers:
Nicki Simmonds

Typeset in Great Britain by
Central Southern Typesetters, Eastbourne
Manufactured in Hong Kong by
Regent Publishing Services Limited
Printed in China by
Leefung-Asco Printers Limited

This book contains material used in previous
publications.

CONTENTS

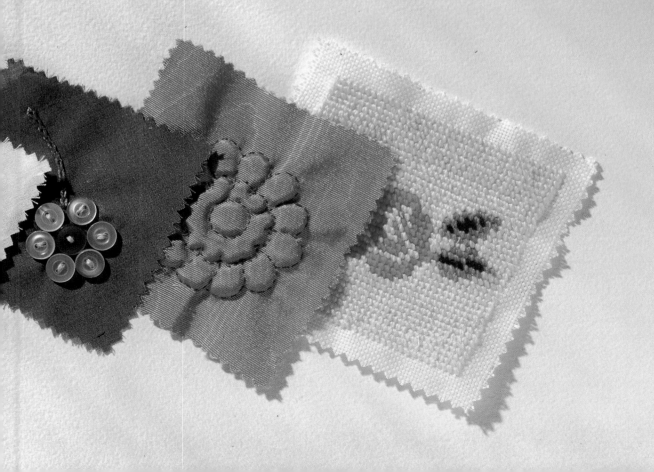

INTRODUCTION

Sewing is an art almost as old as civilization. which has developed through thousands of years of civilization to encompass many techniques.

With a wealth of modern fabrics and threads available, with developments in equipment from the sewing machine to modern lighting, sewing today can take advantage of the centuries of expertize built up by our ancestors, with greater ease and convenience than ever before.

Today there is no longer any need to make clothes or soft furnishings, both of which are mass-produced by industrial methods and readily available to buy in the shops. Yet still the art of sewing these items at home persists, sometimes because it is cheaper than buying them ready-made, sometimes to achieve a personal touch – an exact style or color – and often purely because of the pleasure of creating a well-made item with one's own hands. In addition, purely ornamental sewing, which has a history almost as long as that of functional sewing, continues to be a popular creative art.

This book aims to provide the reader with the necessary information to undertake the basic forms of sewing in use today, both practical and decorative – and to undertake them not merely adequately but to a satisfying level of excellence.

We begin by looking at the practical techniques used in making garments and soft furnishing, such as different methods of sewing a seam and how to finish raw edges. The basic equipment necessary for achieving good results when making clothes or soft furnishings is described, in terms of both machine sewing and hand sewing. Many different types of domestic sewing machine are now available, and it is important to choose the one most suitable for your own needs: this chapter looks at the different types and at the various controls and attachments. We go on to explain the constructional elements of sewing, from the most basic stitching to methods for achieving a professional finish.

From the practical we move on to the decorative techniques – first embroidery, which is covered in three chapters describing every major embroidery technique from blackwork to whitework. The first of these chapters covers the materials, equipment and techniques required for embroidery. The structure of the different fabrics used in embroidery is clearly defined and the potential of each delineated. Many basic stitches are illustrated and we consider how they may be used creatively to express movement, direction, tonal values and line, and how they can create varying textures.

This chapter aims to equip you to follow traditional techniques but also to create your own designs in a contemporary way. Embroidery covers a far wider field than the simple stitching of patterns on to a fabric. Delicate lacy effects can be achieved with cutwork, in which decorative holes are cut in the fabric, or with drawn thread and pulled thread work, in which separate threads of the fabric are distorted or removed. The surface of the fabric can be manipulated by pleating, gathering, folding and smocking to create shadows and a three-dimensional effect.

You can work with the subtleties of monochrome as in blackwork and whitework, or achieve bold effects with all the colors of the spectrum. We consider sources of inspiration for creating your

RIGHT *Making garments at home gives the opportunity for adding a personal touch. These dungarees are enlivened with a patch pocket and knee patches embroidered with simple floral motifs and sewn on to the garment with a decorative edging stitch.*

FAR RIGHT *Embroidery need not be restricted to traditional fabrics; stitching over the details of a printed fabric can be very effective, as shown here. Deeper tones of the printed shades have been used to build up a stronger color effect. Some areas have been left unworked so that the embroidered areas are more prominent and the colors highlighted.*

ABOVE *This bedspread, worked in about 1910, shows a delicate use of crewel embroidery, with much of the background left plain. The center is stitched with wild flowers in subtle colors, and the border is a thin, geometric pattern.*

LEFT *An Italian 16th century border, sewn in colored silks using split stitch and satin stitch on linen, with an edging of silver gilt bobbin lace.*

own designs. This chapter covers crewel work, blackwork, whitework (including cutwork, pulled thread and drawn thread work), smocking, metal thread work and also machine embroidery.

Two counted-thread techniques, cross stitch and sewing on canvas – called variously canvaswork (as here), needlepoint, or needlepoint 'tapestry' (a misnomer since technically a true tapestry is woven) – each have a separate chapter to give full coverage to a long tradition and to a modern popularity which has produced many developments. Under the heading of cross stitch we look at the traditions of sewing samplers, which have recently become popular again. These two chapters also give clear instructions on how to make up or frame the completed work in both traditional and contemporary ways.

Although embroidery is considered essentially a decorative art, like most forms of needlework its origins are functional, the earliest forms probably having arisen as surface stitching to reinforce or repair fabrics. Today this craft still retains its practical element, and the use of embroidery is not restricted to decoration. The embroidery of garments and soft furnishings benefits from reflecting the functional element, with the ornamental stitching used to underline the style or to reinforce the construction. Canvaswork is a hardwearing form of embroidery which is particularly useful for making beautiful and practical soft furnishings such as chair seat covers. The three chapters dealing with embroidery

bear in mind this aspect and help guide you to consider the practical uses of embroidery in your home.

Subsequent chapters cover quilting, patchwork and appliqué, three techniques with a long and often interwoven history.

Quilting, the art of attaching layers of cloth together, arose as a means of providing warmth or protection but developed along ornamental lines. Wadded quilting, where a layer of padding is sandwiched between two thinner fabrics, is the most familiar technique today and remains a practical and attractive method of providing warmth in clothing or bedcovers, but there are other more purely decorative methods. Padded quilting is such a technique and is mainly used for fun nowadays to create such items as three-dimensional pictures; corded quilting is another method used for effect rather than for warmth and providing results which can be delicate or dramatic; and shadow quilting, the daintiest of all, creates soft and subtle colors and textures. This chapter explains each of these techniques and demonstrates their use in traditional and contemporary designs.

Patchwork, the art of making a piece of cloth out of small pieces of various fabrics sewn together, has also developed greatly since it was first used as an economical way of recycling fragments of fabric from worn pieces, and today has developed along a variety of fascinating and beautiful lines. The technique in essence relies on the use of colored fabrics to create patterned surfaces. The varieties of patchwork demonstrated in this chapter include English and American pieced work, shell, Suffolk puffs, crazy work, log cabin, strip, folded star, Mayflower and pleated work. One of the many joys of patchwork is the rich tradition that has built up around the craft, with the evocative names given to the patterns (Road to California, Steps to the Altar, or Drunkard's Path) conjuring up a lost way of life; yet it remains a vital and still developing technique.

Appliqué, a two-dimensional form of needlework achieved by applying small pieces of material onto a background fabric, has been much used to ornament heraldic and ecclesiastical devices and today offers exciting opportunities to the embroiderer. From the familiar standard appliqué, or onlay, have developed a range of techniques of varying elaboration including inlay, which uses several layers of colored fabrics. Appliqué can be padded to give a raised effect, seen at its most extreme in the craft of stumpwork, which has the appearance of a low-relief carving.

Each of these crafts has a long and fascinating history, and each chapter gives a brief description of the historical development of the techniques covered, as well as basic information on equipment, stitches and fabrics. Contemporary developments in design are depicted alongside traditional approaches, providing useful reference for both the beginner and the person who already has considerable expertise. The creative pleasure in making something is increased by an awareness that one is perpetuating and indeed developing a tradition, whether you think of some seventeenth century child poring with intense concentration over her sampler, or a party of nineteenth-century housewives gathered around a quilting frame. It is intended that this book should be a useful source of reference and inspiration to provide the stimulus to develop your own skills and creative approaches.

FAR LEFT *Lettering can be used to add interest to an embroidery design. This panel reflects a memory of a visit to California. The cloudless skies and bright sunshine are suggested by the use of color, and the broken lines of the stitching suggest the shimmering heat. Different types of letter are used for the names, with variation of scale and in the use of capitals and lower case. To give uniformity to the design only straight stitches are used but in varying sizes and directions.*

BELOW *A 19th century Pennsylvanian sampler of motifs. Animals, plants, figures and household items are worked in cross stitch.*

RIGHT *Darning stitch evolved from a method of repairing worn fabric to this elaborative form of decoration, known as pattern darning. The straight stitch is used densely around the front opening of this Spanish shirt to build up interesting patterns, some almost solid and others open, resembling black lace.*

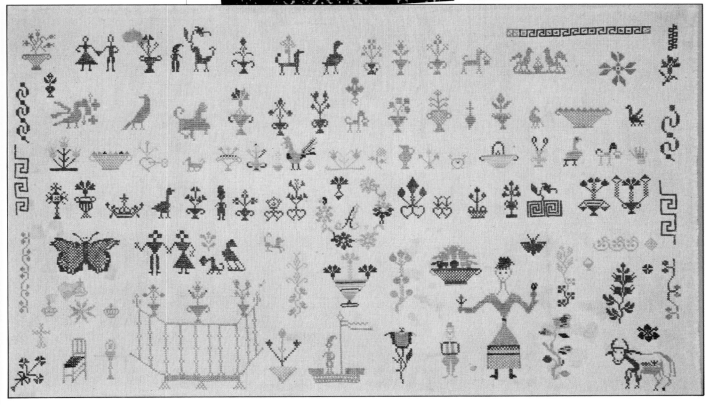

CHAPTER 1

BASIC SEWING TECHNIQUES

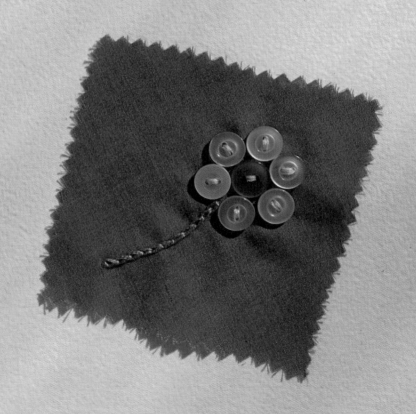

SEWING EQUIPMENT

*G*ood equipment helps to give more professional finish to your sewing. A few basic pieces of equipment are essential, so always buy the best you can afford. There is an increasing range of gadgets available which, strictly speaking, are not essential, although many of them are useful and time-saving.

Scissors

Good quality scissors are a real investment, for they will cut accurately and last longer than cheaper ones. Buy several pairs in different sizes and make sure they are comfortable to hold. Drop-forged scissors are quite heavy, but they can be sharpened repeatedly and, with care, they will last a lifetime. Lightweight stainless steel scissors with plastic handles are comfortable to use and keep sharp for a long time.

Choose a large pair of scissors with 11 inch (28 cm) blades for cutting out fabric. These should be shaped so that the blade rests flat on the table while you are cutting. A medium-sized pair, 4 to 5 inches (10 to 12 cm) long, are useful for trimming seams and cutting small pieces of fabric. A small pair will also be needed for trimming thread ends, clipping fabric edges and cutting buttonholes. Pinking shears for finishing the edges of fabric are useful, but not essential. Look after your scissors and do not cut anything other than fabric with them or they will become blunt.

Needles

The choice of needles for hand sewing is largely a matter of personal preference. Needles are designed for specific purposes, but you may feel comfortable using a certain type.

BETWEENS are short needles used for most types of hand sewing, especially hemming.

SHARPS are longer and are used for tacking and gathering, when more than one stitch is on the needle.

MILLINER'S NEEDLES are very long and are used for stitching through many layers of fabric.

Keep a range of types and sizes of needles and replace them frequently, as they soon become blunt from use. Select the needle size according to the weight of fabric and thread you are using.

Thread

Several types of thread are available for both machine and hand sewing.

MERCERIZED COTTON THREAD is smooth and has a slight sheen; it comes in number 40 for general use and numbers 50 and 60 for fine fabrics and hand sewing. Use this thread for stitching cotton and linen fabrics.

SPUN POLYESTER THREAD is very strong and has more 'give', and should be used on stretch fabrics. It can also be used on wool fabrics.

COTTON-WRAPPED POLYESTER THREAD has a coating of cotton around a polyester core; it is a strong thread, slightly thicker than polyester. Use it on all types of fabric except fine ones.

PURE SILK THREAD is strong and lustrous and very good for hand sewing. Use silk thread on

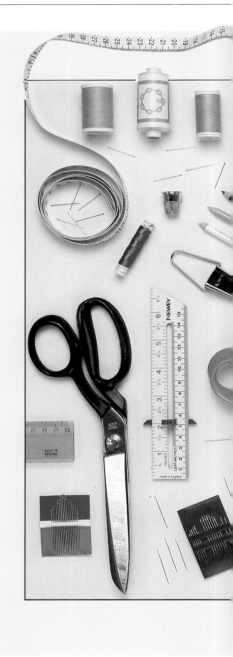

silk and wool fabrics.

QUILTING THREAD is a lustrous, strong thread made of pure cotton or cotton-wrapped polyester. Because it does not tangle, it is ideal for most hand sewing.

BUTTONHOLE TWIST is made from polyester or silk and is used for top stitching, for working hand-stitched buttonholes, and for sewing on buttons.

Pins

Buy good quality pins in a container. Long pins with glass or plastic heads are useful when working with openweave or hairy fabrics, as they are longer than average and easy to see. Ballpoint pins should be used when working with silk. It is useful to keep a pincushion or magnetic pinholder by the machine.

used when making tucks and pleats and for marking buttonholes. A plastic right-angled triangle and a ruler are needed for altering paper patterns.

Tailor's chalk

Tailor's chalk is used to mark stitching lines, darts, and hem-lines. Use white chalk, since this is the easiest to brush out after stitching. Keep the edge of the chalk sharp by paring it carefully with a razor blade. Chalk pencils have a brush at one end for removing the chalk marks from the fabric. A fabric-marking pen with special ink which washes out can also be used to mark single layers of fabric, although it has been found that this may rot some fabrics.

Other sewing equipment

The following items are not essential, but they will all save time and make certain processes easier. A skirt marker will help you mark a hemline by puffing a chalk line onto the garment at a chosen height from the floor. A loop turner is useful for turning narrow bias tubing. Battery-operated scissors are quicker but less accurate than ordinary ones. A needle threader is handy if your eyesight is less than perfect. Dressmaker's carbon paper and a tracing wheel can be used to transfer symbols from a paper pattern to fabric. Iron-on fusible web will hold hems and facings in place. Perforated fusible waistbandings will make the construction of cuffs and waistbands simpler.

Thimbles

A thimble is worn on the middle finger of the hand that holds the needle. It enables you to push the needle through the fabric painlessly, which is important if the fabric is stiff or has a very close weave.

Bodkins

A bodkin is a long, blunt needle with a large eye, used for inserting elastic or cord through a casing. (It is also handy for removing tacking stitches and easing out corners and points to give a sharp finish.) The elastic is tied securely around the groove at the end of the bodkin, and then inserted. An elastic threader, which is a flat, blunt-ended metal needle with a very large eye, is also used for threading elastic.

Measures

Buy a fiberglass tape measure marked with standard and metric measurements. Fabric and plastic tape measures may eventually stretch. A wooden yardstick is essential for accurate long measurements and for marking hems. A metal or plastic seam gauge should also be purchased. This has a movable pointer and can be

Sewing machines

Choosing a machine

The first step when choosing a sewing machine is to decide which type of machine will suit your particular needs, as they fall into quite distinct categories.

A simple zigzag machine with a free arm, semi-automatic buttonhole and a choice of stretch stitches will be adequate for most dressmaking and home sewing needs. A heavier type of machine with good needle penetration and a slow stitch control would be better for heavy fabrics and tailoring processes. If you have to pack your machine away after each sewing session, choose a portable, lightweight model that is easy to lift. Other machines have a range of decorative features, but they will be much more expensive. It is worthwhile remembering that no single machine will include all the features offered by the different manufacturers,

so you must decide which features are essential to you.

The next thing to consider is price. A good sewing machine may seem rather expensive, but a well-made machine will last a lifetime if properly cared for and serviced regularly. Decide how much you want to spend and then look for the most suitable machine in that price range. You should buy your machine from a reputable dealer who offers a thorough demonstration and good after-sale service. Many dealers can provide additional instruction for a complicated machine if necessary. If you do decide to buy a machine from a discount store or by mail order, you may have trouble getting it serviced elsewhere.

Try out as many machines as you can that look suitable, using scraps of your own fabric. Take along a section of different weights and types of fabric, including a thin, slippery synthetic and a stretchy knit, for these can be difficult to sew

on some machines. Stitch through double fabric and check that the machine stitches evenly without allowing the fabric to 'creep' under the foot. Ask the demonstrator to show you the stretch stitches and those for finishing raw edges. Try out the threading and bobbin-winding procedures for ease of use. Other features to look at include the position of the light, which should be directly over the needle, the quality of the instruction book, and response of control.

Straight stitch

These are the simplest type of machines available and are now made by very few manufacturers. These machines sew varying lengths of straight stitch forward or in reverse and, although very limited in scope, are generally reliable. They have a flat bed around the stitching area to provide support for the fabric.

Basic zigzag

In addition to the usual straight stitch these machines will work an adjustable zigzag stitch, up

to ¼inch (5mm) wide. The length of the stitch is also adjustable – a very short length produces a satin stitch, which can be used for working buttonholes, with the fabric guided manually. Straight stitching can usually be done with the needle to the right, centre or left of the needle hole in the foot. These machines have either a flat bed or a free arm, which is useful when stitching openings and small circular areas such as sleeves and cuffs. There are controls for stitch length and width, a pushbutton length and width, a pushbutton reverse, and a limited range of feet and attachments.

Semi-automatic

Semi-automatic machines have more useful features than the basic zigzag type, and they can also do simple decorative stitches. They have straight and zigzag stitch facilities, variable needle positions, pushbutton reverse, and the usual stitch length and width controls. In addition, they have pattern cams which alter the width control automatically to form simple, decorative stitches. The pattern cams are either inserted manually inside the machine or selected by a knob or lever on the outside. The patterns are based on geometric and curved shapes and they can be worked on a close satin stitch setting or opened up by use of the stitch length lever. These machines also offer a semi-automatic buttonhole. The stitch still has to be reversed manually at the end, but the width of the satin stitch is preset by turning a dial. They also have a wider range of feet and attachments and are available as either flat-bed or free-arm models.

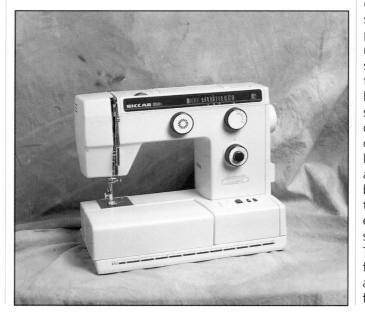

There is a wide range of sewing machines designed especially for home use. At first sight, choosing a sewing machine seems to be a totally bewildering task! This section describes the different types of machines available and their attachments. It shows you how to begin using your new machine, and how to give your sewing a professional finish.

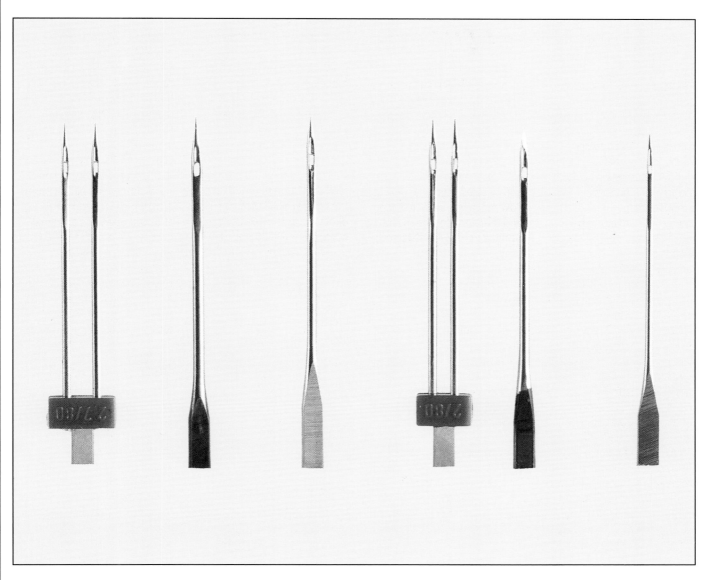

Sergers

Sergers, also called overlocking sewing machines, allow home sewers to reproduce ready-to-wear with ease. These machines stitch, trim, and overcast a seam in one step at twice the speed of a conventional sewing machine. Every major sewing machine manufacturer now has a model of its own and they are proving immensely popular with dressmakers, although not the first choice for machine embroidery.

Automatic

The definition of an automatic sewing machine is one which has a built-in buttonholer, which automatically reverses at the chosen point. The button-hole is worked in two, four or five steps and the width of the satin stitch is preset. The definition means that a machine with an automatic buttonholer and a few utility stitches comes into the same category as a machine with many more advanced features such as automatic patterns and special straight stitch for stretch

fabric. With the advanced machines, the fabric is moved backward and forward beneath the needle, and the needle bar may move from side to side as well, depending on the automatic stitch selected. This gives a range of stretch and overlock utility stitches and a large choice of decorative stitches. New models of this type wind the bobbin through the needle to save unthreading.

Electronic

Electronic machines have all the features of the advanced

ABOVE *Different types of machine needles are designed for different fabrics.*

automatic machines, including mechanical pattern cams, but by the use of electronics they make the physical process of stitching easier. They have an integrated circuit, located either in the machine or in the foot control, which controls the mechanical functions. Some machines use both a circuit in the machine and one in the foot control. An electronic foot control regulates the speed of the motor and provides full needle power even at slow speeds or when stitching heavyweight fabric. It allows

operated pattern cams, as the stitch patterns are stored in the computer memory. The stitch patterns are chosen by touching a button, and the selection is then shown on a visual display panel. Pre-programmed motifs and alphabets can be elongated or shortened without losing the density of the stitches and they can be inverted or stitched in mirror image. A sequence of stitch patterns can be chosen and dialed into the machine, which will then repeat the sequence exactly.

Thread Guide

Tension Disc

Machine Foot

Needleplate

NEEDLE AND THREAD SELECTION CHART

Fabric	Thread	Needle
LIGHTWEIGHT Chiffon, organza, fine lace, lawn, voile	Silk, mercerized cotton, extra fine (any fiber), size 60–100	70
MEDIUM WEIGHT Velvet, gingham, crepe, brocade, line, fine denims, polyester/cotton	Polyester, cotton-wrapped polyester, mercerized cotton, size 50–60	80
HEAVY Wide rib corduroy, tweed, heavy woolens	Polyester, cotton-wrapped polyester, heavy duty (any fiber), size 30–40	90 or 100
VERY HEAVY Canvas, upholstery fabric, heavy denim	Polyester, cotton-wrapped polyester, heavy duty (any fiber), size 20	100 or 110

more sensitive control and has the ability to stop and start immediately. The circuit in the machine provides for stitch-by-stitch sewing, allowing the machine to stop with the needle either up or down.

Computerized

These are the most sophisticated machines available; they are controlled by a built-in micro-processor. They have a full range of features including a one-step buttonhole, but their real advantage is their wide range range of decorative options. There are no mechanically

Needles

Modern machine needles have a rounded shank which is flattened down one side and has a long groove on the opposite side. Thread the needle from the grooved side. Do not use a blunt or bent needle. Needles are made in various sizes to accommodate all weights of thread, and there are different types for specific purposes, most useful being the basic sharp point type. Use the correct size needle for the fabric and change the needle frequently, especially when working with synthetics.

Thread

Select a thread according to the type of fabric you are using. Cotton-wrapped polyester is suitable for most fabrics; it has the strength and 'give' of pure polyester but can take the hot iron required for cotton and linen material. Pure polyester and mercerized cotton can be used for synthetics and natural fiber fabric, choosing one shade darker, because the

thread will appear lighter when stitched.

On all types of thread, the higher the number on the spool, the finer the thread. Select the number of the thread according to the weight of the fabric.

Machine controls

Machine controls may look different from machine to machine but their basic

Bobbin Winder

Balance Wheel

Stitch Selector

Stitch Length Control

functions are the same. All sewing machines require a continuous thread to be fed to the needle at the correct tension and connected to a second tensioned thread from the bobbin. These two threads form the lock-stitch, which is the basis of all machine stitches. The thread spindle, located on the top of the machine, holds the reel of thread for the needle and allows it to unwind evenly.

Some machines have more than one spindle to allow twin and triple needles to be used.

● **Bobbin winder** The bobbin winding position differs according to the machine, but the thread always passes through a tension control to ensure even winding. The balance wheel is disengaged in order to wind the bobbin. Many machines have an automatic cut-off feature when the bobbin is full and on some sophisticated machines the bobbin can be wound directly through the needle without unthreading.

● **Balance wheel** The machine is worked by turning the balance wheel which is usually driven by an electric motor. The balance wheel can be turned by hand to make a single stitch or to raise and lower the needle.

● **Foot controls** can be electric, electronic or worked by air pressure control.

● **Machine feet** All machines, except the straight stitch type, have at least two feet provided with them, one for straight stitch and one for zigzag. Some machines have a selection of special purpose feet which come as standard, while others have a range which can be purchased separately. The feet are hinged to accommodate different weight of fabric, and they can be screwed in place or clipped on a shank.

● **Needle** The needle is fixed into the needle bar by a small screw which should be tightened firmly after inserting the needles.

● **Presser bar** This holds the machine foot and often incorporates a thread cutter at the back of the bar. The pressure can be adjusted to suit different weights of fabric.

● **Presser bar lifter** This is a lever positioned behind and above the foot which raises and lowers the foot. The thread tension is engaged only when the foot is lowered.

● **Bobbins and bobbin cases** Bobbins are circular and vary in size according to the machine, so they are not usually interchangeable. The bobbin thread feeds through a tension spring on the bobbin case which can be adjusted. The bobbin fits snugly into the bobbin case, which either slots in under the needleplate or is inserted from the side.

● **Stitch selector** If the machine features a few utility and pattern stitches, the controls are usually incorporated into the stitch width dial, which will be marked with the appropriate symbols. Automatic machines have a pattern panel with a lever or movable pointer which selectes the stitches.

● **Take-up lever and thread guides** The thread feeds through the eye in the take-up lever and down to the needle. Thread guides are small loops of wire which guide the thread from the reel to the needle. Some machines have a slotted take-up lever and thread guides to make threading quick and simple.

● **Stitch length control** The length of stitch is determined by the rate at which the fabric is fed under the foot. This feeding mechanism is called the feed dog and is regulated by the stitch length control. This control can be a lever with graduated markings or a numbered dial. The feed dog can be dropped on most machines for darning and free embroidery.

● **Stitch width control** This control is found on all machines except the straight stitch type. It controls the width of the zigzag and decorative stitches and may be a graduated lever or a numbered dial. Some machines have a dial or lever marked left, middle and right, which allows the needle to be set in one of these positions.

● **Tension discs** Tension discs are situated on the front of the machine or partially concealed on the top. They act like brakes and control the rate at which the thread feeds to the needle. The tension is altered by a numbered dial or by a plus and minus indicator. There may be a second disc for sewing with two threads. If the thread tension is not correctly adjusted, this will cause either loose stitches or jammed threads. When using the machine for embroidery, however, experimenting with altering tensions may produce some interesting variations of stitch effects.

● **Needleplate** The needleplate surrounds the feed dog and has a small hole for straight stitch and a slot for zigzag stitch. There may be two separate plates provided with the machine which are changed according to the type of stitching in progress, or one plate which can be turned round. The plate is held in position magnetically or by screws or clips, and has fabric guide markings.

● **Controls on computerized machines** All the functions are chosen by touch control, either alone or in conjunction with dialling wheels or stitch lengths and width. Stop start, reverse, stitch selector panel.

Machine attachments

All machines have special attachments for different types of stitching. Some make sewing difficult fabrics easier, some save time and some are used in conjunction with a particular needle. Your machine handbook will give details of those available for your machine and show you how to attach them. Some will come with your machine, while others will have to be bought separately. Attachments are usually a good investment, because they will lend a more professional appearance to the items you make. A selection of machine attachments is shown below.

● **Zip foot** A zip foot is supplied with most modern machines. It is also used to attach cording and is designed for stitching close to the zip teeth or the filled edge of cording. On some machines the needle position adjusts so that it will fit into the indentations on each side of the foot; on other models the zip foot is adjusted to fit to the needle. Special grooved plastic zip feet are also available for use with an invisible zip.

● **Embroidery foot** An embroidery foot is made from clear plastic so that you can see what is happening underneath it. A groove is cut out underneath the foot to allow the thickness of the stitching to pass through it without becoming flattened. Use this foot for all satin stitch and decorative stitching.

● **Binding foot** This foot applies pre-folded bias binding to raw edges. Use purchased binding or make your own from bias strips of fabric using a tape maker.

● **Hemmer foot** A hemmer foot rolls under the raw edge of the fabric to form a narrow double hem which is fed under the needle. This attachment works best with lightweight fabrics.

● **Pin tuck foot** This foot accommodates narrow tucks in the fabric which fit into the grooves under the foot; it is used with a twin needle.

● **Gathering foot** A gathering foot will gather a length of fabric in fixed amounts as you stitch. It can be used to gather a single piece of fabric, or to gather a ruffle and attach it to another piece of fabric in one operation.

● **Roller foot** A roller foot has two or more grooved rollers fitted into the front and back of the foot. Use it when stitching leather, plastic, velvet and slippery fabrics.

● **Overlock foot** This foot is used with stitches that make a seam and finish the raw edges of the fabric in one operation. It is a useful extra to buy if you make a lot of garments and you like this type of seam finish.

General rules for machine stitching

Follow the suggestions given below to obtain a good finish with machine stitching.

● Before stitching press the fabric, using the correct iron temperature, so that it is perfectly flat and smooth.

● Use the correct size and type of needle for the fabric and the stitch.

● Change needles frequently, as they soon become blunt.

● Use the same colour and type of thread for the needle and bobbin.

● Set the stitch length and width to settings that seem suitable. Try out the stitching on a folded piece of extra fabric. Press and check both sides of the fabric to see if any adjustments are necessary. If so, make the adjustments and test the stitching again.

● When using knitted, stretchy fabric, pull it gently to make sure the zigzag width is sufficient to prevent the stitches from snapping.

● After stitching, press the line of stitches on one side of the fabric to flatten and set them into the fabric.

● Trim off any loose, fraying threads from the edges of the fabric.

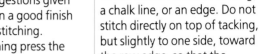

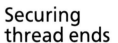

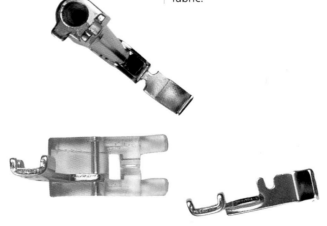

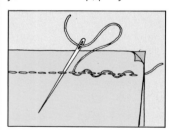

Keeping straight

Always have a guideline along which to sew: a line of tacking, a chalk line, or an edge. Do not stitch directly on top of tacking, but slightly to one side, toward the raw edge, so that the tacking can be removed easily after the stitching is finished. Keep stitching straight by running the edge of the fabric even with the presser foot or by using the guide marked on the needle plate. Work from the wider end of the piece of fabric and stitch the seams in the same direction if possible.

Securing thread ends

It is important to finish the thread ends securely at each end of the stitching. Do this by reversing the direction of the stitching. Start stitching about ⅜inch (1cm) from the edge and reverse to the edge before stitching forward. At the end of the line, when you are approaching the point where you want to stop, put your

hand on the hand wheel to act as a brake and ease off the pressure on the foot control. All machines will stop within one or two stitches. You can use the wheel to make the final stitch by hand. Dot not stitch beyond the edge of the fabric. Reverse the stitching for ⅜inch (1cm) to secure the threads. Then, cut off the surplus at each end of the stitching. When using a fine fabric, fasten off the threads by hand, by running the threads through the stitching on the wrong side with a needle. On fine fabrics reverse stitching tends to pucker and should be avoided.

Turning corners

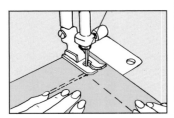

When you reach the corner point, turn the hand wheel, if necessary, so that the needle is lowered into the fabric. Raise the foot and pivot the fabric around the needle so that you can stitch along the seamline. Lower the foot and continue stitching.

On fine fabrics and those which are likely to fray, adjust the stitch to a smaller size just before turning the corner. Work a few stitches past the corner, then return to the original stitch size.

Stitching around curves

On a gentle curve, stitch as usual, but use a slow speed and ease the fabric around gradually. For a tight curve, stop stitching at the beginning of the curve and lower the needle into the fabric. Raise the foot and turn the fabric slightly in the direction of the curve. Work one or two stitches slowly and then repeat the 'stop, turn, stitch' sequence right around the curve. Take care to keep the stitching at an even distance from the edge of the fabric.

When you feel really familiar with your machine, try out the more complicated features such as buttonholes and any automatic stitch patterns. Practise them on a scrap of fabric a few times before using them on a project.

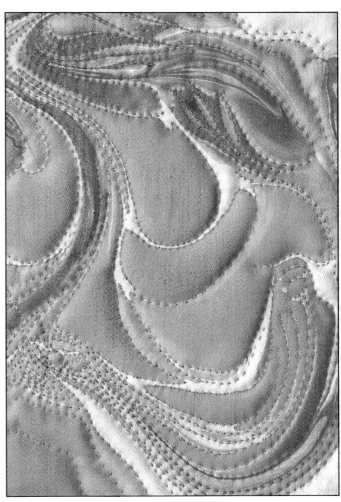

ABOVE *With practice, it is possible to machine curves fluently and accurately.*

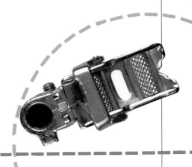

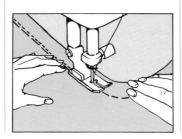

HAND SEWING

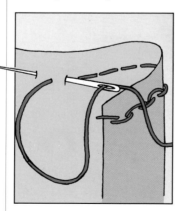

Most garments and items for the home are made initially on the machine and then finished by hand. Hand finishing should be neat and unobtrusive, so take care to use the correct stitch for the job in hand; otherwise the results could be disappointing. If you are not familiar with some of the stitches shown, take time to practice them on a scrap of fabric until you feel confident with your technique. Never try to hurry hand sewing – it should be an enjoyable and relaxed process. The size needle to use when sewing by hand is largely a matter of personal preference, but a fine needle will generally give a neater result.

Starting to sew

Good light is essential when sewing. Sit in a comfortable chair where there is good natural light, or use a directional lamp. Assemble the equipment you will need before you begin sewing and keep it together within easy reach. Make sure that your hands are scrupulously clean and try to use a thimble to prevent wear and tear on the fingers. When sewing white fabrics, shake some talcum powder on your hands to help prevent the fabric from becoming fingermarked.

Use a small knot at the end of the thread unless you are working on a fine, delicate fabric, when a few tiny stitches should be used to secure the end. Hide the knot under a fold or at the edge of the fabric if the stitching is to be permanent. Keep the length of working thread fairly short to prevent it from tangling. Fasten off the thread with two or three backstitches, again hiding them under a fold or at the edge of the fabric.

Keeping the correct tension when hand sewing is just as important as when you are using a machine. It should be correct for the fabric – if it is too tight, puckers and wrinkles will occur. When stitching is loose, the layers of fabric will part and the stitching could eventually break. The secret of even tension is practice and familiarity with the particular stitch you are using.

Backstitch

Backstitch is a strong stitch which can be used to make a garment if a machine is not available. It is also used to stitch parts of a garment that

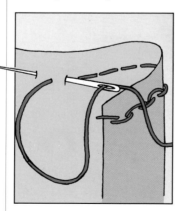

are awkward to reach with a machine. The stitches on the front of the work look like machine stitches, and they should be small and worked perfectly evenly. Two or three backstitches worked on top of each other can also be used to start and finish hand stitching.

Basting

Basting is used to keep layers of fabric together temporarily after pinning and before machine stitching. Use a thread

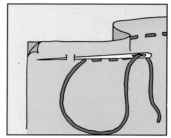

that contrasts well with the fabric to make the basting easy to remove. The stitches should be between ¼ inch (5mm) and ⅜ inch (1cm) long.

Uneven Basting Stitch

Uneven basting is also used to hold layers of fabric together,

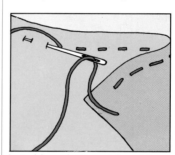

but although it is quicker, it is not as strong as the previous stitch. Take long stitches on one side of the fabric and short stitches on the reverse.

Diagonal Basting Stitch

Diagonal basting is used to hold layers of fabric firmly together within an area. It keeps the fabric flat where a row of ordinary basting could cause a ridge – for example, when attaching interfacing or holding a pleat in place. Take horizontal stitches from right to

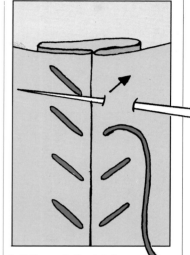

left through the fabric as shown to leave a row of diagonal stitches on the right side.

Running stitch

Running stitch is used mainly for gathering and shirring fabric. It is basically the same as basting, but smaller, and the stitches must be even. Take several small stitches on the point of the needle before pulling it through the fabric. When gathering fabric, make sure that the thread is long enough to make an unbroken line of stitching.

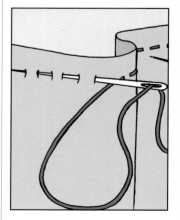

Half backstitch

Half backstitch is similar to ordinary backstitch but a longer stitch is taken on the reverse of the fabric, which spaces out the stitches on the front. From the

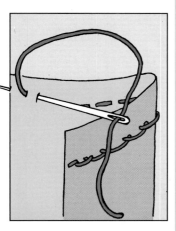

front, the stitches should form a neat, broken line. When the stitches on the front are very tiny, this stitch is known as prick stitch.

Overcasting

Overcasting is used to finish the edges of fabrics that fray easily. Work from either direction, taking the thread over the edge

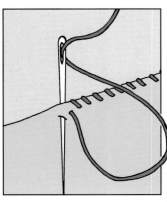

of the fabric. Do not pull the thread too tightly, or the edges of the fabric will curl and make bulges. If the fabric frays badly, work a row of machine

stitching first and trim the fabric close to this stitching before overcasting over the edge and the machine stitching.

Whip stitch

Whip stitch, also called oversewing, is used instead of slipstitch to join two folded edges of fabric when a strong joining is needed. Work from right to left as shown taking a

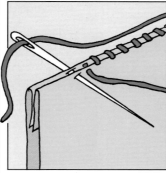

small amount of fabric from each fold. Pull the sewing thread quite tightly to give a neat joining.

Prick stitch

Prick stitch is a small, strong stitch worked through several layers of fabric. It is a good stitch to use when attaching a zipper by hand as it is almost invisible on the right side. Prick

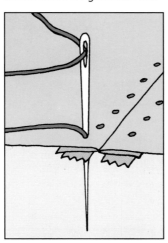

stitch looks similar to half backstitch, but it is worked with a stabbing motion through the fabric layers. Work prick stitch from the right side, since it is untidy on the reverse side.

Blanket stitch

Blanket stitch is a looped stitch used mainly for finishing raw edges. The loops can be close together or spaced apart, depending on where the stitch is used. Open blanket stitch, with the stitches set widely apart, is also used as an alternative to herringbone

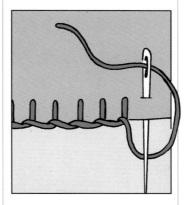

stitch for finishing edges and holding them down. Close blanket stitch is used over bar tacks and button shanks.

Buttonhole stitch

This stitch is used for working buttonholes in preference to close blanket stitch, since it is stronger and more hard wearing. Worked in a similar way, it forms a row of knots against the raw edge. Always keep the stitches close together and make sure that the knots touch in order to keep the edge firm.

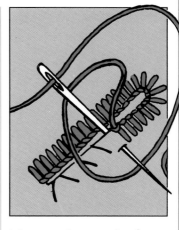

Hemming stitch

Hemming stitch is used to hold down the fold of a hem on light and medium-weight fabrics. This stitch may show on the right side. The thread should not be pulled taut or the fabric may pucker. Work toward

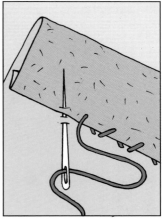

yourself, picking up a thread of the single fabric and then a thread of the fold before pulling the needle through.

Felling stitch

Felling stitch is used in tailoring to attach loose linings to the neckline, seams, and front

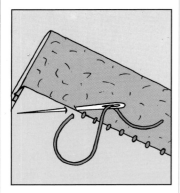

edges of coats and jackets. Baste the lining in position with the raw edge folded under, and work with this fold away from you as shown. The stitches should be neat, tiny, and almost invisible. The joining made will be extremely strong.

Herringbone stitch

Although primarily an embroidery stitch, herringbone stitch is used in hand sewing for securing hems on heavy fabrics. Work it directly over the raw edge; the edge will be finished at the same time. Herringbone stitch is fairly elastic, so it is ideal for use with stretch fabrics and knits.

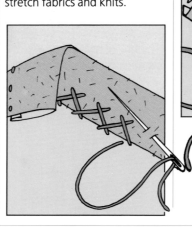

Blind stitch

Blind stitch is worked on the inside fold of a hem and worked from right to left. The stitches are almost invisible,

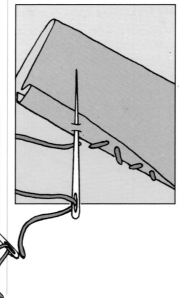

provided the thread is not pulled tightly, which makes it ideal for skirt or dress hems. This stitch can also be used to hold down a fold of fabric which has had the raw edge finished by overcasting or by zigzag stitch.

Bar tack

A bar tack is a strengthening device used to prevent fabric from tearing, for example, at the base of a zipper or across the end of a sleeve opening, either on the right side or the wrong side. A bar of straight stitches is worked through the fabric first. Closely spaced blanket stitches are then worked over this bar without the needle penetrating the fabric. Take care to fasten off the thread securely on the wrong side of the fabric.

Tailor's tacks

Tailor's tacks are the most accurate method of transferring markings from a paper pattern to double layers of fabric. Use them to mark seamlines, darts, and other construction symbols and also to mark delicate fabrics, which may be damaged by using other methods such as a tracing wheel. Always leave the

pattern pinned to the fabric until all marks have been transferred from it. With the point of the needle, slit the pattern across the symbol to be marked before working the tailor's tack and always use double thread. Take care not to pull the tacks out when lifting the pattern off the fabric. After the pattern has been removed, gently separate the layers of fabric and cut the loops with sharp scissors.

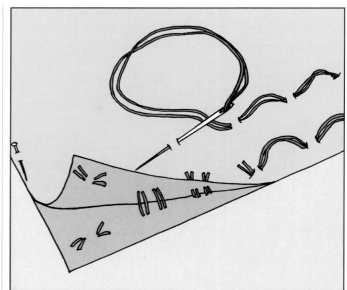

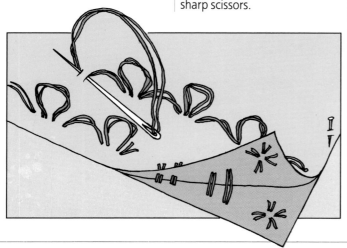

Simplified tailor's tacks

Simplified tailor's tacks are used to mark a line of pleats or a seamline on a single piece of fabric. They consist of a

continuous row of loose stitches in double thread as shown. Cut the thread between each stitch before carefully removing the pattern, taking care not to pull out the markings.

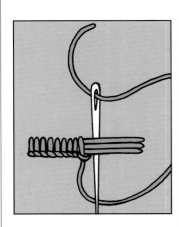

Slipstitch

Slipstich is used to join two folded edges of fabric or a folded edge to a layer of flat fabric. If worked carefully, it should be almost invisible. It can be worked from the right side which makes it especially useful for finishing the ends of

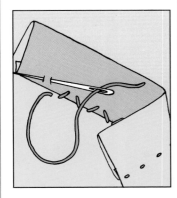

ties, waistbands and cuffs. Pull the thread just enough to join the folds securely; the fabric will wrinkle if the tension is too tight. Slipstitch is also used to finish hems on fine, delicate fabrics.

RIGHT *Attention to the details of construction will give a professional finish to the garment.*

Cotton and Linen

Wool and silk

Man-made fibers

Special fabrics

SEAMS

Seams are formed when two or more pieces of fabric are joined together by a line of stitching. They are the main constructional element in sewing, and should be worked with care. Seams are usually machine stitched, but they can be sewn by hand using backstitch.

Plain seams create the shape of a garment or household accessory and should be almost invisible when pressed. Decorative seams emphasize the lines of shaping and are often used as a strong design feature. The choice of seam will also depend on the weight of the fabric and they type of article being made. For example a flat fell seam used on denim jeans will be more durable and suitable for repeated laundering than a flat seam.

Plain seams

● Flat seam A flat seam, also called open seam, is the basic method used to join fabrics of average weight. It is always sewn with the right sides of the fabric facing, and the raw edges should be finished to prevent fraying. Finish straight flat seams after stitching and pressing open. A plain straight stitch should be used on woven fabric.

Stretch fabric needs to be sewn with a stitch that allows the seam to 'give', otherwise the stitching will break during use. A small straight stitch and polyester thread will often give sufficient stretch, or a very narrow zigzag stitch can be used. Some machines have a special stretch stitch; use this with care, for it is difficult to rip out. A flat zigzag seam will need to be pressed to one side to accommodate the width of the stitching.

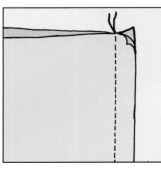

1. Place the two pieces of fabric together with right sides facing and edges even, and pin and baste along the seamline.

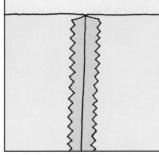

2. Machine stitch along the seamline. Remove basting, and press.

● Crossed seam A crossed seam is formed when two pieces of fabric that each contain a flat seam are joined at right angles to the seams.

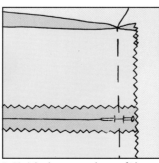

1. Finish the raw edges of the seams before joining the pieces together. Placing the right sides of the two pieces of fabric

together, pin along the seamline, making sure that the crossed seams align by inserting a fine pin through both seams as shown.

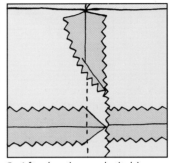

2. After basting and stitching the seam, trim the seam allowances diagonally to reduce any bulk. Remove the basting and press the seam open.

● French seam A French seam is a narrow seam which encloses the raw edges of the fabric so that fraying does not occur. It is normally used on fine, semi-transparent fabric or on medium-weight fabric that has a tendency to fray badly. On heavy fabrics it would be bulky and unsightly. This seam is often used on baby clothes and lingerie. The finished seam should be no wider than ¼inch (5mm). It is always pressed to one side, toward the back of the garment.

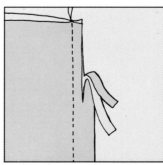

1. Place the two pieces of fabric together with wrong sides facing. Pin, baste and stitch about ⅜ inch (1cm) from the raw edges. Trim both the seam allowances to ⅛ inch (3mm).

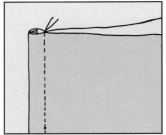

2. Refold so that the right sides are together and the seam is at the edge. Pin, baste and stitch along the seam again, this time ¼ inch (5mm) from the edge.

● Flat fell seam A flat fell seam is a very useful self-finishing seam which is used extensively where a strong, non-fraying seam is needed. Use this seam on medium-weight fabrics such as poplin and challis, since it is rather bulky when used on heavy fabrics. Two rows of stitching show on one side of the seams, these can be in contrasting colours. Denim jeans are usually put together using flat fell seams, because they are durable.

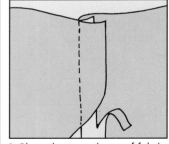

1. Place the two pieces of fabric with wrong sides facing. Pin, baste and stitch about ⅝ inch (1.5cm) from the raw edges. Trim one seam allowance to ¼ inch (5mm).

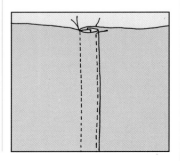

2. Fold the wider seam allowance in half with the raw edge to the seamline. The narrower seam allowance is now neatly enclosed. Press the seam down flat and then baste to keep the folded edge in place. Stitch along the fold to finish.

● **Taped seam** A taped seam is similar to a flat seam, but it is used on areas that will be subjected to strain, especially on garments. It incorporates seam binding or tape, which should always be pre-shrunk to prevent the seam from puckering after it is laundered.

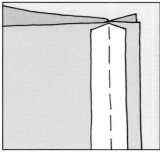

1. Place the two pieces of fabric together with right sides facing, and pin and baste along the seamline. Baste a length of seam binding or tape along the seamline. If you are taping a curved seam, ease the binding or tape carefully around the curve while you are inserting the basting stitches.

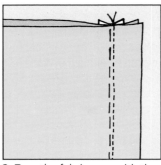

2. Turn the fabric over with the taped side facing down, and stitch close to the tacking. Remove tacking before pressing.

● **Self-bound seam** This seam, also called self-finished seam, is used where one piece of fabric is gathered and one is flat. It is also useful for fraying fabrics, since the raw edges are enclosed, but it forms a rather bulky ridge and is only successful on lightweight fabrics.

1. Place the two pieces of fabric together with right sides facing, with the gathered piece on top. Baste along the seamline and stitch. Remove basting, trim upper or gathered seam allowance only to ¼ inch (5mm).

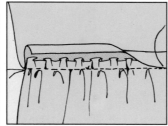

2. Fold the wider edge over twice, bringing it over to meet the line of stitching. Baste and press.

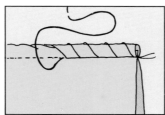

3. For a soft finish to the seam, hand-sew the fold, taking the stitches into the machine-stitched line, rather than through the fabric. Alternatively, machine stitch along close to the fold. This will give a harder ridge, but it will be more hard wearing.
4. When using this seam on flimsy fabric, make the seam narrower by trimming the wider seam allowance to ¼inch (5mm), and the narrower one to about ¹⁄₁₆inch (2mm). Fold down as in step ¼,

and overcast over the edge, bringing the needle through just above the line of stitching and pulling the stitches fairly tight.

● **Curved seam** A curved seam is used to provide shaping. It is used to join two pieces of fabric that differ in shape, for one piece will generally be more curved than the other.

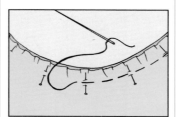

1. Place the two pieces of fabric together with right sides facing, with the more curved piece on top. Pin them together exactly on the seamline with the points of the pins facing outward as shown, picking up a tiny piece of fabric each time. Ease the top piece into position and hold the seam over your hand to pin, keeping the curve even.

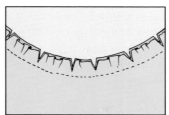

2. Baste along the seamline with small stitches and remove the pins. If the fabric is quite stiff, you will need to clip the seam allowances as you work.

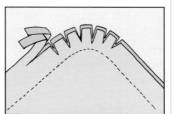

3. Keeping the more shaped piece on top, stitch carefully along the curve, following the

basted line closely. Trim seam allowance and clip further if necessary. Either press this seam open and finish the edges separately, or press it to one side and finish the edges together.

● **Corner seam** A corner seam is used to provide shaping and is usually constructed using an ordinary flat seam. This seam is a little tricky, for it is difficult to keep the corner sharp and neat. If the seam will not be enclosed, finish the edges of the fabric before beginning the seam.

1. Mark the corner points on the fabric with tailor's tacks. Placing the right sides of the two pieces of fabric together, pin along one side up to the corner inserting the pins at right angles to the seamline.

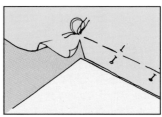

2. Clip the top piece of fabric at the corner point. Stitch the pinned seam to the corner, leaving the point of the needle in the fabric.

3. Pivot the work around the needle. Align both layers of fabric as shown, then pin the second side of the seam and stitch to the end. Remove the tailor's tacks and press the seam flat.

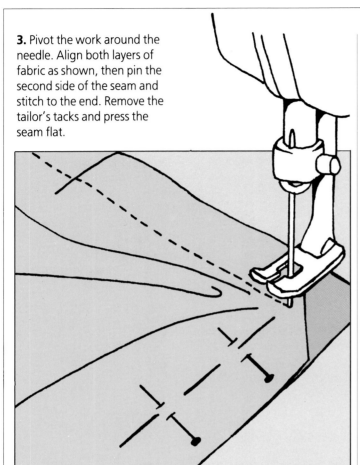

● **Welt seam** A welt seam is extremely strong and is suitable for use on almost all fabrics, apart from fine fabrics, which have a tendency to fray badly. A row of stitching shows on the right side. This can add interest to a solid-colour fabric if a contrasting thread is used.
1. Place the two pieces of fabric together with right sides facing. Pin, baste and stitch along the seamline. Remove the basting and press the seam to one side, depending on where you want the row of stitching to show.

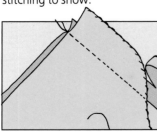

2. Open the pressed seam allowances and trim the lower one to slightly less than ⅜inch (1cm). At this stage, finish the edge of the wider seam allowance unless the item is to be lined.

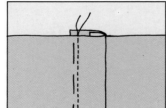

3. Turn the fabric right side up and baste parallel to the seamline, basting through the wider seam allowance as shown. The narrow seam allowance is now enclosed. Stitch or topstitch with a heavier thread from the right side, keeping the line of stitching parallel to the original seam and inside the line of basting. Press the seam again from the right side.

● **Narrow finish seam** A narrow finish seam is used only on lightweight or semi-transparent fabrics. It is an inconspicuous way of joining fine fabrics and can be finished by hand or machine.
1. Place the two pieces of fabric together with the right sides facing. Pin, baste and stitch along the seamline. Remove the basting and press the seam to one side.

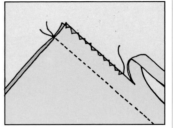

2. To finish by machine, trim the seam allowances to ¼inch (5mm) and zigzag over both together.

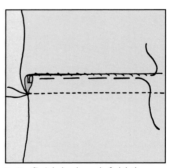

3. To finish by hand, fold the seam allowances in to meet each other, as shown. Baste the folds together, press, and slipstitch neatly.

● **Rolled seam** A rolled seam is used on fine fabrics and is a self-finishing seam. It looks rather similar to a French seam, but only one row of stitching is used. Use rolled seams on loosely fitting garments only, as they could split when stretched as they are not very strong.

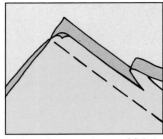

1. Place the two pieces of fabric together with the right sides facing and baste along the seamline. Trim one seam allowance to within ⅛ inch (3mm) of the basting. On a very fine fabric, also trim the wider allowance slightly.

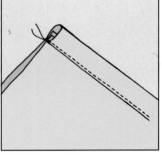

2. Fold the wider seam allowance over once, and then fold it just over the basted line. Baste through the fold along the seamline. Stitch along the edge of the fold, remove basting, and press from the wrong side.

● **Topstitched seam** A plain flat seam can be decorated by topstitching it in a matching or contrasting color, or heavier weight of thread for reinforcement as well as ornament. The stitching can be on one side of the seam or both and can be worked by hand or machine. Decorative machine stitches can also be used. Check the size of the seam allowance before your begin cutting out, and add a little extra if necessary. If you are topstitching along both sides of the seam, always stitch in the same direction or the stitching could pull the fabric and make it pucker.

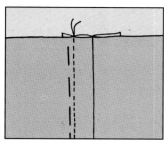

1. Make a flat seam, press, and finish the edges. Baste through the layers of fabric at the chosen distance from the seam, and stitch on the right side close to the basted lines. Remove the basting and press.

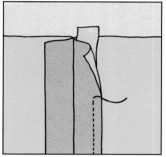

2. To give a raised effect to the seam, cut narrow bias strips of fine fabric and insert them under the seam allowance on the wrong side. Finish the seam as above.

● **Channel or slot seam** A channel seam can be used on most types of fabric, but it will work best on a solid color, fairly firm fabric. It incorporates a backing strip which shows between the seam edges. This can be cut from a matching, contrasting, or patterned fabric. Try to use the same weight of fabric for the backing strip as for the main item, or back a finer fabric with iron-on interfacing for added firmness. The width of the backing strip depends on the weight of the fabric and how much of it will be seen. Usually, the maximum amount that should show through is ¼ inch (5mm), but it could be larger to give a more decorative effect.

When adding this type of seam to a pattern piece, join the seam first, using larger pieces of fabric, and then cut out the complete section, using the pattern.

1. Turn in the raw edges of the two pieces of main fabric along the seamline. Baste, press and finish the edges. Cut a bias strip of the contrasting fabric at least 1¼ inch (3cm) wide. Finish the edges and mark the centre of the strip with a line of basting.

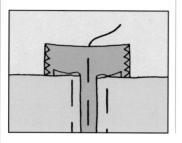

Decorative seams

● **Insertion seam** An insertion seam is used to attach lengths of lace or braid to lingerie and garments made from lightweight fabrics. The insertions can be made almost anywhere on the garment and can be as wide or narrow as you like. They are added after the pattern pieces have been cut out, since no extra seam allowance is needed.

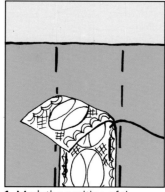

1. Mark the position of the insertion on the right side of the main fabric, using a line of basting or tailor's tacks. Place

2. Baste one folded edge of the main fabric, right side up, to the strip, about 1/16 inch (2mm) from the centre. The top edge of the main fabric should be slightly lower than the edge of the backing strip, as shown. Baste the other folded edge in the same way, keeping both

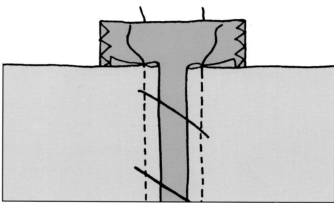

one edge of the insertion along the markings and baste it in place. Holding the insertion flat to prevent puckering, baste it down along the second side.

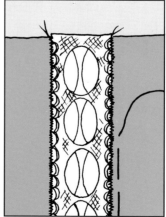

2. Attach the insertion on the right side with straight, zigzag or machine embroidery stitches. Use a matching thread so the stitching is inconspicuous and keep the stitching close to the edges as possible. Remove the basting, then press from the wrong sides on a well-padded surface.

folds parallel. Work a row of diagonal basting across the folds as shown.

3. On the right side, stitch along the folds about ⅛ inch (3mm) away from the edge. Remove the basting and press from the wrong side on a well-padded surface.

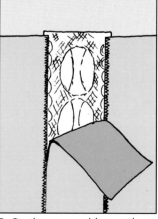

3. On the wrong side, cut the fabric away between the rows of stitching, using a sharp pair of scissors. Trim the edges and finish them with overcasting. When using a transparent insertion, roll the edges back to the main fabric and hand hem. This will prevent them from showing through on the right side and spoiling the look of the finished garment.

● **Fagoted seam** A fagoted seam is very decorative but not particularly strong, so avoid using this seam on garments that are going to be worn frequently: the two pieces of fabric are joined with hand embroidery, leaving a small gap between them. The gap can vary between ⅛inch (3mm) on fine fabric and ⅜inch (1cm) on wool or heavy cottons. Work a fagoted seam on a larger piece of fabric first and then cut out the pattern pieces.

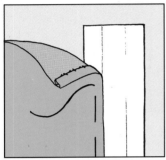

1. Mark the position of the fagoting on the right side of the fabric with a line of basting. Cut the fabric on this line and press a narrow double hem to the wrong side along each edge. Hand-hem each piece.
2. With a pencil and ruler, mark parallel lines the desired distance apart on a piece of typing paper or thin brown paper. These will act as guidelines to keep the fabric even while the embroidery is being worked. Baste one piece of fabric along the left-hand pencil as shown, and then baste the other piece along the

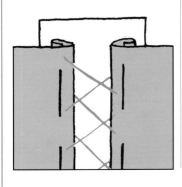

other line. The paper ensures that the gap remains even, and that the stitches are of equal size.
3. Join the edges with fagoting, also known as insertion stitch, using a suitable weight of embroidery thread for the type of fabric. Remove the paper after the stitching is completed.
● **Lapped seam** A lapped seam is simple to construct and relies on the use of a contrasting thread to add decoration. One side of the seam laps over the other. This seam can be used on any type of fabric.

1. After deciding which way the seam will face, turn under the seam allowance on the top layer of fabric along the seamline. Baste along the fold and press. Place this on the other piece of fabric with the right sides uppermost, matching the seamlines, and baste in place.

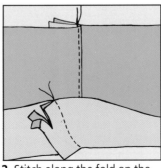

2. Stitch along the fold on the right side using a straight, zigzag, or machine embroidery stitch and a contrasting thread; take care to keep the line of stitching perfectly even.

INSERTION STITCHES

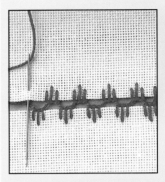
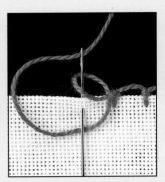

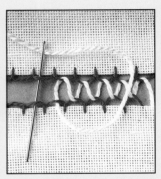

Various insertion stitches may be used for ornamental fagoted seams.
ABOVE TOP *Buttonhole insertion stitch is a simple insertion stitch, which is worked over a fairly narrow space. Groups of three buttonhole stitches are worked alternately from edge to edge. The stitch begins at the right-hand side of the row and the central stitch of each group is made slightly longer than the others.*

ABOVE BOTTOM *Twisted insertion stitch is one of the simplest forms of insertion and it makes a pretty, twisted zig-zag line. Make a simple twisted stitch alternately from one edge of the fabric to the other, ensuring that the needle always emerges from the back of the fabric.*

ABOVE *Laced insertion stitch is a wide, lacy insertion stitch, often worked in two colors. Unlike the other insertion stitches, some of the embroidery is worked before the two pieces of fabric are basted to the brown paper. A row of braid edging stitch (**ABOVE TOP**) is worked along each edge of the fabric before the fabric is basted down; the loops on the top edge should alternate with those on the bottom. The two rows of loops are then laced together (**ABOVE BOTTOM**).*

Although this stitch makes a very pretty join, it is not particularly stable and it is therefore not advisable to use it on an item that is to be laundered.

RIGHT *This cushion shows an imaginative use of piping technique. Curved banks of flat piping have been inserted into the plain front. Twisted cord has been stitched over the side seams to neaten them and to echo the loose covers and curtains.*

Piped seams

Piped seams are used on both garments and household accessories to accentuate the construction lines. The piping can be left unfilled to give a soft look, or filled with a length of cord – when it is known as cording – for a more pronounced line. A matching or contrasting colour can be used for the piping fabric. A piped seam is quite stiff, even when left unfilled, and is unsuitable for softly draped home furnishings or garments.

● **Basic piped seam**

1. Cut bias strips of the piping fabric approximately 1¾ inches (3cm) wide and join them together into a long strip. Alternatively, ready-made bias binding could be used.

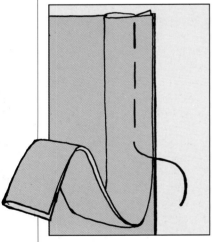

2. Fold the strip in half lengthwise with the wrong sides facing and press. Baste the folded strip along the seamline on the right side of one of the seam edges with the raw edges facing outward.

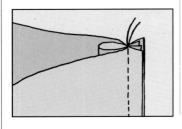

3. Place the second piece of fabric over the strip with the right sides together. Baste through both layers of fabric and the piping seam allowance, turning the fabric back occasionally to check that the seamlines match. Stitch close to the basting. Remove the basting and press. Trim away any excess piping at the ends of the seam and clip corners.

● **Corded seam** In this type of seamline, a bias strip is folded in half around a length of cotton filler or piping cord. This cord is available in several different thicknesses and may need to be pre-shrunk before use. The bias strip needs to be wide enough to accommodate the cord and to leave a seam allowance of ⅝ inch (1.5cm) at each side.

1. Cut bias strips of the cording fabric and join them together. Wrap the strip around the cord with the right side facing outward and pin through both layers of fabric. Stitch, either by hand or by machine, using a zip foot, as close as possible to the cord. Baste the piping to the seamline and finish as for a piped seam.

2. When the cording meets around a shape, trim the ends of the cord so they butt together. Trim the fabric strip, leaving an overlap of ⅜ inch (1cm). Turn under ¼ inch (5mm) on one end, place it over the opposite raw edge and slipstitch along the joining.

Special seams

● **Stretch fabric seam** Stretch fabric must be sewn with a stitch that allows the fabric to 'give', otherwise the stitching may break during use.

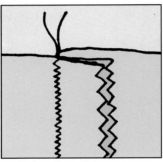

1. Stitch as for a flat, or open seam, using a narrow zigzag stitch, a special stretch stitch setting, or a narrow three step zigzag stitch.

2. If your machine has only a straight stitch setting, stretch the fabric gently with your hands as it passes under the needle. Use a smaller than normal stitch and polyester thread.

● **Lace seam** This seam is used on patterned lace to give an almost invisible joining. Use a thread that matches the color of lace perfectly.

1. Cut out the lace with a slightly wider seam allowance than usual and mark the seamlines with tailor's tacks. Placing both pieces right side up, lap one piece over the other, taking care to match the seamlines exactly. Use a row of basting near the seamline to mark out a stitching line, following the pattern of the lace as closely as possible.

2. Work over the basting line with a close zigzag stitch. Remove the basting and carefully trim away the excess lace on both the top and the bottom piece. Press the joining with the right side down on a well-padded surface.

● **Velvet seam** Use a velvet seam on any kind of pile fabric.

1. Place the two pieces of fabric together with the right sides facing. Baste along the seamline following the direction of the pile. Do not fasten off the basting cotton.

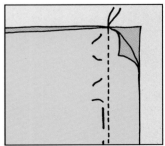

2. Stitch the seam in the same direction, cutting the basting stitches as necessary to allow the top piece of fabric to move.

● **Hairline seam** A hairline seam is used on fine fabrics where a normal seam allowance would show through and look untidy. It can also be used for a full, gathered garment where a bulky seam would be unsightly.

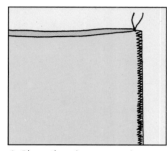

1. Place the pieces together with right sides facing. Pin and baste just outside the seamline.
2. Stitch along the seamline using a narrow, close zigzag stitch. Remove the basting and trim the seam allowance close to the stitching.

Finishing seams

The raw edges that are are left on the wrong side of those seams that are not self-finishing should be finished in order to prevent the fabric from fraying. Cutting out the pattern pieces with a pair of pinking shears will usually be sufficient to prevent most closely woven and some knitted fabrics from fraying. However, if the item is going to be washed frequently or by machine, finish the edges by one of the methods described below. Always finish the edges of fabric that look as if they are likely to fray.
● **Three-step zigzag stitch** This stitch is included on many modern machines. It is very, stretchy which makes it useful for finishing the edges on knits and other stretch fabrics. Work from the right side and stitch along each edge, keeping the row of stitches close to the edge, without taking the

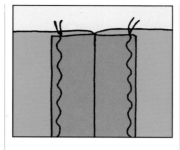

stitches over the edges. Press the seam open.
● **Edge stitching** This is a quick and neat way of finishing the raw edges on light- and

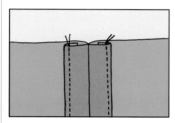

medium-weight fabrics. Fold under ⅛inch (3mm) of the seam allowance and press the fold. Placing the right side uppermost, stitch close to the fold with a straight machine stitch and press the seam open.
● **Zigzag stitching** A zigzag-edged seam is ideal for finishing the raw edges on fabrics that fray badly. Set the machine to the appropriate stitch length and width of

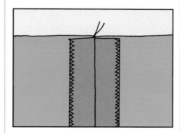

zigzag. Stitch along the right side of the edge so that the needle stitches once into the fabric and then once over the edge. Press the seam open.
● **Finishing by hand** Finish the raw edges by working a row of overcasting over them. Leave

the stitching quite loose, for the fabric edges may curl and make a ridge if the stitching is too tight. Overcasting can be used on most types of fabric.
● **Seam binding** Seam binding can be used to finish the raw edges on heavy, bulky fabrics that fray. Fold the binding in half lengthwise and enclose the raw edge in it. Pin, baste and

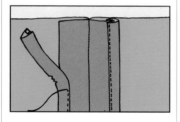

stitch in place. Where the seams are curved, use bias binding in preference to seam binding, since it will stretch around the curve.

Trimming seams

Unless a seam is a self-finishing seam, the seam allowance should be trimmed wherever the seam curves in order to leave a neat, flat seam. On heavy fabric, the seam allowance may also need to be graded to eliminate bulk.
● **Notching** Where the seam allowance lies on the inside of a

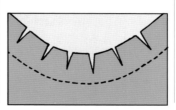

curve, cut out small 'V' shapes at regular intervals almost up to the line of stitching. This is called notching and it allows the fabric to fit into the curve, giving a smooth finish.
● **Clipping** Where the seam allowance lies on the outside of a curve, cut into it at frequent intervals almost up to the line of stitching. This is called

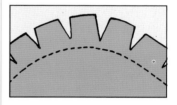

clipping and it allows the fabric to spread out around the curve so that it does not pucker.

● **Grading** Grading is used on seam allowances where bulk needs to be eliminated. This often happens where you have several thicknesses of fabric, such as on collars and cuffs. Trim the interfacing close to the line of stitching. Trim the under layer of fabric to within ⅛inch (3mm) of the stitching, and then the outer layer to within ¼ (5mm) of the stitching.

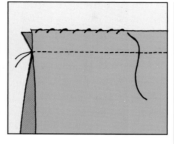

SHAPING TECHNIQUES

*F*abric can be shaped in various ways, depending on the effect desired. It can be cut and joined to create a shape, controlling any extra fullness by means of pointed folds called darts. It can be gathered or folded into tucks and pleats.

The method of shaping used will influence the type of fabric required, and vice versa. A design using gathers or unpressed pleats will need a soft fabric such as silk or cotton jersey, which will drape easily. Crisp fabrics such as linen or cotton piqué can be shaped with darts, intricate seaming, and pressed pleats. Heavy fabrics including woolen tweed, wide wale corduroy and duck will have to be shaped mainly by cutting and seaming, with the addition of darts. Fabrics with bright, bold patterns need careful attention and usually work best with a simple shape, which will show the pattern to full advantage.

Another factor to consider is the extra fabric required to make pleats, tucks, and gathers. This could be important when you are intending to buy an expensive fabric such as pure silk. If you are designing an item rather than following a commercial pattern, remember to allow enough fabric for three times the width of each pleat. For gathers allow one and a half to two times as much fabric, depending on the fullness desired.

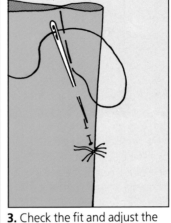

3. Check the fit and adjust the dart. Remove the tailor's tacks and stitch, starting at the raw edge. Reinforce the point by working a few reverse stitches. Press as appropriate.

● Special finishes for darts

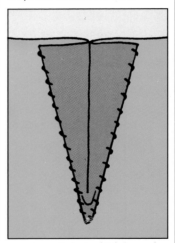

DEEP DART A dart which is made with a deep fold should be slashed along the fold to within ⅝ inch (1.5cm) of the point. Overcast the edges if the fabric is likely to fray, and then press the dart open.

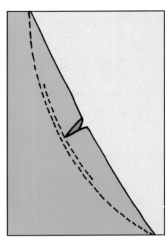

CURVED DART A curved dart should be clipped along the curve, as shown. Reinforce the curve with a second line of stitching, press to one side.

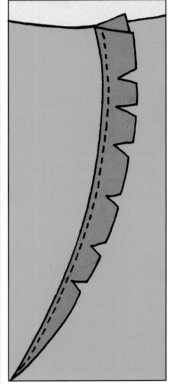

CONTOUR DART A contour dart is pointed at both ends. After stitching the dart, clip it at the widest point almost up to the stitched line and work a second line of stitching along the curve as a reinforcement. Overcast the clipped edges if the fabric is likely to fray.

Darts

Darts are used to provide shaping and can be curved or straight, and single- or double-pointed. The length, width, shape, and position of darts will depend on the design of the garment or item, and they may need to be altered to give a correct fit. Any corresponding darts should be realigned to match if you make such an alteration.

Darts are normally worked on the wrong side unless they are used as a decorative feature. Before stitching a dart, check the fit and adjust the position and shape of the darts as required. Darts should always taper to a fine point to fit well. Slashed darts are pressed flat and other types are pressed to one side, over a tailor's hem if necessary. Always press darts before proceeding to the next stage of assembling.

● Making a simple dart

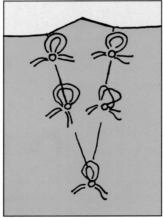

1. Mark the position of the dart with tailor's tacks or a tracing wheel. Fold the dart in half matching the markings carefully.
2. Pin and baste the dart, starting at the raw edge and tapering it to a fine point. Any inaccuracy in finishing the point will show up on the completed garment.

Gathering and shirring

Gathering and shirring are both formed by drawing up a piece of fabric by means of rows of stitching. Gathering is worked near the edge of a piece of fabric which will then be joined to an ungathered piece. Ruffles are made by this method. Shirring is worked in a band across the fabric, producing an effect similar to smocking.

● **Gathering** Gathering can be worked by hand with evenly spaced rows of running stitch or on a machine using the longest stitch length available. Use a long piece of thread for the running stitch so that you can complete each section of stitching without a break.

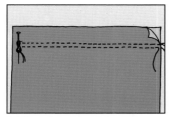

1. Work two rows of small running stitches or machine stitching ¼inch (5mm) apart just outside the seamline. Do not fasten off the ends of the thread.

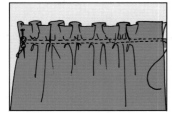

2. Pull up the threads at each end of the stitching until the gathered section is the required width. Arrange the gathers evenly. Fasten the gathering threads by winding them around a pin as shown.

3. Pin the gathered fabric to the ungathered section, placing the right sides together and the gathered fabric on the top. The pins should be at right angles to the stitching. Baste and then stitch along the seamline. A second row of stitching should be worked to reinforce the first if the gathering is at a point of strain – for example at the waistline of a dress. Remove the pins holding the gathering threads, snip the gathering threads at the center and pull them out.

● **Shirring** Fabric can be shirred by working multiple parallel rows of straight machine stitching, using the longest stitch length.

Shirring

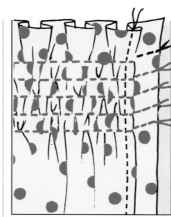

1. Draw up the threads in the same way as for gathering.
2. Fold back the side edges of the fabric and stitch to secure the ends of the shirring threads.
Fabric can also be shirred on the machine using a special elastic thread called shirring elastic. This can either be threaded into the bobbin or couched directly onto the fabric with a narrow zigzag stitch.

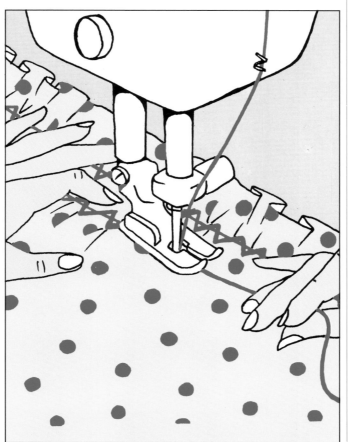

● **Ruffling** Gathering may be used to create a pretty ruffle for pillow-cases or cushion covers.
1. Measure the length and width of the pillow. Cut one back piece to this size, adding 2⅝ inches (6.5cm) to the length and 1¼ inches (3cm) to the width for the hem and seam allowances. Cut one front piece, adding a 1¼ inch (3cm) seam allowance all around. Cut a strip of fabric for the flap: the width should be 7 inches (17.5cm); the length should be two times the width of the pillow including seam allowance. Cut long strips of fabric for the ruffle to make a length twice that of the complete outer edge of the pillow. The width of this strip should be twice the width of the finished ruffle, usually between ¾ inch (2cm) and 3 inches (8cm), plus 1¼ inch (3cm) for seam allowances.
2. Along one short edge of the back piece, turn under 2 inches (5cm) to the wrong side and then turn under ⅜ inch (1cm) along the raw edge. Pin, press, and stitch in place. Pin, baste and stitch the ruffle pieces, right sides facing, into a ring, using plain seams.

3. Fold the ruffle in half lengthwise with the wrong sides facing and pin. Divide the ruffle into four equal sections and mark. Gather each ruffle section in turn.
Divide the complete edge of the front piece into four equal sections and mark. Position the

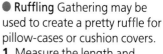

ruffle on the right side of the front with the ruffle inward to the centre. Pull up the gathering stitches of each section in turn to match the sections on the pillowcase front. Match the marks on the front to those on the ruffle and then pin, baste and stitch the ruffle in place.

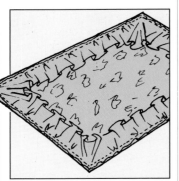

4. Assemble the pillowcase by placing the back on top of the ruffled front with the right sides facing. Align the hemmed edge of the back with the seamline on the front. Place the flap right side down over the back, as shown, matching the long raw edge with the raw edge of the front. Pin, baste, and stitch in place, following the previous line of stitching; take care not to catch the hemmed edge of the back in the stitching. Trim and finish the raw edges, remove the basting stitches, and turn right side out.

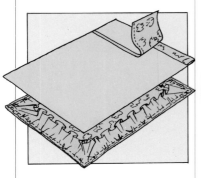

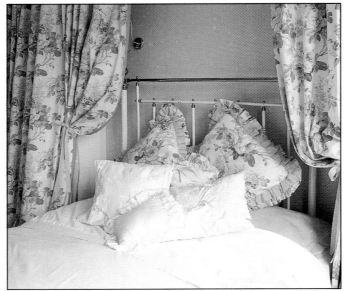

LEFT *Here the neat double frill on the bed cushions is used to echo the canopy fabric. The plain and lace pillows are decorated with single frills and ribbons.*

BELOW *Box pleats provide a professional finish to this bed valance.*

Pleats and tucks

Pleats are folds made in fabric and are used to distribute fullness creating a soft effect without bulkiness. There are three main types of pleat: knife pleats, box pleats and inverted pleats. On crisp fabric, pleats are usually pressed and can be stitched to help them retain their shape in wear. Pleats on soft fabrics look best when they are left unpressed. It is essential to mark the position of pleats accurately so that each pleat takes up exactly the same amount of fabric and the fullness is evenly distributed.

● **Knife pleats** The folds of knife pleats lie in the same direction along the whole pleated section.

1. Mark the position of the pleats on the right side of the fabric with simplified tailor's tacks. Use contrasting thread for the fold lines and the pleat-edge lines.

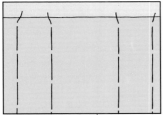

2. Working from the right side, fold the pleats along the marked lines. Pin them in position with the pins at right angles to the folds. Secure the pleats with diagonal basting and remove the tailor's tacks.

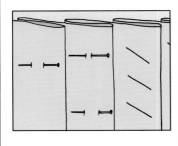

● **Box pleats** Box pleats have two folds of equal width forming each pleat. The fold turn away from each other on the right side of the fabric with the underfolds meeting at the centre to form an inverted pleat on the wrong side. Box pleats are often used singly to add extra fullness, such as at the center back of a shirt.

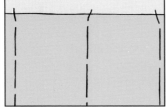

1. Mark the position of the pleats on the right side of the fabric with simplified tailor's tacks. Use a contrasting thread for the fold lines and the pleat-edge lines.

2. Working from the right side, fold the pleats along the marked lines as shown, and pin them in position at right angles to the folds. Secure the pleats with diagonal basting and remove the tailor's tacks.

● **Inverted pleats** Inverted pleats are the reverse of box pleats. The inverted pleats are on the right side of the fabric with box pleats formed on the wrong side. This type of pleat is often used on skirts and slipcovers.

1. Mark the pleats in the same way as for box pleats. Fold pairs of pleats toward each other as shown.

2. Pin the pleats in position at right angles to the folds and secure them with basting. Remove the tailor's tacks.

● **Finishing pleats** All pleats can be pressed, unpressed, or stitched. If the pleats are to be pressed or stitched down to the hem, finish the hem first. When making pressed pleats, use a damp press cloth between the iron and the pleats to avoid making the fabric shiny. Let the fabric dry thoroughly before removing the basting stitches. For stitched pleats, first press the pleats in position; then stitch through the fold only close to the edge of each pleat using a matching thread.

STITCHING KNIFE PLEATS Stitch the edge of each pleat ⅛ inch (3mm) from the fold and finish at the appropriate point down

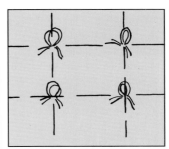

the pleat. Pull the threads through to the wrong side and fasten off securely. Take care to make the stitched lines all the same length.

STITCHING INVERTED PLEATS Stitch each pleat as shown, pivoting at the corners. Pull the threads

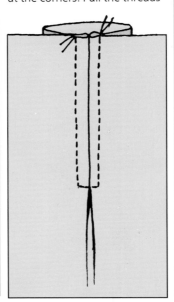

through to the wrong side and fasten off securely.

● **Tucks** Tucks are really a narrow version of knife pleats held in place with stitching. They can be made in different widths; the narrowest tucks are known as pin tucks. Tucks can be placed horizontally or vertically and they are often used as a purely decorative feature on bodices and yokes. Vertical tucks can be stitched down to the hem or seamline, or the fabric can be released at a certain point to give fullness to a skirt or smock. Wide horizontal tucks are often found on children's clothes; they can be removed to lengthen a skirt or sleeves.

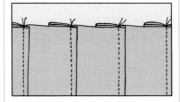

1. Mark the position of the tucks with simplified tailor's tacks, using two colors of thread to denote the different lines.

2. Fold the tucks, matching the markings, and keeping the width of the tucks even. Pin and baste them in position. Stitch along each tuck and remove the basting threads. Decorative pin tucks can also be worked on fine fabrics using a twin needle, pin tuck foot and two colors of thread for an ornamental effect.

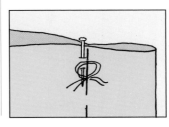

HEMS

inishing the hem is usually the last stage in making a garment or household accessory. Hems are nearly always hand stitched to give a neat finish, but a machine stitched edge is occasionally used on a narrower hem. Use a suitable stitch and take care not to pucker the fabric by pulling the thread too tightly when stitching.

Match seam and center lines carefully and trim down the seam allowance under the hem to prevent unsightly bulges. The allowance left for a hem depends on its position and on the type of fabric being stitched. Heavy fabric such as woolen tweed or drapery fabrics need a deep hem so that the extra weight will help the fabric to hang well. Sleeves and light-weight fabrics will require only a narrow hem. Allow bias-cut garments to hang at least overnight before marking the hem level, since the fabric may drop unevenly.

Marking the hemline

It is best to have help marking the hemline on a skirt or dress. Use a hem marker or a yardstick and tailor's chalk to measure an even distance from the floor. If help is not at hand, pin up the hem and try on the garment in front of a full length mirror. Note any alterations, remove the garment and re-pin the hem. You may have to

repeat this procedure several times before the hem is finally neat and level. Hand-operated hem markers are available which simplify this process.

To mark the hemline on draperies, hang them on the drapery rod overnight, then measure an even distance from the floor using a yardstick and chalk. Pin up the hem, then re-hang the draperies to check that the length is correct and the pattern is level.

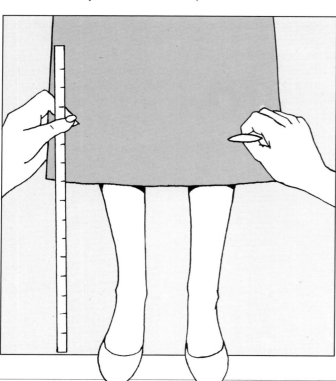

● **Turning the hem** Fold the hem along the chalk line and pin it up, placing the pins at right angles to the folded edge.

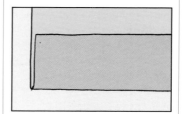

Check that the hem is level and make any further adjustments at this stage. Baste the hem ¼ inch (5mm) above the folded edge and press it to sharpen

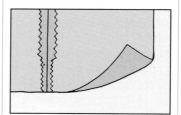

the crease. Cut away any surplus fabric to make the hem the correct depth and trim any seam allowances inside the hem by half.

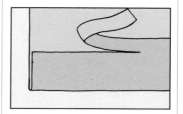

Hem finishes

The shape of the item as well as the weight and type of fabric will determine which method of finishing to choose. Always finish hems by hand if an invisible finish is desired on the right side of the item.

● **Plain hem** This method of finishing a hem is suitable for a straight hem on light- and medium-weight fabrics.

1. Fold ¼ inch (5mm) under along the raw edge and press.

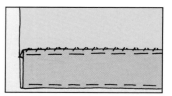

2. Pin the hem edge in place, baste and finish with hemming stitch. Remove the basting and press the hem.

● **Turned and stitched hem** A turned and stitched hem is suitable for articles that are laundered frequently and for linings. Use this method for finishing a straight hem on most weights of fabric.

1. Fold under ¼ inch (5mm) along the raw edge and machine stitch near the edge of the fold.

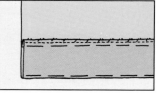

2. Press, pin, and baste the hem in place. Finish with hemming stitch. Remove the basting and press the hem.

● **Blind-stitched hem** This finish can be used on any straight hem and is particularly suitable for use on draperies. Use either seam binding or bias binding to enclose the raw edge.

1. Sew the binding ¼ inch (5mm) from the raw edge of the hem using a narrow zigzag stitch. Press the binding.

2. Pin the hem edge in place, baste and finish with blind hem stitch. Remove the basting and press the hem.

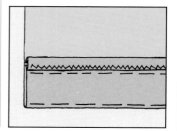

● **Herringbone hem** Use a herringbone hem on both loosely woven and heavyweight fabrics. The raw edge should be cut with pinking shears or enclosed with bias binding, before it is stitched. This hem can also be used on stretch fabrics if your machine does not have a zigzag setting.

1. Pink the raw edge or attach the binding as for a blind-stitched hem. Press, pin, and baste the hem in place.

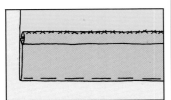

2. Stitch the hem using herringbone stitch, working from left to right. Remove the basting and press.

● **Zigzag hem** A zigzag hem is used on stretch fabrics and knits. It prevents fraying and has the same amount of 'give' as the fabric.

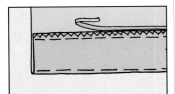

1. Work a row of narrow machine zigzag or three-step zigzag stitch close to the raw edge. Press and trim close to the stitching with a pair of sharp scissors.

2. Pin, baste, and finish with blind stitch. Remove the basting and press the hem.

● **Eased hem** An eased hem is used mainly on garments to finish the hem of a flared or gored skirt. The fullness of the skirt hem is controlled by gathering the edge slightly to ease in the fullness and prevent a lumpy effect.

1. Work running stitches ¼ inch (5mm) from the raw edge. Pin up the hem, matching center and side seamlines. Draw the running stitches up to ease the fullness and fit the skirt shape.

2. Shrink out the fullness using a steam iron. Remove the pins and stitch a length of bias binding to the hem, placing it over the gathering thread.

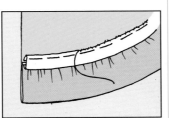

3. Pin and baste the hem in place and press, shrinking the bias binding to the curve. Finish with blind stitch. Remove the basting and press.

● **Circular hem** A circular hem should be quite narrow so that it lies perfectly flat. Always hang a garment with a circular skirt overnight or longer with the hem pinned up before finishing the hem.

1. Mark the hem line and trim away any excess fabric, leaving a hem of approximately ⅝ inch (1.5cm). Pin, baste and stitch a length of bias binding ¼ inch (5mm) from the raw edge, taking care not to stretch the binding as you stitch.

2. Press the binding and then fold the fabric along the marked line. Pin, baste, and press, then finish with blind stitch or slipstitch. Remove the basting and press.

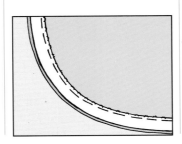

● **Machine-stitched hem** A narrow, machine-stitched hem is useful, since it is quick to sew and strong. The stitching is visible on the right side, so care should be taken to keep the line of stitching straight and to choose a thread either to match perfectly or give deliberate contrast. This hem can be stitched with an ordinary presser foot as described below, or by using a narrow hemming foot.

1. Trim the hem allowance to ¼ inch (5mm). Fold ⅛ inch (3mm) then another ⅛ inch (3mm) over to the wrong side and press.

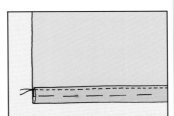

2. Baste along the center of the hem, then stitch close to the edge.

Finishing corners on hems

Finish the corners on hems so they are sharp and square by mitering or facing them. Mitered corners give a good finish to tablecloths and bedspreads; faced hems are usual on garments such as coats and jackets.

● **Mitered corners** Hems with mitered corners can be either hand or machine stitched.

1. Turn under the raw edges of the fabric and then fold the hem to the wrong side. Press it in position and open out the fabric. At the corner point of the hem fold, draw a diagonal line across the wrong side of the fabric with tailor's chalk. Cut off the corner of the fabric ¼ inch (5mm) outside this line.

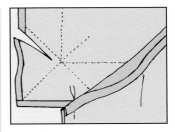

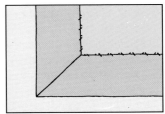

2. With the right sides of the fabric facing and the raw edges turned under, fold the corner. Stitch along the marked diagonal line. Turn the corner right side out, press, and finish the hem as desired by hand or machine.

● **Faced corners** A hem with a faced corner is usually finished by hand.

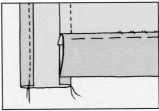

1. Finish the edge of the facing with zigzag stitch, or by folding ¼ inch (5mm) to the wrong side and machine stitching close to the edge. Pin, baste, and finish the hem to the desired depth.

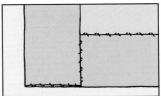

2. Turn the facing back over the finished hem. Slipstitch the lower edge of facing to the hem, and then slipstitch the side of the facing to the hem to secure it.

BINDING

*B*inding is a way of finishing a raw edge by enclosing it in a strip of fabric. A contrasting color pattern or weight of fabric is often used which can make it decorative.

Binding can be either single or double, except on heavy fabrics, where single binding should be used. Single binding can be bought ready for use in a variety of colors and widths; in solid-colour and printed cotton, polyester cotton, mercerized cotton and a shiny rayon blend.

Binding strips can be cut from any type of fabric, although light- and medium-weight fabrics will give the best results. Leftover scraps of fabric provide a good source of binding, but if long lengths are required, buy extra fabric to avoid too many seams. The strips should be cut on the bias of the fabric, rather than along the grain, so that they will stretch easily around curves and fold over smoothly without twisting.

Cutting the bias strips

For single binding, cut strips twice the required width plus a seam allowance on both sides of approximately ¼ inch (5mm). Double bindings should be four times the finished width plus the two seam allowances of ¼ inch (5mm).
1. Straighten the edges of the fabric by pulling the cross threads. Use the selvage as one of the straight edges if you are cutting the binding from a length of fabric.

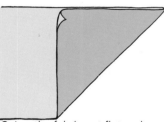

2. Lay the fabric out flat and then fold it over with a straight edge to the selvage, as shown. The diagonal fold is on the true bias of the fabric.
3. Pin along the diagonal, leaving the fold free, and cut along the fold. Mark a line the required distance from the fold and parallel to it. Cut along the line to give the first pair of strips. Continue marking and

cutting in this way, moving the pins away from the edge each time.

Joining the bias strips

Join the strips end to end, as shown, to form a strip 4 inches (10cm) longer than you need.

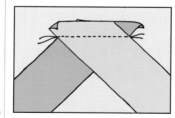

The ends can be machine stitched ¼ inch (5mm) from the edge, or you can work a line of backstitch by hand.

Applying single binding

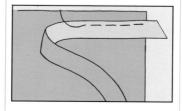

1. Place one edge of the bias strip right side down on the right side of the fabric to be bound, allowing ¾ inch (20mm) of binding to extend over the raw edge as shown. Take a ¼ inch (5mm) seam allowance on the binding and a normal one on the fabric. Pin across the strip at intervals and baste binding in place.

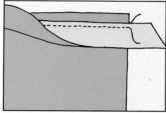

2. With the bias strip on top, stitch along the seamline. Remove the tacking and press the stitching. Trim the seam allowances to slightly less than the finished width of the binding. On the right side, press the binding over the raw edge.
3. Turn the fabric wrong side up, fold under ¼ inch (5mm) of the binding, and bring the fold to the stitching. Baste the binding in place in two sections, working from the center outward.

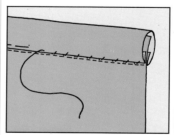

4. Hem into the line of stitching, working stitches about ¼ inch (5mm) apart. Press lightly, taking care not to flatten the binding.

Applying double binding

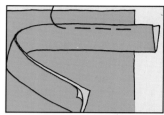

1. Fold the bias strip in half with the wrong side inside and press it lightly. Baste the raw edges of the double strip to the fabric to be bound and proceed exactly as for single binding, until you reach step 3.

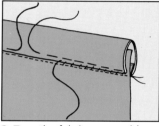

2. Turn the fabric wrong side up, and roll the fold of the binding over to meet the stitched line. Baste it in place in two sections, working from the centre outward. Hem into the stitching and press lightly.

ABOVE RIGHT *This quilted bag is made up of three fabric thicknesses, the top layer, quilting wadding and lining. A bulky finish is avoided by enclosing the raw edges of all layers with bias binding.*

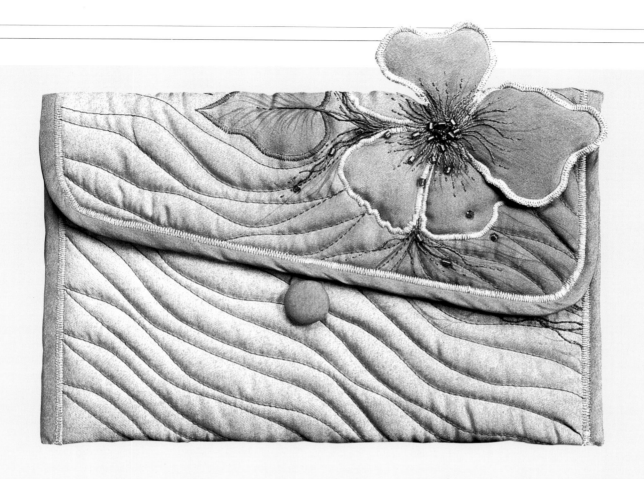

Joining single and double binding

When binding a continuous edge such as an armhole, always make the final joining in an inconspicuous place.
1. Baste the bias strip in place, leaving ⅜ inch (1cm) unstitched at the beginning

and ¾ inch (2cm) overlapping at the end.
2. Fold back the surplus ⅜ inch (1cm) at the beginning of the strip and lay the other end on top, as shown, to overlap the folded end.
3. Baste the ends to the fabric along the seamline. Apply the binding in the usual way.

Flat finish binding

Single binding can be applied to a raw edge in such a way that it is almost invisible from the right side, giving a neat, flat edge.
1. Follow steps 1 and 2 for applying single binding.
2. Turn under the ¼ inch (5mm) seam allowance and fold the binding over to the wrong side, taking it past the line of stitching, as shown.

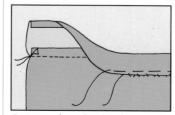

3. Baste the edge in place and slipstitch to hold it down. Press lightly from the wrong side.

Narrow finish binding

This method of applying single binding gives a very neat finish when the main fabric is much heavier than the binding strip.
1. Follow steps 1 and 2 for applying single binding.
2. Trim both seam allowances down to ⅟₁₆ inch (2mm). Fold the free edge of the binding over to the wrong side without turning under the raw edge. Working from the right side, baste below the joining.

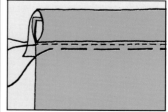

3. Stitch on the edge of the binding or along the seamline.

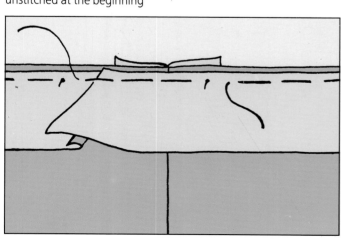

41

FASTENINGS

Zippers

Zippers are available in three basic types: all-purpose, or conventional zippers, which have a stop at the bottom and can be used on most garments and household items; invisible zippers, which lie neatly inside a seam; and separating zippers, which are used wherever two sections of a garment must separate completely – as on a jacket, for example. Some separating zippers, called parka zippers, have a slider at each end.

All three basic types come in a variety of weights of materials. For most clothing and household accessories the usual choice is a lightweight zipper on which the teeth consist of two continuous polyester or nylon coils. When the zipper is closed, the two coils interlock. This type of zipper has the advantage of being unobtrusive and is strong enough for most purposes.

● **General rules** Follow these rules when inserting a zipper to obtain a professional finish.
1. Match the zipper length to the size of the opening.
2. Check that the garment fits correctly before inserting the zipper.
3. Finish and press the seam before inserting the zipper.
4. Pre-shrink a zipper with cotton tape to prevent puckering if the item is to be washed rather than dry cleaned.
5. If the zipper is too long, shorten it at the bottom by working a few stitches over the zipper teeth 1 inch (2.5cm) below the required length and cutting off the surplus.
6. Pin upward from the bottom of the zipper wherever possible.
7. Use a zipper foot when you are machine stitching.
8. Finish the ends of the zipper tape after insertion.

● **Inserting a zipper – Centered method** The easiest method of inserting a conventional zipper is to place it in the center of the seam with an equal amount of fabric on each side.

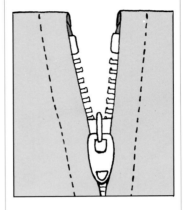

1. Press the finished seam and pin and baste the seam allowances together along the fold lines. Mark the end of the opening with a pin.
2. Pin the zipper in position with the teeth centred over the seam. Insert the pins at right angles to the zipper, changing the direction of every other pin.

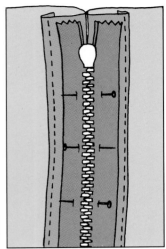

3. Tack ¼ inch (5mm) from the zipper teeth and remove the pins. Stitch close to the basting on the right side using a zipper foot. Begin at the top and stitch down one side, pivot the fabric and stitch across the bottom, and up the other side. Alternatively, stitch the zipper in by hand using a tiny prick stitch and double thread. Remove the basting and finish the ends of the zipper tape.

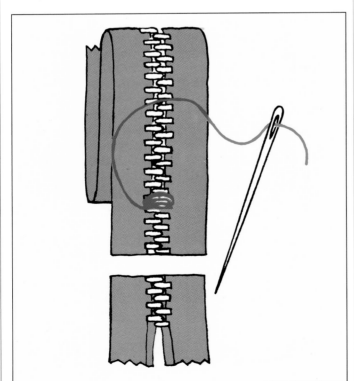

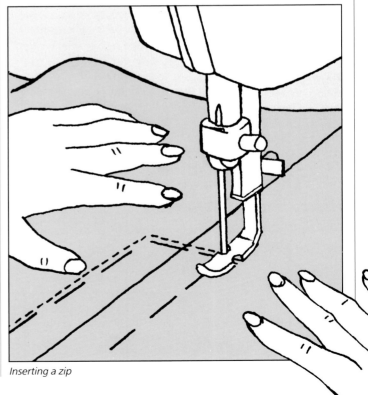

Inserting a zip

● **Inserting a zipper – Lapped method** Here the zipper lies under a flap formed by the seam allowance on one side. Side zippers on garments are usually lapped so that the flap opens toward the garment back.

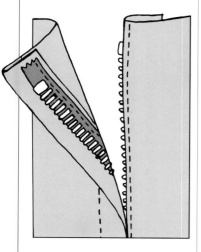

1. Finish and press the seam. Working from the right side, place the zipper under the seam opening. Pin and baste one edge close to the teeth of the zipper, as shown.
2. Lap the opposite seam allowance over the zipper teeth, making sure that they are completely covered. Pin and baste the flap in position ⅜ inch (1cm) from the fold.
3. Stitch by hand or machine as for a centered zipper, step 3.

● **Inserting an invisible zipper**
An invisible zipper is used where a conventional zipper could spoil the line. All that is visible on the right side is a plain seam and the

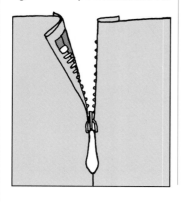

pull tab. An invisible zipper is always stitched in place before the seam is stitched.

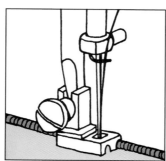

The tapes are stitched to the seam allowances of the garment pieces using a special invisible zipper foot so that none of the stitching shows on the right side. The special zipper foot must be the one recommended for the brand of zipper that is being used.
1. Finish the raw edges of the fabric and mark the seamlines with basting stitches. Open the zipper and press the tapes carefully so that the coils stand away from the tape. This will insure that the zipper will feed smoothly through the foot.

2. Place the open zipper face down on the right side of one garment piece. Position one coil on the seamline with the zipper tape over the seam allowance as shown. Pin or baste in position if necessary. Fit the right-hand groove of the special foot over the coil and stitch as far as the tab of the zipper.

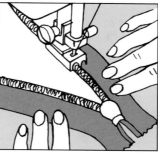

3. Pin the unstitched tape face down to the right side of the other garment piece, centering the coil on the marked seamline. Stitch in place, this time using the left-hand groove of the foot.

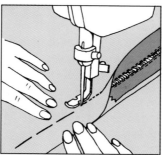

4. Close the zipper, then pin and baste the remainder of the seam in the usual way. Replace the special foot with an ordinary zipper foot positioned to the left of the needle. Lower the needle into the fabric slightly above and to the left of the previous stitching. Stitch the seam.

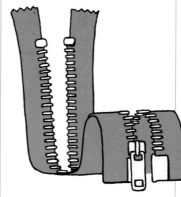

● **Inserting a separating zipper**
A separating zipper should be inserted before any facings or hems are begun. This type of

zipper is usually centered with the teeth either concealed as usual or exposed for a decorative finish.
1. Finish and press the raw edge. Pin and baste the seam allowances together along the fold lines.

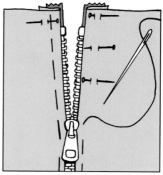

2. Pin the zipper in position with the teeth centered over the seam. Mark the level where the bottom of the garment will be when it is hemmed, and make sure that the end of the zipper is accurately aligned with this level. Insert the pins at right angles to the zipper, changing the direction of each alternate pin.
3. Baste approximately ¼ inch (5mm) or ⅜ inch (1cm) on heavy-weight zippers, from the zipper teeth and remove the pins. Stitch close to the basting on the right side using a zipper foot. Begin at the top and stitch down one side of the zipper. Stitch the second side in the same direction. Alternatively, if you are using this type of zipper on a lightweight garment, stitch the zipper in by hand using prick stitch and double thread. Remove the basting.

● **Finishing** Depending on the position of the zipper, the tape ends may be exposed, on the wrong side, after insertion. In many cases, one end of the zipper will eventually be covered by a facing, hem, or waistband and need not be finished. Exposed tape ends should be attached to the seam allowance with a row of blanket stitch. This will prevent the tape from rolling up and making a ridge.

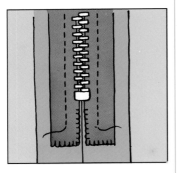

Finish the base of the zipper opening by working a small bar baste by hand on the right side. If this would spoil the look of the finished item, work the bar baste on the wrong side just below the zipper teeth.

● **Zipped cushion covers** Make an opening across the center of the cover back by making a plain seam and inserting a zipper using the centered

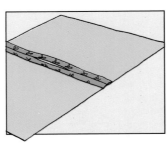

method. This works especially well on a corded cover. You will need to add an extra 1¼ inches (3cm) to the seam allowance on the back when cutting out the fabric to allow for the center seam. Omit the side opening on the cover.

Buttoned openings

Overlapped openings fastened by buttons are found mainly on garments. Shirts, jackets, and coats usually have a buttoned fastening on the front which can be decorative as well as functional. Small openings, especially those on children's garments, can also be fastened with buttons.

Buttonholes can be worked successfully on all fabrics provided that the right type of buttonhole is made. Button loops are much more decorative and can be substituted for buttonholes if appropriate to the style of the garment. They are also useful when a single button is necessary – for example, on a waistband. Button loops suit an edge-to-edge opening particularly well, but like buttonholes, they can also be used for an overlapped opening.

● **Buttonholes** There are three types of buttonhole: machine-worked, hand-worked and bound. Always make the buttonholes before attaching the buttons. Horizontal buttonholes are used on the front of garments and at points of strain such as cuffs and waistbands. Vertical buttonholes should be confined to fastening loosely fitting garments and as a decorative feature, because the buttons tend to come undone if the opening is put under strain.

Calculate the size of the buttonhole by measuring the diameter of the button and then allowing a little extra for the thickness of both the button and the fabric. After calculating the size, make a trial buttonhole on a scrap of fabric in case any adjustments are

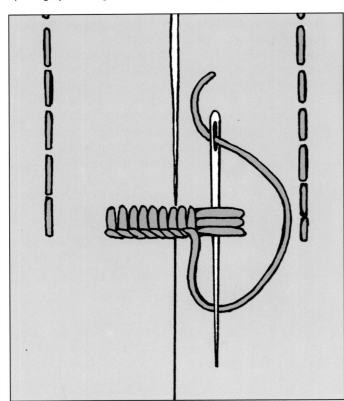

A hand-worked buttonhole

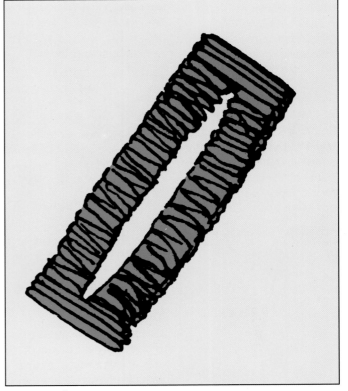

Button opening

needed. When marking the length of the buttonholes, use an adjustable marker set to the right measurement or a small strip of cardboard cut to size.

MACHINE-WORKED BUTTONHOLES

Machine-worked buttonholes are suitable for most types of fabric, and they are quick and easy to work. Work this type of buttonhole after all the other stages of the garment are completed.

1. Mark the position and size of the buttonholes with tailor's chalk. To prevent fraying, press a rectangle of fusible web underneath each buttonhole between the garment and the facing.

2. Using a zigzag foot or buttonhole attachment, stitch around the buttonhole following the instructions in your sewing machine handbook. Cut through the center of the buttonhole using sharp embroidery scissors.

HAND-WORKED BUTTONHOLES

Hand-worked buttonholes are a little tricky, but with practise a neat finish can be obtained. If you enjoy hand sewing, you will probably choose this type of buttonhole, since it is suitable for all types of fabric. Choose a weight of thread to match the fabric and work the buttonholes after all the other stages of the garment have been completed.

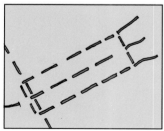

1. Mark the position and size of the buttonhole with lines of basting, as shown. This is preferable to marking with

chalk, since the basting keeps the layers of fabric together while you are working the buttonhole. Insert a pin at each end of the buttonhole and cut a slit between the pins using a sharp pair of scissors. Remove the pins.

2. On a horizontal buttonhole, stitch along the lower edge of the slit toward the edge of the garment using buttonhole stitch.

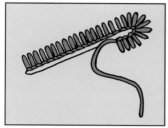

3. At the end of the slit, work five stitches in a semicircle to accommodate the shank of the button. These stitches should

be slightly shorter than those already worked. Work along the second side of the slit in the same way as the first.

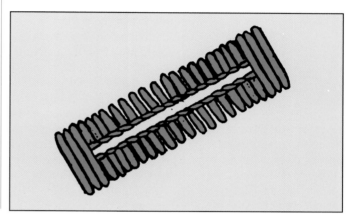

4. Work a bar of satin stitch across the end of the buttonhole to the depth of both rows of buttonhole stitch. For a more durable buttonhole, work a bar tack instead of satin stitch. Fasten off the thread on the wrong side of the garment.

5. On a vertical buttonhole, work around the slit but replace the semicircular stitches with a satin stitch bar.

BOUND BUTTONHOLES

Bound buttonholes are used on light- and medium-weight fabrics. They look extremely neat and professional when worked correctly. The openings are bound with a strip of matching fabric and the first five stages should be completed after interfacing, but before the fabric facing is attached. Finish the backs of the buttonholes after the garment is completed.

1. Mark the position and size of the buttonholes with lines of basting stitches or chalk. Cut rectangles of fabric on the

straight grain at least 1¼ inches (3cm) wider and longer than the buttonhole. Place the right side of the rectangle over the position mark on the right side of the garment and baste in place.

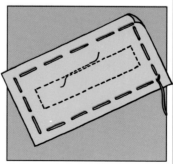

2. Re-mark the buttonhole length on the rectangle. Work a rectangle of stitching around the position mark. The rectangle should be the same length as the buttonhole and three or four machine stitches wide. Work the final stitches over the first ones and cut off

the thread ends. Remove the basting and press.

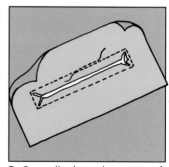

3. Cut a slit along the center of the stitched rectangle as shown, and clip into the corners up to the stitching.

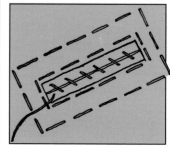

4. Push the rectangle through the slit to the wrong side. Manipulate the fabric until two folds of equal width fill the buttonhole opening, and baste the rectangle to the garment as shown. Press and then diagonally baste the folds together at the center of the buttonhole.

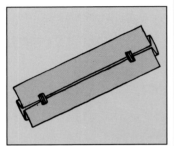

5. On the wrong side, the rectangle has formed an inverted pleat at each end of the opening. Hold the pleats in position with small bar bastes and remove the basting

stitches. Attach the sides of the rectangle to the garment with small pieces of fusible webbing. Press and then finish the remaining stages of the garment.

6. When the garment is complete, a fabric facing will cover the back of the buttonholes. Baste around the buttonholes on the right side of the garment, taking the stitches through the facing. Mark each end of the buttonhole on the wrong side by stabbing a pin through from the front.

7. On the wrong side, cut a slit in the facing between the pins and remove them. Turn the raw edge under with the point of a needle and hem around it to make an oval shape, as shown. Press the buttonholes on the right side and remove the basting.

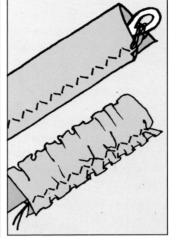

2. Slide a loop turner into the tube and secure the eye to the seam allowance with a few stitches. Ease the tube gently back over the eye of the turner as shown, and pull the turner through to turn the tubing right side out.

● **Attaching button loops**
Measure the diameter of the button and cut the tubing into sections, allowing enough length to fit around the button plus the seam allowance at each end.

1. Mark the position for the loops on the seamline on the right side of the garment. Pin the loops in place and attach them with a row of stitching just inside the seam allowance.

2. Placing right sides of the fabric together, pin and baste the facing in position. Stitch along the seamline. Fold the facing back to expose the loops and press it into position. Slipstitch the facing in place.

BUTTON LOOPS Button loops are more decorative than buttonholes, and they work particularly well on edge-to-edge openings. The loops can be made singly or in strips, and they are inserted between the main piece of fabric and the facing. The loops are made from bias strips which are stitched and then turned right side out to form tubing. The loops can be self-colored or made in a contrasting color and type of fabric for extra effect. effect.

● **Making tubing**
1. Cut a bias strip of fabric the required length and about 1 inch (2.5cm) wide, joining several shorter strips if necessary. Fold the strip with the right side facing and stitch along it 1/8 to 1/4 inch (3 to 5mm) from the fold. The distance from the fold depends on the weight of the fabric, so you may need to work a small sample piece first to make sure that the strip can be turned without splitting. Trim the seam allowances.

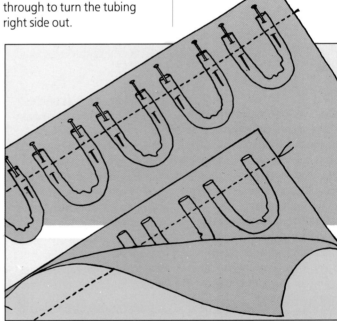

● **Buttons** Buttons can be made from a variety of materials including bone, wood, shell, glass, plastics, ceramics and metals of many kinds, and come in all sorts of different shapes, sizes, textures and colors. Used imaginatively, even a single button can become a focal point; rows of

tiny buttons, used purely decoratively, and in contrasting colors, may become the main feature of a design. The size of the button should be appropriate for its use, for instance small flat ones on babies' clothing and bolder ones on coats and bags. The character of the button – its color, texture, shape – can be chosen to match, complement or contrast with the work in a very positive way.

You can make your own buttons by stretching fabric over a button mold. It may be decorated using any of the embroidery methods, and it is often possible to adapt a small motif from the pattern of the fabric. Rolls of fabric or padded balls covered with detached buttonhole stitch make ideal buttons. Washers or curtain rings can be closely buttonholed, or covered in fabric and quilted. Wooden buttons or toggles can be dyed with a 'fiber-reactive' dye to match exactly. After polishing they will withstand normal washing. Of all the forms of fastenings, buttons will be subjected to the most wear and must be firmly stitched on.

● Frogging This is a bold decorative form of fastening made from spirals of cord or braid, many examples of which can be seen on military uniforms from the Baltic and Hungary. A wide variety of different knot and loop combinations features on European folk costume and textiles from China. The stiffness of the cord or braid affects the way in which they can be coiled and must be designed accordingly. Soft flexible cord such as rouleau can be coiled into tighter, more elaborate frogging. Raw ends can be taken through softly woven fabrics to the back. With firmer fabrics or cords the ends should be tucked under. If the fabric is very stiff, flat braids may be preferable.

FASTENINGS

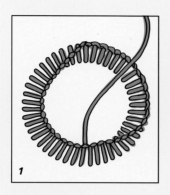

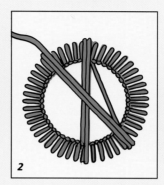

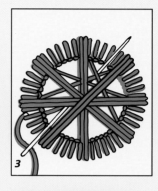

DORSET WHEEL BUTTON
1 Using a metal curtain ring, buttonhole around edge and slip thread through first stitch. Turn looped edge of stitch to inside ring.
2 Take threads from bottom to top of ring, through south east to north west and so on. Finish with a cross stitch in center.
3 With same thread back stitch over each spoke.
4 Repeat until button is filled.
5 Finish off on back.

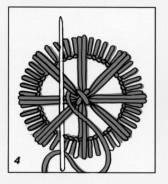

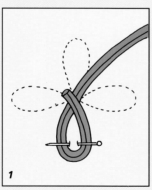

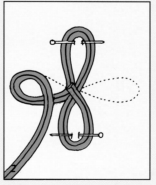

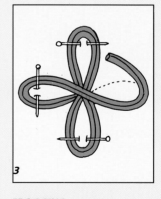

FROGGING
1 Draw design on paper. Place end of cord in middle, extending end about ¼ inch (6mm).
2 Pin loops to paper following design and whipstitch through single fabric only.
3 Trim ends and stitch firmly to hold. Stitches should not show on right side.
4 Remove from paper and place right side up on fabric with button loop extending over edge. Slip stitch in place.
5 Make a second frog for button and attach to button side.

LINING

*L*ining a garment will help to prolong its life, since it prevents the fabric from becoming baggy and pulling out of shape. Lining also finishes the inside by covering the seam edges – essential on a jacket or coat. A lining will also make an outer garment more comfortable to wear, since it will prevent the fabric from sticking to the garments underneath.

A loose lining, which is made separately from the garment and attached later, is the easiest type to make. The lining should be the same size as the garment and made without stitching details such as darts. It should fit without pulling or straining. Fabrics for lining should be slippery and quite soft. The most commonly used materials are fine synthetics and inexpensive silks.

On lined skirts and dresses, the hem of the lining is finished separately from the garment hem.

General rules

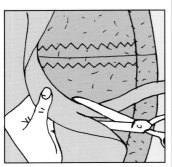

1. Finish the hem of the garment in the appropriate way. Turn the garment inside out and fold back the excess lining at the hem, so that the fold of the lining hem is 1 inch (2.5cm) from the hemline of the garment. Trim away any surplus lining from the hem.

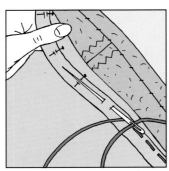

2. Tuck under the raw edge and pin and baste the lining hem in place. Take care not to catch the fabric hem in the stitches.

Machine stitch around the hem to provide a durable finish.

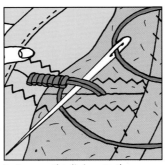

3. Secure the lining to the garment at the side seams by making three or four long stitches, as shown. Reinforce the stitches by working over them with a blanket stitch.

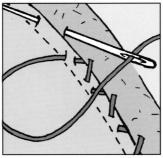

4. The linings of jackets and some coats are slipstitched to the finished garment hem, as shown.

INTERFACING

Interfacing is an extra layer of fabric placed between layers of the garment fabric. It adds body and permanent shape to the garment as well as reinforcing on the fabric. The type of interfacing to use will depend both on the type of garment and on the fabric from which it is made. Interfacing should never be heavier in weight than the garment fabric.

Interfacing comes in various weights and degrees of firmness; some types may be sewn in and others are ironed onto the fabric. Your paper pattern will tell you which garment pieces will need interfacing. The chart shows suitable types of interfacing for garments and fabrics.

INTERFACING		
Fabric Weight	Suggested Fabrics	Recommended Interfacing
Delicate fabrics	Voile, chiffon, crepe de chine, georgette, lawn, silk, cotton, polycotton, polyester	Very soft iron-on
Soft, delicate or lightweight	Voile, chiffon, crepe de chine, georgette, silk, lawn, knits, jersey, polycotton	Light iron-on or Light sew-in
Light to Medium	Challis, jersey, double knits, poplin, wool, woolblends, linen, corduroy, velvet	Medium iron-on or Medium sew-in
Medium to Heavy	Gaberdine, tweeds, double knits, suit and coat weight wools and woollen mixtures	Heavy iron-on Heavy sew-in
Light to Medium	Cotton and cotton blend fabrics	Soft iron-on
Medium to Heavy	Cotton and cotton blend fabric	Firm iron-on

LEFT *Lining a jacket will cover up construction details such as seams, as well as helping the garment to hang better. With all the care that has gone into this elaborately worked evening jacket with its feature smocking and appliquéd leaves, it would be a pity to leave raw seam edges and the underside of the ornamental stitching showing on the inside.*

FACINGS

*O*penings at the neck or sleeves of garments may be finished by attaching a matching piece of fabric called a facing. Armholes on sleeveless garments are also often fiished with a facing. Darts and shoulder seams should be finished and zippers inserted before the facing is added. Interfacing can be added to the facing pieces before stitching to give the neckline a firmer finish.

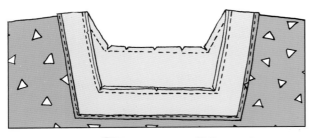

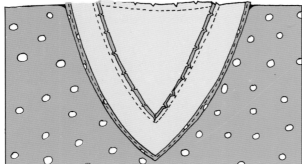

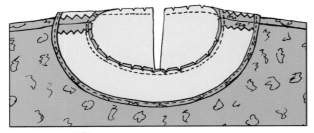

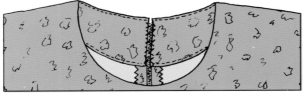

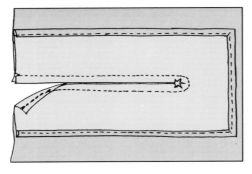

Facing a square neck

Follow the instruction for facing a round neck, but pivot the fabric when stitching the corners, and clip the corners to within ⅛ inch (3mm) of the seamline.

Facing a 'V' neck

Follow the instruction for facing a round neck, but pivot the fabric at the point of the 'V' and clip the edges as shown.

Facing a round neck

1. Join the facing at the shoulder seams and finish the seams. Press the seams open. Finish the edge of the facing that will not be attached to the garment by turning ¼ inch (5mm) to the wrong side and stitching it in place.

2. Pin the facing to the garment with the right sides together, matching the shoulder seams and notches. Baste and stitch it in place.

3. Trim the facing seam allowance to ⅛ inch (3mm) and the garment seam allowance to ¼ inch (5mm). Clip the curves and trim away excess fabric where the seams cross the stitched line. Press seam.

4. Pull the facing to the outside of the neckline. Stitch around the neckline through both the facing and the seam allowances. Stitch as close to the seamline as possible and press the stitching.

5. Turn the facing to the inside so that the seamline lies inside the neckline. Baste the facing in place and press it well.

6. Slipstitch the facing to the garment at the shoulder seams. Fold in the edges along the seamline at the ends of the facing and slipstitch them in place along the zipper.

Facing sleeve openings

Cuffed sleeves require an opening in the sleeve to allow your hand to go through easily. The opening should be finished before the cuff is attached. Sleeve openings are placed on the side of the sleeve toward the back. They can be faced or bound.

1. Cut a strip of the garment fabric 1¼ inches (3cm) longer than the opening and 2¾ inches (7cm) wide. Finish the two long sides and one short one by turning ¼ inch (5mm) of the fabric to the wrong side and stitching in place. Placing right sides together, baste the strip over the opening with the centre of the strip over the cutting line on the sleeve.

2. Stitch around the opening ¼ inch (5mm) from the cutting line as shown, curving the stitching at the top of the opening. Cut to the top of the stitching.

3. Turn the facing to the wrong side of the sleeve and baste it in place. Press the opening and slipstitch the facing to the sleeve. Do not remove the basting stitches until the cuff has been attached.

BINDING OPENINGS

Alternatively, openings for necklines, armholes and sleeves may be finished by binding.

Bound sleeve opening

1. Cut the opening to within ¼ inch (5mm) of the top. Cut a bias strip of fabric twice as long as the opening plus ¾ inch (2cm). The strip should be about 1⅜ inches (3.5cm) wide.

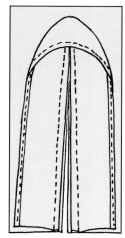

2. Placing right sides together, position one edge of the strip along the left-hand edge of the opening. Stitch along this side and then curve the strip at the top of the opening and stitch around the curve. Continue stitching along the right-hand side.

3. Reinforce the curve with a short row of smaller stitches and then finish the binding in the usual way.

RIGHT *Cuffed sleeves require an opening above the cuff to let the hand pass through easily. This opening needs to be faced or bound for a neat finish.*

BOTTOM RIGHT *A neckline without a collar must be neatened by facing.*

CHAPTER 2

EMBROIDERY

INTRODUCTION

*I*n the previous chapter we looked at the basic techniques of functional sewing. This chapter covers the basic techniques of decorative sewing, and looks at some of the principal categories of embroidery on fabric.

An introduction is given to crewel work, blackwork, whitework, smocking, metal thread work and machine embroidery. Cross stitch and canvaswork (needlepoint) are covered in more detail in separate chapters.

Embroidery has a long history as a decorative art. It has been used for ceremonial purposes to create magnificent displays in areas ranging from military uniforms and heraldic costumes to ecclesiastical work. Embroidery of the highest order has always been associated with the church, for example the rich silk and metal thread work of the thirteenth and fourteenth centuries known as Opus Anglicanum. Modern altar frontals, copes and banners carry on this tradition.

On a domestic level, embroidery has been used to adorn garments and soft furnishings, where it has often included a functional element in strengthening and repairing fabrics. Until modern times embroidery was the principal means to add splendor to clothes, ranging from the traditional decoration of peasant costume to the magnificence of Regency waistcoats.

The use of embroidery to create pictures is also a traditional art: one of the early examples that springs to mind is the Bayeux Tapestry, in which the story of the Norman Conquest of England is depicted in crewel work.

The contemporary needleworker has access to a far wider range of fabrics and threads than was ever available before, as well as to a wider range of designs and techniques; and today embroidery is seen as a rewarding hobby rather than the household duty it once was.

RIGHT *This section is only a small part of an 18 foot (6m) hanging depicting scenes from Chinese court life. It was made with colored silks and metal threads on silk in the late nineteenth century. Detailed observation and rich embroidery make it a remarkable piece.*

ABOVE FAR RIGHT *This machine-embroidered landscape achieves a sense of distance through clever use of color and texture.*

ABOVE RIGHT *This French sixteenth-century valance is a very intricate piece of embroidery. The animal, plant and bird motifs are cross and tent stitches, in silk and wool on linen.*

BELOW FAR RIGHT *A pair of mittens from the seventeenth century show fine decorative work in silver, silver gilt and silk threads on satin. Because they have remained in good condition, the long-and-short and satin stitches with couching are easily visible.*

MATERIALS AND EQUIPMENT

*I*t is not necessary to have an extensive collection of sewing equipment. Decide which items are most important, and build on these basics over time. It is too easy to be seduced by dazzling displays of threads.

Fabrics and threads can be bought from department stores and specialist shops throughout the country. Some shops and small firms run mail order services; their addresses can be found in embroidery magazines.

The basic tools are quite simple. You need a selection of needles for different uses; pins; a bodkin; a thimble; a stiletto; tape measure and tacking cotton. Apart from dressmaking shears, fine embroidery scissors with sharp points are essential. Beeswax is necessary for metal thread work. An embroidery frame will help with some techniques; it is essential when using metal threads.

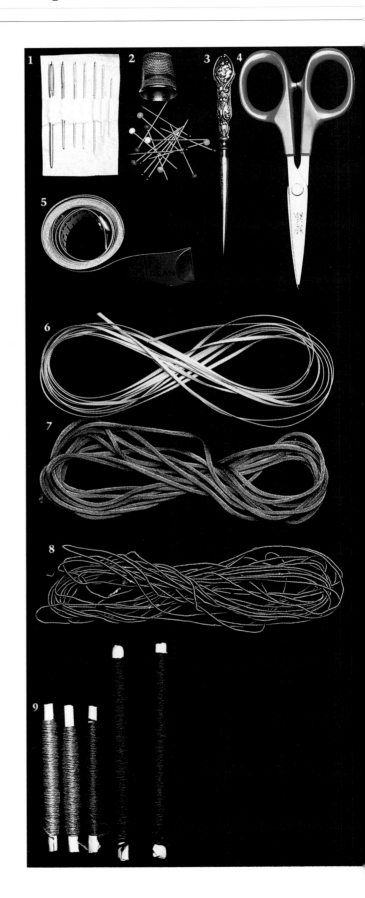

For creating your own embroidery designs, the only essentials are pencil and paper, but you can build up your range of design tools to meet your needs.

The range of drawing, coloring and painting materials is almost endless. Get a variety of materials which make different kinds of marks, rather than spend all your money on dozens of different colors in the same medium. Drawing equipment can range in use from the freedom of charcoal drawing to the precision of the technical pen. Felt-tip markers, for fast free work in color, are cheap and readily available. Technical pens are expensive, but they give a fine clean line. Non-clogging ink is essential. Conté crayons, charcoal and chalk are good for free sketching. Pencils, in a range of hardnesses, are indispensible.

The basic paints are watercolor and gouache. Watercolor is transparent, gouache opaque. A small pocket box of watercolors will do to start; gouaches can be bought in tubes as needed. Choose brushes carefully, and take care of them in use. Three will be enough: sizes 1 (small), 4 (medium), and 7 or 8 (large). Sable is best, but expensive; however, with care, sable brushes will last for years.

Paper is available in a huge variety of weights, colors and textures. A basic minimum of sheets of cartridge for drawing and painting; tracing paper and squared paper, for ready measurement, and for scaling work up and down to size.

You may also find a setsquare useful for drawing true right angles, and a pair of compasses, not only for drawing circles but also for constructing and bisecting angles.

RIGHT 1 *Selection of needles, including a bodkin, tapestry, crewel, sewing and beading,* **2** *Thimble and glass-beaded pins,* **3** *Stiletto,* **4** *Embroidery scissors.* **5** *Tape measure,* **6** *Narrow ribbon,* **7** *Rat tail cord,* **8** *Bourdon cord,* **9** *Linen threads,* **10** *Flower threads,* **11, 12, 13** *Pearl cotton,* **14, 15** *Stranded cottons (shaded),* **16, 17** *Cordonnet,* **18, 19, 20** *Machine thread* **21, 22, 23** *Coton à broder,* **24, 25** *Stranded cottons,* **26** *Crewel wool,* **27** *Persian wool,* **28, 29** *Tapestry wool,* **30** *Bouclé* **31** *Knitting yarn.*

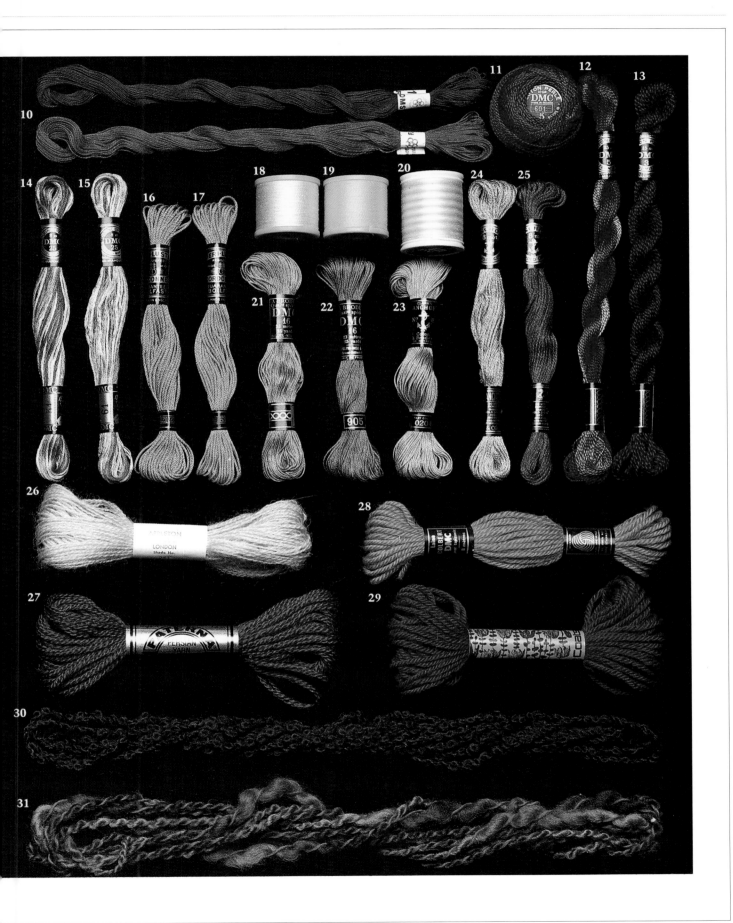

RIGHT *A selection of stranded cottons.*

Fabrics

The traditional fabrics which used to form the background for embroidery are continually being supplemented by new textiles to the extent that the selection can become overwhelming. The wrong choice of background fabric often leads to a disappointing piece of work, so selection with discrimination will save many hours of wasted effort. An understanding of the basic construction of different fabrics, together with handling samples of as many different fabrics as possible, will help considerably. The various techniques of embroidery relate closely to the qualities of the fabrics and threads used, and often to their availability in specific geographical areas. For example, the fine linens of northern Europe have formed the background for many of the lovely whitework and counted thread techniques. The rich endowment of natural fibers – wool, cotton, linen and silk – is now joined by the many synthetic yarns, all of which have their own specific qualities and characteristics.

Different fabric structures create a variety of surfaces to work on. WOVEN fabrics can range from a simple warp and weft to more complicated patterns such as herringbone, twill and damask. These strong patterns can be more difficult to use and in some instances it is hard at first to see whether the patterns are woven or embroidered. Embroidery on evenweave fabrics includes blackwork, canvaswork, cross-stitch, pulled work, pattern darning and drawn thread. The simple regular weave of the background fabric influences the characteristics of those methods.

KNITTED fabrics are constructed with a continuous yarn, and are therefore more malleable and stretchy than woven structures. FABRICATED or non-woven fabrics are firm and do not fray. They range from the natural forms, leather, kid, and suede, to felt, vinyl and bonded interfacings. Other non-woven fabrics include both cotton and synthetic waddings. MESH fabrics have a twisted structure. They range from simple nets to the complicated lace patterns.

The texture of fabrics can vary enormously, depending on their construction and density, and the type and weight of the yarn. Fabrics can be fine or coarse; smooth or rough; thin or thick; dull or lustrous; loosely or firmly woven, and endless combinations and variations of these characteristics exist. The construction yarn can be plied, slubbed, woven to a complicated structure like bouclé or chenille and so on. The surface can also be affected by the finishing processes, such as napping and glazing, applied to textiles.

By collecting and comparing as many fabrics as possible you will learn their different qualities, and, almost certainly, personal preferences will start to develop. Try combining fabrics that are similar in color to make use of the varying effects of light on the surface. Consider the direction of the pile of velvet and corduroy and observe the apparent tonal change that takes place at different angles. Think about fabrics that have a different color warp and weft, such as Thai silk. Again there is a rich variety of tone and color to be seen and exploited in the single piece of fabric. Consider the use of transparent fabrics, exploring the change of tone and color which can be achieved by layering one fabric on another.

To gain further appreciation of the exciting potential of the many types of fabric, try disturbing the surface and structure: firstly by displaying the threads, then removing them altogether, making holes, cutting, tearing and fraying edges so that the fabric is entirely altered. Obviously different constructions will react differently to these treatments, and you will learn how a certain fabric will suit a certain embroidery technique. Some fabrics are particularly amenable to a variety of techniques, and so become dependable favorites.

Many fabrics produced for embroidery backgrounds are found in neutral colors, but exciting effects can be achieved with the use of a colored ground fabric.

Before selecting your fabric, bear in mind the function of the end product, how much wear it will have to stand, whether it will be required to fall in soft folds or to retain a stiff texture, and so forth. A cushion, for example, will have to put up with a surprising amount of squashing and pushing around, so that too soft a material will quickly begin to look tired; an embroidered dress for a child must withstand repeated washing.

Threads

Embroidery threads are available in a wide range of weights and colors. The most common threads are made from cotton and wool, but pure silk, linen, synthetic, and metallic threads can also be bought. Some threads are tightly twisted and cannot be divided, whereas others are made up of several strands which can be separated to give a finer thread. The strands can be put together to give different weights and color combinations, or mixed with another thread. Some threads are not colorfast so take this into consideration if the embroidered item is to be washed. If in doubt, work a few stitches on a scrap of fabric and wash it to check that the color is fast.

Two of the most useful threads are embroidery floss, which can be divided into separate strands (most stitches are worked best with three strands), and pearl cotton which is twisted and must be used as a single thread.

Some people prefer to cut an entire skein into suitable lengths before they begin to stitch. The easiest way of doing this is to cut a piece of cardboard to the required length (say, 15 inches/38 cm), then wind the thread round and round the cardboard and cut through at both ends.

You can store cut lengths by looping them through the holes of a palette – the plastic rings of the top of a pack of

beer cans make a good and inexpensive palette. You can also store cut or whole skeins in a clear-fronted tool cabinet or in the special looseleaf files with clear pockets availble on the needlecraft market.

You can stitch with one, two, three, four, five or all six strands of stranded cotton. Regardless of how many strands you require, you should always 'strip' a cut length before stitching. This entails

carefully extracting each strand, one by one, until all six strands have been separated. As many strands as are required can then be put back together again. This results in smooth, untwisted stitching and the thread will cover the ground fabric better.

Stranded cottons have no nap, so you can stitch from either end of a cut length. Wools on the other hand, usually do have an easily

discernable nap. If you cannot find it by any other means, you can pass the thread over your upper lip. When you have found the nap, make sure that you thread the needle so that the smoothness runs down from the needle along the main thread length.

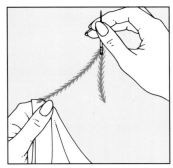

FINDING THE NAP
*1 The easiest way to identify the direction of the nap on the thread is by passing a taut section between the lips both ways.
2 In one direction the thread will feel much rougher. When sewing, make sure that the spines of the nap point are in the opposite direction to the needle.*

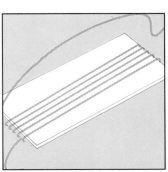
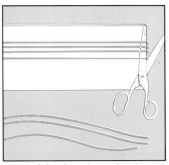
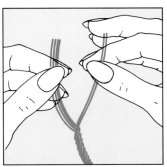

MEASURING THREAD LENGTH
1 The optimum thread length for embroidery is approximately 15 inches (38cm). Longer threads may become tangled.

2 Wind the thread round a piece of cardboard 15 inches (38cm) long as many times as the number of thread lengths required.

3 Cut through all the loops at either end, for a handy bunch of threads, all the same length.

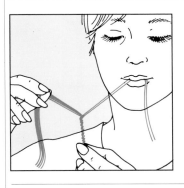
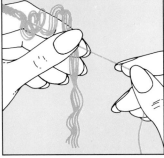

PREPARING THE THREAD
Work with as many strands of the thread as required, separating them out as shown. Do this even when using all the strands.

PREPARING WOOL YARN
Strands must be separated to obtain a smooth working thread.

NEEDLES

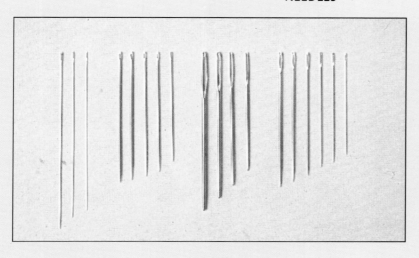

LEFT *A small selection of needles. There are many hundreds on the market, of every conceivable combination of length and thickness. The blunt-ended ones with large eyes are known as tapestry needles and are generally used for canvaswork. The long thin needles are beading needles. Several beads can be threaded on to the needle at once, before it is pulled through. It is impossible to work fine embroidery with a coarse needle, or to penetrate several layers of tough fabric with a needle that is too small, so it is important to select needles carefully.*

Needles

Crewel and chenille needles are used for embroidery on fabric. They have larger eyes than ordinary sewing needles to accommodate a thicker thread. Crewel needles are of medium length and are used for fine and medium-weight embroidery. Chenille needles are longer and thicker, and have larger eyes than crewel needles, which makes them suitable for use with heavier threads and fabrics. Tapestry needles, which have blunt points, are used for working through the surface of some stitches.

All needles are graded from fine to thick with the lower number denoting the thicker needle. The size of needle to use is really a matter of personal preference, but the eye should be large enough to let the thread pass through it without fraying. Always use a fine needle if embroidering on a light, delicate fabric.

Specific needle requirements are listed later in this book for each technique of

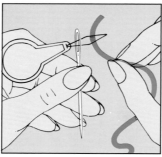

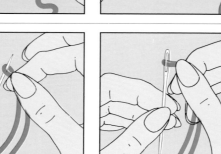

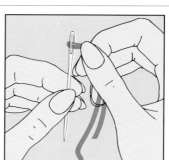

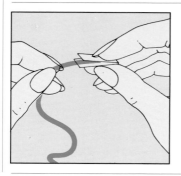

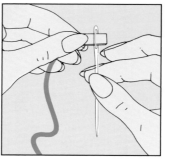

NEEDLE THREADER
1 A needle threader can make needle threading much easier. Thread the diamond of wire through the eye of the needle as shown above.
2 Thread the cotton or wool through the diamond of wire. Draw the needle back over the wire diamond, and it will force the thread through.

LOOP METHOD
1 An alternative method of threading is to use a loop. Wrap the cotton or wool tightly round the eye of the needle in a loop.
2 Ease the loop off the top of the eye, and attempt to thread the needle loop-first. The loop will be stiffer and easier to thread than the limp end.

PAPER METHOD
1 If there is no needle threader to hand, you can use the paper method. Place the end of the thread in a piece of folded paper.
2 The paper can then be pushed through the eye of the needle with the thread inside it. The paper must be small enough to fit and relatively stiff.

FRAMES AND HOOPS

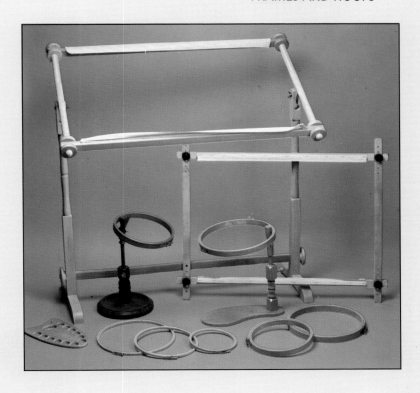

LEFT *A selection of needlework frames that can be used for embroidery, canvaswork and quilting. The advantage of the largest stand is that both hands are left free to work. The fabric must be laced into position, whereas on the square frame without a stand, tacks or drawing pins can be used. The smaller circular frames are only used for fine needlework. They are made from two loops that can be tightened by a screw, between which the fabric is trapped. Whenever a frame is being used, make sure that the fabric is evenly stretched with no wrinkles or buckling. The small palette can be used to keep lengths of thread tidy, separate and accessible.*

needlework. Most experienced needlecrafters have their own favorite needles, and you will quickly discover which size needles, and which type, suits you best.

Today needles are made of stainless steel and should not tarnish easily. If they do discolor it should not affect the fabric or threads with which you are working.

Store the needle you work with most often with a length of thread through it. This way you will be able to find it more easily if it falls. It is not a good idea to store your needle in your mouth, even temporarily.

Embroidery hoops and frames

All embroidery will be more successful if the fabric is held taut in an embroidery hoop. Not only is it easier to handle, but the stitches will be more regular and distortion of the fabric will be kept to a minimum. If the area of embroidery is quite large, the hoop can be easily moved along the fabric after a portion of the stitching has been completed.

Today, frames are generally square or rectangular, whereas hoops are most often circular, sometimes oval. If you are working some counted thread forms, you do not necessarily need to have your material held taut on a frame or hoop; if you are concentrating on canvaswork, you definitely need a square or rectangular frame. In some other techniques it is a matter of your own personal preference whether you work with the piece held in your hand or with the material held taut.

In the past, canvas and other materials had to be laced in place on the square or rectangular frames, a painstaking process known as 'dressing'. Nowadays, a simple range or roller bar frame is available; another inexpensive alternative is to use pairs of artists' stretchers, hammered together. The canvas is held by staples or drawing pins.

When putting canvas or fabric on a frame, it is best to pin one center point of one side first and then pin the center point of the opposite side, followed by the center points of the other two sides. Next, pin outwards from one central pin to a corner point; pin the diagonally opposite section in the same way and continue in this manner until all sections are held firmly. If you are using drawing pins, make sure they lean slightly away from the canvas.

One of the advantages of the two-ringed circular or oval hoop is that it can easily be moved along from one area of the fabric to another. The lightweight plastic hoops available today are particularly easy to set up. The smaller ring is placed beneath the fabric and the larger, screwed ring is placed above it. When the screw is tightened, the fabric is held taut between the ridge on the outside of the smaller hoop and the ridge on the inside of the larger hoop. The tension of the fabric may need to be adjusted from time to time as you sew.

Scissors

Most needleworkers only need two pairs of scissors. One should be large dressmaking scissors with long enough blades to cut fabric and canvas. The other pair should have short, very sharp blades. Needlework scissors should be reserved for sewing and not used for any other purpose.

Working area

Good light and comfortable surroundings are all too often ignored, but both are essential for producing fine work. The best type of light is a gooseneck type, positioned so the light comes over the left shoulder (lefthanded people may find it better to have the light over their right shoulder).

An upright chair with good back support enables you to sit comfortably while you are stitching. If the chair has arms make sure they are not too high. Low and wide arms can conveniently hold pins, scissors and threads. It is quite tempting, when you are progressing well with a piece, to sit and stitch for a long time. Regardless of how comfortable your surroundings and how keen your enthusiasm, it is not a good idea to sit for too long. Try and force yourself at least to stand up and stretch every so often.

Other equipment

There are other pieces of equipment in which you could invest but they are not strictly necessary, as long as you have fabric, threads, needles and perhaps a frame or hoop, scissors and good surroundings. If you do want to add to your range of equipment, a needle-threader is useful, as is a neck-hanging magnifier or a floor-standing magnifying light. Frames and hoops can be held on gadgets that you sit on; at greater cost, some floor-standing models are available. A simpler and less expensive method is to hold the frame on a convenient table or ledge with a handyman's clamp.

You probably already have a container of dressmaking pins and sewing threads useful for basting. You may even have a loop-turner, intended for turning narrow fabric cords and straps right side out. Pencils, a ruler and an eraser should also be to hand. If you are lefthanded, you should also have a mirror nearby to follow diagrams drawn for righthanded needleworkers, using the mirror's reflection to reverse them.

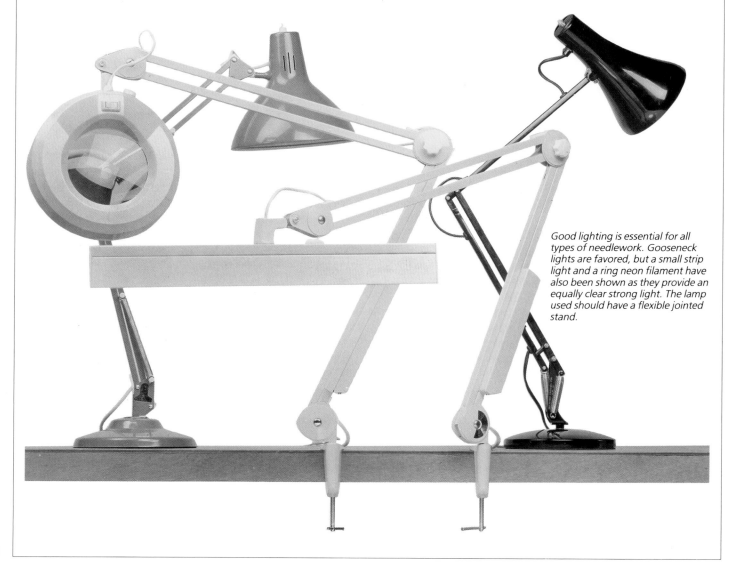

Good lighting is essential for all types of needlework. Gooseneck lights are favored, but a small strip light and a ring neon filament have also been shown as they provide an equally clear strong light. The lamp used should have a flexible jointed stand.

USING A ROUND FRAME

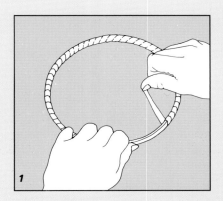

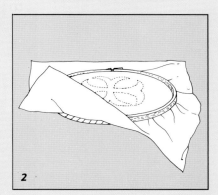

LEFT *Using a frame*
1 To prevent damage to fine fabric, wrap a length of cotton tape around the inner ring. Make sure it is tightly wound, then secure the ends with masking tape.
2 Place the fabric over the inner ring with the design facing upwards. Then place the outer ring over the top and adjust the screw so that it will fit lightly around the inner ring.

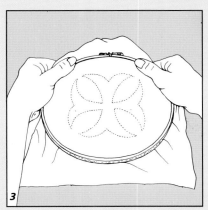

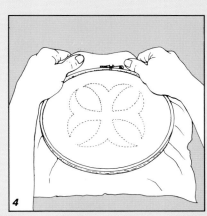

3 With your hands, gradually work your way around the ring, pressing it down over the fabric and inner ring, making sure the fabric is kept taut by pulling it outwards with your fingers and thumbs.
4 You may find that the outer ring rides up as you are pulling on the fabric. In this case push the ring down over the inner circle so that it is securely fitted. When the fabric is evenly taut, tighten the screw to hold the outer ring firmly in place.

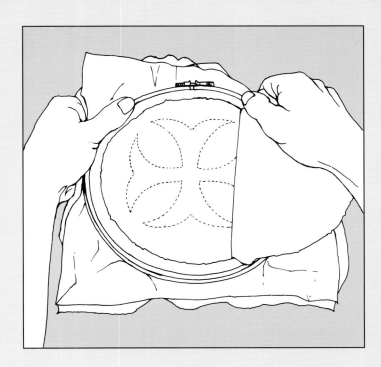

LEFT *The rings may damage the fabric or stitching already worked. To avoid this, lay a piece of tissue paper over the fabric. Put the outer ring in place and secure it. Tear away the paper in the center.*

TECHNIQUES

STARTING AND ENDING THREADS

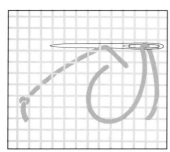 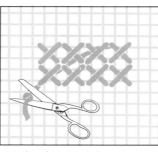 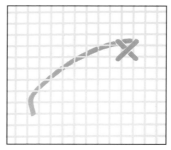 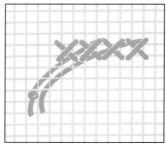

1 To secure the thread end when starting make a knot and leave it on the right side of the fabric.

2 Make a long stitch from the direction in which you will work. The embroidery stitches will hold the thread and you can cut off the waste knot.

3 When ending a thread, secure it in a similar way, by making a waste tail and taking the tail to the area you will be covering with stitches.

4 The tail will not need knotting. It will be bound at the same time as the waste knot of the next thread by that thread's first stitches.

BINDING FABRIC

 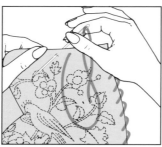 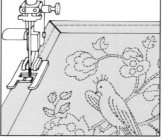 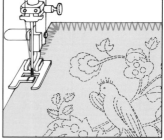

1 To prevent fraying while the piece is being worked, bind the edges temporarily with masking tape as shown.

2 Alternatively, raw edges can be neatly secured with overcast stitching. Overcast by hand, along each edge.

3 A neater and more reliable way of binding the raw edges is to turn them over to the depth of 1 inch (2.5cm) and machine stitch around on the wrong side.

4 If there is a hem, machine straight stitch can be used. Use machine zigzag stitches to bind raw edges, if there is to be no hem.

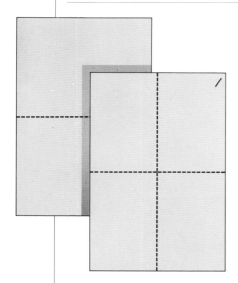

It is often necessary to find the exact center of the fabric in order to organize the design effectively. This can be done by folding the fabric lengthwise and breadthwise. The center of the fabric will be where the two creases cross.

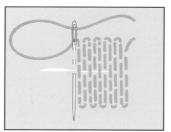

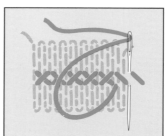

MENDING
If there is a tear in your fabric, you can mend it with small basting stitches worked up and down over it.
Once the basting is in place, the desired stitches can be worked over the basting.

can also be done with one or two little holding stitches, or with the waste tail method.

Waste knots and waste tails are particularly appropriate on canvaswork and other dense stitch techniques. If you finish off a thread by weaving in and out of the back of worked stitches, you are stretching those stitches. By forming waste knots and waste tails each subsequent stitch accommodates the extra thread.

Care of the fabric

The time and labor that goes into a piece of embroidery can all be wasted if care is not taken of the fabric while it is being worked. Simple precautions such as keeping the hands clean and putting the work away in a bag or basket in between stitching sessions will prevent the grubby look that embroidery worked over a long period so easily acquires. Take care when cutting threads not to make an accidental snip in the fabric. If this does happen, you can either work one or two little holding darning stitches and subsequently stitch over them or you can add a small patch, either to the front or the back of the surface, and stitch over it. If you are working a crewel or raised work piece it might be better simply to add another motif, to cover the snip or hole.

Preparing the fabric

When you cut your canvas or fabric make sure to cut exactly between warp and weft threads. If you are cutting linen, you can withdraw a guide thread first to help you cut exactly.

Bind the edges of the cut material to prevent fraying or unravelling. Among the methods are machine zig-zagging and binding with tape; either a serger overlocking machine or a professional tape binder is very useful for this operation. For projects such as tablecloths, it is often easier to miter the corners of the fabric and hem the cloth before beginning the main decoration.

It is always helpful to find the center of your area before you start to stitch. To do this, thread up a length of basting thread, preferably in a pale color that will not show if accidentally caught in subsequent stitching. Measure the halfway point across the top of your area and, from that point, baste from top to bottom of the area, making sure you do not cross any vertical warp threads. Similarly find the halfway point on one side of the area, and from that point, baste from one side to the other, and do not cross any horizontal weft threads.

Beginning and ending thread

It is better not to start stitching with a holding knot. You can secure the end of the thread with one or two little back or running stitches in a space that will subsequently be covered with stitching. An alternative method is to make a waste knot. A knotted thread is taken in from the front of the material, a short distance from where you will begin stitching. The subsequent stitching will then bind the holding thread on the reverse of the work so that the holding knot can be cut without having to turn the material over. Ending a thread

MAKING UP

MOUNTING ON A STRETCHER

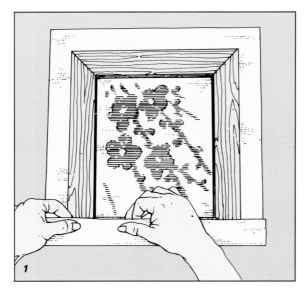

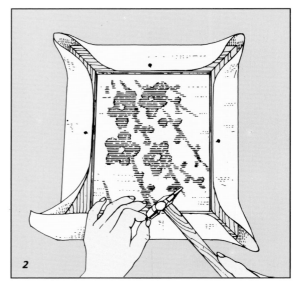

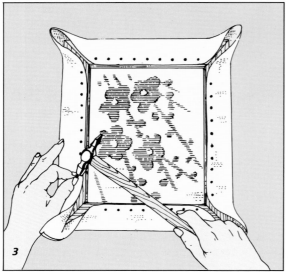

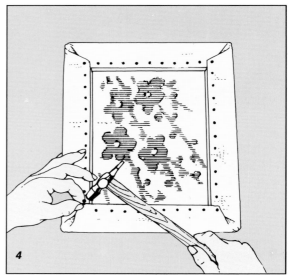

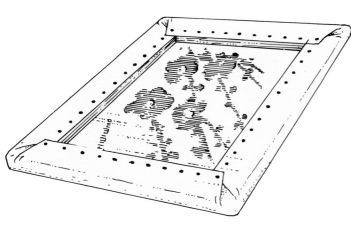

1 Lay the finished piece of embroidery face downwards on a flat surface. Position the stretcher on top of the work and fold the unworked edges of the canvas back over the sides.
2 Insert a tack in the unworked canvas at the center of each side, making sure that the canvas threads are not distorted.

3 Gently hammer in further tacks along the edges, working from the center of each side to the corners. Make sure the embroidery is evenly stretched.
4 Miter the corners with a triangular fold. When the canvas is fully stretched, hammer in the tacks securely.

DAMP-STRETCHING

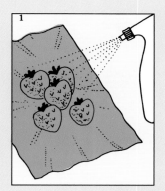
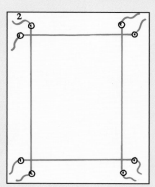
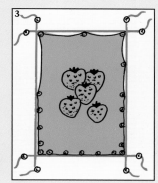

1 Dampen the embroidery by spraying with water.
2 Cover a board with several sheets of clean absorbent paper. Using lengths of string, pin out a rectangle to the finished size. Dampen the paper.
3 Place embroidery on top, right sides aligning the edges with the string. Then working from the middle outwards and on opposite sides, gently stretch and pin to shape with drawing pins. Allow to dry naturally.

*E*mbroidered items for use often need lining, to strengthen the fabric and to cover up the wrong side of the stitching. Some items, for example embroidered panels for an evening bag, can be made up professionally. Most simpler items can be made up easily at home.

Mounting and framing

Before framing, a piece of work must first be mounted on either a wooden stretcher or a sheet of hardboard. Embroidery can be displayed unframed using any of these methods, but framing behind glass will protect the work from dirt and damage, especially important if the fabric and thread are light in color. If you are going to frame the work after it has been mounted, make sure that the stretcher or hardboard is slightly larger than the finished area of embroidery, otherwise some of the stitches will be covered by the overlapping lip (rebate) of the frame.

If the fabric has been pulled out of shape during embroidery, it should be stretched until it is even, as shown.

Mounting on a stretcher

This is probably the easiest method of mounting embroideries. One disadvantage is that the thickness of the stretcher will not fit into a readymade picture frame so you would have to make your own or have one made professionally. As you can see from the diagrams, it is a very simple process.

Mounting on hardboard

This can be done in two ways. The embroidery can be stitched onto a fabric-covered piece of hardboard, or it can be stretched directly over the hardboard and laced at the back with fine string or linen carpet thread. The first method takes longer but is good for mounting work on fine fabrics.

Framing

Once the piece of work is mounted, framing behind glass will protect it from the dirt and dust in the atmosphere. You can make your own frame, buy one ready-made or take your mounted piece to be framed professionally.

It is important that the glass does not touch the embroidered surface or the stitches will be flattened. To avoid this, small strips of wood, mitered at the edges, should be placed in the corners of the frame between the glass and embroidery to keep them apart. These strips of wood should be small enough not to show under the frame. An alternative method of separating glass and embroidery is to use a colored window mount made of acid-free cardboard. After framing, make sure a backing sheet (usually made of brown paper) is firmly stuck over the back of the frame to exclude all dirt and dust.

● **Fabric frames** There are several different ways of making fabric frames. A simple fabric frame can be used on its own, or treated as another opportunity to add either embroidery, screen printing or raised work to the surround. The basic frame should be cut from hardboard or plywood, which is stronger than cardboard – hardboard is recommended by conservators for supporting the back of embroidery as it is a neutral fiber and will not mark fabric over the years.

worked on evenly woven fabric can be cut on the straight grain and back stitched to another piece of fabric, leaving a border to act as a frame. Both fabrics can then be mounted onto a board using the lacing method.

A piece of embroidery laced to a board can be stitched onto another larger board covered with fabric. A curved needle will be needed to do this accurately. If the embroidery is heavy, screws or fixings will be needed to hold both pieces of board together for added support, and to prevent the backing fabric from being dragged down with the weight. On thicker mounts, metal or wooded strips can be added round the edges as a final finish.

MOUNTING ON HARDBOARD

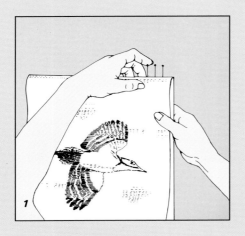

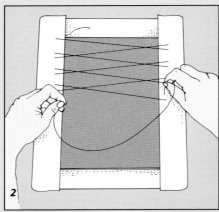

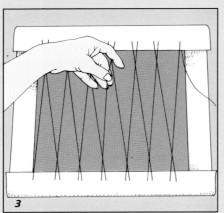

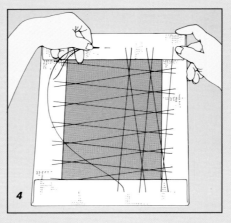

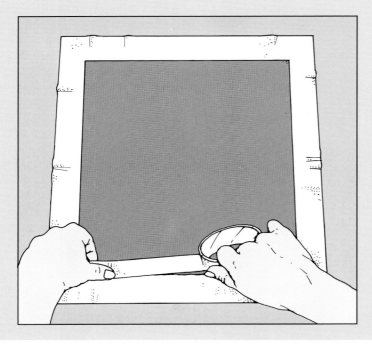

MOUNTING DIRECTLY ON HARDBOARD

1 Place the embroidered piece on the board, face upwards. Fold back two opposite unworked edges of canvas, and put pins through the canvas into the outside edge of the board.

2 Turn the board over and, starting from the top lefthand corner, sew the two overlapping edges of canvas together with large interlacing stitches. With each stitch, go back to the starting point and pull the threads to tighten up the stitches along the way.

3 When you have reached the end, remove the pins. Knot the thread at the starting point and move along the stitching, tightening it up as you go. The fabric should then be firmly stretched.

4 Turn over the other two unworked edges of the canvas and sew these together in the same way. Make simple box corners. Remember to go back and tighten the stitches at each stage, making sure the canvas is evenly stretched.

MOUNTING ON COVERED HARDBOARD

Cut out a piece of lightweight linen, allowing a margin of 3 inches (7.5cm) all round the sides of the board. Stretch it over the board, fold back the edges and stick them down. Position the work face up on the covered surface. Stretch it evenly, pin it and then sew it securely to the fabric.

FRAMING

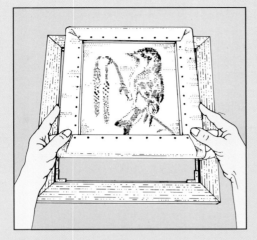

1 Insert small strips of wood in the corners of the frame before dropping the mounted work into the frame. The strips of wood must be small enough to be hidden in the frame, but substantial enough to separate the stitching from the glass and thus prevent flattening.

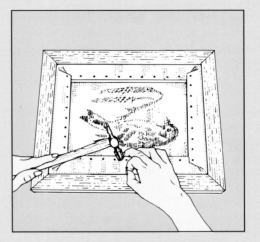

2 To hold the work in the frame, hammer a fine nail into the center of each side of the frame, making sure the nails are angled over the mount.

3 Turn the frame over to check that the embroidered design is positioned, then turn back and insert several more nails at regular intervals around the frame.

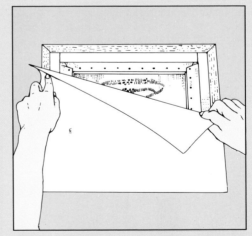

4 Seal the edge between frame and mounted work with cellophane tape to exclude dust. Finish off with a protective sheet of brown paper glued or taped over the back of the frame.

FREE HANGING

*L*arger embroideries are often better displayed by hanging. Traditionally, large textiles were hung using brass rings and hooks, or a pole passed through a fabric sleeve sewn to the back of the textile. The pole should be thick enough to carry the weight of the hanging without bending. Very heavy embroideries will need brackets screwed into the wall. Lightweight fabrics may need weighting at the bottom.

An interlining is necessary for this type of hanging, and for banners, to prevent areas of embroidery or appliqué from pulling the background fabric out of shape.

For strong pieces, these methods may be satisfactory, although the uneven tension created by using hooks and rings may eventually cause damage. Delicate pieces are best displayed using a strip contact fastener (for example, Velcro). This has the advantage of giving even support, and the hang and drape of the piece can be easily adjusted.

Velcro consists of two strips – one soft with a looped pile, the other with a rough barbed surface. A piece of contrast fastener should be cut to fit the entire length of the top edge of the hanging. For ease of handling, the soft strip may then be machine- or hand-stitched to woven tape, wider than the contact fastener itself. The tape, with the Velcro attached, can then be hand-sewn along the top edge of the hanging. Two lines of stitching are necessary – one along the upper edge of the tape, and one along the lower edge. For effective support, the stitching should go through to the front of the hanging, or be fixed as an extension of the lining, and care should be taken to use matching thread and even stitching. The matching barbed strip can be nailed to a wooden batten which is then fastened to the wall. The textile is then hung from the batten by pressing the two strips firmly together.

Large hangings often benefit from being lined, as this helps to prevent soiling of the textile. Curtain lining materials and techniques are normally suitable.

Displaying

It is important when deciding where to hang your framed or unframed piece of embroidery, to choose a position that eliminates the risk of damage during long periods. Always avoid hanging an embroidery where it can be faded by direct sunlight or bright lights. If you hang it over a fireplace or radiator, the constantly changing temperature and humidity will weaken the fibers of the fabric and damage the piece. A large embroidery can make a stunning centerpiece hung alone on a plain wall, or a collection of smaller pieces can be grouped together.

PICTURE FRAMING

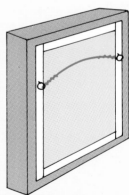

1 If using glass, the embroidery should not be too deep. First stretch the embroidery over cardboard as shown in Mounting and lacing.
2 Decide on the color and type of mount; cut out. Place the cleaned glass inside the frame, then the mount with the embroidery secured to it. Then cover with the frame back.
3 Secure with panel pins and gummed paper strip. Attach rings and cord for hanging.

LEFT *The machine-stitched embroidery of a young Edwardian lady is set in a commercially manufactured plastic frame which has been molded and treated to produce a finish similar to that of an antique wooden frame.*

ABOVE *The frame displaying Grandma and Grandpa, a pair of machine-embroidered portraits, was made from a small block of untreated yew, cut in half and joined with a leather strip at the back. The frame can be closed and clasped like a locket.*

CUSHION COVERS

MAKING UP A PIPED CUSHION COVER

*C*ut a piece of backing fabric the same size as the embroidery. Put the embroidery and backing fabric right sides together and pin the edges. Machine stitch seams on three sides, 1¼ inch (3cm) from the edges, and turn the stitching just around each corner on the further side. Clip diagonally across the corners of the seams, turn the cover to the right side and press the seams, paying special attention to the corners which should be pushed out to square off the shape cleanly. Insert the cushion pad and close up the open side of the cover with handstitching. To make a removable cover, sew snaps or Velcro inside the open edge, or insert a zipper (see page 44).

1 Arrange the piping around the right side of one section of the cover. Baste it down and trim the seam allowance at the corners. Stitch the piping in place.

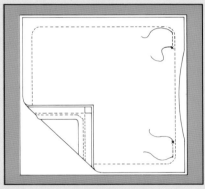

2 On the wrong side of the same section, mark the opening for the zipper. Put the two sections of the cover right sides together and machine stitch on either side of the zipper opening, as far as the corner seams.

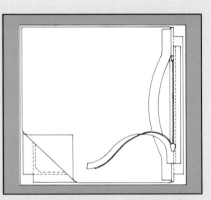

3 Open the zipper and pin one side to the seam allowance of the zipper opening. Machine stitch it in place.

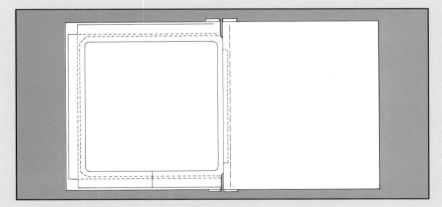

4 Close the zipper and baste across the width at either end. Open out the cover sections, right side up. Stitch the free end of the zipper to the second seam allowance of the zipper opening. Remove the basting threads and open the zipper.

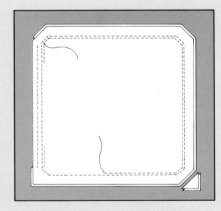

5 Fold the sections of the cushion cover together with the right sides facing and align the edges. Start machine stitching from one side of the zipper opening and work right round the cover, sewing through both layers of fabric and the piping seam allowance. Clip the corners and turn the cushion right side out through the zipper opening.

EMBROIDERY

STITCHES

Stitches are the embroiderer's alphabet; each one has its own characteristics. Practice working them in a medium weight smooth thread, such as perlé no. 5 or cotton à broder, to learn the character of the stitch. Try each stitch in as wide a variety of thread as you can, noticing how the stitch is influenced by the thread that is used.

Choose a needle to suit the thread being used. The needle makes the hole in the fabric for the thread to slide through, so too large a one will leave an ugly gap; too fine a needle will be difficult to sew with and to thread.

Soft cotton fabric is easy to work on. Put a piece of fabric on a frame, and try a variety of stitches and threads on one sampler.

Basic stitches

● **Holbein stitch or Double running stitch** is a simple line stitch used mostly as an outline stitch in free-style embroidery.

It is a very old stitch and is an important component of two distinct types of counted thread embroidery: Assisi work and blackwork. Assisi work evolved in the town of that name in central Italy, probably during the fourteenth century, and is characterized by an unworked design and an embroidered background. The designs, often heraldic, were

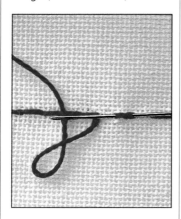

outlined by a row of Holbein stitch worked in black thread, with the background areas solidly filled in with cross stitch in one colour only, traditionally red or blue.

Blackwork, also known as Spanish blackwork or Spanish

work, was worked in a black thread on a white or natural fabric, using Holbein stitch extensively as an outline. The designs were very formal, with strongly outlined shapes and regular geometric fillings, and were sometimes enlivened by the use of metal thread or spangles. The designs were probably of Moorish origin and blackwork spread from Spain to England and the rest of Europe some time during the fifteenth century when it was used as a decoration for clothing.

Holbein stitch is extremely easy to work and is a useful stitch, both for outlines and for intricate linear details. It is worked in two operations. Begin by working evenly spaced running stitches on the traced line. Then using the same colored thread, work running stitches in the spaces left. Unlike back stitch, Holbein stitch is quite reversible.

● **Back stitch** is used extensively for outlining, and is one of the most adaptable stitches in this book. It can be used as a line stitch on common- and even-weave fabrics; as a firm foundation row for composite stitches, such as Pekinese stitch and herringbone ladder filling stitch; and occasionally on

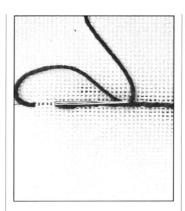

canvas in conjunction with another stitch, where a well-defined outline or center line is needed. When used alone it should be worked in small, even stitches to look rather like machine stitching. This stitch follows intricate curves well if the stitches are kept tiny to let the curve flow. The front of the work is similar in appearance to Holbein stitch (see above) but, where Holbein stitch is quite flat, backstitch is slightly raised.

Working from right to left, bring needle out on line, make a short straight stitch to right and bring needle out on line to left – the same distance from the starting point. Insert needle at starting point and repeat along line working even stitches close together.

● **Blanket stitch**, as its name implies, is used as an edging stitch but it can also be used for borders and outlining in both free-style and counted thread embroidery. It is a looped line stitch worked on common- and even-weave fabrics in exactly the same way as buttonhole stitch (see below). The only difference between the two stitches is the spacing between the uprights: in blanket stitch, a space is left between each upright. Blanket stitch is frequently used as an edging stitch to cover a turned-over surface of the fabric, blanket stitch can be made more

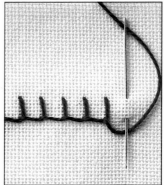

raw edge and makes a good appliqué stitch. The name probably originates from the use of the stitch, sometimes worked by hand but more often by machine, as a method of finishing the edges of blankets. As a line stitch on the

decorative by altering the lengths of the uprights; a simple variation is to make the stitches alternately long and short, either single or in groups of two or three. The lengths can also be varied to form pyramid shapes or the loops at the bottom of the stitch can be whipped with a contrasting color. Blanket stitch also forms the foundation for composite stitches such as barb stitch.

Working from left to right, bring needle out on bottom line. Insert it on top line, to right, and bring out directly below with thread under needle. Repeat along row and

ASSISI EMBROIDERY

LEFT *A stitch detail from an early example of Assisi work, using back stitch and long-armed cross.*

This type of embroidery originated in Assisi, Italy; it is a variation on cross stitch. Its main characteristic is that the design is reversed, with the background stitched and the motifs left unfilled or voided.

Long-armed cross stitch (or plaited Slav stitch) was originally used, but modern interpretations use simple cross stitch. The work is started by outlining the design with back or Holbein double-running stitch. All the outline stitches must lie vertically or horizontally, so that the entire fabric between the motifs is covered.

Plan the design on graph paper, and choose an evenweave fabric whose threads can be easily counted.

finish by inserting needle on botton line.

● **Buttonhole stitch** is ordinarily used to give a firm edge to handmade button holes, but it is also used for cutwork and free-style motifs. Variations of this stitch are used for many types of decorative embroidery, including cutwork, couching and filling. The stitch is equally successful worked in straight lines or following curves, and the size of the vertical stitches can be graduated to give a wavy line or a sawtooth edge at the top of the row. The stitches are placed close together so that no ground fabric shows between them; if they are widely spaced, the stitch is known as blanket stitch (*see above*).

It is worked like blanket stitch but with the stitches

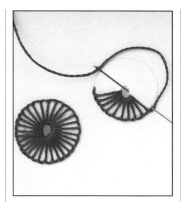

placed close together. For a buttonhole stitch wheel, take the needle through the same central hole, spacing the outer stitches evenly. For a firm edge, work over a row of split stitch.

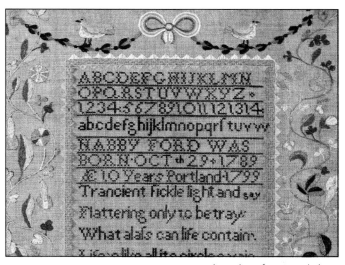

ABOVE *A portion of a cross stitch sampler with a crewel work border, worked in 1799 by a 10 year-old American girl, Nabby Ford.*

● **Chain stitch** is one of the oldest embroidery stitches. Its use is widespread, and examples of the stitch can be found on many antique and contemporary textiles throughout the world.

Chain stitch usually forms a thin line. It can also be worked solidly to produce a dense filling, which lends itself well to shading. It is a simple stitch to work, but care should be taken to keep the stitches even and of the same size. Chain makes a good outline stitch and is very useful for defining curves and intricate shapes when worked

quite small. Any thread is suitable, but the size of the stitch will depend on the weight of the embroidery thread used. Chain stitch can be used as a filling in either of two ways: it can be worked in close rows to fill the shape, or the rows can be worked from the centre outward in a spiral,

using one or more colors or textures. Chain stitch can have a row of backstitch worked down the center, in either a matching or a contrasting thread. Chain stitch can also be worked singly as an isolated stitch and it is then known as detached chain stitch or lazy daisystitch.

Bring needle out and make a straight stitch downwards inserting a needle at starting point. Pull through with loop under needle point. Repeat, inserting needle where thread emerges. Finish row with a small stitch over last chain loop to secure.

● **Cross stitch** is probably one of the oldest and best known of all embroidery stitches. It has many variations and has been known world-wide for centuries. Cross stitch is still used on traditional embroideries in many areas, including the Greek Islands, Scandinavia, Central and Eastern Europe, and India.

It is an extremely quick and easy stitch to work and is used mainly on even-weave fabrics where the threads can be counted to keep the crosses even. The stitch can also be used on other plain-weave fabrics but guidelines will need to be marked on the fabric unless a commercially produced transfer is being used. Among its many uses, cross stitch is excellent for outlines, solid fillings, formalized motifs, borders, and lettering (see Chapter 3). The top diagonal stitches must always fall in the same direction, unless a deliberate light-and-shade effect is required, in which case the direction of stitches can be varied to catch the light. Work a complete cross stitch before proceeding to the next stitch to

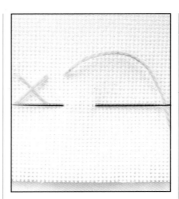

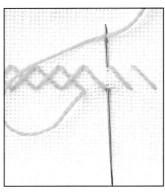

form neat, slightly raised crosses.

Working from right to left, bring needle out on bottom line, take it to top left and bring out directly below on bottom line. Complete row of diagonal stitches. Working from left to right, complete crosses by making diagonal stitches in opposite direction. For a single cross, work from bottom right to top left, then from bottom left to top right.

● **Herringbone stitch** is a line stitch that makes a pretty, crossed zigzag line. The stitches must be perfectly regular. It is worked from left to right and is very easy and quick to work. Guidelines may need to be marked on the fabric to keep the row straight. When the stitch is used as a filling, the rows can be placed so that the tips of stitches on each row touch those on the row immediately preceding them. This will give a light trellis effect. For a heavier look,

arrange the rows underneath each other so that the zigzags interlock. Herringbone stitch is also used as the foundation row for a number of more complicated stitches. Any type of thread can be used for this

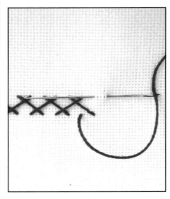

stitch, the choice depending on the size of stitch required and the weight of the ground fabric.

Working from left to right, bring thread out, take it diagonally upwards and make a short back stitch on top line. Repeat making a similar stitch on bottom line, bringing needle out directly under starting point of stitch above. Continue in this way along row working evenly spaced stitches.

● **Fancy herringbone** is a wide, ornamental stitch. It makes a rich border, particularly if a metallic thread is used for the interlacing, and it can look stunning if worked in spaced multiple rows, using a carefully chosen color scheme.

It is simple to work, in spite of its rather complex appearance. Each row is worked in three journeys. First, a foundation row of herringbone stitch is worked, using guidelines marked on the fabric. A row of upright cross stitches is then worked over the top and bottom crosses of the herringbone rows, taking care that the horizontal bar of the

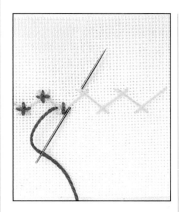

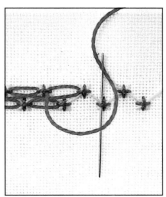

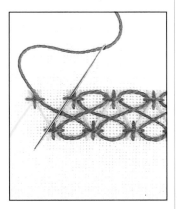

cross stitch is always worked over the vertical one. These two journeys can be worked in the same color threads, or two contrasting threads. On the third journey, the horizontal bars are interlaced without the ground fabric being picked up. Use a tapestry needle for the interlacing to avoid splitting the stitches on the two preceding rows.

● **Satin stitch** is used for filling shapes and sometimes for borders and is one of the oldest embroidery stitches. It consists of straight stitches worked side by side. Although it appears to be an easy stitch to work, it requires some practice before it can be worked evenly. It should be worked on fabric stretched in an embroidery hoop to prevent the material from puckering, and the stitches should lie evenly and closely together to cover the ground fabric completely. When used for a border, it is worked between two lines with the stitches either slanting or at right angles to the lines to give a perfectly smooth surface.

When worked to fill a shape, the stitches are taken right across the shape and can be worked vertically or diagonally,

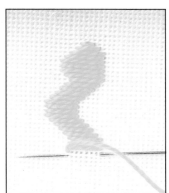

with changes of direction giving the effect of light and shade. This effect is enhanced by the use of a lustrous thread such as embroidery floss or silk thread but any embroidery thread can be used, the choice depending on the effect required and the weight of the ground fabric.

1. Begin on bottom line and make a short upright stitch (not longer than ¾ inch (2cm). Bring needle out close to starting point.

2. Make second stitch close to first.

3. Complete the row keeping an even tension.

SATIN STITCH

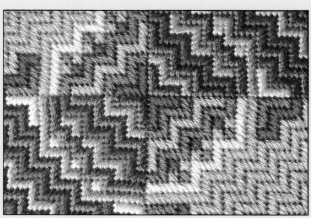

Satin stitch is a versatile filling stitch.

ABOVE TOP *On canvas it can be used for outlines or small shapes, with the stitches running vertically, horizontally or diagonally, to create a dense texture.*

ABOVE BOTTOM *On common-weave fabric, satin stitch has long been a favorite stitch for working flowers, as in this exquisite piece of 19th century Chinese embroidery.*

GROUPING STITCHES INTO FAMILIES

Outline Stitches

The main characteristic of this family of stitches is the linear quality, developing from the simplicity of running stitch to the raised and cord-line appearance of scroll stitch. They are useful when stressing the linear aspect of a design. They can also be used closely packed to fill an area.

● **Scroll stitch or coral stitch** is a line stitch used on common- and even-weave fabrics. It makes a simple knotted line which flows around curves and follows intricate details well, and is often used to depict areas of water. Any type of embroidery thread can be used with scroll stitch, provided that it is compatible with the weight of the ground fabric. A stranded thread gives a much flatter effect than a rounded thread such as pearl cotton. It is

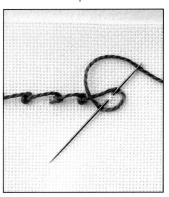

very quick and easy to work and runs from left to right along the line. It consists of a series of simple knots which are linked together. The knots should not be pulled tightly and they can be worked close together or spaced quite widely apart, depending on the effect required.

● **Split stitch** is a line stitch used on plain- and even-weave fabrics. It is used for outlines, as it follows intricate designs well, and it is also worked solidly as a

shaded filling, especially for figurative embroideries, because of its brush-stroke quality. The type of thread suitable for use with split stitch is confined to a soft, untwisted thread which can be split by the

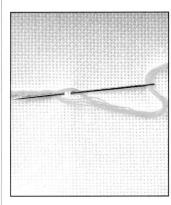

needle. The method of working this stitch is similar to stem stitch (see below) but in this case the thread is split by the needle as it emerges from the fabric. The result is rather like chain stitch (see page 74) in appearance.

Split stitch was used during the Middle Ages for embroidering figures, particularly hands and faces. Examples of 'opus anglicanum' still exist which show the extensive use of this stitch.

● **Stem stitch** is one of the most frequently used outline stitches. It is quite easy to work and follows curves and intricate linear details well. It can also be used for filling and shading areas.

The stitch is simply worked with a forward and backward motion along the line. The stitches should be evenly worked and equally sized. The working thread must always be kept at the right of the needle; if it is at the left, the effect is slightly different. A slightly wider stem stitch line can be made by inserting the needle into the fabric at a slight angle

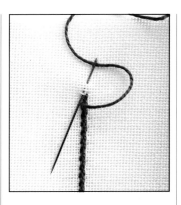

to the line instead of directly along it. Any type of embroidery thread can be used, provided that it is compatible with the size of the stitch and the weight of the ground fabric.

Stem stitch filling is a way of using rows of stem stitch to make a very useful solid filling for a shape of any size on plain and even-weave fabrics. It makes a closely packed filling with a woven appearance, and any type of embroidery thread can be used, from a fine crewel yarn to a heavy pearl cotton. The lines of this stitch should follow the contours of the shape quite carefully, and the stem stitches should be of an even size on each row. The first stem stitch of each row should be a little shorter than the first stitch of the preceding row in order to give the effect of a pattern of diagonal lines across the surface.

Stem stitch shading is worked in exactly the same way by following the contours of the shape carefully. The colors should be evenly shaded and changed on every second or third row.

Looped stitches

When working stitches from this group the method requires the thread to be looped under the needle to form the stitch. Simple buttonhole and blanket stitch are worked in rows, whereas fly stitch can be worked singly or in groups. Cretan stitch is particularly versatile.

● **Feather stitch** is a decorative line stitch. This stitch has been extensively used on traditional English smocks, both as a smocking stitch and as surface embroidery; it is also used as a decorative joining stitch on hand-sewn crazy patchwork.

It makes a pretty, feathery line, which is equally effective

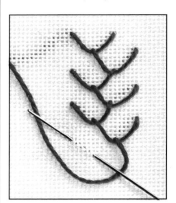

when worked in straight lines or following curves. Worked downward, it is a quick stitch, easy to perfect. Thread is brought through at the top of the line to be covered and a slanting loop stitch is made alternately to the left and to the right of the line. Any type of embroidery thread can be used with feather stitch but the desired effect and the weight of the ground fabric must be taken into account.

● **Fly stitch** is an isolated stitch often worked in rows. Each stitch is worked very easily: a V-shaped loop is made and then tied down with a vertical straight stitch. The tying stitch can vary in length to produce different effects. The fly stitches can be arranged side by side to make a horizontal row, or worked underneath each other to make a vertical row. The stitches can touch one another or be spaced apart at a

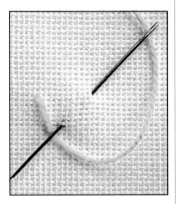

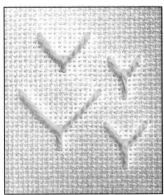

regular interval. Isolated fly stitches can be used to make a pretty powdering, either spaced evenly or scattered at random over a shape. Each stitch can be decorated by the addition of a Chinese knot in a contrasting thread. Any type of thread can be used for this stitch, although stitch size and fabric weight must be taken into account.

● **Cretan stitch** is a line stitch or filling for narrow shapes, used on common- and even-weave fabrics. The name is derived from the island of Crete, where the stitch has been used for centuries to decorate clothing. It is also found on Persian embroideries, and the stitch is called Persian stitch in France.

When used as a filling, the stitch is worked from alternate sides of the shape to completely cover it. A plait forms down the centre of the space to make a very decorative filling. This stitch can be worked with the stitches close together, or they can be spaced apart to let the ground fabric show through. Whether it is used as a filling or as a line stitch, different effects can be achieved by varying the amount of fabric picked up and by altering the slant of the needle. When used as a line stitch, it is usually worked with an open finish, and it makes a pretty, spiked line, which follows curves well. Any type of embroidery thread can be used with Cretan stitch, but when it is being used to fill a shape solidly, a stranded silk or cotton will give better cover.

● **Vandyke stitch** is a border stitch and filling used on plain- and even-weave fabrics. It makes a wide line with a raised plait in the center, and

looks very attractive worked in multiple rows to create a heavy border. By graduating the length of the stitches on each side of the plait, it is also used to fill narrow shapes. It is worked downward between two parallel lines, and guidelines may need to be marked on the fabric if the threads cannot be counted to keep the stitch an even width. The top stitch picks up a tiny amount of fabric at the center to anchor the whole row. The second and subsequent stitches cross the line from left to right, passing behind the preceding

stitch at the center; no ground fabric is picked up. The stitches should be worked close together to make a solidly stitched row that covers the fabric completely. A lustrous embroidery thread, such as stranded silk or cotton floss shows Vandyke stitch to its best advantage and accentuates the central plait.

TRANSLATING A DESIGN INTO STITCHES

ABOVE In this section of a landscape, areas of densely worked French knots contrast with smoother areas of overlapping cretan and straight stitches. The rich texture of stitches is complemented by the areas of smooth unworked background fabric.

Flat stitches

There is a wide range of stitches that are built up from the simple straight stitch. When repeated this can become satin, long and short or brick stitch, creating smooth areas of thread. The simple variations of cross stitch can develop into herringbone, leaf or chevron.

● **Leaf stitch** is a filling stitch used on common- and finely woven, even-weave fabrics. It is a light, open stitch suitable for filling small areas, such as oval or leaf shapes. It is always worked upward and consists of slanting straight stitches, which pass from one side of the shape to the other and make a loose plait down the center. An

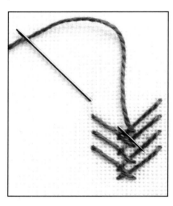

outline stitch, such as backstitch (see page 72) or stem stitch (see page 76), is worked around the edge to define the shape more distinctly. Leaf stitch can also be worked between parallel lines to make a border and the length of the stitches can be varied to give an undulating line. A lustrous embroidery thread, such as stranded floss, shows this stitch off to its best advantage, although any type of thread can be used.

● **Long and short stitch** is a variation of satin stitch (see page 75) which gives a gradually shaded effect and is much used in naturalistic

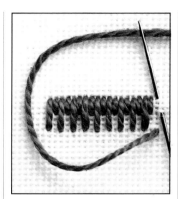

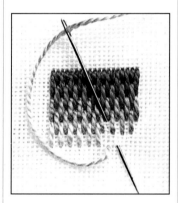

embroidery. It is also used to fill an area that is too large or irregularly shaped to be covered neatly by satin stitch. It can be worked on all types of fabric and on mono canvas. The first row is made up of alternately long and short stitches which follow closely the outline of the shape to be filled. The subsequent rows are worked in satin stitches of equal length. The stitches should lie closely together and cover the ground fabric.

● **Fishbone stitch** is a filling stitch used on plain and even-weave fabrics. It is often used to fill petal and leaf shapes when the stitch lengths are graduated to follow the outline of the shape. It also makes an attractive solid border when the stitches are of equal length, and it makes a flat, solidly stitched surface in which the stitches cross one another at the center. A central vertical straight stitch is worked at the

top and then slanting straight stitches are worked alternately from the center to each side of the shape. The stitches should be worked evenly and very

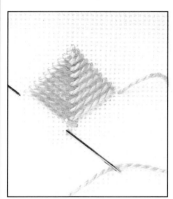

close together so that no ground fabric is visible. A lustrous embroidery thread, such as stranded floss or silk, will emphasize the different directions of the stitches. The stitch can be striped by threading two needles with different colors and using each color alternately.

● **Chevron stitch** is a line and filling stitch used on common- and even-weave fabrics. It is

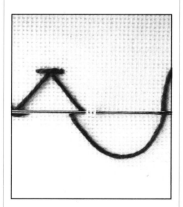

also used as a smocking stitch to make both the diamond and surface honeycomb patterns. Chevron stitch is worked from left to right between two parallel lines, in a similar way to herringbone stitch (see page 74), and makes a pretty zig-zag line. This stitch does not follow

curves well unless they are very gradual. It is composed of diagonal stitches set at an angle to a shorter horizontal stitch worked where these stitches meet. To keep the width of the stitches even, guidelines need to be marked on the fabric, unless the threads can be counted.

When used as a filling stitch, the rows are placed close together to give a lattice effect, which benefits from being worked neatly and regularly. An isolated stitch such as daisy stitch (see page 74) can be worked in the center of the diamond-shaped spaces to make the filling more decorative. Chevron stitch can also be threaded with a contrasting color.

Chained stitches

This is a comprehensive group of stitches and contains numerous variations. Most of them have a linear quality and the more complicated forms gives a decorative raised line. Detached chain and wheatear stitch are worked separately. Simple chain is also used to give a solid filling.

● **Open chain stitch** is a line stitch worked downward on common- and even-weave fabrics. A variation of chain stitch (see page 74) it is quick and easy to work. Carefully follow the sequence shown and anchor the last chain in each row by a tiny straight stitch through each of the bottom corners. Open chain stitch can be worked to give either an open or closed effect by simply adjusting the spacing between the stitches. It can be worked between parallel lines to make a heavy outline, and can couch down cords, narrow ribbons or other threads. This stitch is also suitable for filling

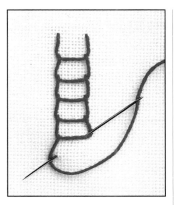

narrow shapes of graduated widths, or it can be worked solidly row upon row to fill a larger area. It is essential that the line should be of an even width and guidelines may need to be marked on the fabric when the stitch is worked in a straight line if the fabric threads cannot be counted.

When this stitch is spaced so that the ground fabric shows through, the space in the center of each chain stitch can be decorated with an isolated stitch. Running stitch or chain stitch can be worked down the center of each row in a contrasting color or a different weight of embroidery thread. Open chain stitch worked close together to make a solid line with no ground fabric showing through is characteristic of both Indian and East European embroidery, particularly that of Hungary and Yugoslavia.

● **Broad chain stitch** is a line stitch used on common- and even-weave fabrics. It makes a bold, broad line suitable for where a heavily defined outline is needed. A firm thread should be chosen so that the individual stitches keep their shape well. Begin the row by working a short straight stitch; this will anchor the top chain. Bring the needle out of the fabric further along the line and then work the top chain through the straight stitch; work the second

and subsequent chains as shown. When the needle passes under the chain loops,

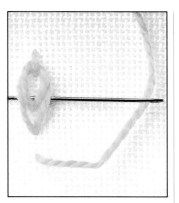

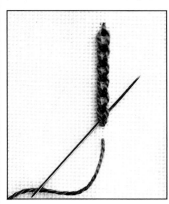

no ground fabric should be picked up: the chain stitches should be left quite loose on the surface of the fabric to make the line flat and broad.
● **Heavy chain stitch** is a solid line stitch used on common- and even-weave fabrics. It makes a heavy, cord-like line which is useful where a well-defined outline is needed. It is similar in construction to broad chain stitch (see above) and is also worked downward. The row starts with a vertical straight stitch worked in exactly the same way as broad chain stitch; the second and subsequent chains are then worked as shown. The difference between this stitch and broad chain stitch is that the needle is passed back under the previous two chain loops, rather than just the previous

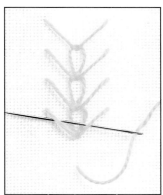

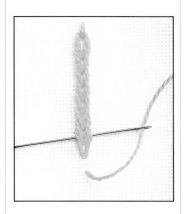

one, to form the next stitch. When the needle passes under the chain loops, no ground fabric should be picked up. This stitch can be worked row on row to fill an area, but the effect can be rather solid and uninteresting, and choice of thread is important. Any type of embroidery thread can be used when heavy chain stitch is worked in a single row, although a round, twisted thread will make the line stand out best from the background. A stranded floss will create a flatter, wider line.
● **Wheatear stitch** is a decorative line stitch used on common- and even-weave fabrics. It makes a branched line with a heavy central strip and looks rather like an ear of corn, especially when used in short lengths. The stitch follows a gentle curve but is normally used on the straight. Wheatear stitch was often used as a

surface decoration on traditional English smocks. The stitch is worked downward and consists of two diagonal stitches set at a right angle and

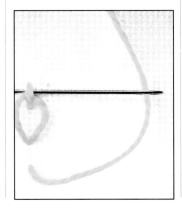

then joined by a broad chain stitch (see above), as shown. The length of the diagonal stitches can be varied to give an attractive irregular line, and any type of embroidery thread can be used.

Designing with stitches

Throughout the past centuries the use of stitches has been influenced by the fashion of the day, and the availability of fabrics and threads. Embroiderers often copied designs and patterns from books of designs printed especially for craftsmen and women, or drawn out by professional designers who toured the country. Fortunately, embroiderers today are released from these inhibitions, and the number of ways of creating a personal design is infinite.

Knotted stitches

These form a useful group as they contrast with the flatter, smoother stitches. The single units of French knots and bullion knots can be worked closely together or scattered in a random manner. The knotted linear stitches like coral or knotted chain give a decorative effect.

● **French knot** is an isolated stitch used on common- and even-weave fabrics. It is a neat, raised knot, which has many used. It can be used as an accent stitch, as a powdering, massed together to make a solidly textured area, and worked closely in rows to make an outline. It can also be used over an area of canvas stitching, where extra texture or dots of contrasting colors are needed. Any type of thread can be used and the weight of the thread will determine the size of the finished stitch.

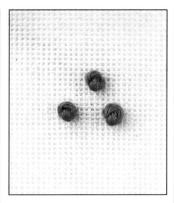

Interesting effects can be made when French knots are massed together. To achieve this, work each knot with three or four contrasting threads placed through the needle at the same time.

A French knot is a little tricky to work and some practice will be needed to perfect the stitch. Work the knot with the fabric stretched in an embroidery hoop or frame to leave both hands free for the working. Bring the thread through the fabric and, if you are right-handed, hold it taut with the left hand, while twisting the needle around it two or three times with the right hand. Then tighten the twists, turn the needle and insert it back into the same place in the fabric, still keeping the thread taut, and pull the needle through. The thread slides through the twists to make the knot.

● **Bullion knot** is an isolated stitch used on common- and even-weave fabrics. It is a long, coiled knot which can be used as an accent stitch; as a powdering; massed together to make a densely textured filling; worked close together to make a heavy outline; or used on top of an area of flat needlepoint, where extra texture or splashes of color are needed. Any type of embroidery thread can be used; the weight of thread

determines the size of the finished knot. Three or four contrasting fine threads can be threaded through the needle at the same time to create some interesting effects with this stitch.

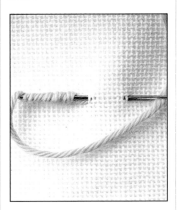

A bullion knot is a little tricky to work and some practice will be needed to perfect it. It is better to work bullion knots on fabric which is stretched in an embroidery hoop or frame, thus leaving both hands free to work the knot. Bring the thread to the surface and insert the needle a short distance away, so that the point emerges at the same place as the thread. The distance between the point where the needle is inserted and the place where the thread emerges determines the length of the knot. Coil the thread around the needle six or seven times and then pull the needle carefully through the coil,

which should be held down firmly on the fabric with the left thumb (if you are right-handed). Gently pull the working thread in the opposite direction to tighten the coils and insert the needle in exactly the same place as before. The coil of thread should now lie neatly on the surface. A rather thick needle with a small eye should be used so that it will pass easily through the coil. By coiling the thread many more times around the needle a different type of bullion knot can be created. The coil will be too long to lie flat on the fabric and will make a small hump instead of a long knot.

● **Double knit stitch** is a line stitch used on common- and even-weave fabrics. Characteristic of Italian embroidery, this stitch makes an attractive knotted line with a beaded effect. It is used for outlines, linear details, curves

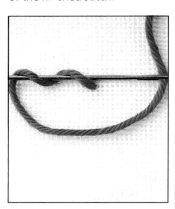

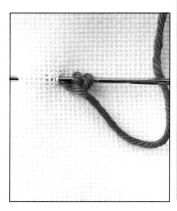

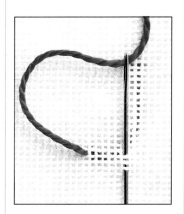

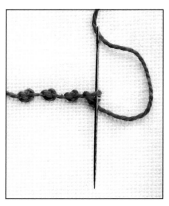

and, by working it solidly, as a textured filling. It can also be worked as an isolated stitch and be used as a powdering. Work the stitch from left to right: make a straight stitch and loop the thread under and over it to form a knot at the end. The knots can be arranged more closely together and the straight stitch made very small to give a heavy line. Use a round, twisted thread, such as pearl cotton, for this stitch to show the knots to their best advantage.

● **Coral stitch** is a knotted line stitch used on common- and even-weave fabrics. It is one of the oldest embroidery stitches, and many examples of it can be

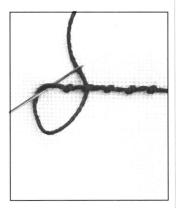

found on seventeenth- and eighteenth-century English crewel embroidery work. It is worked from right to left.

Hold the thread loosely on the surface of the fabric with your left thumb (if you are right-handed) and pull the needle through the fabric and over the thread to form a knot. The stitch can be varied by altering the angle of the needle as it takes up the fabric, and by changing the spacing of the knots along the row. Any type of embroidery thread can be used; the effect made depends on the weight and composition of the thread. Coral stitch is used for outlines, as it follows

curves well, and for linear details. It can also be worked solidly to cover an area with a pretty, knotted filling. The knots can be arranged so that they form lines across the filling, or they can be set alternately on every row.

Filling stitches

A number of ways can be used to shade in an area of design. Individual stitches like seeding and sheaf give a speckled appearance, whereas cloud filling stitch makes a more regular effect. Couched laid threads give great variety and stitches like cretan and long and short are equally suitable.

● **Sheaf filling stitch** is used to fill a shape of any size on common- and even-weave fabrics. It makes an extremely attractive light filling when worked in a regular pattern, and each stitch looks like a tiny sheaf of corn. The sheaves are usually arranged in rather

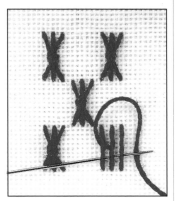

formal rows but they can also be scattered in all directions. Each sheaf consists of three vertical satin stitches (see page 75) bunched and tied around the center by two small horizontal stitches. The needle should emerge from the fabric behind the satin stitches to work the overcasting, without picking up any ground fabric, before taking the needle to the

back of the work. Any type of embroidery thread can be used, the choice depending on the size of sheaves required.

● **Seed stitch** is a filling stitch used on common- and even-weave fabrics. It makes a light speckled powdering for an area, and is extremely quick and easy to work. Work tiny backstitches (see page 70) in any direction over the area to be filled. They should all be of even length, but should be

scattered irregularly and should not make a pattern. The size and spacing of the backstitches can be varied, depending on the type of thread used and the effect required.

● **Tête de boeuf** filling stitch is used on common- and even-weave fabrics. It looks like a bull's head, complete with the horns. A fly stitch (see page 77) makes the horns, and a daisy stitch (see page 74) anchors the

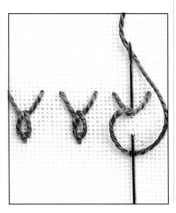

fly stitch and makes the head. It is usually worked in formal rows to make an attractive light filling but the stitch can also be worked in horizontal rows to form a border.

● **Cloud filling stitch** is a composite filling stitch used on common- and even-weave fabrics. It is a quick and

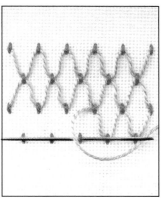

effective way of filling a shape, and it has an attractive, lacy appearance. any type of embroidery thread can be used, the choice depending on the effect desired. A foundation of regularly spaced, vertical stitches is worked over the entire area to be filled. The stitches can be placed close together or be widely spaced, but they should be worked perfectly evenly. If a common-weave fabric is used, the position of these stitches will need to be marked on the fabric before they are worked. A second thread of contrasting color or weight is then laced through these stitches in rows. The needle enters the fabric only at the beginning and end of each row. Use a blunt-ended tapestry needle for the second thread to avoid splitting the stitches on the foundation row. The delicate trellis pattern that is made can be decorated by working an isolated knot stitch, such as French knot (see page 80), in the spaces.

Couching stitches

Threads to be couched are laid on the surface of the material and held in place. A number of embroidery stitches like cross detached chain or buttonhole can be used as well as the usual small straight stitch. Many of the decorative laid fillings are based on the couching technique.

● **Couching** takes its name from the French word 'coucher', meaning to lay down. The technique involves laying a thread or group of threads on the surface of a common- or even-weave

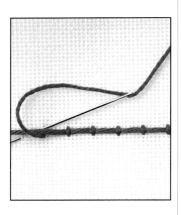

fabric, and then tying them down by means of a second, often finer, thread. Couching was extensively used on medieval embroideries to keep scarce and expensive threads, especially those made from precious metals, on the surface of the work to avoid any waste. It was also used to attach threads to the fabric when they were too thick, rigid or textured to be stitched directly into the fabric or thread. Couching can be used to work linear designs, to cover the edge of an appliquéd shape, or to fill an area solidly.

This technique should always be worked with the fabric stretched in an embroidery hoop or frame. It is

worked from right to left, usually along a guideline marked on the fabric, unless it is being worked as a filling. The thick thread (or group of threads) is brought to the surface of the fabric, laid loosely along the line to be couched and, if you are right-handed, held in place and guided by the left hand. The couching thread is brought through, and small, straight stitches are taken over the thick thread and back through the fabric. The line of thick thread should lie evenly on the surface after it has been couched. When the line is completed, all the threads are taken to the back of the work and secured. When working curves, arrange the couching stitches closer together so that the curved line lies flat. An extra stitch or two may need to be worked when negotiating an angle to make sure that the corner of the couched thread lies flat. When this stitch is used solidly, row on row, for filling a shape, the couching stitches can be arranged so they form parallel rows across the laid threads. They can also be placed alternatively on each row, or arranged to make a small geometric pattern.

● **Couched filling stitch**, also known as *Jacobean couching*, is a composite stitch used for filling shapes on plain- and even-weave fabrics. It has a pretty, lattice appearance and can be worked in two or more colours. It should always be worked with the fabric stretched in an embroidery hoop or frame to keep the foundation grid perfectly regular. The grid is worked first and consists of long horizontal stitches placed at regular intervals across the shape. Long vertical stitches are then

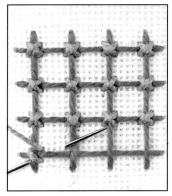

worked to cross the first set of stitches at right angles. Keep the foundation grid as even as possible or the beauty of the stitch will be lost. These long stitches are then anchored or 'couched down' at each intersection by a tiny cross stitch *(see page 74)*, usually in a contrasting color of thread.

● **Bokhara couching** is a solid filling stitch used on common- and even-weave fabrics. It is a couching stitch which uses a continuous thread for both the laid and the couching stitches. It will fill any size and shape of

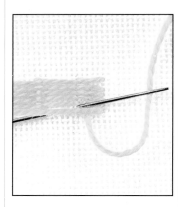

space well and it looks best when worked with a lustrous stranded thread, either cotton or silk, to catch the light. Adjoining areas of Bokhara couching can be worked with the laid threads running in alternate directions to enhance the light and shade effect the stitch makes. It is straightforward to work but a

little practice will be needed to keep the couching stitches even. The stitch should always be worked with the fabric stretched in an embroidery hoop or frame to keep the laid threads parallel. The thread is laid across the shape from left to right and then couched down on the return journey with small, slanting stitches placed at regular intervals. The slanting stitches can be arranged to form lines across the laid threads, or they can be set alternately to give a woven effect.

Composite stitches

The stitches in this group are worked in two or more stages. A foundation is worked on the fabric and onto this subsequent threads are looped or woven. Many basic stitches can be embellished in this way, including threaded back, chain and herringbone.

● **Threaded backstitch** is quick to work and gives a decorative outline on common- and even-weave fabrics; the line is heavier and wider than a plain

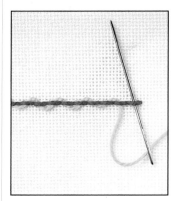

backstitch line. A foundation row of ordinary backstitch is worked, although the stitches should be slightly longer than usual. Using a blunt-ended tapestry needle, a second thread is then passed alternately up and down behind these stitches, without entering the fabric. A third thread is then used to fill in the spaces left on the first journey to create a richer, heavier line. Threaded backstitch can be worked in one, two or three colors and will give an embossed effect if a much thicker yarn is used for the threading than for the foundation row. If the backstitches are made fairly large, textured threads can be used for the threading to give an interesting effect on delicate fabric.

● **Laced herringbone stitch** is a decorative, composite line stitch used on common- and even-weave fabrics. It makes an attractive border stitch and has an unusual circular threading. If the threads cannot be counted, guidelines may need to be drawn on the fabric to keep the

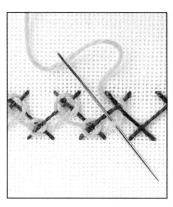

rows an even width. This stitch can be worked in one or two colors: a contrasting color, weight or texture of thread can be used for the lacing. A metallic lacing thread will also look attractive.

A foundation row of herringbone stitch *(see page 74)* is worked first, and should be at least ¾ inch (1.6cm) wide to show the lacing to its best advantage. The work is then turned upside-down before the lacing is begun. This will ensure that the 'unders' and 'overs' of the herringbone stitch follow the correct sequence. The circular threading is quite complicated, so follow the sequence shown very carefully. Laced herringbone stitch should be worked with the fabric stretched in an embroidery hoop or frame, otherwise the lacing will tighten the stitch and pucker the fabric.

● **Threaded chain stitch** is a composite line stitch used on common- and even-weave fabrics. It consists of a foundation row of spaced daisy stitches *(see page 74)*, all facing the same direction. These stitches are then threaded with a similar or contrasting color thread along the row from left to right. For a more decorative line, a second threading can be made, perhaps in a third color, with the second thread filling

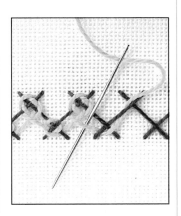

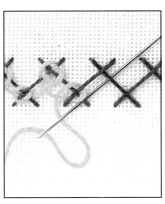

STITCHES AS MARKS

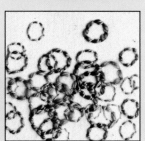
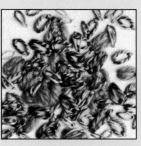
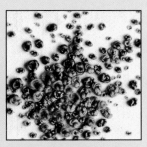

Every stitch can be used to create countless patterns and textures. The left-hand column shows, from the top, seeding, fly stitch and detached chain stitch. The right-hand column shows blocks of straight stitch, circles of back stitch and French knots.

the spaces left on the first journey. Any type of embroidery thread is suitable for this stitch, and a metallic thread can be used for the

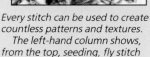

threading. A blunt-ended tapestry needle should be used for the threading to avoid splitting the stitches on the foundation row. Extra decorative touches can be added after the threading, by working isolated French knots *(see page 80)* or cross stitches *(see page 74)* between the daisy stitches.

DESIGN

Using purchased designs

When first learning to embroider, it is always wise to begin with a charted design, a transfer or even with a purchased kit. When stitching from a chart or graph, make sure that you read all instructions carefully before you begin. On some graphs one square equals one stitch. In other cases, one line equals one thread. Check on the size of the stitches (over one, two or more threads). If the chart is black-and-white, you will find it much easier to follow if you take time to color it before you begin to embroider.

Transfer designs consist of a pattern on tissue paper. To transfer the design, lay the paper, design side down, above the chosen fabric, and apply a heated iron. Transfers are available as inserts in specialty and other magazines, and from needlework suppliers and other shops. They are used especially for crewel and other surface embroideries which do not need the warp and weft threads of the fabric to be exactly aligned.

Pencils are available for making your own transfer. Draw the reverse of your pattern on paper, lay the paper design side down, and iron it. An easier method of making a transfer pattern, however, is to draw the design the right way round on thin paper. Lay dressmakers' or carbon film paper (the type used in electric typewriters) above, carbon side down, and the tracing above. Make sure you do not pin through all three layers as pin marks will show carbon spots: cut the carbon to a smaller size than fabric and paper, pin the paper to the fabric along the

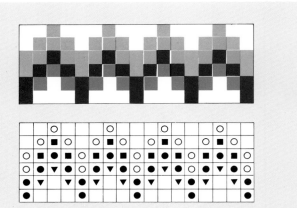

Plot out the pattern on squared paper, using symbols for the different colors as shown. Repeat using different symbols for the stitches to gain a thorough understanding of the colors and textures of a design before embarking on the actual stitching. It is obviously much easier to make alterations at the drawing stage.

top edges and loosely insert the carbon. Carefully press out the outline pattern, say with the end of a blunt needle.

Although some needleworkers object to commercial kits, for beginners such kits often make economic and practical sense. The complete package should include enough material, embroidery threads, needle and full instructions. As many

materials are only available in standard widths, if you want to work a small piece of embroidery, buying your own fabric can be very wasteful. Beginners, too, are apt to misjudge the amount of thread required. Running out of thread may mean that you cannot get more supplies from the same dye-lot. Another advantage of kits is that they can encourage you to have

Find the center of the background fabric and use it to plan the design. Avoid a concentration of heavy shapes too near the top or bottom of the design. Cut the proposed shapes out of paper, and move them around until satisfied.

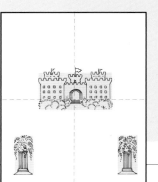

the confidence to progress to making your own designs.

Some techniques described in this book have special design instructions and ideas. Blackwork, for instance, has special affiliation with tiles and wrought-iron patterns. Needlepoint similarly has its own design inspirations. A wealth of other ideas can be taken from the patterns on furnishing, photographs in magazines and from nature.

Creating your own designs

Most embroidery techniques share some basic design considerations. Although some people stitch creatively without first planning a design, it is a good idea, unless you are utterly confident in your own talent, to make a preliminary sketch. When you are satisfied with a few basic shapes, cut these out of newspaper. Cut the same shape out several times from different parts of the newspaper, in order to vary the tone. Lay these shapes on a sheet of white paper and move them around until you achieve a balance in tone and composition. You will find that the darker shapes seem heavier and these should not all go at the top of the design. The bottom should be slightly heavier in tone than the top, while each side should be roughly equal in tone. If there is any unevenness, the eye will better accommodate it in the righthand side. When you have decided on the composition, fix the shapes to the paper with pins or tape. Lay tracing paper over the paper collage and mark the outlines through. When the tracing is complete, color the outlines in using the appropriate colors.

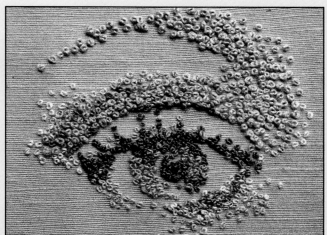

LEFT *The bright primary and secondary colors of the hot-air balloons and their geometric patterns are translated with stitchery. The embroidery is worked in silks on a silk background.*

ABOVE *A magazine cutting inspired the drawing and embroidery of an eye. It is worked entirely in French knots, in threads of varying thicknesses.*

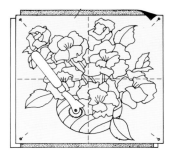

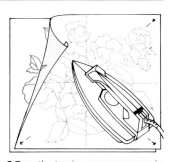

TRANSFERRING DESIGNS WITH CARBON
1 Place the carbon paper, carbon side down on the right side of the fabric. Pin the pattern down on top, design side up.

2 Trace over the lines of the pattern using a small tracing wheel. Try to avoid repeating areas as the final line may become blurred or messy. Remove carbon and pattern.

HOT IRON TRANSFER
1 Copy the design onto thick tracing paper, turn it over and trace around the outline again with a transfer pencil.

2 Turn the tracing paper over again, place it on the fabric and iron the design into position with a cool iron. Iron ready-made transfers on in same way.

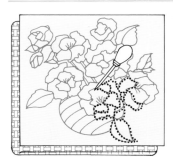

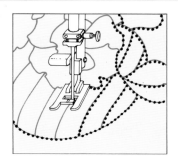

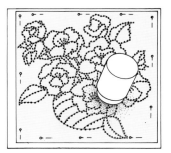

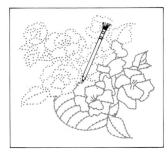

PRICKING AND POUNCING
1 Place the design on some newspaper or rags, and prick along the lines of the pattern with a pin or sharp implement.

2 The pricked holes must be fairly close together, so the process is time-consuming. It can be done more quickly with a threadless sewing machine.

3 Having pricked out the design on the pattern, pin it right side up onto the fabric. Use a small felt pad to rub special pounce powder over the holes.

4 Take the paper off very carefully so as not to blur the pounce powder. Join up all the small dots that have been marked with a dressmaker's pencil.

CORNERS

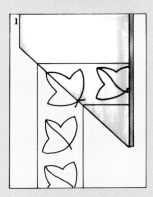

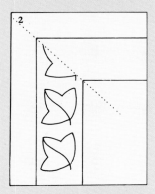

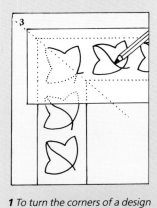

*1 To turn the corners of a design or border, place a small hand mirror diagonally across the design. Look at the reflected image and adjust the mirror to give a pleasant, even design.
2 Mark the diagonal line.
3 Trace the original border up to the line and reverse the tracing paper, as shown. Retrace the second half and repeat as needed. This gives a mitered corner effect.*

ENLARGING AND REDUCING PATTERNS

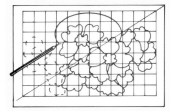

1 It is relatively easy to enlarge a pattern if it is on graph paper. Box off the sides and draw in a diagonal as shown.

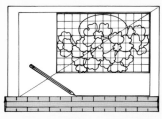

2 Extend the diagonal to the new required height, and draw in the new sides to the design.

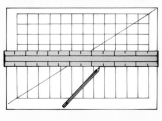

3 Rule in the same number of squares as in the original design, and draw the design in square by square.

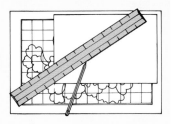

4 Use the same procedure to reduce a pattern.

CURVED DESIGNS

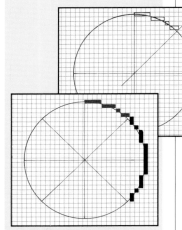

*1 Difficulties are often encountered in reproducing circular designs. Draw the proposed circle onto graph paper as eight segments.
2 Block round the curve, one section at a time, making each segment a mirror image of its opposite number. Block in less rather than more squares initially.*

Transpose this design to the fabric, either using the carbon method or the old-fashioned 'prick and pounce' method. This involves making pinpricks around the outlines of the tracing, placing it above the fabric, and pushing a powder (pounce) through the outline holes.

Your design might not be the right size for your fabric. If this is the case, the most professional method of enlarging or reducing a design to the required size is with a pantograph, which can be obtained from an art supplier. This device is a complicated system of levers – follow the outline of your shape and, when the pantograph is set to the required size alteration, it draws the shape accordingly.

If you do not have a pantograph, you can use the blocking method of enlarging or reducing. Divide your drawing into quarters horizontally, and quarters vertically, to give sixteen equal shapes. Similarly, divide a piece of paper of the required size into sixteen shapes. Carefully copy the pattern in the top lefthand shape of the original pattern, drawing it in the top lefthand shape of the correctly sized paper. Continue until you transpose all the shapes' patterns.

If you want to transpose a freeform design to a chart, the easiest way is to lay a piece of graphed tracing paper over the drawing, and block off the design. A clear plastic sheet with marked graph can also be used instead of graphed tracing paper. Lay the plastic over the design and, noting where the pattern shows through the clear graph, copy it onto another piece of ordinary graph paper.

If you are making your own graphs, you might find curves and circles confusing. Use a compass or an appropriately shaped plate or saucer to draw the required curves and then block these off. If you are not sure whether to block off one or two squares at each 'step' on the curve, it is better to do too few rather than make too many stitches. If you are still in doubt, stitch on the outside rather than the inside of the marked line.

To form a circle, first block off one-eighth of the whole. Segments either side of this first blocking are then mirror images of that blocking. Continue in this manner around the whole circle.

ABOVE *The design for this panel is based on the strata of the Grand Canyon in Arizona. The sun and shadows on the layers create subtle differences in color. Rows of straight stitches are worked in tones of rust and purple, to interpret this effect. The embroidery is worked in fine silk thread on a background of handwoven silk.*

LEFT *An apple worked in running and split stitches. The use of color and direction of line emphasize the roundness of the form.*

● **Designing from photographs and sketches.** Inspiration for designs can be drawn from photographs and sketches. From these a selection can be made and the actual design can begin to take shape on paper. The method of designing is a personal preference; but small 'thumbnail' sketches will help to get the plan started. As you sketch, select samples of fabrics and threads; you are effectively making a palette from which to work. By taking different areas of the design and working small samples in fabric and thread, many problems can be resolved before the larger-scale work is tackled. It will quickly become apparent which are the most effective, and these can be used as a reference for the final piece of work.

When you are faced with a complicated shape, such as for instance a plant with many overlapping leaves, it will be helpful to make an outline drawing, treating the subject as a shadow cast upon a wall. You can add details within this simplified shape. Do not forget that the spaces between the leaves, as revealed in the drawing, may also be made into a feature of the design.

Of all the ways of collecting information, drawing is the most immediate and useful. A simple diagram is often all that is needed to record an idea. Those who 'can't draw' need not despair; everyone can draw to some extent, and can certainly make marks. Children match marks to images in a lively and instinctive way.

In addition to the use of a sketch book, a camera is a useful way of recording interesting shapes and textures. Experiment by photographing objects from unusual angles, reflected images, silhouettes and structural details. A photograph makes a good starting point for a simple design – whether you use an image from a magazine or one you have taken yourself. Choose one which features strong lines, simple shapes and contrasting tone. Make a viewfinder by cutting two L-shapes from paper or thin cardboard; move these around to frame a suitable area to develop a design. Using tracing paper, trace the main lines within the selected area to give the basic structure and guidelines for the embroidery. Transfer the design onto a plain-colored background fabric with a firm smooth weave.

In this example, a photograph of ivy leaves (above) *provides the basic idea for a simple design worked in cutwork. Several tracings are taken before choosing one to develop* (below). *The shapes are simplified and then enlarged to make a suitable motif for the chosen technique, bearing in mind that* areas of the background will be cut away (right). *The larger solid area is balanced by the smaller negative shapes of the cutwork. Several designs may be developed from the same basic idea and it is useful to keep all the tracings for future reference.*

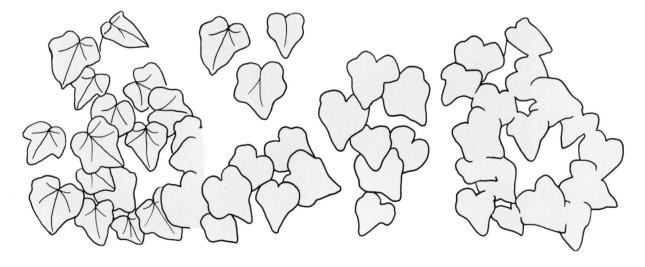

CUTWORK DESIGN FROM A PHOTOGRAPH

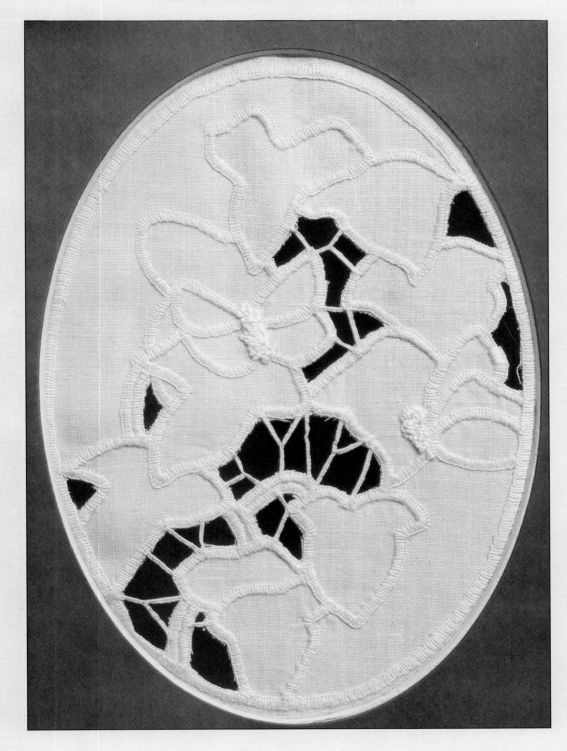

CREWEL

The Bayeux Tapestry is one of the oldest surviving examples of crewel work. It is over 230 yards (210m) long and 20 inches (50cm) wide, but it was worked on several pieces of linen, probably to enable many people to work on it at one time. The pieces were joined together after the embroidery was finished.

The main story is told in the center band, while in the narrow borders at the top and bottom, there are heraldic beasts. Where the battle is shown at its height, the story overlaps onto the borders and many decapitated bodies are depicted in the lower border. There is no perspective in the embroidery – men, horses, trees, buildings and ships are all roughly the same size.

The embroidery was worked in laid work, which are long stitches taken across an area on the surface and caught down with small stitches, and couching. Only eight colors were used – terracotta, buff, yellow, two blues and three greens.

The section shown here (right) depicts the troops about to join the battle at Hastings.

Crewel embroidery is generally defined as a variety of different surface or above-surface stitches worked in colored two-ply woollen yarn on closely woven linen fabric, the threads of which are not counted. The word crewel is believed to have come from the Anglo-Saxon word *cleow* meaning a ball of thread. There is evidence that embroidery using a wool thread has a history going back thousands of years, particularly in Britain, where it has always been a notable embroidery medium.

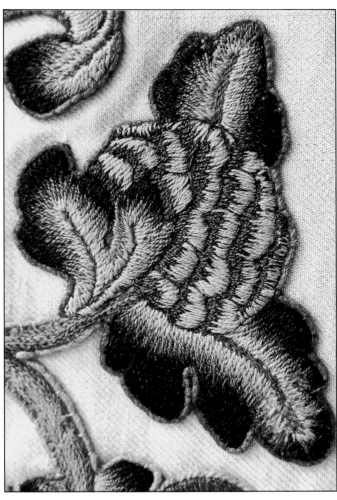

Little is known to us today of the early wool embroideries, but one piece of work which has survived is the famous Bayeux Tapestry. This is not a tapestry at all, but an embroidery worked in a worsted thread on linen, which tells the story of the Battle of Hastings and the events leading up to it. It was thought to have been commissioned by Odo (c.1036–1097), the Bishop of Bayeux and half-brother of William the Conqueror, for his cathedral which was dedicated in 1077.

Today, crewel work is often rather mistakenly called Jacobean work, from the style of design which developed in the seventeenth century and which remains a major influence in modern crewel work. The characteristic Tudor fascination with floral shapes was combined with Eastern influences as the beginnings of the overseas trade, and the formation of the East India Company by London merchants in the early 1600s, made exotic goods from India and China available.

The Jacobean embroiderers developed the Tree of Life motif design, which consists chiefly of unnatural-looking leaves and floral forms on a central tree-like growth rising from rounded hillocks. Quaint, almost grotesque, animals and birds, such as rabbits, deer, squirrels, peacocks and birds of paradise, were introduced, as well as English flowers such as the rose, the national emblem, the carnation, which was a symbol of the Stuart family, honeysuckle, marigolds, irises and the potato flower, together with other exotic many-petalled flowers.

Jacobean style embroidery remains popular today as a technique for filling large spaces with a bold pattern. The many hued coloring may have been simplified, but the Tree of Life motif remains popular with its characteristic sweeping and complexly filled leaves.

LEFT *The most famous of all the seventeenth-century crewel work must be the bed hangings made by a certain Abigail Pett in 1675. Her identity still remains a mystery, despite many attempts to find out who she was. The scale of the work she undertook was vast by any standards, and on the bed curtains and valances there are no two motifs exactly alike in stitch or color. Here, again, the effects of trade with the Far East are apparent in some of the exotic birds that are portrayed. It is difficult to imagine anyone today embarking on such a large project – and completing it.*

The section illustrated gives some idea of the extraordinary range and scope of vision employed.

ABOVE *The leaf motif pictured here is part of a Jacobean bed hanging. The crewel embroidery was worked with long-and-short stitches for the shading, stem and split stitches and block shading. The motif is outlined with couching.*

Materials

● **Fabric** With the wide range of fabrics available today, choosing an appropriate material can be difficult, but there are a few guidelines to remember. It is always best to use as good quality a fabric as you can afford. The weave should be firm and close, but avoid a very tightly woven fabric, as this will make stitching difficult.

Traditionally, linen is the best material for crewel work. In the eighteenth century, a linen and cotton twill weave fabric was used. Many furnishing fabrics can be suitable, but ensure that the material is firm enough to bear the weight of the embroidered wool.

Denim and ticking can be used to good effect. Beware of using lightweight fabrics, such as cotton or lawn, as these materials will pucker under the weight of the crewel wools.

If you have a piece of fabric that you particularly want to use, but think it might be too fine, you can mount it on a backing material like firm muslin or old sheeting before starting the stitchery. This also applies to loosely woven fabrics. Fabrics should be chosen carefully when you are embarking on a project that is to receive any amount of wear and tear such as chair seats or cushions.

● **Thread** Crewel yarns are the most suitable and can be bought by the skein, or in hanks if a quantity of one color is needed. These are available in a large range of colors, and are generally color-fast and moth-proofed. Crewel yarn is a fine two-ply yarn but can be used singly, or with several strands together.

Three-stranded Persian yarns can be separated to suit your needs and to give contrast of texture. When working on very coarse materials, it is also possible to use rug wools, or some of the bulky knitting wools that are on sale today.

Always use wool in short lengths – a thread that is too long will eventually weaken and break from the strain of passing to and fro through the material.

● **Needles** There are basically two needles used in crewel work. The first are crewel needles, which are short with long eyes. The sizes most frequently used are sizes 4 to 10. The second type are chenille needles, which are used for coarser threads. These have large eyes and sharp points and come in sizes 18 to 24.

Remember to choose the size of needle in relation to the thickness of thread and fabric. The needle should pass through the fabric without any strain. If the thread breaks, the needle is probably too small. If you are working with a fairly fine thread and your stitches are uneven, your needle is probably too big.

Tapestry needles with blunt ends should be used when working a laid filling stitch where threads are woven on the surface, since these needles will not split the thread. If you do not have a tapestry needle, it is also possible to push a crewel or chenille needle through eye-first, which has the same effect. A point to remember when buying needles is that the higher the number, the smaller the size.

● **Frames** A frame is essential when working most of the techniques associated with crewel work. It is always much easier to keep work neat and even, when the background fabric is held taut. When doing laid work or working the various laid filling stitches, frames are essential – it is impossible to work these stitches in the hand as the threads have to lie flat on the surface of the material. A frame is also preferable when couching or working long-and-short stitch.

Any kind of frame can be used for crewel work. A ring frame is suitable for small

LEFT Samples of crewel yarn, arranged by shade.

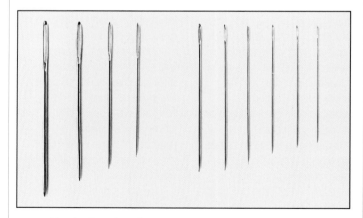

ABOVE This selection of needles shows the variety generally used in crewel work. On the left are chenille needles, size 18, 20, 22 and 24, with large eyes and relatively sharp points. On the right are crewel needles of sizes 5, 6, 7, 8, 9 and 10. These are used for stitching fine strands of crewel wools.

pieces, but if this will flatten areas of stitchery, it is better to use a slate or square frame, which enables larger areas of work to be completed at a time. A square frame only governs the width of the stitching area, as any excess length can be wound on the rollers. For a bedspread or another large item, it is easier to work in strips and join them together later, unless you have access to a large quilting frame.

Design

There have been many different styles of crewel work over the centuries, from the simple, lively approach of the Bayeux Tapestry, the large Jacobean hangings with their Oriental motifs and the delicate floral designs of the Queen Anne period to the bold naturalistic style of William Morris' hangings. A good deal of crewel work is still based on traditional stitches and the laid fillings used on those wall and bed hangings of the seventeenth century, although your designs should not be straight copies from early techniques. Photographs of gardens and seed catalogues are useful for designing flowers and foliage, and leaves are a marvellous source of design. When you have found a leaf you like, take a tracing and then make a paper cutout. Leaf designs are ideal for pockets or handbags, or you could cut out several identical leaf shapes and repeat the design as a border on a dress or a pair of curtains. A single motif can adorn a cushion.

Crewel work has often been associated with large-scale work such as wall hangings and panels, but it is also ideal for cushions and curtains, and can be worked on a much finer scale for clothes and accessories. Eyeglass cases, purses and belts are all suitable projects but your first piece of crewel work does not have to be small. Crewel work grows relatively quickly and a wall hanging could be very satisfying to do.

William Morris headed the nineteenth-century revival of crewel work, designing many large-scale embroideries which were worked by skilled needlewomen.

ABOVE LEFT *These bed hangings from Kelmscott Manor were designed by William Morris and worked by his daughter May in the late nineteenth century. They show an interesting mixture of stylization and realism. Extravagant birds of paradise as well as the more familiar shapes of Western birds in bright colors perch on the boughs of an intensely worked flowering tree, and on a rose-covered trellis among a variety of other recognizable plants. The colors are an integral part of the design.*

ABOVE RIGHT *Recently worked by Audrey Francini, this piece of American crewel embroidery shows delicate stitchery. She made use of an inventive variety of stitches, so creating eye-catching textures and unusual effects.*

LAID FILLINGS

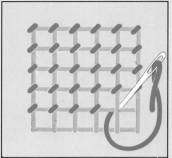

1 Work this laid design with long stitches placed to form a lattice, and tiny slanting stitches over the crossings.

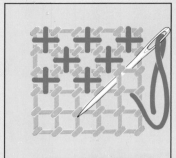

2 Work straight cross stitches in a contrasting color into every alternate square of the original lattice to produce this variation.

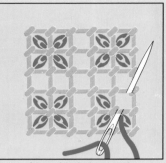

3 To achieve this design, stitch a block of four detached chain stitches into the corner squares of the lattice.

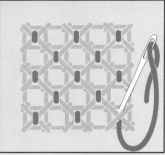

4 Over the original lattice, lay diagonal threads, and secure them at the intersections with small vertical stitches.

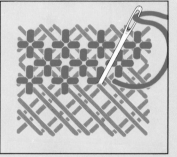

5 Lay pairs of diagonal threads to form a diagonal lattice base, then work four small straight stitches at the intersections.

ABOVE *Block shading has always been popular in crewel work. It consists of rows of satin stitch in tones of one color or graduating colors. It is best worked with a single thread of crewel or Persian yarn. Start with an outline of split stitch. Bring the needle up into the material and down just over the outline. The following rows are worked by bringing the needle up into the fabric and taking it down into the extreme end of the previous row.*

Stitches

Many standard stitches can be used in crewel work, and any freehand stitch can also be combined with the special stitches associated with crewel work. These can be worked on different scales, in threads other than wool. The stitches most commonly used in crewel work are stem, split, long-and-short, satin, block shading, coral, laid and couched work, with a variety of fillings. French knots are also frequently used *(see page 80).*

Stitches are used to make lines, solid and semi-solid shapes, and open fillings. Once you have learned the basic form of each stitch, experiment. Where the whole design is to be worked in wool, it is important to create texture, and apart from choosing stitches to complement each other, this can be done by working the same stitch in different directions, or using different thicknesses of wool. You can change the scale of your work or even combine more than one stitch, possibly to make a new one.

RIGHT *Worked in 1930, 'St Francis' involved the embroidering of split, long-and-short, satin and chain stitches with couching on a linen twill.*

ABOVE *This is a piece of nineteenth-century American crewel work. The designs developed in the United States were often influenced by those prevalent in England, but were lighter, leaving a considerable amount of plain ground fabric, partly due to the fact that yarn was not easy to obtain. The preferred stitches were those which used as little yarn as possible: laid work was popular. This piece was embroidered in 1851, with a beautiful, fresh floral design in rich yet subtle coloring.*

COUCHED AND LAID WORK

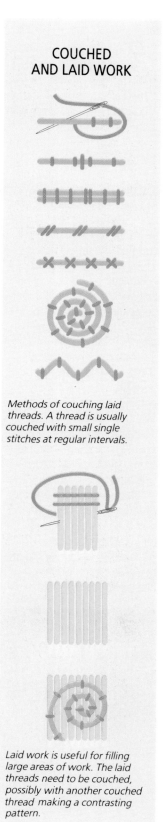

Methods of couching laid threads. A thread is usually couched with small single stitches at regular intervals.

Shading is very much a feature of traditional crewel work. Block shading, which consists of rows of satin stitch worked in tones of one color or in graduating colors, and long and short stitch are two of the most popular methods. Remember that it is important to keep stitches even. Quite a bit of practice is needed to achieve good results.

Interesting textures are also characteristically developed by use of a wide variety of filling stitches. Laid and couched work was frequently used as fillings for the large leaf shapes so popular on the embroidered bed curtains and hangings of the seventeenth and eighteenth centuries. The Bayeux Tapestry was also worked partly in laid work. Today, laid work can be used to advantage for backgrounds, when economy in time and material has to be considered. It is quickly worked, and as all the threads are on the surface, no materials are wasted. Another advantage of laid work is that the colors can be blended. Designs should be bold, important and large.

Crewel work does not have to be worked solely in wool. Experiment with different threads, such as stranded cottons, cotton perlé, silks or textured yarns and with unusual fabrics.

ABOVE *This piece of crewel embroidery shows an interesting and varied selection of textures and patterns made with laid work. The central leaf motif is filled with laid threads, couched in straight lines. Others have been couched producing brick and lattice effects. Split and stem stitches have also been used, with French knots completing some details.*

Laid work is useful for filling large areas of work. The laid threads need to be couched, possibly with another couched thread making a contrasting pattern.

BLACKWORK

*B*lackwork is a form of counted thread embroidery, that is, with the stitches worked over a counted number of warp and weft threads. It takes its name from the characteristic form in which black thread is used on a white or natural fabric. It can, however, be worked in monochrome coloring – traditionally dark green, brown or blue – or enlivened with metal thead or sequin work, and it can also be worked in freeform designs rather than as counted thread.

It is said that Catherine of Aragon brought blackwork from Spain when she married Henry VIII in 1509, but black counted-thread embroidery on a white ground was practiced in England before that date. Originally it was used for dress decoration, particularly on the very full sleeves of women's dresses. It can be seen in Tudor portraits by Hans Holbein (1497–1543): so many portraits by Holbein show people wearing clothing decorated in this way that double-runnng stitch, one of the main blackwork techniques of that period, is still called Holbein stitch.

Blackwork soon came to be used for a wider range of domestic items, including bed-hangings, cushions and curtains. By the beginning of the seventeenth century, blackwork was used with more freedom, and a greater variety of stitches. Designs varied from the pictorial to geometric patterns, from isolated natural motifs to continuous scrolling leaves and flowers. Many of the geometric designs show Arabic influence; fillings for leaf and flower motifs are similar to those of needlepoint lace. Isolated plant designs were influenced by the botanical woodcuts which illustrated contemporary herbals.

Modern blackwork has developed a much freer style, moving away from the originally limited range of stitches and experimenting with the use of color.

BELOW *This linen shirt, attributed to Dorothy Wadham, wife of the founder of Wadham College, Oxford, was embroidered in blackwork designs in pale purple silk. Early seventeenth-century blackwork was often worked in colors other than black.*

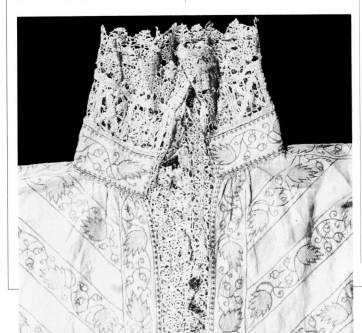

LEFT *This detail of seventeenth-century blackwork embroidery is part of a sleeve panel, where geometric patterns were used to fill the floral and leaf motifs. Sometimes pieces were further embroidered with gold and other metal threads skilfully woven or threaded on the right side of the fabric, so as little as possible was wasted on the back.*

LEFT *A modern panel based on a design of figures in action. Threads in different thicknesses are used to build up a variation in tone, and are emphasized by the interplay of stitch patterns.*

Notice that the figures in the central section are unworked areas. Their shapes are created by the patterned background. The contrast between these and the figures either side provides an interesting example of counterchange.

MODERN STYLE BLACKWORK

ABOVE This design of buildings is worked out on isometric graph paper in pen and ink. Cross-hatching is used in addition to outlining, to achieve gradations of tone which give the illusion of three-dimensional form.

By varying the spacing between the lines of cross-hatching — and also the thickness of the line — a wide range of tone can be suggested.

The blackwork technique is ideally suited to carry out this design in stitchery. Tone can be built up by the use of different thicknesses of thread, ranging from fine sewing cotton, silk twist, coton à broder to pearl cotton, and by varying the stitch patterns. The many gradations of tone built up in this way give interest and variety to the embroidery.

Materials

● **Fabrics** Should be evenweave linen or cotton, loosely or closely woven, with easily countable threads. Lawn will suit very fine work, and 'square' net gives interesting transparent effects. Hessian, canvas or regularly woven tweeds can be used for bold designs, if suitable thread is selected. Other fabrics can be applied as required.

● **Needles** For fine work, use size 26 tapestry needles; size 18 for coarse work. Avoid sharp-pointed needles, as these are liable to split the thread of the fabric.

● **Threads** Use basting thread of a contrasting color for transferring the design. For the work itself, a range of thicknesses from 60 machine silk to number 8 or 5 cotton perlé may be used. A smooth thread, which maintains the precision of the stitch pattern, is most effective. If free stitchery is introduced, thicker threads may be used; but textured threads, if used, must be couched down. With coarse work, knitting wools, cotton à broder, strings, and heavy pearl cotton are appropriate.

Designs

Part of the fascination of blackwork is forming repeating patterns with varying density. Before beginning stitching it is a good idea to sketch out various patterns on graph paper, filling some of them in. You might prefer to have greater density of stitches at the bottom, in the middle, or around the edges of an area of pattern. Colour in some of the motifs to see if you would rather work in strict blackwork or use a color.

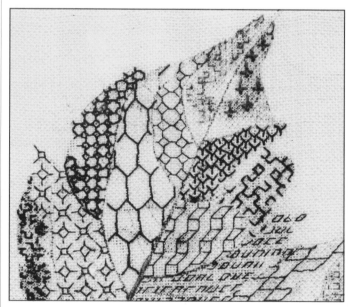

It is important to see a design in terms of areas of tone, without unnecessary detail. Look at a photograph with half closed eyes, for example. Tracing and basting is a simple way of transferring this type of design. Alternatively ink an object, for example a leaf, and press it on to the fabric. This gives an irregular outline on which to build. Establish an overall idea of tone values before concentrating on detail. Areas of lighter and darker tone are built up with fine or thick threads, or light or dense stitch patterns. Dark areas can be worked into later. Perspective, depth and overlapping are

achieved by control of the stitches. Stitches worked on a large scale, with thick thread, come forward, while less detailed, smaller stitches in fine thread will recede.

TOP *This piece of embroidery was worked from a design taken from an ink impression of a leaf.*

ABOVE *This is a detail from a linen panel c.1600. The scrolled pattern was marked in blue pencil and the embroidery partially enhanced with straight stitches along the design outlines. Silver-gilt thread was woven through the straight stitches.*

EMBROIDERY

BLACKWORK PATTERNS

1 Aim for variety in the density of blackwork, to achieve diverse effects. Both patterns above are of a light overall density.

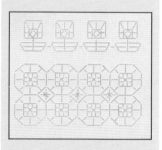

2 By adding slightly more detail to these basic designs, a denser effect can be achieved as shown in the two repeating patterns above.

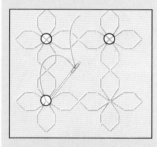

3 Add in still more details to darken the design further. Although the scale of the outlines have remained the same throughout, the overall effect has altered radically.

Stitches

Traditionally, the two basic stitches for blackwork are double-running or Holbein stitch *(see page 70)* and back stitch *(see page 70)*. Double running stitch produces a smoother line, and reduces the tendency to distort the fabric by pulling the thread too tight. Back stitch is sometimes appropriate; both stitches can be used in one piece of work.

Stitches may be worked horizontally, vertically or diagonally: buttonhole stitch, chain stitch, coral stitch, Pekinese stitch and seeding or speckling among others may be used for variety.

During the first half of this century, blackwork embroiderers kept closely to traditional stitch patterns, outlining each section carefully with chain, whipped chain, stem or back stitch; as a result, they made tight designs with little freedom to experiment. Today, although traditional stitch patterns are usually followed, to maintain the character of the technique, it is acceptable to invent or adapt them to achieve broader effects of texture, mood and contrast. Outlining is no longer obligatory; line can be used in conjunction with mass, and other techniques, such as appliqué, free stitchery and canvaswork stitches, can be added. When used pictorially, blackwork images are built up of varying blocks of contrast and tonal values to create three-dimensional effects.

STITCHES

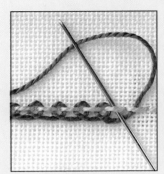

Traditionally, blackwork has achieved telling effects with a limited range of stitches. Most of the basic stitches have been described earlier in this chapter.
ABOVE *Pekinese stitch is a composite line stitch which makes an attractive braided line which follows any linear design well. It is worked on a foundation of backstitch the stitches should be left fairly loose, as the threading wil tighten them. A second thread, of a contrasting weight, color or texture, is then laced through the backstitch foundation. The needle should enter the fabric only at the beginning and end of each row. Use a blunt-ended tapestry needle for the lacing to avoid*

splitting the foundation stitches. The lacing thread should be tightened slightly after each loop has been formed to make a neat, textured line.

ABOVE *Whipped chain stitch is a simple line stitch which gives a neat, slightly raised, line. The whipping thread can be of a contrasting color, weight or texture.*

A foundation row of chain stitch is worked first, and then whipped at regular intervals with a second thread (do not pick up any ground fabric). The whipping stitches fall across the junctions of the chain stitches. Use a blunt-ended tapestry needle for the whipping to avoid splitting the stitches on the foundation row.

SPANGLES

A traditional way of decorating blackwork was to sew on small spangles, with radial stitches, at focal points in the design. Contemporary blackwork tends to avoid this glittering effect, but it could be put to good use on, for example, an evening blouse. Today sequins are made in metallic finishes, gold, silver, brass or copper, and in a wide range of colors including black and white; pearly and iridescent finishes are also made. They are usually round with a central hole for sewing down, although other shapes, for example stars, flowers, leaves and ovals, are available.

LEFT *Example of blackwork dating from the sixteenth century. The design is outlined in couched metal threads, and the shapes are filled with blackwork patterns embroidered in fine silk on an evenweave linen.*

LEFT This detail shows part of an unfinished nightcap, worked in a curling feathered design on a fine linen ground. The bottom line of design is worked in reverse, ready to be turned up into a brim. The blackwork stitches have been embroidered in green silks in this case, and decorated with metal threads and spangles in part.

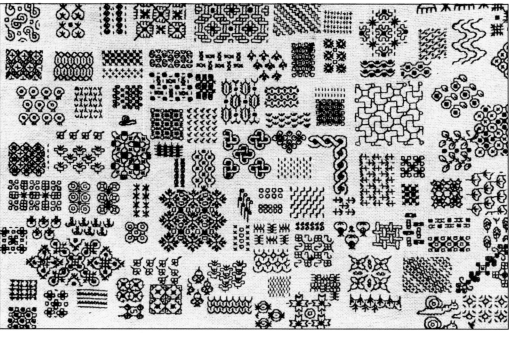

LEFT This is a modern blackwork sampler, which was embroidered with many of the most popular filling patterns from historical pieces. It measures 13 × 8¼ inches (33 × 21cm), which gives some indication of the size of the detail.

WHITEWORK

Whitework is a generic term covering the many styles of embroidery carried out using white threads and stitches on white fabrics. As well as surface embroidery, many forms of whitework make use of small ornamental holes in the fabric to create a lacy effect. On drawn thread work, threads are withdrawn from a loosely woven ground fabric and the spaces left are then filled or edged with different stitches. Pulled thread work (sometimes called drawn fabric work) creates a pattern of tiny holes in the fabric by pulling stitches tightly so that the threads of the ground fabric are distorted. In cutwork, patterns are outlined with close buttonhole stitching and the ground fabric is cut away in various sections of the design.

The stitches and methods have developed and become interrelated over the centuries, to produce yet more types of work, many identified by the areas where they originated. These include broderie anglaise, Ayrshire, Ruskin or Langdale linen, Mountmellick, Dresden and Madeira. Hardanger and Hedebo are other distinctive types of white embroidery.

Whitework has a long history. In the Middle Ages, sumptuary laws forbidding the use of color and rich work in embroidery and textiles led to

elaborate development of white embroideries to express richness and delicacy. By the sixteenth and seventeenth centuries, whitework had become one of the three main methods of embroidery used on clothes, the others being blackwork and silk embroidery. Techniques continued to develop. The development of the cotton industry led to the growth in the nineteenth century of regional cottage industries such as Ayrshire embroidery in Scotland, and Mountmellick and Carrickmacross work in Ireland.

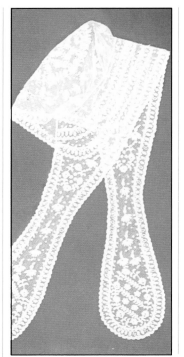

LEFT *A beautifully worked Carrickmacross bonnet. The long lappets display the different techniques used in this kind of whitework.*

Carrickmacross work is another type of Irish white embroidery, named after the town where the technique was established as a cottage industry in the 1820s. It was revived in 1846 to help relieve poverty after the great potato famines. Carrickmacross work resembles lace, and consists of floral designs of fine cambric, cut and applied to a ground of hexagonal net. The cambric motifs are overcast onto the net; sometimes further decoration is added with chain stitches and pulled fabric work. This work is still produced commercially by outworkers who are managed by sisters of a convent in the town. The main items for sale are handkerchiefs, collars and cuffs, and wedding veils.

LEFT *A man's waistcoat in white embroidery and pulled work made in the early eighteenth century. It is a delicate piece of work that has remained in very good condition. Waistcoats and modern vests can be very decorative garments, and this is acknowledged in the extravagant curlicues of the design.*

ABOVE *A Piña cloth mat from the Philippines. This is one of the finest and most delicate varieties of whitework.*

Floral motifs are embroidered in pulled fabric stitches, satin and buttonhole stitches on to a very fine lawn type of cloth woven from pineapple leaf fiber, using a matching thread. Table linen, shirts and blouses are produced for export.

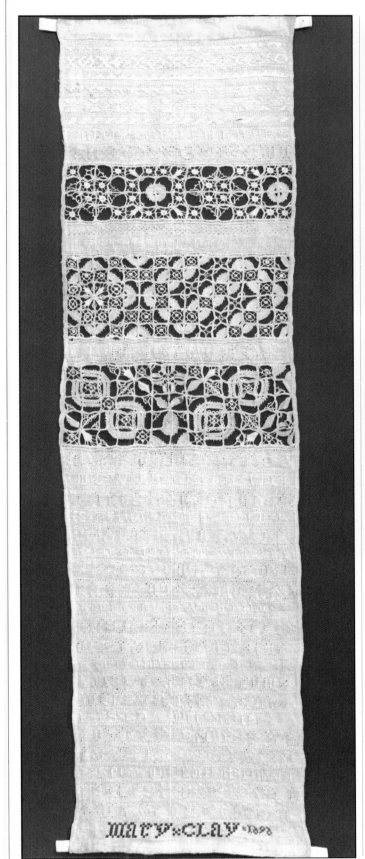

LEFT *Mary Clay put her name to this whitework band sampler in 1696. The name and date have been sewn in colored silk, but the 34 horizontal bands of different styles of alphabet are simple whitework on linen.*

ABOVE *A nineteenth-century English bonnet with alternating bands of Ayrshire embroidery and Valenciennes lace. Ayrshire Whitework, also called 'The Flowering' from its use of floral motifs, was one of the few forms of whitework to develop on a commercial scale, flourishing from the 1820s to the 1860s. White cotton threads on white cotton muslins, lawns or cambrics were worked in padded satin stitch, stem stitch, eyelets, and fine needlepoint or drawn thread filling stitches so intricate that they resembled lace. Ayrshire whitework is particularly notable on baby clothes, christening gowns and bonnets as well as women's dresses and men's shirts, and was also worked on collars, cuffs and caps.*

RETICELLA

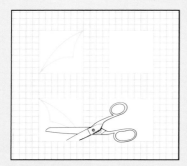

1 Select the square and baste around the outline with small even running stitches. Cut out four windows as shown.

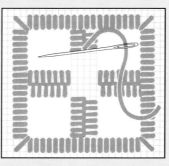

2 Over stitch carefully around the outline, working a diagonal over stitch at each corner, and continuing through the bars as shown.

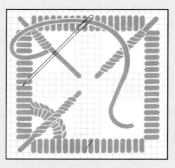

3 Work the bars as woven bars. A small square of canvas will be left in the center. This basic unit can then be further decorated as required.

OVERCAST BAR

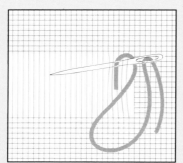

1 Align working thread with the vertical threads that will make up the overcast bar. Start to bind them all into a bundle as shown.

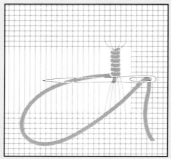

2 Keep coil neat and firm by pushing the wrapping threads close together without letting them overlap. Make sure the remaining thread stays taut.

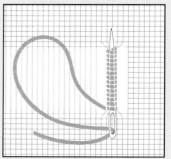

3 Having wrapped the bar to the bottom of the drawn thread area, take the needle straight back up the bundle to anchor it and pull it through.

WOVEN BAR

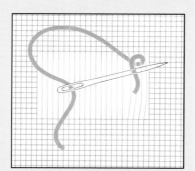

1 Align working thread with the four fabric threads to be used for the first bar. Work the needle over two, under two and back in a figure of eight.

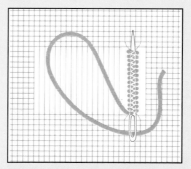

2 Work tightly down to the bottom of the fabric threads, pushing the figures of eight up against each other. End off as for the overcast bar shown above.

Materials

The choice of materials and threads will depend on the purpose of your work, how it is to be used, how durable it has to be in wear and laundering, and the scale of design. It is always a good idea to work a sampler and experiment with threads and fabric.

Whitework usually demands a smooth fabric to emphasize the texture of stitches, and traditionally is worked in fine cotton or linen threads on fine cotton or linen lawn, muslin and cambrics. It is worth considering the contrast of matt cotton threads on a shiny satin fabric, or a wool fabric stitched with mercerized cotton threads like Sylko perle, especially for Mountmellick work. Several types and weights of thread could be used in one design.

Techniques

The best work is achieved by putting the fabric into an embroidery frame. When the work is completed and ready for pressing, cover the ironing board with a soft cloth or blanket and place the embroidery *face down* so that the pressing is done on the back. This ensures that the raised textures are preserved. Whitework can quickly become grubby if care is not taken to keep hands clean and dry.

Design

The essence of designing for whitework lies in the creation of different areas of light and shade. These are made by padded and knotted stitches and the contrasts of textures produced by stitches and threads.

Sources of ideas include natural objects, such as flowers, leaves, tree shapes, lichens and butterflies, and buildings, the texture of brick and stone, and wrought-iron. It is always useful to keep a notebook for cuttings from magazines and sketches.

Using a brush and white paint on a tinted paper is an effective way of producing designs for white embroidery, as is cutting paper shapes and moving them about until a pleasing pattern is achieved. Background spaces are important for emphasizing the design; it is also important to remember that the design can be altered or added to.

Stitches

Trailing stitch is a characteristic of whitework and is used for lines, stems, or veins of leaves. It is worked by laying three padding stitches and then overcasting with tiny stitches to completely cover the padding. *Raised chain band* is a strongly textured line stitch, also used for finishing edges.

STITCHING TECHNIQUES

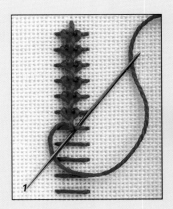

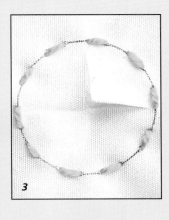
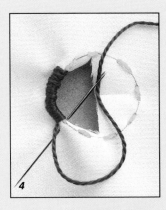

Raised chain band (1) is a composite line stitch worked downward on common-and even-weave fabrics. It can be given a more raised appearance by working a padding of laid threads underneath the foundation stitches. The foundation of evenly spaced, short, horizontal stitches is worked first. These can vary in width to accommodate one, two or three bands of the top stitch, depending on the width of line required. The chain-like stitching is worked over the foundation threads, without picking up any of the ground fabric.

Sew running stitches around and make cuts across the center. Fold the corners back and overstitch the edges. Turn the fabric over and cut off the corners. The finished circles should be neat. Use the same method for an oval, making one end pointed. A triangle must have longer overstitches at the corners with deep cuts.

Trailing stitch (2), or satin stitch couching, is a variation of ordinary couching in which the laid threads are used as a padding and are completely covered by couching stitches. It is used exclusively as a line stitch; it follows both tight and gradual curves well, and can be used for very intricate linear patterns. To give a varying diameter of line, vary the weight of the laid threads. Bring the laid threads to the surface and guide them with your left hand (if you are right-handed) along the line to be stitched. Then bring through the couching thread, and work small close satin stitches (see page 75) over the laid thread. The satin stitches can be worked either at a right angle to the laid thread, or they can be slanted, depending on the effect required.

Broderie anglaise can be distinguished from Ayrshire whitework by the simplicity of its design. It consists of repetitive eyelets (3 and 4), round or oval in shape. Sometimes designs are entirely worked in these open eyelets, but other designs include solid satin stitch spots or simple leaf sprays. Stems and scrolls are worked in overcast or stem stitch, and scalloping is the usual method of finishing edges.

The transverse stitches are worked first to provide a foundation for the looped top stitch. *Chain, stem and back stitch* are also used as line stitches *(see pages 74, 76 and 70)*. *Cretan stitch* is versatile and interesting to use because its appearance can be varied by the spacing or closeness of stitching. *(see page 77)*. *French knots* and *bullion knots* can be used as scattered fillings or closely textured as in Mountmellick work *(see page 80)*. *Seeding* and *sheaf stitches* are just two of many scattered filling stitches. Seeding consists of small back stitches worked in random directions and spaced as required. Sheaf stitch is composed of groups of three or four long stitches tied across the center by two back stitches *(see page 81)*. *Padded satin stitch* is a whitework stitch giving a rich, raised effect. Satin stitches are worked over a padding of rows of chain, running or stem stitches.

Cutwork

In cutwork parts of the background fabric are cut away to emphasize the design. There are several types. In *simple cutwork,* the outlines are embroidered in buttonhole stitch, and some of the shapes cut away. *Renaissance* work is more elaborate; the cut-away areas are larger, and are decorated with 'bridges' or 'bars'. Still more elaborate is *Richelieu* work; the bars are embellished with 'picots', producing a lacy effect.

More intricate forms of cutwork, which are Italian in origin, include *reticella,* where large areas of the background are cut away, and the spaces filled with needlelace patterns.
● **Materials** It is essential to use a closely woven background

fabric, otherwise the cutaway edges are liable to fray. If the embroidery is to be purely decorative, and thus will not require constant washing or handling, then light-weight iron-on interfacing can be applied to the wrong side. Traditional cut work uses self-colored embroidery thread, and relies on the cut areas to give the design its character. If colored threads are used, great care should be taken that they do not overpower the design. A pair of sharp-pointed embroidery scissors is essential.
● **Techniques** Work the bars at the same time as the running stitches, before the buttonhole stitches are worked and the background fabric cut away. Carry the working thread across the design, at the point where the bar is to be worked. Make a tiny holding stitch, and take the thread back across the space. Make a second holding stitch, and return the thread once more, so that the bar consists of three threads. These must be pulled fairly taut. Anchor the thread firmly.

The bar must now be covered closely in buttonhole stitches, detached from the back-ground fabric. Continue outlining the shapes in running stitch. The outline buttonhole stitches can then be worked as before.

To work picots, buttonhole to the center of the bar and insert a pin into the bar and the background fabric, at right angles to the bar. Loop the working thread under the pin, without piercing the fabric, then up over the bar and out underneath. Slip the needle under the loop and over the bar, and twist the thread around the needle before pulling it through. Pull the thread tight and remove pin.

LEFT *An elaborate sachet made between 1880 and 1890 and decorated with Mountmellick work.*

Mountmellick work originated in Ireland as a cottage industry. It differs from other types of whitework in as much as there are no drawn or open spaces. The majority of the stitches lie on the surface with very little showing on the wrong side; the bold surface stitchery is sewn with coarse cotton thread on linen or sateen.

Traditionally it has either a knitted fringe or a heavy buttonhole edge. It has been used mostly for household or church linen. The designs are based on flowers and leaves; a variety of stitches is used, including Gordian knot, thorn, bullion, fern, feather and trellis, and the work has a raised effect.

ABOVE *A cutwork mat in the Richelieu style owned by the Embroiderers' Guild.*

HEMSTITCH AND SIMPLE TWIST

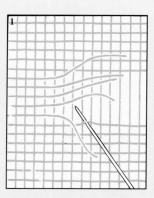

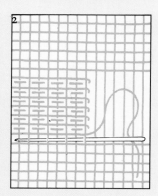

(LEFT) Withdraw sufficient threads for the depth of the border required, starting in the middle and working outwards. With a pin, lift one thread in the middle and cut. Withdraw it on both sides back to the end, leaving threads long enough to thread into a needle.

Neaten the edges of the border on the wrong side weaving the ends back into the main fabric for about ¾ in (2cm).

Neaten the opposite end of the border ready for hemstitching.

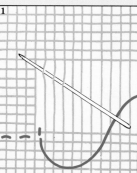

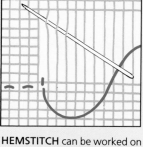

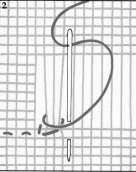

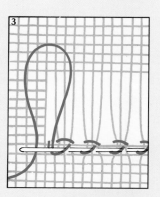

HEMSTITCH can be worked on single fabric, without a hem, from the wrong side (**ABOVE**).
1 Begin by running the thread into the bottom left corner leaving a 4 inch (10cm) length of thread. Make a single stitch over the first thread. Pass needle behind three threads.

2 Bring needle out, pass it behind two horizontal threads and bring through, pulling firmly.

3 Neaten threads through hem stitching on wrong side.

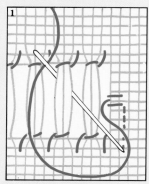

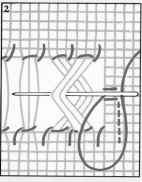

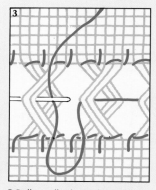

SIMPLE TWIST (ABOVE):
1 Make from the right side on evenly hem-stitched border. Secure working thread to edge of fabric. Place needle behind second group of threads with needle tip on first group.

2 Press needle tip on first group and slip it behind twisting the first group to left of second.

3 Pull needle through keeping thread tight and twisted threads in place. Complete the border.

Drawn thread work

Drawn thread work is of peasant origin. In the nineteenth and early twentieth centuries, a great deal of drawn thread work was done, mainly for household linen; because modern methods of laundering are unsuitable for delicate work it is now less popular for such articles.

Any strong fabric from which threads can easily be drawn is suitable. Experiment with loosely woven furnishing fabrics and unusual threads. If the work is intended for tablelinen, an even weave linen is the best choice. The threads are withdrawn from the fabric horizontally or vertically, and the remaining threads are decorated and strengthened by binding and additional stitches.

As the threads are withdrawn from an evenly woven fabric, designs are based on straight lines or rectangular shapes, which should not be too large; if too many threads are withdrawn from one place the fabric is considerably weakened. Design the whole area in blocks of tone – the darkest blocks representing areas which will have the most threads removed. Working with cut paper is a good design method for this technique, as squares and rectangles of paper can be moved around easily.

In the simplest form of drawn thread work the threads are withdrawn in one direction only and neatened with decorative hemstitching. This method is traditionally used for finishing the hems on evenweave fabric.

Pulled thread work

Pulled thread work is another name for drawn fabric work; the former name helps avoid the confusion between drawn thread and drawn fabric work. In pulled work, the threads of the fabric are pulled or drawn together to make lacy patterns, whereas in drawn thread work threads are actually withdrawn from the fabric.

Pulled work has always been popular in Britain, particularly during the eighteenth century, when it was used on coverlets and gentlemen's waistcoats. These were sometimes quilted to give extra warmth. Traditionally, it was worked in self-color, relying on contrasting area of texture produced by the stitches to give the work its characters. However, there is no reason not to experiment with color in pulled work.

The method is used mainly for functional purposes, and is still used a great deal for tablelinen of all kinds. An evenweave fabric, on which the threads can be easily counted, should be chosen. Linen, which launders well, is excellent for household articles, but you may experiment with many dress and furnishing fabrics which, provided they are not too tightly woven, will pull into the lacy patterns. Scrim is a very good fabric to experiment with; it looks well in its natural color, and also dyes well.

The stitching thread must be strong, as there is a considerable strain on each stitch. It should be about the same weight as the threads of the background fabric, but experiment with thicker and thinner threads to see the difference in effect. Heavier

threads will give greater contrast, especially when working stitches in the satin stitch group. Linen threads, if available, are good, but fine cotton perlé or crochet cotton can also be used. Use a fine tapestry needle, which will separate the fabric threads without splitting them. Take care to get the correct tension; if working in a frame, do not stretch the fabric too tightly.

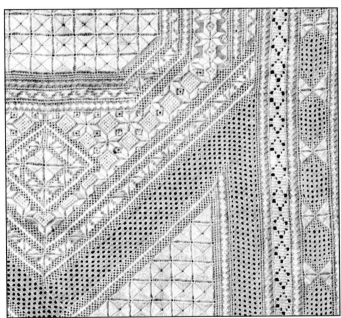

TOP *Hardanger work, from western Norway, uses geometric designs composed of drawn thread squares and cross-shapes, edged with blocks of satin stitches called 'kloster' blocks. This hard-wearing style of embroidery has not changed very much since the eighteenth century.*

ABOVE *In this detail of a Persian cover, the use of stitched geometrical patterns in contrast with a filigree of pulled holes exploits the way in which the light falls on a complex surface.*

COIL FILLING STITCH

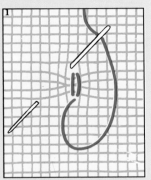

1 Working from right to left, make three straight stitches upwards over three threads. Pull thread firmly, pass needle diagonally behind four intersections and bring out.

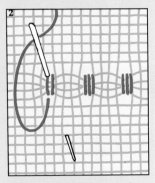

2 Repeat to end of row and bring needle out four threads down and two to right.

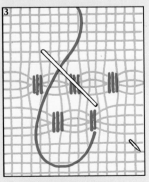

3 Repeat stitch sequence, working from left to right and continue in this way to fill area.

SMOCKING

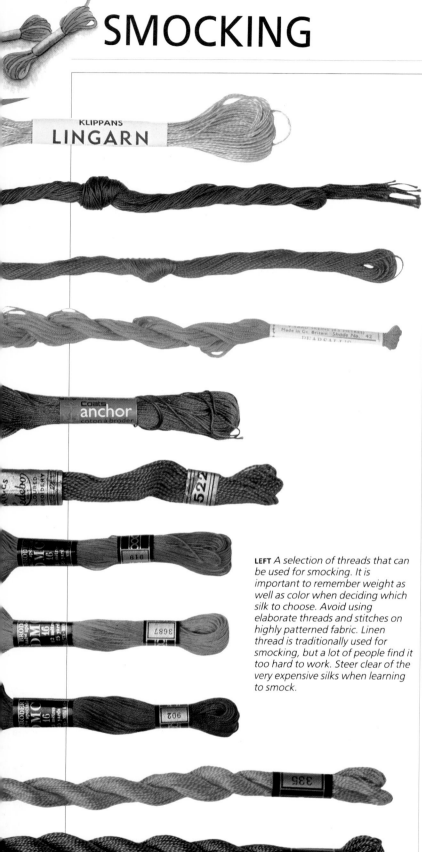

Smocking could be described as an elaborate and decorative form of pleating. It evolved as gathering held in place by rows of stitches worked over the pleats, very regularly and evenly. Traditionally it was often worked on linen with self-colored linen thread, to control fullness and allow stretch across the back and chest, and to shape the sleeves of landworkers' smocks. A wealth of diamond, rope, and wave patterns developed from a combination of four simple stitches – stem or rope, cable or basket, vandyke and chevron. A further two stitches, honeycomb and feather, were later additions. The beauty of smocking relies on the way in which the various stitches arrange the pleats into different groupings and directions; how spaced at intervals and in varying proportions, decorative bands and units of pattern are created. The fretwork of pleats remaining un-stitched is as important to the elasticity, tonal effects, textures and patterns of smocking as the embroidery itself.

The complexity of the embroidered designs reached a peak in the middle years of the nineteenth century, and included boxes (the areas either side of the front and back panels of smocking) of complementary patterns worked in single, double, treble feather stitch and eyelet holes, stem and chain stitches. These were worked both for decorative effect and to strengthen the places most subject to wear. Pleated and embroidered epaulettes over the shoulders also gave extra protection from rain and the rub of yokes.

Versions of the landworker's smock and smocking are to be found throughout the world and vary in decorative detail and function.

There have been several revivals of interest in the traditional smock (for instance, by some of the followers of William Morris) in reaction to the goods and values of industrialization. More recently fashion designers, particularly designers of children's clothes, have made many decorative and effective innovations in smocking by selecting and combining different fabrics, methods and styles and by using colored fabrics and threads.

LEFT *A selection of threads that can be used for smocking. It is important to remember weight as well as color when deciding which silk to choose. Avoid using elaborate threads and stitches on highly patterned fabric. Linen thread is traditionally used for smocking, but a lot of people find it too hard to work. Steer clear of the very expensive silks when learning to smock.*

Materials

● **Fabric** Any fabric which will gather easily is suitable. The width of the fabric required depends on the type of fabric, the distance between the pleats and the tension of the stitches. As a general rule allow three times the width of the finished piece but test this by working a small amount of smocking on a measured piece.

If a fabric is sufficiently firm to hold the preparatory gathering threads, then it can be smocked. Smocking on a very stiff fabric will result in work that will not stretch. On a limp or floppy fabric, the smocking will not be resilient and the fabric will return to its original shape having been stretched. Traditional fabrics such as linen and cotton drill, with their firmness of weave and creasing properties, will form neat 'tubes' more readily than a loosely woven fabric.

Smocking need not be confined to clothing; many

FABRICS

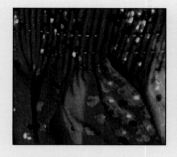
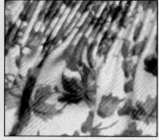

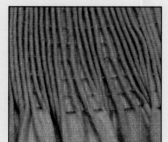
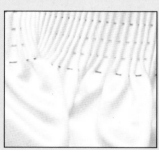
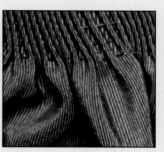

Smocking can look effective on a variety of different fabrics.
1 Silk georgette is a luxurious diaphanous fabric which will gather up very tightly.
2 Viyella is popular, particularly for children's clothes.
3 Hessian is an ideal fabric to experiment with. Use in conjunction with applique for cushions, bags and wall-hangings.

4 Tussore silk is a gorgeous fabric that can be smocked on luxury garments such as evening dresses or jackets.
5 Polyester satin is both floppy and slippery. Only the most experienced smocker should attempt to work on it.
6 Cotton drill is tough, inexpensive and will pleat up firmly.

embroiderers have adapted the technique to textiles generally. Hessian, P.V.C. and other unconventional fabrics are used for wall hangings and collages, and smocking has also been combined with screen-printed and painted fabrics.

● **Thread** Twisted threads are strong and less likely to shred than a stranded variety. D.M.C. and coton-à-broder are available in a wide range of colors; these are versatile threads suitable for many fabrics, used singly or doubled in the needle, and are particularly good for beginners and children. Pearl cotton is also an attractive twisted thread with a high luster and can be combined with other threads. Hard twisted linen threads are ideal for traditional smocking, but are difficult to use. Softly twisted embroidery silks are rare and expensive, but a good alternative is firmly twisted buttonhole silks.

LEFT *In the latter half of the nineteenth century, farmers would go into town on market days wearing top hats and smocks as in this early photograph of Samuel Sinfield of Moulsoe. They could be made from a variety of different fabrics; in 'Under the Greenwood Tree' Thomas Hardy wrote in 1871, 'Some were as usual in snow white smocks of Russian duck and some in whitey brown ones of drabbet.'*

BELOW *A shepherd's smock made from blue linen with smocked cuffs, shoulders and front panel. The wavy pattern on the shoulders and collar is formed by working smocking on the underside of the material.*

SMOCKING STITCHES

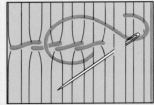

OUTLINE STITCH
Work this stitch from left to right making a small diagonal stitch in each tube. The thread can be kept consistently under or over the needle throughout.

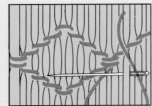

WAVE AND TRELLIS STITCH
When working these diamond shapes keep the thread above the needle when stitching downwards and below for stitching upwards.

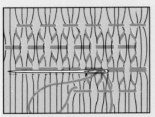

VANDYKE STITCH
Anchor the tubes with small horizontal stitches on alternate levels as shown, worked as a continuous back stitch from right to left.

HONEYCOMB STITCH
Stitch two rows at once, working backwards and forwards and catching up two tubes with each horizontal stitch that is made.

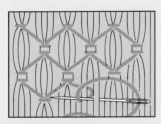

CHEVRON STITCH
Work the horizontal stitches across two tube widths each, positioning the ends of the diagonal linking stitches between the joined tubes.

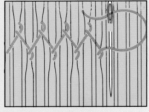

CRETAN STITCH
To achieve this diamond effect, work alternate rows upside down and aligned as shown. Try to work an even number of rows.

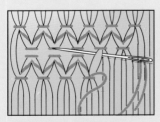

SURFACE HONEYCOMB STITCH
Sew each tube to its neighbor above and below, working from right to left. Then only work full back stitches along the bottom.

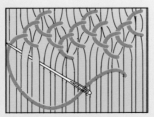

FEATHER STITCH
Work from right to left, marking two feather stitches upwards followed by two downwards and linking them as shown.

Techniques

The fabric is basted across in rows on the wrong side and drawn up into even pleats with the basting threads which are then tied securely to pins.

Work along each row. On the completion of a row, unthread the needle and leave the thread loose. Baste the required number of rows, then draw up the pleats by holding, the loose ends of the threads in pairs, carefully easing each row along its gathering thread until the right width and distribution is settled. Secure the ends around pins or knot them in pairs.

Make sure you have enough thread to complete each line. Secure the embroidery thread on the wrong side with a knot, or a double stitch into the back of a pleat. On the right side, work the smocking stitches, regularly and with even tension, by picking up a small portion of the top edges of the pleats. Put the last stitch through to the wrong side and fasten off into the back of the last pleat. When complete, draw out the gathering threads.

Stitches

The traditional nineteenth-century smocking stitches are strong and firm, being variations of the simple outline stitch. Chevron and honeycomb stitches are the techniques used on the luxury fabrics of the twentieth century; these stitches are more resilient than the first group and take up less fabric. These differences should be taken into consideration when combining the two types of stitches in one piece of work. The greater elasticity of the chevron group is ideally suited

to the lower edge of the smocking on a curved yoke or child's garment.

The traditional stitches worked in broad bands of texture divided by single rows of outline stitch still give a satisfying result. Do not overcrowd the rows of smocking, as well-formed tubes have a pleasing effect unadorned. It is a good general rule to start the work with a row of outline stitch to organize or 'set' the tubes to lie parallel. Endeavor to work at an even tension, bearing in mind that the natural tendency is to pull the stitches too tight, thus reducing the elasticity of the finished article. The

retaining threads of the gathers are visible between the tubes and provide a guide for keeping the smocked lines straight.

Most stitches are worked from left to right. Start with a small knot carefully concealed in the first tube, then pick up each tube in turn at a regular depth. Avoid finishing off threads within the line of smocking, particularly on fine fabrics where the finishing stitches will be visible from the right side. At the same time it is important that the initial length of thread should not be so long that it becomes woolly in appearance towards the end of the row. Finish off the line of

smocking with three or four overstitches securely worked into the last tube.

Outline stitch is a simple interpretation of stem stitch, which can either be worked with the thread above the needle, or below the needle for a neater rope-like effect. *Cable stitch* is similar to outline stitch except that the needle is inserted at right-angles to the tubes and the thread is held alternately above and below the needle. *Wave or trellis stitch* is a combination of the previous ones. Using the visible gathering threads to determine the size of the wave or trellis, keep the thread below the needle on the upward movement. On the downward movement keep the thread above the needle. *Vandyke stitch* is worked from right to left. Each tube is backstitched to its neighbor making a very strong resilient stitch, but it is slow to execute. *Honeycomb stitch* is the quickest method of smocking as two rows are worked simultaneously. It needs some care in execution. As the majority of the thread is on the underside, it is ideal for patterned or piled fabrics. Beads or sequins can be applied to the work with chevron or honeycomb stitch. *Chevron stitch* is the most versatile of smocking stitches; it can be varied in depth and width and combined with other stitches. It can be worked in a single row or reversed upon itself to form diamonds. *Surface honeycomb stitch* is a minor variation of chevron stitch. Each tube is oversewn to its neighbor, first above and then below. It is a very stretchy stitch. *Feather stitch* is very attractive on children's clothes.

Finishing

When the smocking is complete, the pins holding the retaining threads can be removed. Flatten the work on a surface with the palm of one hand and withdraw the retaining threads by firmly pulling each knot with the other hand. Excessive handling while working smocking and embroidery will fray some fabrics. Stay stitching across the top of the fabric will help to prevent this. Stretch the smocking gently and steam press on the underside to improve its appearance. Use small sharp scissors to 'layer' the tops of the tubes, reducing the bulkiness where they are to be set into a yoke or cuff.

Always smock and embroider each piece of fabric before making up a garment. Laundering is no problem; cotton and linen garments can be machine-washed and even boiled, but subsequent steam or damp pressing will be necessary.

LEFT *Child's coat smock from Hereford. The embroidery is beautifully worked in feather stitch. Originally, extended epaulettes were added to laborers' smocks as extra protection against the weather. On this smock however, they simply provide additional room for the embroidery.*

GATHERING

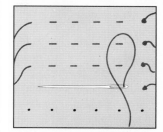

1 Work rows of running stitch over each line of dots, covering each dot with a small stitch as shown. Allow plenty of thread for each row.

2 Pull the threads in pairs to gather the fabric into tubes ready for smocking. Space them as evenly as possible. Secure the thread ends round pins as shown.

BELOW *The smocking on this jacket was randomly worked to create a dense and exciting texture. Applique work and fine seeding stitch extend the pattern.*

METAL THREAD

*O*ne of the earliest mentions of gold for in-darning and weaving is in a description of an ephod (a surplice worn by a Jewish priest) made for Aaron (Exodus XXXIX 2–3). Embroidered and in-woven golden textiles are mentioned in both the Iliad and the Odyssey, and throughout the centuries writers have thought it worth mentioning the use of gold for robes and cloths. The majority of the threads used were silver-gilt or pure silver, pure gold being rarely used. The Durham stole and maniple (A.D. 909–916) is pure gold thread, but all the *opus anglicanum* ('the English work' as it became known throughout Europe) was in silver-gilt. From the mid-thirteenth century to the middle of the fourteenth century, this mainly professional, largely ecclesiastical work reached an exceptionally high standard of design and technique, excelling in underside and surface couching. During the fourteenth century, following the Plague and the death of so many embroiderers, there was a noticeable decline in skill. The emphasis changed to secular and domestic embroidery, as the vigorous designs of the Tudor and Elizabethan period developed. Braid and plaited stitches, buttonhole fillings and interlaced knotted stitches were worked in a fine passing thread. Metal threads found their way into canvaswork and blackwork; plate, cut purl and spangles were used to enrich garments. Metal thread work designs were influenced by imports from India and China during the seventeenth and eighteenth centuries respectively – some embroideries showing large-scale figurative compositions. The nineteenth century saw a deterioration in both design and technique with braids, fringes, tassels and cords doing much of the embellishing. Laid work is to be found on Victorian ecclesiastical robes and cloths, still in use today.

The beauty in a piece of metal thread work lies not only in the perfection of the technique but in the design. As in other types of embroidery, the area is broken up into varied shapes that combine to make a pleasing and harmonious whole. It is a temptation in any form of embroidery to use too many different threads, fillings and textures, which may make an excellent sampler for reference but which do not build up into a unified piece of work. The temptation is even stronger in metal thread embroidery as it so often depends on one color with variation of tone. The beauty of the technique lies in the play of light over the varied undulating surfaces of the threads and cords, giving highlights and depth of tone in pleasing shapes. The lay of the threads should follow the form of the design, giving it life and movement. Areas of richness are often set off to advantage by being laid against simpler ones.

As metal thread work is a slow, time-consuming technique, the beginner is too often tempted to fill large areas with metalized leather or kid which can never give the same effect of movement as laid thread. Leather certainly has its uses, but should be kept to small areas, or be well-broken by threads or manipulation such as pleating and shaping, padding and decoratively cutting.

Materials and equipment

● **Fabrics**

BACKGROUNDS can be of almost any type, weight or finish. It is difficult to work metal thread well on a heavily textured fabric, but the embroidery can be worked onto a smoother fabric and then applied onto the selected background. BACKINGS should be closely woven cotton or similar fabric.

● **Threads**

SEWING THREADS. Since the

ABOVE Opus anglicanum, *a style which reached its peak at the beginning of the fourteenth century, makes beautiful and delicate use of metal thread with silk yarns. This example is part of the Marnhull orphrey – a band of gold embroidery – and the design is similar to religious paintings of the time. There is some use of shading in the figures and their clothing, but no indication of perspective. The silver gilt and silver threads were couched to outline the robes and Christ's halo.*

disappearance of Maltese silk, a matching twisted sewing silk or embroidery thread is the best for couching metal threads. An invisible thread gives good results but is difficult to handle.

METAL THREADS Can be bought in a wide range of shades of gold, silver, aluminum and copper, but the antique colors and more subtle tones and textures take some finding. Even then one must be prepared to make one's own twisted or finger cords in the unusual shades, as only very fine threads are available. Jap gold and silver have a core of threads around which is wrapped a fine covering of metal. Imitation silver-gilt is only now available. Strips of metal, beaten flat, called 'plate' are available in gold and silver. Purls are coiled wires of different size and texture which are cut into short lengths and sewn down like beads. Pearl purl, a heavier coiled wire, is couched down as a continuous length, which is slightly pulled out to give it stability. Crinkle, passing, tambour and twist are some of the wide choice of imitation gold threads. Cord and braids are made in different sizes and patterns, both real and imitation. Metallic colored yarns are also widely available.

● **Other materials**
FELT, of a near-matching color, is used for padding.
STRING, dyed with a waterproof ink to match the thread, is used for padding and fillings. It should be smooth and tightly twisted.

● **Equipment**
A FRAME must be used, as both hands are required to handle the threads. The background fabric and backing should be at a firm tension, but not drum-tight, as this can cause

problems if the embroidery is to be free-hanging on completion.
NEEDLES Crewel needles size 8-10, are suitable for most metal thread work. A large chenille needle is used for taking metal threads through to the wrong side.
A STILETTO is useful for making a hole to take the larger threads through to the back.
SCISSORS with short, strong, straight blades are needed to cut the wires.
TWEEZERS help with handling short lengths of purls, wire or beads.
FELT COVERED BOARD approximately 6 × 4 inches (15cm × 10cm) helps to control the purls when they are being cut.
BEESWAX protects the sewing thread. It also helps to prevent knotting.

Design

The use of metal thread embroidery has usually been limited to decorative work due to its fragility. It may be used alone or to enrich silk embroideries.

Much of the best metal thread work has been made for use in churches; vestments, altar-cloths, banners and so on. The great difference when working ecclesiastical embroidery after working domestic objects is the change of scale in both design and treatment. The whole has to read at a very great distance, and yet still excel in technique and detail when studied at close quarters. Consequently, you should not rely on variation in weight of the threads and cords, or the contrasting lay of the threads, to give the necessary tonal variation to make the work read at a

distance. Take full advantage of the range of shades available in threads, cords and leathers. The brightness of metal threads and cords can be brought out by laying dark cords alongside or among them, giving an accent to the finished texture. The or nué technique, with its subtlety of color, and more important, variation in tone, can be used to great advantage. Try padding and raising important areas; this creates real shadows, which can be of the greatest value.

Take care that vestments are not so weighted with embroidery that they become stiff and uncomfortable to wear; and that none of the materials or techniques you use will catch, rub, pull threads or otherwise become unsightly with regular use.

Where metal thread work is combined with silk embroidery, the metal threads can be used to outline shapes, to emphasize particular details and to brighten the whole effect. Using small purl chips, or pieces, backgrounds can be made to glitter. Small articles such as pincushions can be delicately worked with metal thread hearts, for example. Starting from the outside shape, the threads to be couched, perhaps passing thread, pearl purl and rows of Japanese substitute, can be alternated, then the center filled with a mixture of check and rough purl chips. If initials or other lettering are required, they can be traced or copied, then couched from the outside to the center, perhaps filling the central space with seed beads. There is great scope for experimentation with different combinations for different effects.

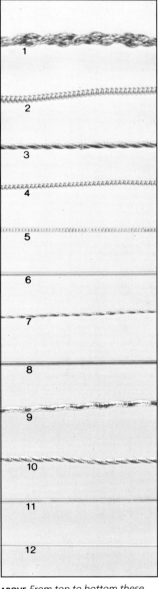

ABOVE *From top to bottom these metal threads are: 1 an 8-ply gold lurex; 2 a no 3 gold pearl purl; 3 a no 10 twist gold; 4 a no 1 gold pearl purl; 5 a gold check purl; 6 a smooth gold purl; 7 a thin gold rococo; 8 a rough silver purl; 9 a thick silver rococo; 10 a no 10 twist silver; 11 a smooth silver purl; 12 a silver passing thread.*

EMBROIDERY

UNDERSIDE COUCHING

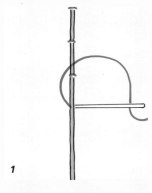

1

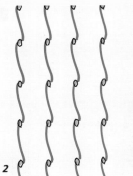

2

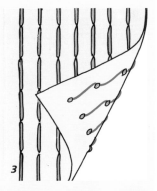

3

1 Secure laid thread on wrong side at top left. Bring couching thread out a little below, take it around laid thread and insert into same hole.
2 Pull firmly taking a small amount of laid thread through to wrong side.
3 Keep an even tension throughout. Continue to work like this covering the fabric surface as needed.

BASKETWORK

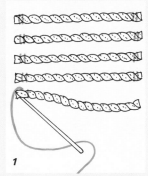

1

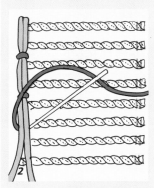

2

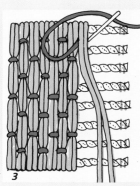

3

1 This form of padded metal threadwork has a basketweave appearance. First cut lengths of string to size and place them evenly in the opposite direction to which metal thread will be worked. Couch down with fine thread, securing ends firmly.
2 Using two strands of metal thread, take it over two strings and tie down with a single stitch.
3 For next and every other row make the first couching stitch over one string.

CIRCULAR COUCHING

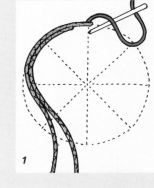

1

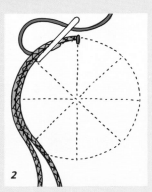

2

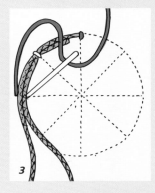

3

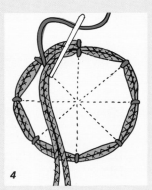

4

5

6

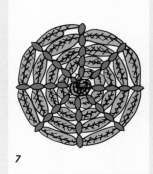

7

1 Begin by folding metal thread in half. Bring out couching thread on edge of traced circle, pass needle through loop and reinsert at starting point.
2 Bring needle out on straight line and couch with a small stitch.
3 Bring needle out on next straight line.
4 Couch in a similar way.
5 Continue couching in this way until the circle is filled.
6 Keep stitches on straight lines.
7 Neaten threads on wrong side.

118

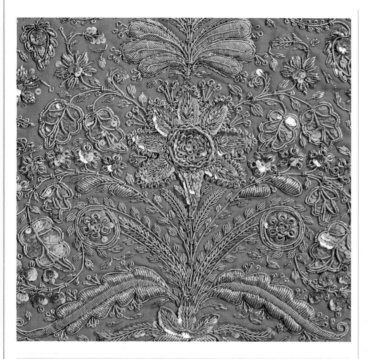

Stitches

Metallic yarn embroidery is a surface embroidery, the yarns being laid on the fabric, or over other stitches and couched into place. Simple couching may be used (see page 82), or underside couching, in which the couching thread is on the wrong side of the work.

When couching, the metal threads need to be held firmly and very slightly pulled to keep it taut. At the same time it should be turned to tighten its own twist. This is especially important with Jap gold, as otherwise the orange thread core will show between the gold. Metal threads may be couched singly, or in pairs, for which a very fine thread is used. The couching stitches can form their own design over the laid threads (lozenges, scrolls or squares) as seen in pieces of *opus anglicanum*.

Raised work can be created using couched work over padding of cardboard, string or felt.

TOP *A gold thread and sequin embroidery from the nineteenth century, this is a detail of an Indian cover. It is carefully worked with the threads couched to emphasize the textures and directions of growth of the leaves and petals. Despite the difficulty of working solely in metal, the detail is remarkable.*

LEFT *A tradition of naval and military uniform using metal threads became established during the eighteenth century. This elaborate cap was worked for a grenadier of the 43rd Foot, c.1745. The gold thread, some of which is raised, was stitched to delineate George II's initials and his crown, with thistles and roses interwoven around the edge.*

PADDING WITH CARD

1

2

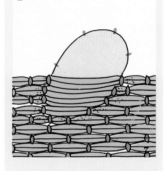

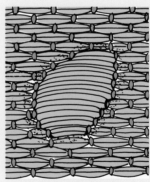

1 Small, individual padded motifs can be made using thin cardboard cut to a simple shape. Attach cardboard to ground fabric with one or two stitches at each side.
2 Secure end of metal thread to wrong side and continue couching up to cardboard.
3 Take metal threads over cardboard, hold down with small stitch at edge taken into same hole. Complete the couching.

MACHINE EMBROIDERY

Machine embroidery has today acquired the status of a creative form. With patience and practice, the machine can quickly produce original embroidery that has great individuality. Machine embroidery on its own offers tremendous scope, together with speed of working, which is much appreciated by busy designer embroiderers. Used in conjunction with hand embroidery, which it can complement and in some cases imitate, it provides many creative possibilities.

Contrary to popular belief, even straight stitch machines can be used for many decorative techniques; zigzag models offer limitless possibilities. With the continual updating of sewing technology, intricate designs can be carried out rapidly with minimum effort.

The domestic sewing machine forms a lock stitch, that is, two threads are used, one from below and one from above. When the tensions are even the stitch is formed in the middle of the fabric, so that the top thread is not seen below and the bottom thread is not seen above. Altering these tensions can produce exciting textures and enables thicker threads to be used in the bobbin.

Successful machine embroidery depends largely on practice, enthusiasm, and a thorough knowledge of the working of the machine, especially the different settings for each technique. The machine handbook will supply the answers to most problems; if not, the manufacturer or a local sewing machine dealer may be approached to give advice. By experimenting with settings, machine embroidery's potential can be explored.

Materials and Equipment

● **Sewing machine** When choosing a machine for embroidery there are certain factors to be considered. Some machines are becoming so automatic and self-regulating that it is difficult to use them freely. Check whether the feed (or teeth) can be lowered easily – this is usually done by pressing a button. If, instead of lowering the feed, a cover plate is needed to cover the teeth, the distance under the shank is reduced and the needle can catch on the embroidery hoop. Check that the bottom tension can be altered – it needs to be loosened to work whip stitch. In addition to a free arm, see that there is a good sized 'bed' to the machine, which can be easily attached to provide a support for the hoop.

● **Threads** Any fine sewing thead may be used on top. Coats and DMC also produce a fine machine embroidery cotton size 50 and 30 – the latter being the thicker.

● **Fabrics** Most fabrics are suitable except the knitted ones, which would stretch when pulled tight in a hoop. You should also avoid very closely woven cottons, as they can cause the top thread to break.

● **Frames** The best ones are the narrow wooden ring frames with a screw adjustment that can be tightened. For practice purposes or when using fine to medium-weight fabrics, small frames with an outer ring of plastic and a sprung metal inner ring are ideal. Bind the inner ring of wooden frames with bias binding. This keeps the fabric tight and clean and helps to keep the weave even.

Techniques

● **Preparing the machine** The machine handbook will usually list this under 'free darning'. On some machines, the feed can be lowered, and, on others, it is covered with a plate. Others have an extra needle plate or incorporate a device to raise the needle plate. In each instance, the feed is put out of action.

Free embroidery is a development of free darning. All domestic machines are capable of being used for this purpose. On old machines when there is no apparent way to put the feed out of action, small washers can be placed around the screw holes under the needle plate to raise it above the level of the feed. Failing that, tape can be placed over the feed, leaving the space through which the needle passes exposed.

Remove the sewing foot and holding screw and put them in a safe place. Thread the machine with the same thread top and bottom, setting tensions to normal and other controls to zero.

● **Framing the fabric** The success and pleasure in free machining depends upon the way the fabric is framed in the hoop. The fabric should be larger than the hoop, and stretched very tightly until like a drum, pulling across the grain of the fabric, stretching and tightening alternately (this is where a screwdriver is needed). If the fabric is not too tight, it will flap about and cause missed and broken stitches. Place the stretched hoop under the needle, with the fabric sitting on the bed of the machine.

● **How to begin stitching** Place the framed fabric under the needle with the fabric flat against the working surface, opposite to the way in which hand embroidery is worked. Lower the presser foot take-up lever, even if there is no foot to place on the fabric. This lever also tensions the top thread and if left up, causes loose stitches or jammed threads. Bring the bottom thread up through the fabric by turning the wheel towards you while holding the top thread. This is the starting procedure for all free embroidery. Stick self-adhesive labels, on which you have written brief reminders of instructions, to the front of the machine where they will be in constant view.

Before starting to embroider, check the top and bottom tensions are even. The bottom tension is regulated by the small screw on the bobbin case and for normal stitching should be neither too loose nor too tight. If the bottom tension is loosened the bottom thread will be pulled through to the surface. If the upper thread is loosened the top thread will be pulled through to the underside. While experimenting use different coloured threads top and bottom so that it can easily be seen from where the thread is coming. Try altering the stitch length for different effects.

Holding both top and bottom threads under your left index finger, and the frame on the rim at either side, with fingers just over the edge, start to run the machine. After

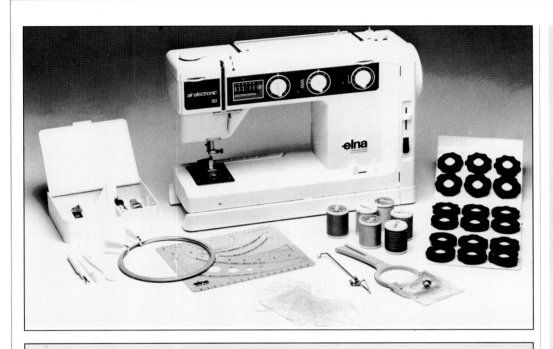

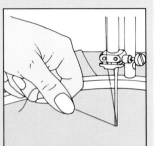

1 Holding the upper thread firmly in the left hand, place the needle in the desired position and make a stitch.

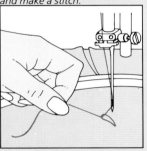

2 When the needle passes back through the fabric, it will have looped the lower thread beneath the fabric. Pull the taut upper thread to bring it through.

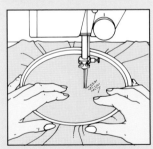

This diagram illustrates the correct position for controlling a frame when machining. The hands should be well in front of the needle.

making a few stitches, cut away the ends of the threads to avoid their becoming entangled with the stitching. With the feed out of action, stitching will only show when you move the frame. Run the machine fairly fast and move the frame smoothly and control will become progressively easier. It helps to practice with the machine unthreaded. Move the frame from side to side, back and forth, and counterclockwise. Practise writing your name and drawing. Move the frame to describe oblongs, squares and triangles in the same manner.

The slower the frame is moved, the shorter the stitch length, and vice versa. With the feed out of action, the stitch length is entirely dependent on the operator.

TOP *The selection shows a plastic box for storing equipment including a choice of feet; a stitch ripper; a cleaning brush; a stiletto; a needle threader; a plastic hoop frame; templates; aids for holding the templates in place while stitching; a selection of threads; some stitch or pattern programmers.*

ABOVE *This postcard was worked during the First World War.*

ZIGZAG STITCH

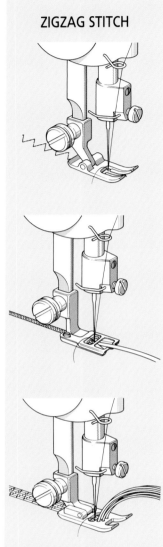

These illustrations show three uses of the zigzag stitch. The first shows plain zigzag; the second shows the couching of a single cord, keeping the cord centered with a special foot. The third shows multiple cord couching, using a foot capable of guiding up to five cords at a time. Each cord is secured singly under large zigzag stitches.

● **Stitches** Free machine embroidery is based on two stitching sequences – free running and free zigzag. Variation are brought about by altering tensions, using threads of different textures and thicknesses, and by subtle frame movements.

FREE RUNNING STITCH is the straight stitch used to form lines of stitching. You can experiment with the speed at which you move the frame, in conjunction with the speed at which you run the machine. Run the machine slowly, and move the frame around, and back and forth to produce more angular effects. Develop a rhythm so as not bend or break the needle.

FREE ZIGZAG STITCH is carried out using any of the stitch widths and the same frame movements as free running stitch. Move the frame smoothly and slowly, and satin stitch will result. Hold the frame still and a satin stitch bead will form. Groups of these worked close together will produce beautiful textures and if the stitches are cut, tufting will result. Small flowers can be worked by radiating zigzag stitches from one central point. If, when one flower is complete, the needle is left in the fabric on the outside of a petal, another flower can be started beside the first, and so on, without fastening off each time.

ZIGZAG TEXTURES If zigzag stitches are worked side by side, encroaching on each other, around in circles or squarely or diagonally on top of one another, an infinite variety of textures can be achieved. These are ideal as filling stitches, to offset bolder hand techniques, to produce repeat patterns.

AUTOMATIC STITCHES In similar manner, intricate patterned textures, unrecognizable as automatic stitches, can be produced effortlessly by selecting from the numbers of preset sequences offered by automatic machines. Experiment with threads, speed and frame movements.

Machine drawn thread and pulled fabric work

Wide zigzag, when used on loosely woven fabric, such as crim or muslin, can produce counterparts to hand techniques. Threads can be removed from the fabric at random, or in definite patterns, and those left can be drawn together in clumps, moving the frame slowly when blocks of satin stitch are wanted. Working into the same fabric with narrow or wide zigzag, or any of the satin stitch-based automatic patterns, will form open lace-like textures.

Machine cutwork

Cutwork is an extension of the way the machine can be used to mend a hole. First, practice mending a hole, following the instructions in the machine handbook.

First attempts are easier when medium-sized circular or oval shapes are used. The neatest effects can be achieved on closely woven natural fabric, like organdie. Matching the thread color to the fabric, stitch circles of small free running stitches. Run over these three or four times, superimposing one row upon the other. With the fabric still framed, cut away the centers of each circle taking care not to cut the stitching.

PULLED WORK

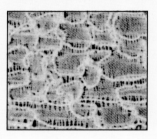

Choose a loosely woven fabric such as muslin in an embroidery hoop using zigzag stitch and both tensions fairly tight. The example (TOP) shows a narrow stitch worked evenly, creating a pattern between the lines of stitching. The stitch size is changed to give a freer effect (ABOVE).

Using the same or a different color thread, and making sure that the fabric is tight, start the stitching on the edge of one hole. After making a few stitches to fasten on, cut away the thread ends to prevent them becoming entangled. Stitch across the hole to the opposite side, catching the threads to the fabric. Cross the circle again and continue until a trellis of threads has been formed. This can be in a spider's web or a random design. On this mesh, further stitching can be worked. The edges of the circles can be neatened with any neat finishing technique.

Eyelets can be made by punching out small circles with a stiletto, and with no. 50 machine embroidery thread radiating fine.

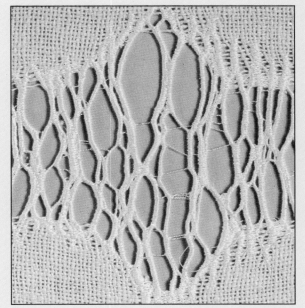

ABOVE LEFT *Japanese Lady in Grey is a free interpretation of a Japanese print. It was embroidered using straight stitch on the domestic Bernina sewing machine with D.M.C. machine cotton and Natesh Indian rayon. The picture has been worked with great delicacy, and is beautifully mounted.*

LEFT *Example of drawn thread worked by machine.*

ABOVE RIGHT *Designed and stitched by Rebecca Crompton in the late 1930s, this machine embroidery was created in free running stitch.*

BELOW *Machine embroidery need not be the restricted medium that is commonly imagined. It can be used in conjunction with other techniques to produce a variety of subtle and three-dimensional effects.*

CHAPTER 3

CROSS STITCH

INTRODUCTION

Cross stitch is probably one of the oldest forms of embroidery. It is used all over the world, particularly in peasant communities. The stitch is made in two stages with two diagonals worked over each other to form a cross. It is usually worked on canvas or evenweave fabric. When working on canvas the stitches should cover the ground completely, while on linen or similar fabric the crosses form a pattern on the surface. Sometimes cross stitch is worked on a fabric whose threads are not easily countable, for example velvet. In this case tack a canvas or net of suitable mesh onto the fabric to be worked and work the cross stitching through both layers without piercing the threads of the canvas or net. When the embroidery is complete the strands of the overlaid material are pulled away without disturbing the stitches. Cross stitches must cross in the same direction.

The earliest known example of a complete cross stitch is thought to date from 500 AD or a little later, and was discovered in a Coptic cemetery in Upper Egypt. The embroidery is worked in upright crosses on a linen background.

Some historians suggest that the development of cross stitch owes much to the craftsmanship of the Chinese, as this form of embroidery is known to have flourished during the T'ang Dynasty between 618 and 906 AD. From China, the skills and designs may have spread via India and Egypt to Greece and Rome, and from there throughout the countries of the eastern Mediterranean and the Middle East. Other schools of thought believe that the spread of cross stitch embroidery may have been in entirely the opposite direction, as it was notable that the first great migration of foreigners into China took place during the T'ang Dynasty. Persians, Arabs and travellers from Greece and India followed the silk routes to China and many settled there, influencing the designs used in Chinese arts and crafts, particulaly those for textiles. Many Chinese textiles bear motifs that show great similarity to those found on Persian fabrics.

What is certain, however, is that from many of these countries the techniques and designs of cross stitch ultimately spread through Europe. The Crusaders probably brought home embroidered textiles from the Middle Eastern countries visited during the Crusades: the trade and spice routes carried not only articles for sale, they were traversed by emigrants who would practise their various craft skills wherever they settled.

It was in the Tudor period in England that cross stitch first rose to prominence, when gentlewomen began to stitch domestic needleworks while professionals worked ecclesiastical pieces.

By the sixteenth century, the lady of the house was producing pillow and cushion covers, coverlets, carpets and other pieces with the aid of her staff and friends. Counted thread purses were popular products. Stitching was done with wool thread, which could nave been produced locally, and silks imported from the Middle East. A soft linen fabric, known as 'canvas', was used and designs were copied from a number of sources which included the many herbals and gardening books then available.

Emblematic designs were also popular, and these more

RIGHT *A detail from the Dowell-Simpson sampler, thought to be the world's largest sampler and worked in the second half of the nineteenth century by the family and friends of Mrs Edward Dowell. Because it was worked over several decades, ending at a length of 41 feet (12m), it illustrates the progress of Berlin woolwork, the designs of which changed from simple, colored patterns to garish and extravagant. The domestic scenes, animal and bird motifs and geometric patterns are worked in cross stitch on several different pieces of soft canvas which were then pieced together.*

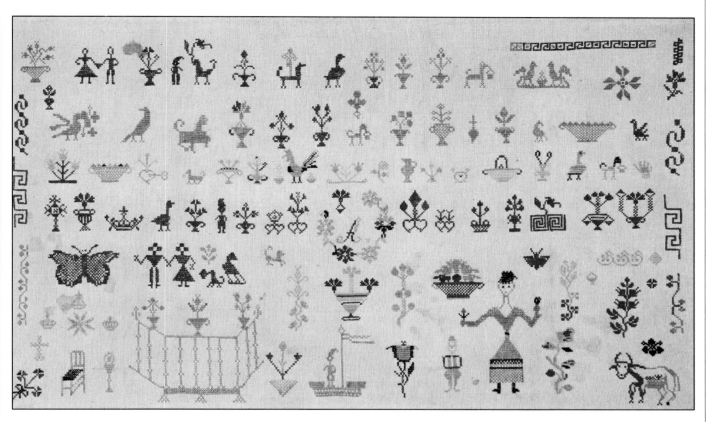

RIGHT *This sixteenth-century octagonal panel is one of the panels worked in cross stitch and applied to a screen. The initials stitched in the corner stand for Elizabeth, Countess of Shrewsbury, more commonly known as Bess of Hardwick.*

ABOVE *This engaging sampler of individual motifs was not signed or dated by the embroiderer, but it is thought to be a nineteenth-century piece from Pennsylvania. It is entirely worked in cross-stitch, and although it resembles the randomly worked spot samplers, the design is highly organized and the colors are logically spread throughout the rows of animals, plants, figures and household items.*

This highly decorative Mexican sampler combines satin, stem, cross and Hungarian point stitches with drawn thread work on linen cloth. Unusually for a sampler of this type, where the main objective was merely to try out stitches, a central pictorial design has been combined with geometric motifs and border sections.

abstract motifs were usually copied from examples of European embroidery that found their way to England. Queen Elizabeth I was a very skilled needlewoman, as was Mary Queen of Scots, who

filled the long months of her captivity producing exquisite examples of canvas embroidery, often using cross stitch, some of which survive today.

By the beginning of the

seventeenth century the lines between cross stitch and canvas work (see chapter 4) were becoming blurred as basic cross stitch was mingled with or gave way to cross stitch variants and unrelated stitches.

In the eighteenth and nineteenth centuries, cross stitch was used primarily in samplers, needlework exercises worked at this period largely by children, and came to be known as 'sampler stitch'.

MATERIALS AND EQUIPMENT

Fabrics

Fabrics for embroidery fall into three distinct categories: common-weave fabrics, even-weave fabrics and canvas.

Certain common-weave fabrics with a regular woven or printed pattern such as gingham, polka-dots or stripes provide a useful grid for working crossed stitches neatly and evenly. However, in the main it is best to work with even-weave fabrics with easily seen warp and weft threads. These should be the same thickness, or a distorted pattern will result. One of the most popular fabrics is Glenshee, an evenweave with 29 threads per inch. Counted stitches can be worked best over two threads (resulting in 14½ stitches per inch) or three threads (resulting in just under 10 stitches per inch).

There is a large range of similar even-weave fabrics available, some finer and some coarser than Glenshee, and they are usually made from linen, cotton or wool, or blends of these with polyester or other synthetics. They are mainly produced in white, cream or pastel colors. Special types of even-weave fabrics suitable for counted thread techniques are Hardanger, Aida and Binca. Hardanger fabric has pairs of threads woven together while Aid and Binca have four threads woven together to form distinct blocks in the weave over which the stitches are formed. These fabrics come in different thread counts and are usually made of pure cotton, or cotton and synthetic blends. The color range includes pastels and bright colors such as yellow, red and green.

The third fabric group consists of different types of canvas. Canvas is made of vertical and horizontal threads woven together to produce precisely spaced holes between the threads. Because canvaswork, although closely related, is a technique in its own right, cross stitch on canvas is treated separately in the next chapter.

Threads

Embroidery threads are made in a wide range of weights and colors. Some are twisted and must be used as one thread, while others are made up of several strands which can be separated and used singly or put together in different weight or color combinations. For cross stitch embroidery on common- or even-weave fabric, the following threads are suitable:

Stranded cotton – a loosely twisted, slightly shiny six-strand thread which can be separated for fine work. A good all-purpose thread with an extensive color range.

Pearl cotton – a twisted 2-ply thread with a lustrous sheen, which cannot be divided. It comes in sizes 3, 5 and 8, 3 being the heaviest, and in a good range of colors.

Soft embroidery cotton – a tightly twisted 5-ply thread, fairly thick and with a matt finish. It is used as a single thread on heavier fabrics.

Coton à broder – a tightly twisted thread which is similar to cotton perlé, although softer, finer and with a less lustrous finish.

Stranded pure silk – a seven-stranded, shiny thread which can be divided. It comes in an extensive color range including many brilliant shades not available in stranded cotton. It is also available as twisted thread, in a much narrower color range. Pure silk is difficult to work with and must by dry-cleaned.

For canvaswork, wool yarns are usually preferred.

Needles

Crewel and chenille needles may be used for fine and medium-weight embroidery on some common-weave fabrics, but as a general rule it is best to use a tapestry needle, which has a blunt end instead of a

LEFT *A variety of stranded cottons from different manufacturers. They should always be stripped, that is separated out and reassembled in the required combination, to avoid a messy finish.*

RIGHT *This selection of evenweave fabrics includes white cream and tan scrims of jutes or linen; a linen huck; an 18 mesh cotton; 4 evenweave linens of 20, 25, 30 and 35 meshes; and a linen cotton crash.*

LEFT *Here a simple block motif is worked on white Hardanger, an even-weave fabric.*

RIGHT *This cross stitch border uses the natural grid of gingham fabric. The stitching is quite simple – a large Leviathan stitch is worked over each square on the fabric and then each of these stitches is overworked with a small cross stitch. The careful use of color imposes a pattern of vertical stripes upon the fabric's check.*

BELOW *This photograph shows four tapestry needles: size 18, 20, 22 and 24, crewel needles sizes 5, 6, 7, 8, 9 and 10. The blunter tapestry needles are useful when working on large meshes; the finer crewel needles should be used on close-meshed linens and cottons.*

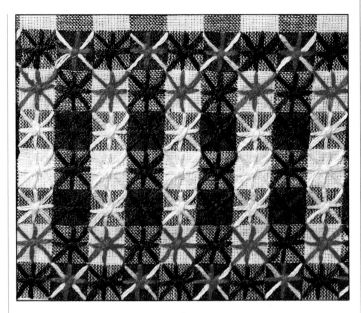

sharp point, on even-weave fabrics. The blunt end separates the threads of the fabric to pass through, whereas a sharp needle would split them.

Tapestry needles come in a range of sizes suitable for different fabrics.

Hoops and frames

Like other forms of embroidery, cross stitch is best worked with the aid of a hoop or frame to prevent the fabric from pulling out of shape. The easiest way to do this is to pin or staple the fabric to a simple wooden stretcher a few inches longer than the finished size of the piece of work. C-clamps can be used to hold this type of frame securely on the edge of a table, leaving both hands free for working. Work on common-weave fabric can be stretched on a two-ringed circular hoop which can be moved easily from one area of fabric to another. More sophisticated frames, some with integral stands are also available *(see page 61).*

Good lighting, preferably from a gooseneck lamp, is important and you need a comfortable chair of the right height for you to work easily at a frame without overstretching.

Other equipment

Every embroiderer will accumulate a personal collection of particularly useful items of equipment and these may vary according to the type of work and the materials preferred. There are a number of general sewing aids which will invariably be useful – dressmaking scissors, a small, sharp pair of embroidery scissors with short blades, a thimble, a tape measure, ordinary sewing needles and threads for basting and a box of dressmaking pins. For design work and preparing the fabric yu will need drawing pins or a lightweight but strong staple gun; pencils, felt-tip pens, markers and acrylic paints; a good supply of tracing and graph paper; a ruler and a set square; and last but not least, a small mirror which enables you to work out reverse motifs and the corners of borders.

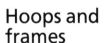

DESIGN

*W*orld-wide traditions of cross stitch have provided us with a whole lexicon of motifs and styles. The peasant embroideries of other nations provide an immediate source of new ideas for contemporary stitchers and can provide the confidence to risk unusual or unfamiliar techniques and design features.

Peasant embroidery has never sought to be more than a domesticated craft, passed down from mother to daughter. The stitches are very simple to work and the fabrics used – usually linen, varying in color from white to dark fawn and in texture from fine to coarse depending upon the locality – have been readily available to every household.

The colors were often limited but the dyes very brilliant: two or three hues might be the maximum number, with the addition of brown or black for outlines. In China, peasant cross stitch is even today almost exclusively worked in dark blue thread on white fabric. Embroideries stitched in monochrome are perhaps the richest of all, as they show off

BELOW FAR LEFT *This modern example of free cross stitch varies the weight of thread and the size and direction of the stitches to create this almost impressionistic picture of pink poppies.*

ABOVE FAR LEFT *This nineteenth century Turkish border uses several bright colors and definite motif designs, rather than the more dense repeating patterns often seen. It is cross stitched in wool on handwoven linen or cotton.*

LEFT *A modern panel from Thailand. Straight-forward cross stitch has been worked on an even-weave fabric. The symmetrical, geometric design and lack of motifs are perhaps typical of contemporary pieces.*

ABOVE *Detail of a Central European shirt, closely worked in cross stitch on even weave.*

BELOW *Yugoslavian peasant embroidery is often characterized by simple border patterns in just one or two colors. The section of a sleeve is modern work but within a characteristic tradition. Dark and light blue threads have been worked in cross stitch to great effect.*

the design to best advantage.

The apparently complex and closely worked border patterns which appear in peasant embroidery all over the world are achieved in the simplest possible way. Motifs used on their own are almost unknown they are usually repeated to form border patterns stitched in rows, one above another. Sometimes as many as six or seven rows are put together to form an intricate design. These can vary from narrow to wide borders and it is rare to find more than two rows alike in a single piece of work. Greek stitchers have been particularly skilled in creating enormously complicated border patterns from fairly simple components. When sufficient depth of border was filled, the work was usually finished with a pattern that created a broken outer edge and, if further decoration was needed, single motifs were

This motto sampler was completed by 10-year-old Eliza Richardson in 1837. It is cross stitch worked with colored silks on woollen fabric. The motto has been divided into two by naturalistic motifs, and formalized by a geometric repeat border. The central motifs provide relief from the more regimented surround, and successfully break up the block of writing.

repeated above the border, widely spaced apart in rows or just dotted in at random.

Most cross stitch embroidery is worked on evenly woven fabric, but in some areas, in India, for example, where a regularly woven fabric was unusual, the designs in cross stitch were all spaced by eye rather than counted out. Most peasant stitchers were not troubled if the borders did not fit exactly into the required space; they adapted the patterns, added sections or missed out motifs, and these irregularities are an intriguing characteristic of peasant embroidery. This free arrangement and the lack of design considerations as we know them give each piece of peasant embroidery its strong individuality and the delight of the unexpected.

Contemporary design need not be restricted to traditional ideas, however. An example of what can be achieved with free style cross stitch is shown in the almost Impressionist embroidery of poppies (*see page 130*), whilst on the other hand the apparent formality of counted-thread work lends itself to almost any design that takes your fancy by the use of graph paper (*see below*). In particular, geometric forms lend themselves to this style, hence the popularity of house samplers with formalised representations of the embroiderer's own home.

LEFT *Geometric patterns lend themselves well to counted thread work, precision being relatively easy to achieve on a canvas. This modern sampler shows how architectural forms can similarly be simply transferred to a canvas, which is the reason many samplers illustrate churches, houses or homes, as well as the alphabet, numbers and mathematical designs.*

LEFT *Greece and the Greek Islands are famous for their crossed stitch embroideries, traditionally worked in home-produced bright-colored silks on linen clothes and many domestic items. Large, complicated designs are loosely worked to give the cross stitching a characteristic raised texture.*

BELOW *Greek motifs are characterized by their geometric order. This Ionian piece, taken from a linen bed valance, is no exception. The highly symmetrical and organized pattern has been worked in plain cross stitch. The vertical stress of the inner border motifs is complemented by the horizontal outer border. It dates from the eighteenth century.*

TECHNIQUES

Transferring designs

Before starting work on your piece of embroidery, you will need to decide how to transfer the design to the fabric. There are several methods of doing this, depending on the type of fabric you have chosen as a background. On common-weave fabrics, guidelines for the areas of stitching should be accurately drawn. If you are using cross stitch on an even-weave fabric or canvas, the usual method is to work from a color chart by counting the threads to determine the placing of the stitches.

Transferring a design onto a common-weave fabric

USING CARBON PAPER This method will work well on smooth fabrics and is simple and quick. Place a sheet of dressmaker's carbon paper between the fabric and an outline tracing of your design, making sure the design is centered. Pin them to a flat surface and draw round the outlines with a hard pencil or use a tracing wheel for simple shapes. Use blue or red carbon paper for light fabrics and yellow carbon paper for dark fabrics.

BASTING THROUGH PAPER This is the best method to use on an uneven fabric or a pile fabric such as velvet or towelling. Trace the design outlines carefully on tissue paper or waxed paper, center the tracing on the fabric and pin it in place. Baste around the traced line with small stitches, using a fine thread that contrasts with the fabric. When the basting is completed, tear the paper away gently, leaving the outlines basted through the fabric. If the embroidery does not completely hide the basting

when the piece is finished, remove the basting thread carefully, using a pair of tweezers.

USING A LIGHT SOURCE This method works only with fine, smooth fabrics such as cotton or silk. Rest a sheet of glass or acrylic sheet between two dining chairs and place a strong light underneath the glass, pointing upwards. A lamp with the shade removed, a gooseneck or similar adjustable lamp are best. Trace your design outlines onto tracing paper or waxed paper and fix this to the top of the glass with masking tape. Center the fabric over the tracing, securing it with more tape. The light will reflect the design on the fabric and you can carefully trace it with a sharp pencil.

● **Enlarging and reducing designs** Patterns may be easily enlarged or reduced to suit your purpose by marking them out into squares and scaling these squares up or down as required (see page 86).

● **Transferring a design onto an even-weave fabric**

USING INK OR PAINT For open-weave fabrics which will be covered by the embroidery, you can mark the design directly onto the fabric, using a fine brush and waterproof ink for the outlines and acrylic paints or waterproof inks to color in the shapes.

You may find that the stitch you have chosen for a particular area cannot be worked right to the edge, as there is too little space left to fit in another complete stitch. The shape can be altered slightly to compensate for this, or the small gaps can be filled with tent stitch in the same yarn.

USING GRAPH PAPER When you use cross stitch on even-weave fabric and canvas, the best way

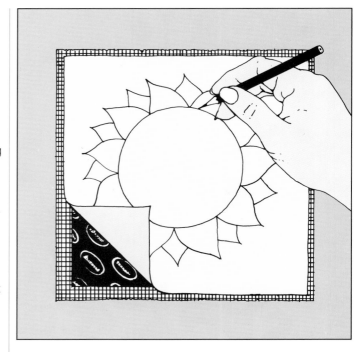

USING CARBON PAPER
Having traced your design on tracing paper, lay a sheet of dressmaker's carbon over the fabric. Place the tracing paper on top of the carbon, making sure the design is centered on the fabric. Using a pencil, draw over the design. Make sure that you press firmly so that the design transfers to the fabric.

USING A LIGHT SOURCE
Having set up a glass-topped surface, place the gooseneck – or other similar light source – underneath, directing the light upwards through the glass. Place the sheet of tracing paper, with the design on it, over the glass surface and fix it with masking tape. Take your piece of fabric and centre it over the design on the tracing paper. The light shining up from below will enable you to see the design through the fabric.

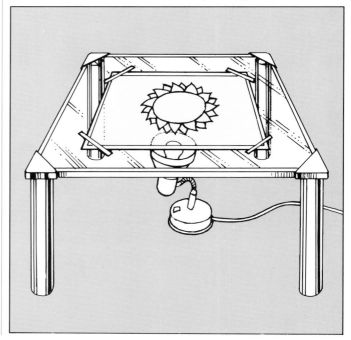

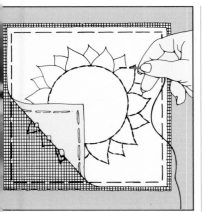

BASTING THROUGH PAPER
Trace your design on tissue paper, then lay this paper over the fabric. Baste around the outline of the design, using small stitches to retain the detail. Tear away the tissue paper, leaving the stitched outline on the fabric. The basting may be left on the fabric underneath the finished stitching, or can be plucked out with a pair of tweezers.

to follow the design is to make a chart and use it as reference for working directly on the fabric. You interpret the chart by counting the threads in the fabric. This method also has the advantage of leaving the fabric or canvas unmarked, so changes to the design can be made while the work is in progress.

● **Making the chart** The first step in making a chart of your design is to square it up onto graph paper. The easiest way to do this is to work on ready-printed, graphed tracing paper, or you can rule a grid on plain tracing paper. Lay the tracing paper over the design and trace the outlines with a fine black felt pen, adjusting the shapes to fit the printed squares. This will give you a squared outline design which you then copy, square for square, on graph paper. Do not use opaque paint for this process as it will obliterate the lines on the graph paper. Each colored square represents one cross stitch to be worked on the fabric. If you are using ready graphed motifs or borders, draw these directly on the graph paper to work out their placing on the fabric. Border corners should be worked out by using a mirror.

● **Calculating the dimensions** The finished size of the piece will depend on whether you work the stitches over one thread or a group of threads, and the gauge of canvas or even-weave fabric you have chosen. Experiment with stitch size and types of thread on a spare piece of background fabric to get the effect you like. You can then work out the finished size of the stitching. Suppose the design on the graph paper chart is 40 squares wide and 60 squares deep; if you plan to use even-weave fabric with 10 threads to the inch (2.5cm) and work each cross stitch over two threads, you will fit five complete stitches into each inch of the fabric. The finished design will measure 8 × 12 inches (20 × 30cm). Then decide whether you will mount the piece over hardboard to display it, or frame it behind glass. For mounting and framing purposes, an extra 5 inches (12.5cm) all around is needed, so your piece of fabric or canvas should measure 18 × 22 inches (45 × 55cm). If you intend to make the piece up into a cushion or table-cover or it is a piece of fashion embroidery for use on a garment, a 3 inch (7.5cm) margin all around is sufficient.

● **Using a chart** Prepare the fabric and mount it in a frame. The first step is to mark the center of the fabric. From the half-way point along the top of the fabric, baste down to the bottom with a contrasting thread being careful not to cross any vertical threads. Mark the center horizontally by basting in the same way from side to side. Do exactly the same if you are using canvas. Rule corresponding lines across the chart to find the center. Begin stitching at the center of the fabric, working outwards in each direction, following the chart square by square.

Preparing the fabric

Any type of fabric or canvas should be finished at the edges before the embroidery is begun, to prevent its fraying and to strengthen the edges for mounting the fabric in a frame. When working out the size of the fabric needed for a design, allow 3 inches (7.5cm) extra all around for unframed pieces and 5 inches (12.5cm) for framed ones. Cut the fabric to the correct size, using sharp scissors, following the grainlines or canvas threads carefully. To finish off the raw edges, turn them over and hemstitch them by hand or machine. On closely woven fabric the raw edges can be finished with a row of machine zigzag stitches. To neaten and secure canvas, cotton tape should be folded over the edges and stitched down firmly.

Preparing threads

Working threads should be used in lengths of

approximately 15 inches (38cm). Longer threads will tend to fray or lose their sheen because they are pulled through the fabric too often. A skein of thread can be cut into convenient lengths before you begin to stitch. Cut a piece of cardboard 15 inches (38cm) long, wrap the thread around and round the length of the cardboard, not too tightly, and cut through the thread at each end. Cut lengths can be loosely plaited to prevent them tangling and each length removed as needed by gently pulling one end from the plait.

Starting and finishing the thread

When you start stitching, do not use a knot as this may show through the finished piece or make a bump on the right side, especially if the work is to be framed. Anchor the thread by making one or two tiny back stitches in a space that will be covered as the stitching progresses. Alternatively, leave a tail of approximately 2 inches (5cm) of thread which can be darned in later. If you are continuing to work an area which is partly stitched, anchor a new thread by sliding the needle under the wrong side of a group of stitches, securing about an inch (2.5cm) of the thread underneath them. To finish a thread, slide the needle in the same way under a group of stitches and cut off the loose end of thread.

STITCHES

Cross stitch consists of two diagonal stitches which bisect each other. It does not matter if the upper diagonal goes up to the right or to the left as long as all stitches are consistent. Neighboring stitches share common holes. Rows share holes with those above and below. It is important to maintain an even tension throughout to avoid 'dropped' stitches. The work can be handheld, but it is often preferable to have the fabric held taut in a frame or hoop.

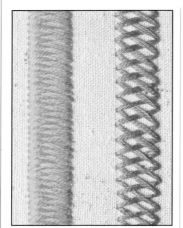

ABOVE *Basket stitch*

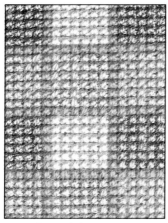

ABOVE *Cross stitch*

Cross stitches can be worked over one, two, three, four, or as many fabric threads as you like – the main consideration is consistency. When working stitches over one fabric thead, it is important to avoid every alternate stitch 'slipping through' to the back of the work. Form each row in four stages. First, work the first diagonals of alternate stitches.

On the return journey, fill in the first diagonals of the other stitches. Then work alternate upper diagonals and fill in the other upper diagonals on the return.

Regardless of how large your stitches are, an alternative

ABOVE *Cross stitch – alternate*

way of working stitches is to make them in two stages, with all the first diagonals stitched first and all the upper diagonals worked on the return. It is also possible to work a row by forming one complete cross stitch at a time. The main advantage of the latter method is that if you have to undo work – as even the best needleworkers must from time to time – you can take out complete stitches simply by snipping through each upper diagonal.

Begin cross stitching with a waste knot, coming in from the area of the fabric that you are

ABOVE *Cross stitch – diagonal*

next going to cover with stitches. Finish a thread in the same way, with a waste tail going to an area to be stitched over.

Cross stitch can be worked as an edge binding. It can also be worked on a closely woven or matte ground by using 'waste canvas' temporarily tacked onto the main fabric. (If you do not have any waste canvas, soak an area of single-thread, mono canvas to remove the stiff sizing and, when it is dry, use this instead.) Stitches

ABOVE *Cross stitch: Victorian panel in wool framed as a picture.*

are formed over the waste canvas and, when the pattern is worked, threads of that canvas are removed one by one. This does result in looser stitching, but it allows the counted thread technique to be used with a great number of fabrics.

Although the actual construction of crossed diagonal stitches remains the same, there are different methods of working ordinary cross stitch, depending on the choice of ground fabric or canvas. One rule applies to all methods: the top diagonal stitches must always fall in the same direction, unless a deliberate light and shade effect is required, in which case their direction can be varied to catch the light.

The variations of crossed stitches included here are elements of design that enable you to produce different effects – a linear motif or a mass of color; a flat surface and restrained texture or a dense mass of interwoven threads to radiate or project from the background. Some stitches are only suitable for certain types of fabric or thread, while others offer scope for considerable inventiveness in manipulating color and texture to create a complex, multi-layered design.

Before starting a project, you may find it helpful to familiarize yourself with the effects of the different cross stitch variants by working a stitch sampler, as children and even adult embroiderers used to do.

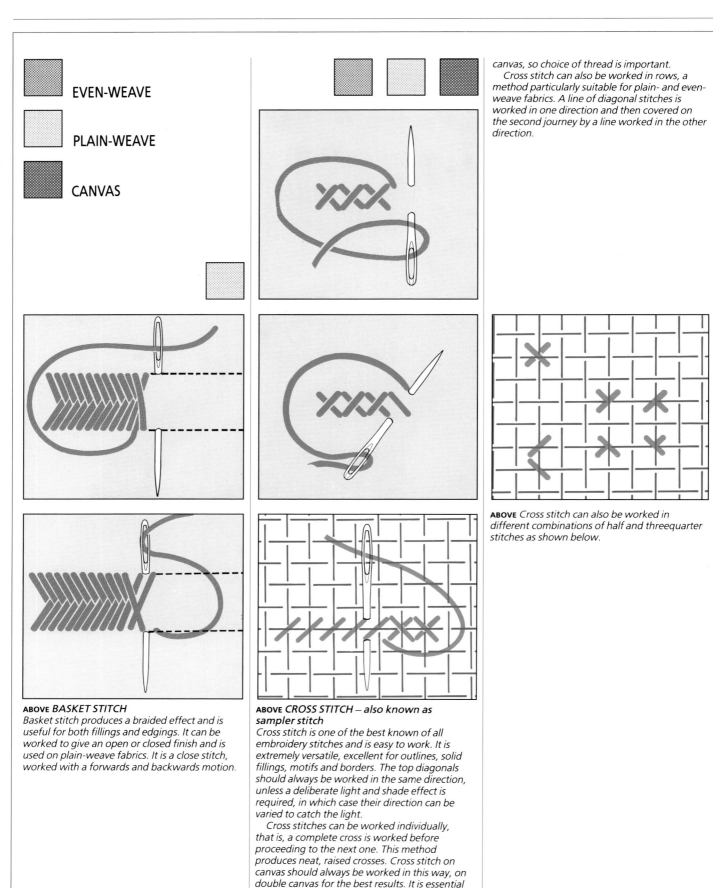

EVEN-WEAVE

PLAIN-WEAVE

CANVAS

canvas, so choice of thread is important.

Cross stitch can also be worked in rows, a method particularly suitable for plain- and even-weave fabrics. A line of diagonal stitches is worked in one direction and then covered on the second journey by a line worked in the other direction.

ABOVE Cross stitch can also be worked in different combinations of half and threequarter stitches as shown below.

ABOVE BASKET STITCH
Basket stitch produces a braided effect and is useful for both fillings and edgings. It can be worked to give an open or closed finish and is used on plain-weave fabrics. It is a close stitch, worked with a forwards and backwards motion.

ABOVE CROSS STITCH – also known as sampler stitch
Cross stitch is one of the best known of all embroidery stitches and is easy to work. It is extremely versatile, excellent for outlines, solid fillings, motifs and borders. The top diagonals should always be worked in the same direction, unless a deliberate light and shade effect is required, in which case their direction can be varied to catch the light.

Cross stitches can be worked individually, that is, a complete cross is worked before proceeding to the next one. This method produces neat, raised crosses. Cross stitch on canvas should always be worked in this way, on double canvas for the best results. It is essential that each cross stitch completely covers the

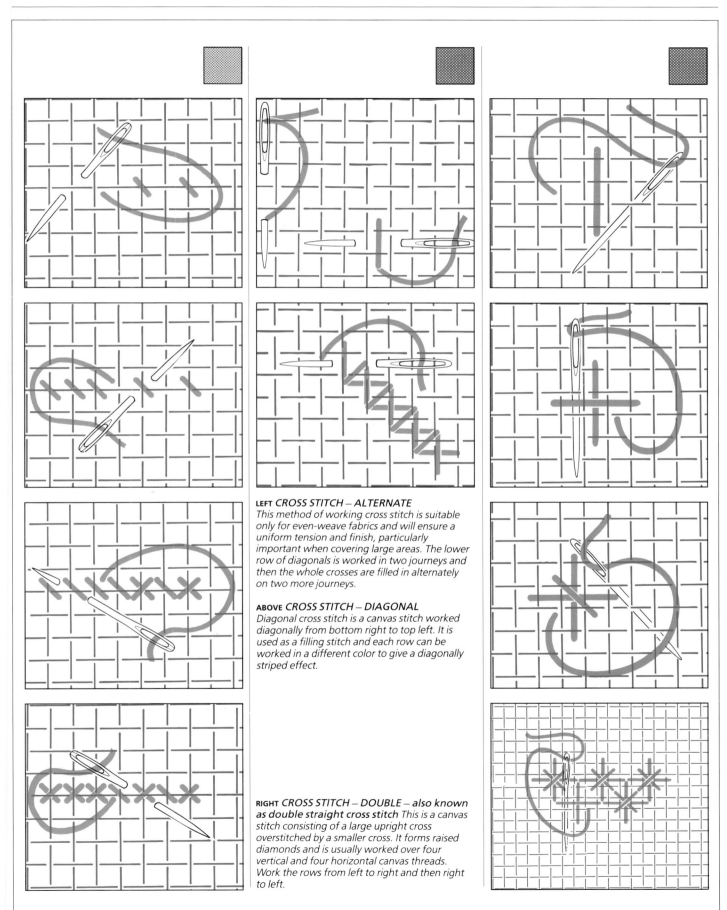

LEFT *CROSS STITCH – ALTERNATE*
This method of working cross stitch is suitable only for even-weave fabrics and will ensure a uniform tension and finish, particularly important when covering large areas. The lower row of diagonals is worked in two journeys and then the whole crosses are filled in alternately on two more journeys.

ABOVE *CROSS STITCH – DIAGONAL*
Diagonal cross stitch is a canvas stitch worked diagonally from bottom right to top left. It is used as a filling stitch and each row can be worked in a different color to give a diagonally striped effect.

RIGHT *CROSS STITCH – DOUBLE – also known as double straight cross stitch* This is a canvas stitch consisting of a large upright cross overstitched by a smaller cross. It forms raised diamonds and is usually worked over four vertical and four horizontal canvas threads. Work the rows from left to right and then right to left.

Cross stitch – double

Cross stitch – oblong

Cross stitch – double sided

Cross stitch – oblong with back stitch

Cross stitch – long armed

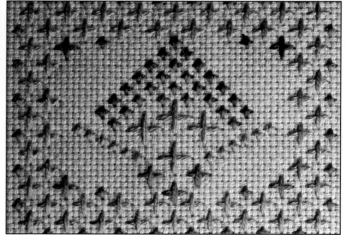

Cross stitch – St George

Long armed cross stitch can be used both as a border and as a textured filling when it has a pretty, plaited appearance, as shown by this seventeenth century border in silk on linen.

It is worked in rows from left to right and consists of long diagonal stitches crossed by short diagonal stitches; the long stitches are worked over twice the number of threads as the short stitches. Long-armed cross stitch is straightforward to work and looks equally effective on fabric or canvas. Any type of embroidery thread can be used with this stitch, provided that the weight of the thread is compatible with the fabric or canvas.

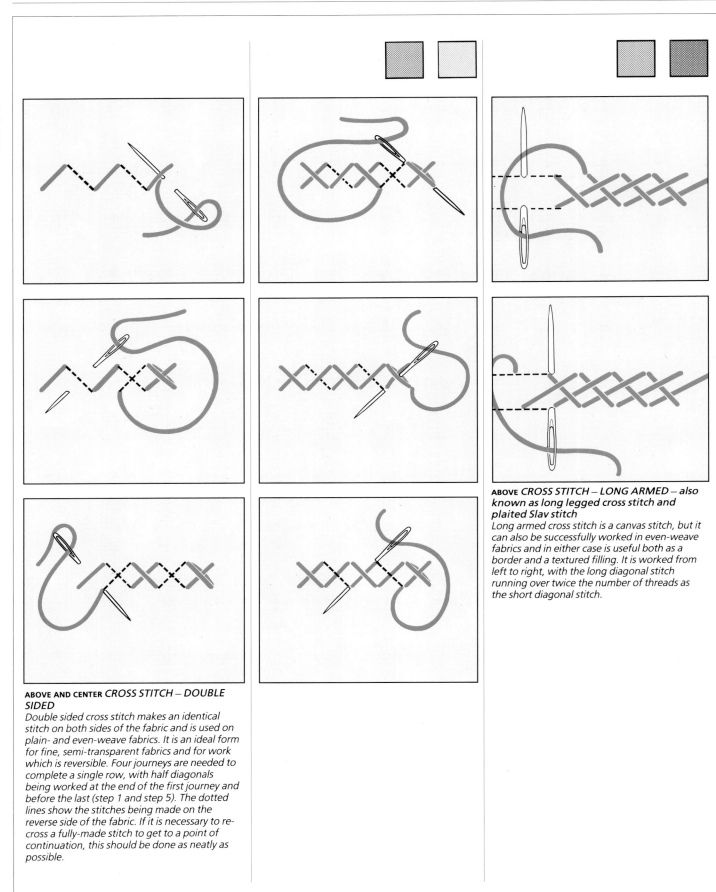

ABOVE *CROSS STITCH – LONG ARMED – also known as long legged cross stitch and plaited Slav stitch*

Long armed cross stitch is a canvas stitch, but it can also be successfully worked in even-weave fabrics and in either case is useful both as a border and a textured filling. It is worked from left to right, with the long diagonal stitch running over twice the number of threads as the short diagonal stitch.

ABOVE AND CENTER *CROSS STITCH – DOUBLE SIDED*

Double sided cross stitch makes an identical stitch on both sides of the fabric and is used on plain- and even-weave fabrics. It is an ideal form for fine, semi-transparent fabrics and for work which is reversible. Four journeys are needed to complete a single row, with half diagonals being worked at the end of the first journey and before the last (step 1 and step 5). The dotted lines show the stitches being made on the reverse side of the fabric. If it is necessary to re-cross a fully-made stitch to get to a point of continuation, this should be done as neatly as possible.

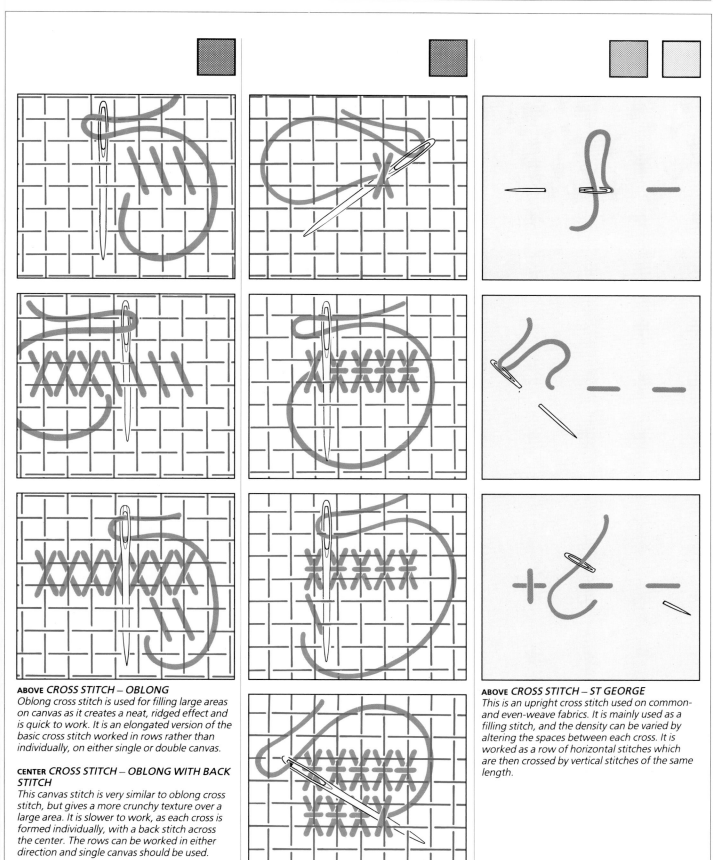

ABOVE *CROSS STITCH – OBLONG*
Oblong cross stitch is used for filling large areas on canvas as it creates a neat, ridged effect and is quick to work. It is an elongated version of the basic cross stitch worked in rows rather than individually, on either single or double canvas.

CENTER *CROSS STITCH – OBLONG WITH BACK STITCH*
This canvas stitch is very similar to oblong cross stitch, but gives a more crunchy texture over a large area. It is slower to work, as each cross is formed individually, with a back stitch across the center. The rows can be worked in either direction and single canvas should be used.

ABOVE *CROSS STITCH – ST GEORGE*
This is an upright cross stitch used on common- and even-weave fabrics. It is mainly used as a filling stitch, and the density can be varied by altering the spaces between each cross. It is worked as a row of horizontal stitches which are then crossed by vertical stitches of the same length.

143

Ermine stitch

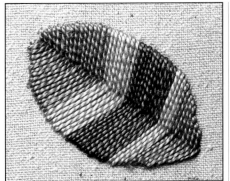

Flat stitch

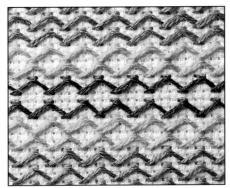

Herringbone stitch

Fern stitch

Fishbone stitch

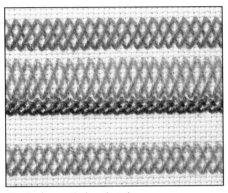

Herringbone stitch – closed

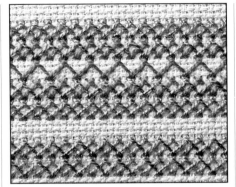

Herringbone stitch – double

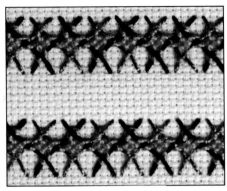

Herringbone stitch – interlaced

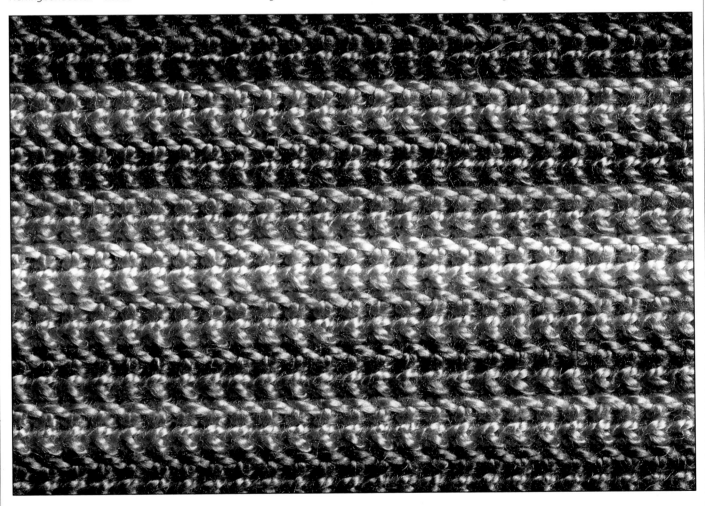

Greek stitch

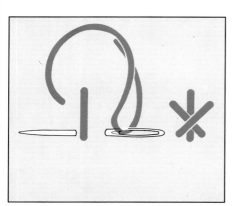

ABOVE *ERMINE STITCH*
Ermine stitch is used on common-weave fabrics for fillings and borders. Its name comes from the ermine tail effect it makes when worked in black thread on a white background. It consists of a long vertical stitch which is then covered by an elongated cross stitch about one-third shorter. The cross should be placed above the base of the vertical stitch.

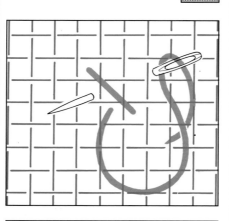

ABOVE *FERN STITCH*
Fern stitch is a canvas stitch which forms plaited, vertical ridges and should be used on double canvas. Each row of top-heavy crosses must be worked from the top to the bottom of the canvas.

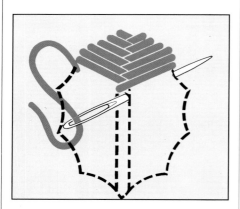

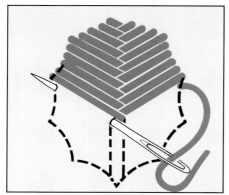

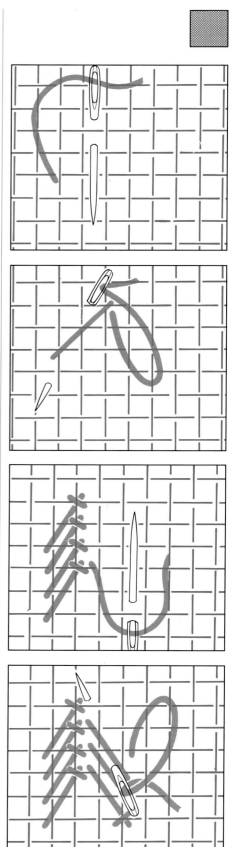

LEFT *FLAT STITCH*
Flat stitch is worked with a fairly thick thread on common-weave fabrics. It is used for filling small shapes solidly or can be worked in parallel rows to give a heavy outline to a shape. It is always worked from the inner margin to the outer margin.

RIGHT *FISHBONE STITCH*
Fishbone stitch makes an attractive chevron pattern and is worked on double canvas. Each stitch consists of a long diagonal held down at one end by a short crossing stitch.

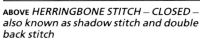

Front

Back

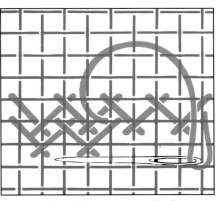

ABOVE *GREEK STITCH*
Greek stitch is a canvas stitch which should be worked in a fairly coarse thread on either single or double canvas. It is similar to herringbone stitch, although the crosses are not spaced symmetrically, and it gives the effect of a plaited texture when applied over large areas.

ABOVE *HERRINGBONE STITCH – also known as Russian stitch, Russian cross stitch and Mossoul stitch*
Herringbone stitch is very simple and can be used on common- and even-weave fabrics and canvas. It can be worked in single rows or as a filling and it forms the foundation row for a number of more complicated stitches.

ABOVE *HERRINGBONE STITCH – CLOSED – also known as shadow stitch and double back stitch*
Closed herringbone stitch can be used in two distinct ways. It can be worked on common- and even-weave fabrics as a border stitch to give a plaited effect. It is also used for shadow work on semi-transparent fabrics, with the rows of straight stitches appearing on the front of the work and the herringbone showing through the fabric in shadow form. It is worked in the same way as herringbone stitch, but the diagonals touch at the top and bottom.

Knotted stitch

ABOVE *Knotted stitch*
Sometimes called Persian cross stitch or Pangolin stitch, this is quick and easy to work. A pretty, broken striped pattern is created by the use of contrasting threads.

RIGHT *Leviathan stitch*
Worked in tapestry yarn, this stitch makes an extremely hard-wearing surface, suitable for chair seats.

Leviathan stitch

Herringbone stitch – overlapping

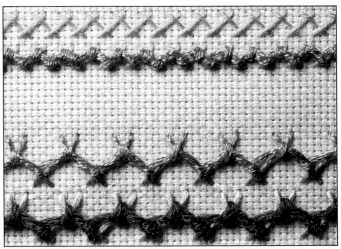

Herringbone stitch – tied

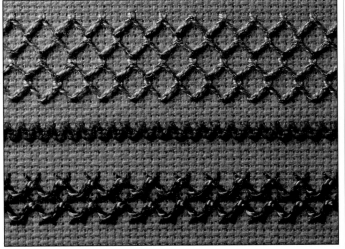

Herringbone stitch – threaded

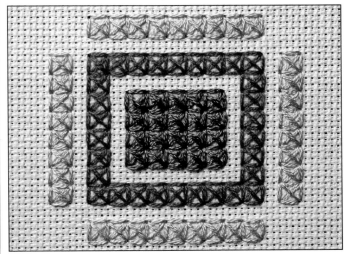

Italian stitch

The three Herringbone stitch variants are useful to give a variety of rich fillings. Italian stitch gives a dense texture on canvas, but can also be used on loosely woven even weave to produce an open-work effect by pulling the stitches tightly together. Leaf stitch can be used for filling small shapes or as a decorative border.

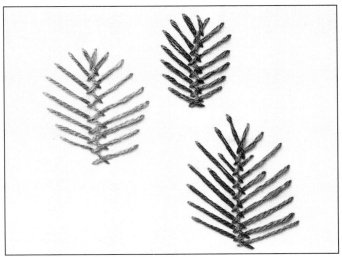

Leaf stitch

149

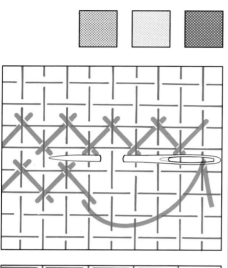

is slightly different from the normal double herringbone stitch as the stitches on the second row are worked over and under those of the first row. The trick in working the stitch correctly is to study its formation carefully from the diagram and make sure the foundation herringbone is correct before proceeding to the interlacing. Work the foundation rows fairly loosely, as the interlacing will draw the stitches together. Thread the interlacing by working along one side and the middle of the row, and then work the second side and the middle.

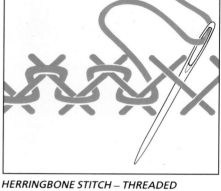

HERRINGBONE STITCH – THREADED
Threaded herringbone stitch can be used on common- and even-weave fabrics as a simple two-color border, or a rich background filling which can be laced with metallic thread. A row of basic herringbone stitch is worked first, then a second thread is laced upwards and downwards through the foundation stitches. When worked as a background, the foundation rows should touch at the tips of the crosses. The color of the lacing thread can be varied to give a gradual color change over the area.

HERRINGBONE STITCH – DOUBLE
Double herringbone stitch can be worked on common- and even-weave fabrics and canvas. It consists of a foundation row of basic herringbone with a second row, often a contrasting color, worked over it.

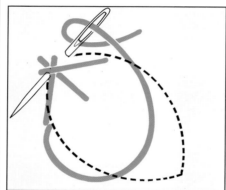

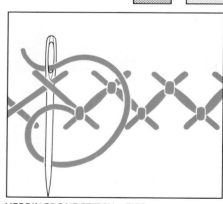

HERRINGBONE STITCH – TIED
Tied herringbone stitch is very similar to threaded herringbone. A row of basic herringbone is worked first and then the crosses are tied together using a contrasting thread and a simple knot.

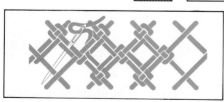

HERRINGBONE STITCH – INTERLACED
Interlaced herringbone stitch can be used as a rich border on common- and even-weave fabrics, or as an insertion stitch to make a decorative seam joining two pieces of fabric together. The interlacing thread can contrast with the herringbone foundation and the stitch looks very rich when interlaced with metallic thread. The herringbone formation of the base

HERRINGBONE STITCH – OVERLAPPING – also known as raised fishbone stitch
Overlapping herringbone stitch is used only on common-weave fabrics and is a filling for shapes such a leaves and petals, triangles and lozenges, to give a padded and raised effect. It is worked over a straight central stitch at the top of the shape and built up with overlapping diagonal stitches worked from side to side and crossing in the center. These stitches should be evenly placed and as close together as possible, to give a smooth surface to the raised area.

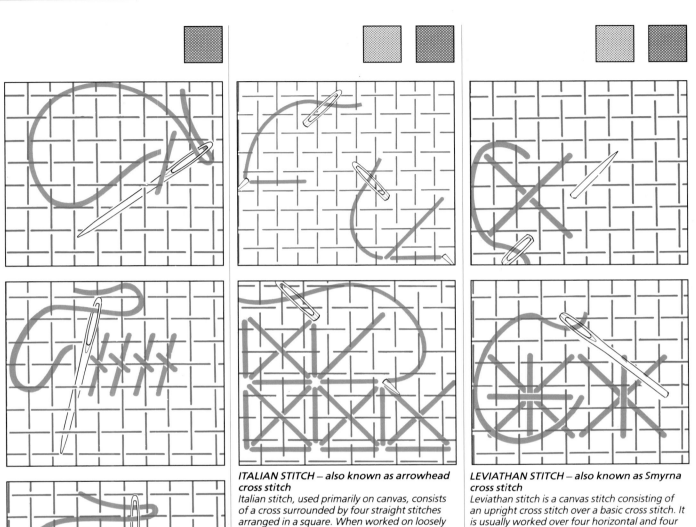

ITALIAN STITCH – *also known as arrowhead cross stitch*

Italian stitch, used primarily on canvas, consists of a cross surrounded by four straight stitches arranged in a square. When worked on loosely woven even-weave fabric, the stitches can be pulled together tightly for an openwork effect.

LEVIATHAN STITCH – *also known as Smyrna cross stitch*

Leviathan stitch is a canvas stitch consisting of an upright cross stitch over a basic cross stitch. It is usually worked over four horizontal and four vertical canvas threads and each stitch forms a neat, raised square unit. These units can be worked in alternate colors to give a checkerboard effect. Leviathan stitch is suitable for even-weave fabrics providing a fine thread is used.

KNOTTED STITCH

Knotted stitch is used on double canvas for backgrounds and large areas. It consists of a long slanting stitch tied down by a short diagonal crossing stitch. The rows of stitching overlap to give a closely packed, ridged appearance.

RIGHT *LEAF STITCH*

Leaf stitch is a light, open stitch suitable for filling regular shapes, and is always worked upwards. It is only used on common-weave fabrics. It can also be used as a border and if the lengths of the stitches are varied the border is given an undulating line. An outline stitch, such as back stitch, is often worked around the edge of leaf stitch to define the shape disinctly.

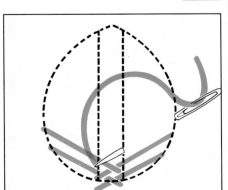

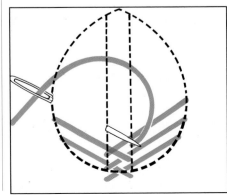

151

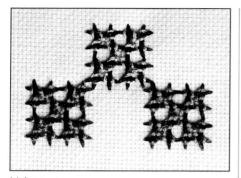

Maltese cross

Rococo stitch

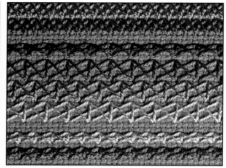

Montenegrin stitch

Leviathan stitch – double

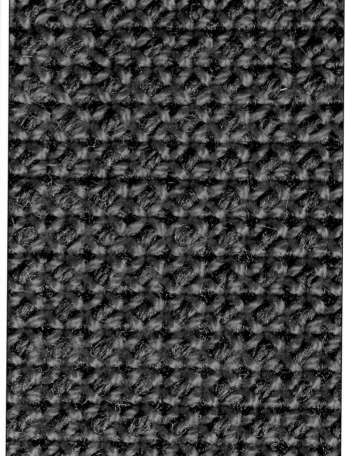

Rice stitch

Maltese cross stitch is a motif stitch making an intricate, interlaced cross shape. It can be used alone or as a striking border, or worked as a square by setting the foundation stitches vertically and horizontally, rather than diagonally.

Rococo stitch, sometimes called queen stitch, is a dense background stitch which was highly popular in the nineteenth century for articles such as pincushions and purses.

Montenegrin stitch is quick to work, which makes it a useful filling stitch for large shapes and backgrounds. When worked in the correct sequence, it is reversible, with a back pattern of ordinary cross stitches alternating with vertical stitches.

Double Leviathan stitch is a more complex variation of Leviathan stitch, making a larger, more raised pattern of square blocks which can be worked in two colors.

Rice stitch is another dense filling stitch. Very effective results can be achieved by experimenting with shading and texture, for example combining tapestry wool with pearl cotton for the corner stitches.

Montenegrin stitch: English sampler of 1656 in colored silks

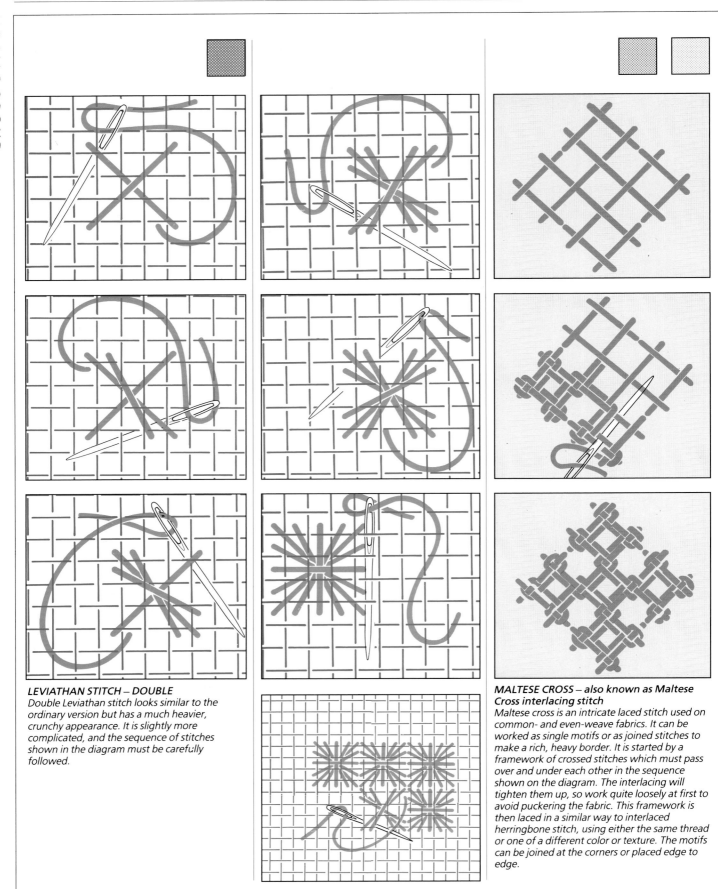

LEVIATHAN STITCH – DOUBLE
Double Leviathan stitch looks similar to the ordinary version but has a much heavier, crunchy appearance. It is slightly more complicated, and the sequence of stitches shown in the diagram must be carefully followed.

MALTESE CROSS – also known as Maltese Cross interlacing stitch
Maltese cross is an intricate laced stitch used on common- and even-weave fabrics. It can be worked as single motifs or as joined stitches to make a rich, heavy border. It is started by a framework of crossed stitches which must pass over and under each other in the sequence shown on the diagram. The interlacing will tighten them up, so work quite loosely at first to avoid puckering the fabric. This framework is then laced in a similar way to interlaced herringbone stitch, using either the same thread or one of a different color or texture. The motifs can be joined at the corners or placed edge to edge.

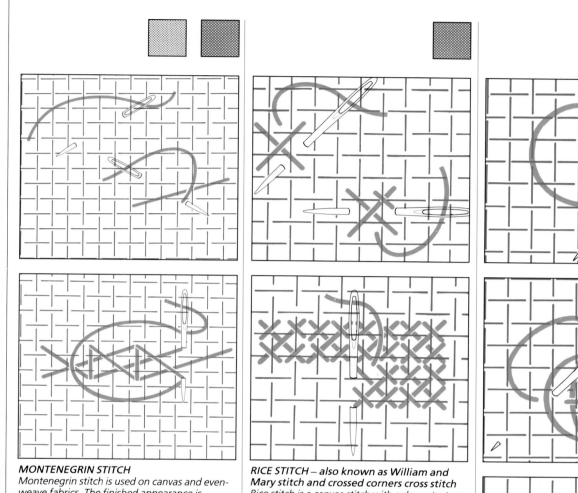

MONTENEGRIN STITCH
Montenegrin stitch is used on canvas and even-weave fabrics. The finished appearance is similar to long armed cross stitch with the addition of vertical bars. When this stitch is worked on canvas, a fairly coarse thread is necessary to cover the canvas completely.

RICE STITCH – also known as William and Mary stitch and crossed corners cross stitch
Rice stitch is a canvas stitch with a dense texture and, as it covers the canvas well, can be used for large areas. It can be worked in two colors or two thicknesses of thread by forming the large crosses first and then stitching the corner diagonals with a second thread. If using two thicknesses of thread, use the thickest thread for the large crosses and the thinner one for the corners. Interesting shaded effects can be achieved by working an area of large crosses in one color, and varying the colors of thread used for the corner stitches.

ROCOCO STITCH
Rococo stitch makes a dramatic background in canvaswork and should be worked on a wide mesh canvas with a fairly thick thread. It consists of four vertical stitches worked into the same space, tied down individually over one thread each with short crossing stitches. The vertical stitches curve when anchored into place on the canvas and make globe-shaped units.

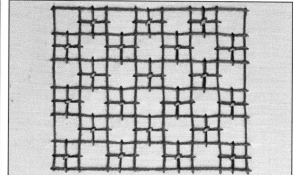

Torocko stitch

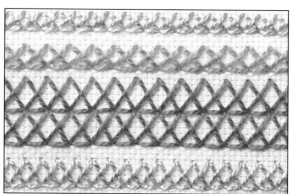

Underlined stitch

Velvet stitch

LEFT *Rococo stitch: sometimes called cross couched filling stitch or Hungarian cross stitch, is most successfully worked on a closely woven fabric stretched on a frame.*

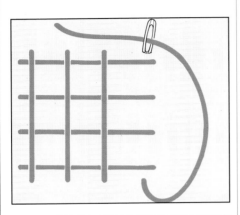

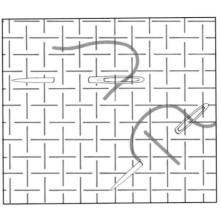

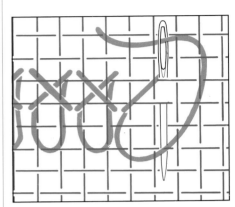

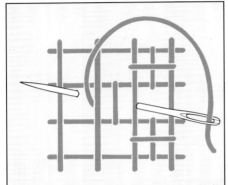

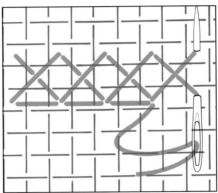

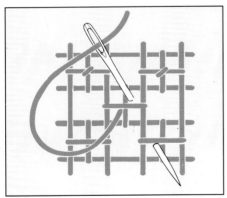

TOROCKO STITCH

Torocko stitch is a quickly worked filling stitch used only on common-weave fabrics. A foundation grid of evenly spaced stitches is worked first, across the whole shape, and then covered with diagonal rows of upright crosses, with a short diagonal stitch worked from bottom left to top right to finish. The crosses can be worked in a different color from that used to form the grid, with a third color being used for the anchoring diagonal stitches.

UNDERLINED STITCH

Underlined stitch is worked on canvas (mono or double) or even-weave fabrics, the latter requiring a fairly fine thread to be used. It is worked in horizontal rows and each cross stitch is underlined by a horizontal straight stitch before the next cross stitch is formed. Any type of embroidery thread can be used but care should be taken to match the weight of the thread to the gauge of the canvas to make sure that the canvas is covered by the stitching.

VELVET STITCH

VELVET STITCH — also known as rug stitch, tassel stitch, raised stitch, Astrakhan stitch, plush stitch and Berlin plush stitch. Velvet stitch resembles the pile of a carpet and is usually worked on double canvas. It became very popular during the Berlin woolwork craze in Europe and America during the middle to late nineteenth century. It was used to give a three-dimensional quality to animals, birds and flowers, against a flat cross stitch background. At that time, chenille thread (a thick, furry thread) was often employed to augment the dense textured effect.

When working velvet stitch, use one strand of a thick, soft yarn or several strands of fine wool through the needle at the same time. The loops are cut and trimmed to length after the stitching has been completed. If the stitches are worked very close together on the canvas and a thick wool is used, the resulting pile will be dense enough to be sculptured into different levels with a sharp pair of scissors.

The Victorian firescreen panel on the left shows a typical deployment of velvet stitch to make the main subject stand out sculpturally from the one-dimensional background.

Velvet stitch: Victorian firescreen panel with cross stitch background.

SAMPLERS

Samplers, or needlework test-pieces, are particularly important in the history of cross stitch. Although cross stitch was only one of the stitches worked in samplers until the eighteenth century, by then some pieces, perhaps worked by girls only six years old, were exclusively cross stitched. Eventually cross stitch became the most popular sampler stitch, and remains so today.

The earliest samplers were worked as reference collections by adult needlewomen; later the function changed as the sampler became an exercise pursued by young girls in the course of their studies. The inclusion of alphabets and numerals suggests that the sampler became increasingly more important as an educational tool. The samplers were usually signed and the age of the embroiderer was often given, together with the date of completion. This evidence indicates that the majority of pieces were worked by girls between the ages of five and fifteen.

Today the sampler has become a purely decorative work in which the modern embroiderer seeks to translate the old-fashioned charm of early pieces into a contemporary style.

Traditionally, sampler patterns are copied from a chart, a worked example, or counted by the embroiderer. Many samplers have an outer border enclosing at least one alphabet and a set of digits, an inscription, the name and age of the embroiderer and the date. Other popular motifs include a range of crowns, recognizable houses and other sites, and a wide variety of flowers.

Elements of design

The motifs and designs used in samplers vary considerably and often reflect the country of origin, though many are traditionally shared. In the seventeenth century flower motifs were popular all over Europe. The rose had particular significance in England; first the red rose of Lancaster and the white rose of York, then the two combined in the Tudor rose. In the United States, the widespread appearance of the Tudor rose, strawberries, carnations and tulips is testimony to English influence during the colonial period. Plant motifs are ubiquitous and

Averil Colby has identified the symbolic meanings of the some of those most commonly used:

Rose – earthly love
Lily – purity or chastity
Honeysuckle – faith
Pear or apple – forbidden fruit
Olive tree – peace and goodwill
Cherry – fruits of Heaven
Pomegranate – hope of eternal life.

Coronets and crowns appeared in embroidery in the eighteenth century, first above initials on household linens and then above initials on samplers. The original function of these motifs may have been to denote noble rank, but it is unlikely that this genuine symbolism would have produced so many. As samplers became increasingly pictorial during the course of the eighteenth century, they featured buildings, landscapes,

LEFT *This map of Europe was probably worked by Elisabeth Hawkins, an English schoolgirl, as an exercise in both stitching and geography. Chain and satin stitches are used to show the countries in red and the towns in black. The blue-grey of the sea seems to have been dyed into the fabric.*

RIGHT *Reworking some typical seventeenth-century designs for the textile study room at the Victoria and Albert Museum, London, Louisa Pesel (1870-1947) embroidered this sampler in cross stitch with the horizontal bands in back stitch. The figures in pink at the top are known as 'boxers' or 'amorini', and are often found on cross stitch samplers.*

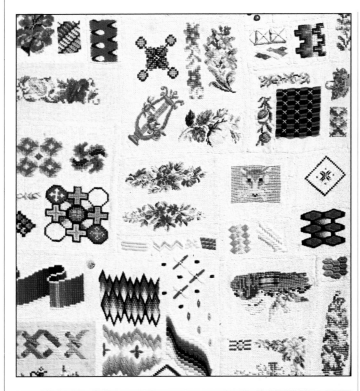

TOP *Section from the Dowell-Simpson sampler.*

ABOVE *This ordinary-looking sampler, stitched with linen threads on a linen ground, is interesting for its expertise. The sampler was stitched by a six-year-old, in cross stitch and eyelets. Practising her alphabet was probably more difficult than creating neat stitches.*

figures and animals, all portrayed in quite a naturalistic way. These were not randomly scattered spot motifs, but were arranged in balanced compositions and motifs were often matched in pairs.

A curious motif that appeared in the seventeenth century and transmuted gradually over many decades was the boxer, a small figure, originally nude except for a fig leaf, often repeated in rows. The description 'boxer' may have derived from the figure's stance – a stiff pose with arms extended, suggested an aggressive attitude. Oddly enough, it is possible that the origin of this figure was a popular sixteenth-century design showing a lover with his beloved. Modesty or fashion prompted seventeenth-century embroiderers to clothe the figures and it seems that the female figure gradually disappeared, leaving the man represented by himself. In some designs he is holding out a trophy, which he seems to be offering to a stylized form of a tree. The tree has sufficient signs of human shape to suggest that it may be a corruption of the original female figure.

Decorative borders were introduced into sampler design in the eighteenth century and these included geometric patterns derived from scrolls and Greek fret designs, together with elaborate, interwoven fruit and flowers. In American work, these borders sometimes assumed such importance that they threatened to swamp the central design. The border continued to be an important feature of nineteenth-century samplers where it always enclosed all four sides.

The map sampler originated in schools, combining needlework with geography, which was a subject of increasing public interest in England from around the middle of the eighteenth century. Not until the following century did maps become popular in the United States, and there some surprising misconceptions were revealed. In one map of Europe, the embroiderer shows a common land boundary between England and France.

The variety of subject, motif, pattern and border is endless; as samplers have progressed over the centuries, all of these design elements have been used with increasing ingenuity. More detail about the other common forms in sampler design – alphabets and numerals, mottoes and verses, the family tree, houses and public buildings – are included in the second part of this chapter, as is the original and often most abstract form, the technical sampler. The embroiderer today has unlimited scope in both design and materials and plenty of encouragement to express individuality, whether traditional motifs and alphabet forms are preferred, or more modern ideas of design are incorporated in the work.

Designing and making your own sampler

Designs for samplers can be taken from many different sources, such as fabrics, oriental carpets, china, lace and Fair Isle knitting patterns. It is also possible to adapt designs from the many exquisite samplers exhibited in museums. When studying

ABOVE *This design updates the pictorial sampler tradition and the subject matter and stitching techniques have been carefully matched. It demonstrates the use of beadwork and fabric painting combined with embroidery; the stitches are flat and satin stitch, cross stitch, back stitch, closed herringbone and French knots. The background fabric is a close-weave canvas that makes a particularly good ground for fabric painting. Plain and shaded embroidery cottons are used to vary the color effects.*

existing motifs you may find that you can use part of a composition and omit or rearrange elements of it, with a view to interpreting the original design rather than merely copying it. Reference can also be made to the large variety of embroidery books that are available, some which present charted cross stitch designs for motifs, borders and alphabets. All designs, whatever their origin, will naturally draw your eye either from top to bottom or from side to side and this factor should be taken into consideration.

If you are going to work on a fabric that offers a natural grid, even-weave or a patterned common-weave such as gingham, the designs

for all these features can be charted on graph paper. Each square of the graph paper represents one square of the fabric and both are available in several gauges which relate to the number of squares per inch (2.5cm). In commercially produced charts you will find that the color of the stitch is indicated either by the color of the square or by a symbol; symbols also designate the sort of stitch to be used. This type of design is suitable for cross stitch but can also be combined with freely worked stitches; in this instance you should work on a close-weave linen using the counted thread method.

Once the basic design has been completed the next thing to consider is the choice of color, which will greatly affect the finished piece. It is advisable to select a neutral color for the background as this will allow the design to be seen quite distinctly. If the background color is too strong, it will dominate the finished work and 'drown' the design. Your decisions about color will be made easier if you produce several different colored versions of your original design on paper; bear in mind that slight modifications may have to be made when matching the color of the threads with the color of an inked design.

Colored threads can be applied in different ways depending on the effect you want to create. For instance, when working with natural subjects you can blend and mix the colors in order to recreate their subtle tones in a manner similar to painting. To achieve this result you can either use one strand from each of several colors in your needle at once or use the 'shaded cottons' that

are commercially available and are particularly suitable for blended areas.

As well as solving design and color problems, you must make decisions about the techniques and materials that can translate the design into embroidery. The threads you choose must be compatible with the weight of your fabric but the design can be enriched by using a selection of different threads, and other materials such as net, beads and sequins. When common-weave fabrics are used, techniques such as appliqué and fabric painting can be introduced to suggest different textures; examples of this type of work can be seen in some American samplers. Texture and depth can also be created by the careful choice of stitches – flat stitches, such as satin stitch, can be worked on objects to suggest they are in the background, whereas an abundance of French knots forms a textural surface which appears to move to the foreground.

Interesting results are achieved by combining different ways of using both color and texture. Obviously your choice will be dependent upon the theme of your design, the background fabric and your own personal preferences. The possibilities in the selection of designs, materials, colors and textures are endless. There are no rules or set combinations to work from; the final decisions are based upon your own taste and inclination. The sampler was originally a personal piece of reference material, and although today samplers are more decorative than educational, they should still reflect your own ingenuity and style.

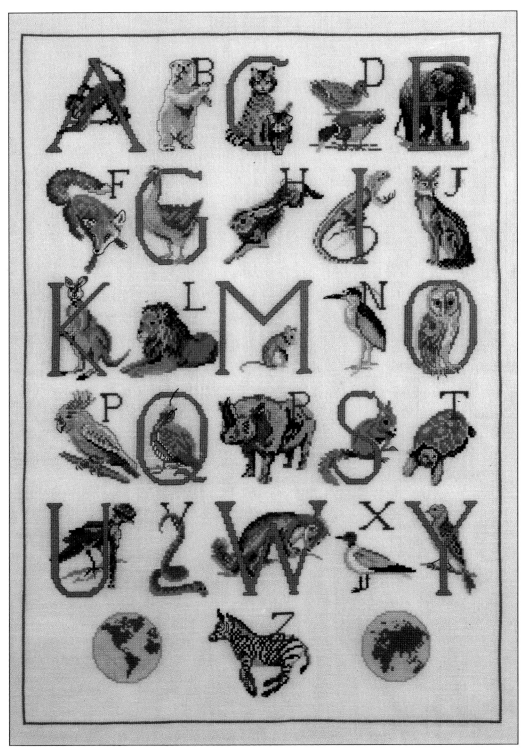

This sampler is worked from an embroidery kit and is a modern interpretation of ornamental alphabet design. The letters and animal motifs work closely together so that each animal is fitted to the initial letter of its name. The pictorial element is a method of enlivening this type of sampler and the motifs are represented naturalistically. The whole piece is worked in cross stitch.

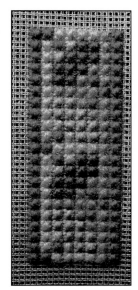

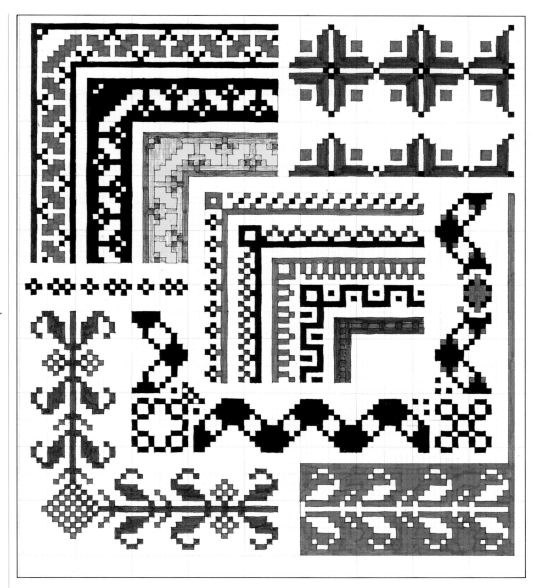

The chart (**RIGHT**) shows a variety of border patterns, arranged as corner sections to show how the design can be interrupted with a featured motif filling the right angle. It also demonstrates the effect of altering the colorways, or reversing the pattern out of the background. A simple border section (**ABOVE**) stitched in woolen threads and bright colors is a striking contrast to the more delicate work in stranded cottons, shown overleaf.

Borders, alphabets, numerals and motifs

When adapting a historical design or working to the traditional sampler format, you will need a border pattern, an alphabet and/or numerals and a variety of different motifs which can be placed either at random or asymmetrically in your design; these motifs usually appear in abundance in the lower part of the work. It is

important to consider the scale of all these elements, as a degree of consistency is necessary if the overall composition is to appear balanced.

● **Borders and corners** Borders are used to create a frame for a rectangular shape, such as a tablecloth, cushion or sampler, and as an edging device for a strip of fabric or the hem of a garment. They are a valuable feature of design for all sorts of embroidered items, as the border can be made narrow or deep, according to the

dimensions of the object and other motifs in the design, and you can also use the border to elaborate a simple framework or create a neat, unobtrusive edging for more complex pictorial work.

The border pattern can be simple or complex and is usually repeated on all four sides of the work. These border patterns are either abstract or derive from natural subject matter and in some cases they combine elements of both.

There are various different ways of creating a border

pattern. A narrow border might be two or three rows of cross stitch in different colors, to form stripes or an alternating checkered effect. There are many designs incorporating simple geometric motifs repeated along the strip; a one-way design can be turned at the center of the border strip, to enliven a basic pattern. Pictorial motifs can be used to construct a border, repeated in rows or matched in pairs with one motif reversed. More complicated designs include twining borders, in which the

LEFT *This is a stitched sample of the border sections shown in the top left corner of the chart on page 164. It is worked in stranded cottons on even-weave fabric. The slightly openwork effect of the cross stitches creates textural interest. Each strip shows exactly the same pattern worked in different colors: the pattern stitched in two colors; the pattern in silhouette on a black background; the border completely filled with stitching; the same colors as the previous sample, but with the background to the design left plain.*

This is usually solved in one of two ways: by using a mirror to reverse the border and turn the design at a 45° angle, or by filling the corner with a block of pattern or a single motif that breaks the sequence of the strip border. If a corner block is used that stands out from the basic pattern, it can be made a special feature or integrated with the rest of the design by careful use of the same colors.

A long, continuous border is often more interesting if it is split up into sections. You can run the sections along the length with a small gap in between, or inset a motif to break up the continuity.

● **Alphabets and numerals**
Alphabets and numerals are chosen according to the role they are going to play in the work. If they are to be arranged in horizontal rows, they can include a variety of capital letters, lower case lettering and numerals usually ranging from 1 to 9, which can be as ornate or as plain as you wish. When letterforms are being considered for a verse or inscription, the design should be fairly simple so that the lettering can be easily read, but it is acceptable to use ornate capital letters in conjunction with simpler lower case ones for effect.

length of each section is altered to fit different patterns and motifs together, or heavy composite borders, effectively used in Greek peasant work, where bands of patterns and motifs are stitched one above the other to create a deep border with many variations in the design.

There are different ways of treating the colors of a border. It can be stitched in a single color on a plain background of even-weave fabric, or in several different colors on a single-toned background, which can be left plain or filled with stitching.

Scale and texture are important aspects of embroidery design that can be used to vary the qualities of border patterns. The size of the border should be in keeping with the scale of the whole item. If used as a frame it should not overwhelm the central section of the design and can be kept quite simple, but if it forms the main body of the design, in a skirt hem or table runner, for example, it can be as complicated and colorful as you like. The scale can be altered in the stitching,

by using a naturally larger stitch or working a simple stitch across four blocks of the fabric weave instead of only one. The texture can be varied by offsetting flat areas of cross stitch with more elaborate raised stitches. The textural qualities will also be different according to the texture of the base fabric – a fine common-weave, light or heavy even-weave, fine or coarse canvas.

When border patterns are used to frame a design, there is the problem of what to do with the corner, where one section of the border runs into another.

ALPHABETS

The need to fit the letters into a regular grid need not constrain you to a limited range of alphabet styles, as these examples show. The letters can be worked directly in cross stitch on an even-weave fabric or canvas by the method of counting threads, or you can copy them on graph paper to make up a chart as a stitching guide to your own design.

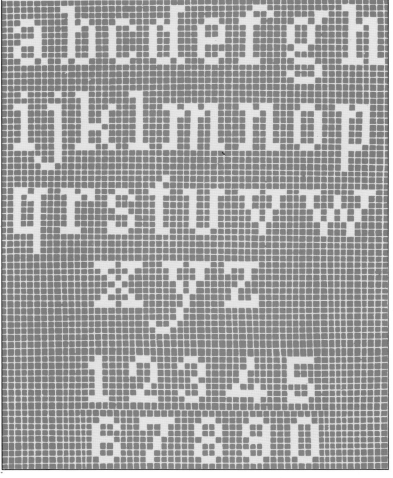

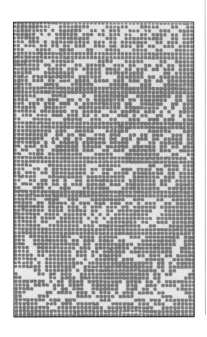

167

LEFT *This sampler has been designed with the inexperienced stitcher in mind. The lettering is bold, the design enlivened by changes of style and scale within each row of letters, to keep the stitcher's interest alive. A very basic but effective cross stitch border frames the alphabet, deliberately kept plain to point up the detail of the lettering. The color scheme exploits the contrast of blue and pink, lined by a mauve related to both colors, but the tones are kept reasonably close so that no one row of characters dominates the design.*

The design could easily be altered by the substitution of other alphabet styles and a different border. Study the scale and color relationships carefully so that your own choices are balanced.

TOP RIGHT *A simple family tree with spot motifs and border makes a highly personalized sampler.*

BOTTOM RIGHT *Motto samplers have retained their popularity. This is a modern example.*

Lettering is used in these examples to create a simple alphabet sampler, a motto sampler and a family tree sampler. Mottoes and verses became a feature of the sampler from the seventeenth century on. Family tree samplers also have a tradition dating back to the early eighteenth century.

MONOGRAMS Letterforms worked in cross stitch have been a traditional feature of embroidery for centuries, notably as a practical form of identification in initials stitched on household linen. They are also familiar from the neat rows of alphabets that were so often part of the stitching exercises carried out in samplers. Frequently, initial letters were overlapped, locked or intertwined to form a

monogram. Today, monograms are favoured more as decorative devices for clothing and can be used to personalize accessories or gift items, such as a fabric bag or belt, handkerchiefs or table linen. A stitched monogram is also an attractive and unusual decoration for a greetings card. If the fabric edges are finished neatly, the embroidery can be glued to the card, or framed in a window mount.

Simple monograms are easily designed from any alphabet adapted to a grid form that serves as a stitching guide.

An effective monogram must be legible and of a suitable size for the particular item to be decorated. A small, well-defined motif is ideal for a shirt pocket, for example, but

to fill the back of a jacket, you need a design that is not only much larger, but also more complex. You can elaborate the device with different colors and textures of thread, or by using more complicated stitches to vary the surface qualities in each section of the design. If you are working on a handkerchief, sheet, or similar item in which both sides may be visible, you might prefer to use the cross stitch variation known as double-sided cross stitch, because the embroidery forms a neat row of crosses on both sides of the fabric.

If you want to make a monogram from letterforms which are not already adapted for cross stitch, you will have to make up a chart on graph paper, modifying the shape of the letterforms as necessary to

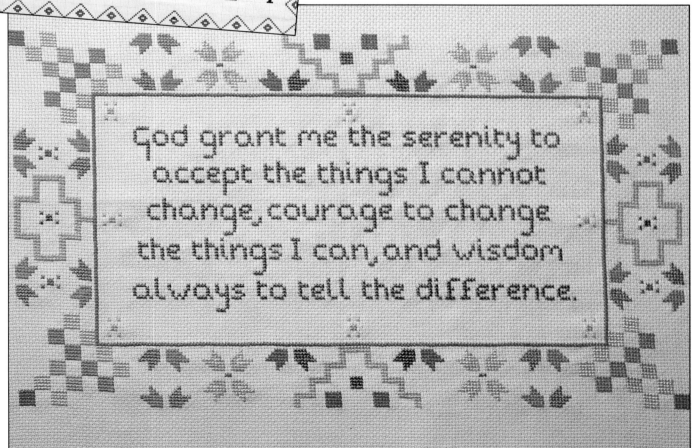

MONOGRAMS

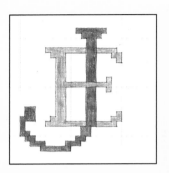

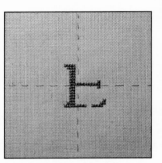

grid for the stitches. The canvas is afterwards trimmed close to the stitches and the remaining threads are pulled out from underneath.

RIGHT *A plain initial letter is an attractive marking for clothes and personal possessions and the design is simpler than intertwining the forms for a monogram. This example, worked in stranded cotton on even-weave fabric, is simply boxed with a black square of single crosses and elaborated with a zigzag device, in the same green as the initial, at top and bottom.*

ABOVE AND CENTER *This monogram is stitched on a plain-weave fabric with irregular warp and weft. To work the stitching evenly, the device is charted on graph paper and then a piece of closely woven canvas is tacked over the plain-weave to provide a corresponding*

ABOVE *One of the simplest ways to form a well-balanced monogram is to align the vertical strokes of two letters. This example, stitched on even-weave fabric, is given a decorative garland and color scheme is a pairing of opposites.*

fit the grid. As shown here, even curved and curling letters can be adapted for cross stitch, but the more exaggerated the form, the more difficult it may be to achieve satisfactory outlines on a squared chart. You can also decorate the lettering with tiny abstract or floral motifs, or add a narrow border to underline or surround the monogram, to make a simple design seem more detailed.

It is easy to work the embroidery on canvas or even-weave fabric, but if the monogram is applied to clothing, the pattern or weave of the fabric may not be sufficiently regular to provide a stitching grid. You can then

tack a piece of canvas in place and work the stitching through both the canvas and the base fabric. when it is complete, cut the surplus canvas close to the stitching and use a pair of tweezers to pull out the canvas threads that remain beneath the stitches.

● Motifs Pictorial motifs can be derived from virtually any source. Historical examples offer a wide variety of subjects, and the choice of motifs is largely determined by the theme of the work.

HERALDIC SYMBOLS Heraldry developed primarily as a functional rather than a decorative art. Heraldic devices were used to establish ownership, through the use of

carved seals, and identity in tournaments and on the field of battle, by the wearing of a coat of arms. The coat of arms was passed from one generation to another and signified historical continuity, a heritage more important than the individual bearer. At the present time, this symbolism is still fulfilled in heraldic devices belonging to royalty and aristocracy, and many corporate bodies – commercial and local government institutions – possess heraldic insignia which are a mark of identity and stability of tradition. Symbols derived from heraldry are also used in the badges and emblems of schools and universities.

While the granting of a hereditary coat of arms requires official sanction, heraldic imagery is an interesting source of motifs for less formal designs. The lion and unicorn, a crown, coronet or crest, a national emblem, and the basic element of the shield which bears the coat of arms, are all items that can be interpreted as motifs for embroidery and there are a number of stylized plant and animal forms. In essence the symbols stand for continuity, therefore heraldic design has been traditional rather than innovative. The devices and colours were originally bold and stylized, to serve as immediate identification, and this

This sequence shows the different stages of designing a monogram and adapting it to a grid for cross stitching. The letterforms chosen for the device are highly graphic, with exaggerated contrast between thick and thin strokes in the body of the letter and the heavily curved serifs and tails. In the charted version the slanted and curving outlines have become stepped and to balance the weight of the single cross stitches in the fine lines, the solid areas are made slightly heavier, especially in the serif on the top curve of the C. The final version, stitched in stranded cottons on even-weave fabric, shows the complete transition and the characteristic style that cross stitching brings to lettering and motifs.

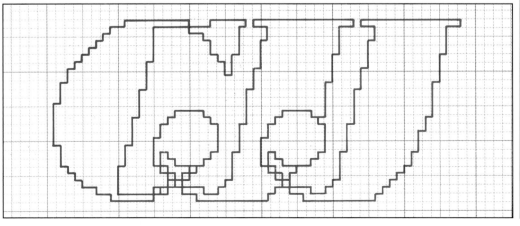

SAMPLE MOTIFS

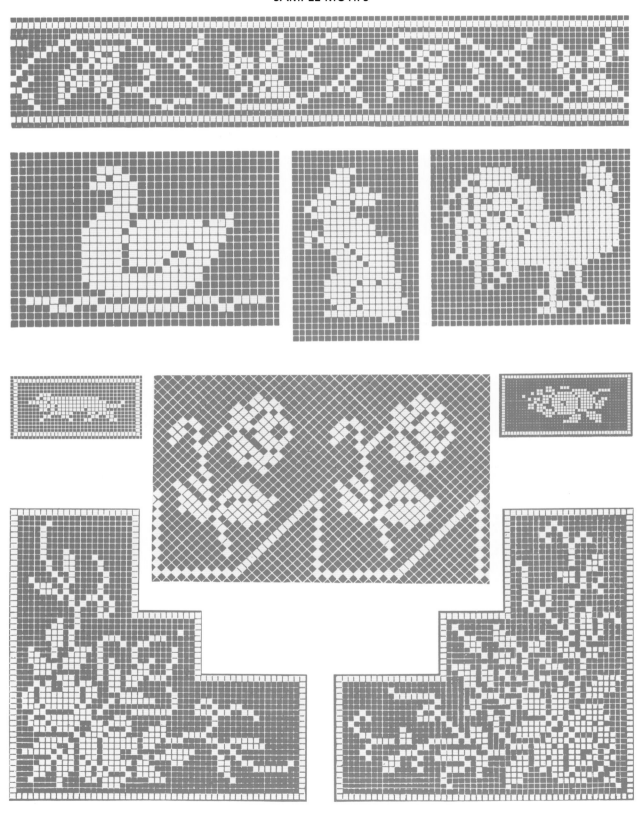

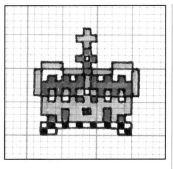

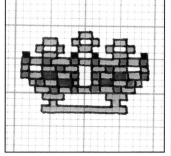

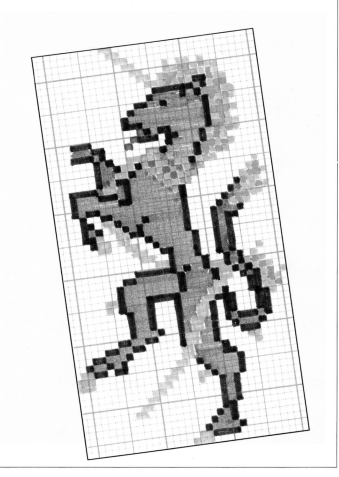

simplicity is a useful rule for interpreting the motifs in small-scale designs.

As heraldic design has been elaborated over centuries, a distinctive feature is the curvilinear style, with flowing contours and intricate decoration. Much of the detail can be abandoned in design for cross stitch, as a fussy motif is ineffective unless worked on an unusually large scale, but the most important modification is the translation of curving shapes to the angular grid of a chart for cross stitching. The design is inevitably simplified and made more geometric, but sympathetic charting and careful choice of threads and stitches will give the motif a decorative character of its own.

Stranded cottons and pearl cotton are the most appropriate threads, as they have a natural sheen that enriches the design. A more flamboyant touch can be added with metallic threads; these can be stitched separately or combined with strands of cotton, depending upon the effect you require. The background fabric should be either canvas, if you intend to stitch the whole surface, or a suitable even-weave fabric providing a neutral or colored based for the motifs. The stitching should be kept small and even, so closely woven fabric is a better choice than a coarse mesh, but you can develop the textural qualities of the design by varying the

Three different heraldic devices are here adapted to cross stitching. Each is worked out on graph paper to translate the curves into a geometric design.

The crown (**FAR LEFT**) is worked on a colored even-weave fabric, so the background needs no stitching.

The shield with the heraldic lion (**LEFT**), worked on canvas, is fully stitched in stranded cottons and metallic thread.

The unicorn (**BELOW**) is designed with flowing curves that do not at first sight suggest the geometric restraints of cross-stitch. However, the curving shapes can be charted on graph paper (**BOTTOM LEFT**) to angularize the design. Stitched on a close-weave canvas (**RIGHT**), this successfully translates the original into the cross stitch mode. The bold outline sharpens the effect and adds elegant definition.

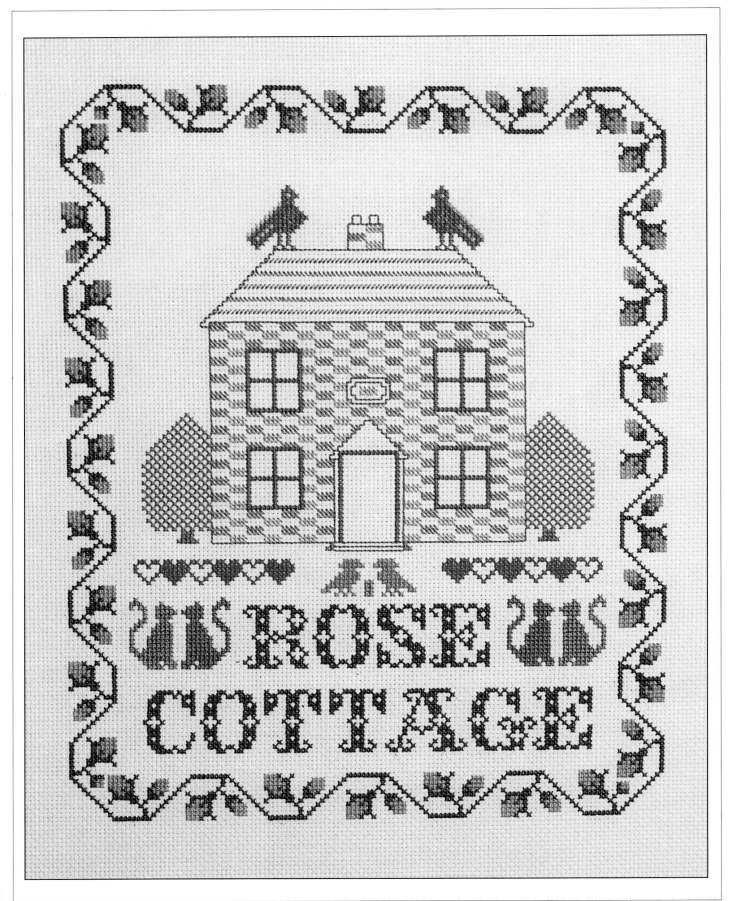

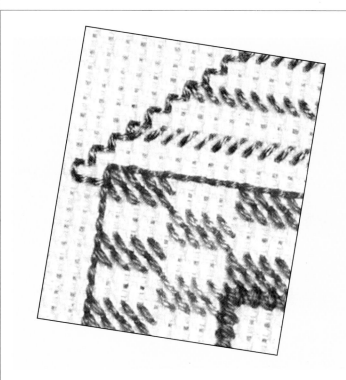

ABOVE *This detail of the sampler shown on the left shows the roof outlined in back stitch and the tiles and bricks indicated with half cross stitch. All other motifs are worked in cross stitch.*

BELOW *The house sampler stitched by Charlotte Glubb in 1813 is a combination of cross and satin stitches, straight stitching and couched work.*

BELOW RIGHT *Mary Pether's house sampler, dated 1839, is worked in a combination of cross stitch, satin stitch and Algerian eye, worked in colored silks on woollen fabric, with a repeat border on all four sides to frame the piece. The lower half of the work, containing the house, is much more heavily embroidered than the top section with the inscription and flower motifs. The fine detail provides a very good picture of the style of architecture and mode of dress that was fashionable at the time.*

stitches, for example, combining tent stitch with basic cross stitch and its simpler variation.

Heraldic symbols were occasionally used in sampler design, as individual spot motifs or repeated to form intricate borders. The devices shown on these pages demonstrate the principle of adapting the shapes from a drawing or photograph to the graph paper grid, and this can be applied to any formal device or decorative emblem that could be used as an alternative motif for your own projects.

HOUSE SAMPLERS The most popular subject for American samplers in the second half of the eighteenth century was the embroiderer's own home, shown in a two-dimensional, frontal view, or from slightly to one side with a simple indication of perspective. The designs would include members of the family, pets and domestic animals, stylized views of the garden and background landscape, or plant motifs suggesting the surroundings. House samplers have a particular appeal from the point of view of color and design, but in addition they are a fascinating and revealing record of changes in styles of architecture and costume, and can provide unexpected details of the habits of everyday life in town and country.

In England, many Victorian samplers portrayed buildings with great exactitude. A piece worked by Mary Pether in 1839 shows a rather grand house, its grounds, and members of the household. Three women, a man and a dog are all worked in extraordinary detail. There are also pots of flowers, latticed garden seats and a lawn which is naturalistically rendered through grading of the green tones of the thread. Although mansions and large houses were common on nineteenth-century samplers, smaller houses and cottages in country surroundings are also depicted, as well as castles, ruins and archways.

The contemporary sampler (far left) shows a simply but effectively stylized rendition of a modern home.

CHAPTER 4

CANVASWORK

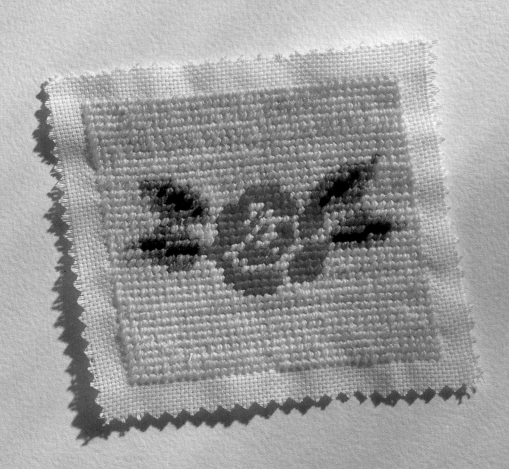

INTRODUCTION

Canvaswork, or needlepoint, is any kind of decorative needlework on canvas. It includes tent stitch and Florentine or Bargello work, and, as we saw in the preceding chapter, cross stitch, which can also be employed as a canvaswork technique.

Canvaswork is often incorrectly called 'tapestry', particularly with reference to pictorial works. True tapestry is, of course, a woven technique. The misnomer arises from the fact that many early pieces of canvaswork copied tapestry designs to simulate expensive woven tapestries.

Canvaswork has a long history. Some stitches which are today almost exclusively associated with canvaswork have been known for hundreds of years; originally they would have been worked on evenweave linen. Historically, the most popular stitch is tent stitch. The name comes from the French *tenter* 'to stretch'; it refers to stretching the background fabric on a frame for working. Fine tent stitch appears on pieces from the middle ages; during the reign of Elizabeth I it was used for furnishings, bags, pin-cushions and book covers. Table coverings, wall hangings and bed hangings were produced in the most elaborate canvaswork. Much of the work came from professional workshops but a great deal was done at home.

Canvaswork furnishings again became popular towards the end of the seventeenth century. Examples of furniture upholstered with canvaswork survive from the seventeenth century; many can be seen in stately homes in their original setting. Canvaswork was also used for smaller pieces, such as polescreens and pocket books.

By the end of the eighteenth century, a great many changes had taken place. Ready-made fabrics and furniture started to be available in greater quantities and, especially in the towns, people had a good choice of alternatives. Canvaswork was only used for firescreens, pictures and other small objects. The excellent training in all forms of needlework given to women in the past was no longer available, as other leisure pursuits took precedence.

Very early in the nineteenth century colored charts, published in Berlin, began to be imported into Britain, together with wools and canvas for working them. Eventually 'Berlin woolwork' and 'canvaswork' became synonymous. By the 1830s it became a craze which swept Britain (and later the USA). Slippers, bags, cushions, upholstery and innumerable small items were produced.

Tent and cross stitch were still popular; there was also a form of raised pile (sometimes called plushwork) which gave a three-dimensional effect. Beads were often incorporated. Another trend was the copying of popular Victorian paintings in canvaswork. Although much of the early work was charming, and Berlin woolwork samplers contain many delightful patterns, the introduction of chemical dyes in the mid-century led to the use of harsh, strident colors, and design deteriorated. With the changes in taste which followed the work of William Morris and his followers, Berlin woolwork lost ground, though its echoes are still with us today.

Canvaswork has enjoyed a reawakening of interest in the last 20 years. Many guilds have become established and traditional techniques have been re-examined. A major feature of this renewal is the willingness to experiment with techniques, stitches and materials, often combining canvaswork with other forms of needlework in the same piece.

It seems that canvaswork never completely lost its appeal. Perhaps the regularity of the traditional stitches has a therapeutic quality. (Canvaswork was in fact used in the First World War as therapy for shell-shocked soldiers.) Many people make their first attempt at embroidery through a canvaswork 'kit', and from there progress to making their own designs. Canvaswork may now be combined with other techniques in experimental work. A variety of threads and materials are used together; stitches other than canvaswork stitches are included; parts of the canvas may be left unworked or may be painted.

Typical uses to which embroidery was put in the past are shown below. **LEFT** *The panel is a piece of English work completed around 1865. Cross stitch has been embroidered in wool and silk threads onto linen, with the addition of glass and metal beads to supply a level of finery. Besides hanging wall panels, chair seats were popular subjects for embroidery.* **BELOW** *Another English example dates from the second quarter of the eighteenth-century. Wool and silk threads have been worked in cross and tent stitches on linen.*

TOP *The Finding of Moses, an early seventeenth-century panel. Biblical and allegorical subjects were often used at this time. The panel is worked in tent stitch with a fine silk thread on canvas; the colors are shaded to give form to the subjects.*

ABOVE LEFT *An extremely solid wing chair, with canvaswork upholstery embroidered in 1760. The pattern is worked over the back of the chair and across the seat, and the colors have remained remarkably bright.*

ABOVE RIGHT *A typical example of Berlin woolwork — the central motif from a late nineteenth-century cushion cover. Rose and floral designs were extremely popular during this period; many charts showing similar designs, which were given away with women's magazines, survive. This piece is worked in wool, on a double thread linen canvas, in tent stitch. A small section of the canvas can be seen on the white rose.*

MATERIALS AND EQUIPMENT

*O*f all needlework techniques, canvaswork probably needs to be made the most hard-wearing as it is most often used for items which receive a great deal of use. A patchwork or appliqué bedspread can be folded up every evening, a dress with smocking or whitework will probably only be worn occasionally, silk embroidery often just hangs on the wall, but a piano stool, set of dining chairs, or even cushions worked in canvaswork, will be used constantly.

Always plan your projects carefully and buy the best possible materials. When you compare the cost of the canvas and wools with the number of hours that you will be stitching, the materials represent a small part of the result. By buying the best possible materials you will enjoy the project more, it will look better when complete and will last longer.

Canvas

There are two kinds of canvas: double thread or Penelope canvas, and single thread or Mono canvas.

Double thread canvas is used when working a large piece of canvas if it is wished to work the background and border in a large tent stitch over the double thread, and give finer detail to the main subject area by working small tent stitches over single canvas threads.

It is also used for trammed work, where threads of the right color are run horizontally across each part of the design before tent stitch is worked over them. Tramming gives a double thickness of wool and was once widely used in the belief that it made the work more durable, but many modern needleworkers have abandoned the practice.

Single thread canvas is more adaptable as double thread may distort some stitches. It is available in evenweave and interlock constructions which have different uses. With evenweave (which is the canvas stocked by most suppliers), the single horizontal and vertical threads are woven over and under each other; this canvas has a certain amount of give and is the right choice for all upholstery, cushions and pulled thread work.

Interlock canvas has two vertical threads bounded, not woven, round each horizontal thread; it is more stable and can be trimmed very close to the finished work without unravelling. It is good for small objects, where the seams are bound with an overcasting stitch which is part of the pattern, or when the edges of the canvas are bound with another material.

Canvas is available in a variety of gauges, that is, the number of threads to the inch. Popular sizes are 14, 16 or 18 threads to 1 inch (2.5 cm). Larger gauge canvas does not give so much detail in the same sized piece because the stitches are larger. On the other hand, 24 gauge, which is the finest of the readily available canvases, would be excellent for realistic shading or work in silks. If, when working from a chart, you use a larger gauge canvas than suggested, it will automatically increase the finished size; conversely, a finer canvas will reduce the size of the completed piece.

Most canvas is made from cotton but there are exceptions. Linen canvas is available in 13 and 17 mesh and is the best for pulled thread stitches. Polyester canvas, though not widely available, is very soft and good for clothing or pieces that need to be gathered. Silk gauze, which is available in gauges up to 72 mesh, is the one to use for very fine work. Plastic or PVC canvas comes in 7 and 10 mesh sheets as well as circles, hexagons and squares. It is rigid, so that baskets or boxes can be made by joining pieces together. Children enjoy using plastic canvas becuase it is easy to hold. Cotton canvas is suitable for panels and small items but linen canvas wears better for items such as chair setas. Rug canvas is suitable for large-scale work.

The standard cotton canvas is available in white and ecru. White is more satisfactory for working with pale colors; ecru is better for dark colors because the canvas is not so likely to show through the yarn. With very dark colors it may be necessary to paint the canvas to match, to avoid any pale canvas threads showing.

Canvas comes in various widths; check the widths available in the mesh you need and take the most economical for the particular project, for example a yard (about 91 cm) of 36-inch (91 cm) or 40-inch (102 cm) wide canvas will make four good cushions, whereas a yard of 27-inch (69 cm) will not.

Look for canvas with tightly twisted round threads, and no knots or irregularities in the thickness of the threads.

Thread

Tapestry and crewel yarns are the traditional yarns and they are best for upholstery and items in constant use. Otherwise a variety of yarns can add interest to the work; examples include carpet thrums, silks, linen threads, stranded floss cottons, soft embroidery, pearl cotton and knitting yarns. If a thread does not cover the canvas, more than one strand can be used.

It is important to obtain the right amount of wool from the same dye lot because dye lots can vary and the difference will show in a large area of one color. As a rough guide, 14 inch (36 cm) square sampler cushions take approximately

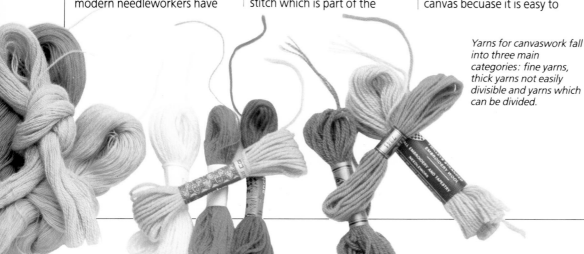

Yarns for canvaswork fall into three main categories: fine yarns, thick yarns not easily divisible and yarns which can be divided.

CANVASES

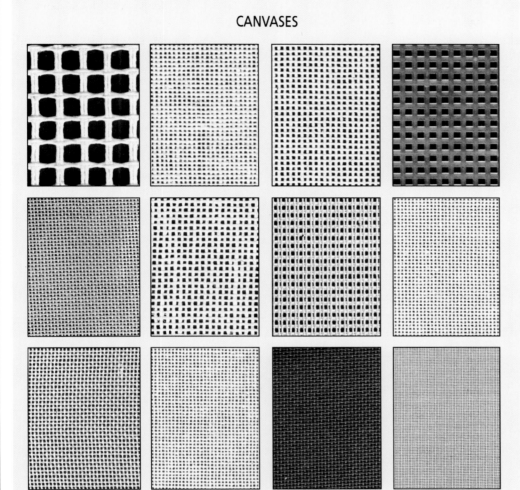

A selection of canvases, including: very fine silk gauze with 48 meshes to the inch, plastic canvas and interlock canvas. They are all pictured life-size. Beginners should not attempt to work a fine gauge canvas until confident on the medium meshes. Single or mono canvas is increasingly popular today and is appropriate for most canvaswork items. Double canvas, with its paired threads, can be useful if two different sized stitches are being used extensively in a piece of work.

CANVAS TYPES

Even-weave canvas

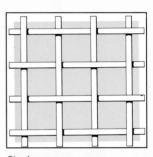

Single or mono canvas

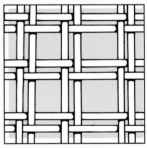

Penelope (Double) canvas

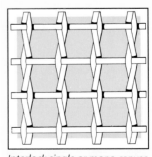

Interlock single or mono canvas

5 ounces (142 g) on 14 mesh canvas. When planning a large piece or a matching set of furnishings, it is worth working a test area in the stitch on the same mesh canvas and calculating the full amount you will need.

If it seems likely that the yarn will run out, despite careful planning, take the remaining hank of wool to the shop for matching. Having found the nearest color match, introduce it gradually into the work, a strand at a time every so often. This will make the transition as unnoticeable as possible.

Crewels are sold by the ounce (28 g) and by the small skein; they are cheaper by the ounce if you need anything more than the smallest quantities. By cutting a length at each end of the skein you have a working length for 14/18 mesh canvas: about 30 inches (76 cm) is best to work with. If the canvas is fine, shorter lengths will be easier.

FRAMES AND STRETCHERS

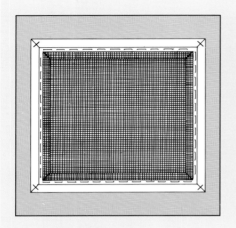

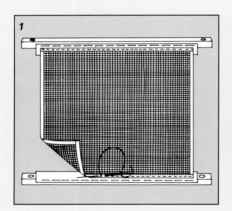

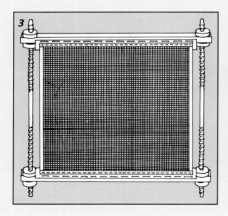

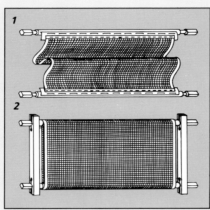

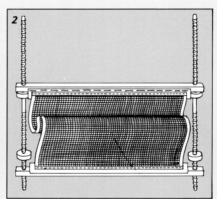

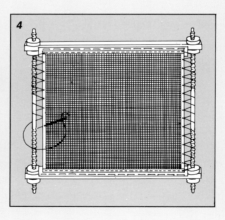

FAR LEFT CANVAS STRETCHER
This simple rectangular frame is made from four wood battens. The fabric is fastened lengthways, and then across the frame.

LEFT ROTATING FRAME
1 Sew the top and bottom of the canvas to the webbing.
2 Loosen the nuts on the side arms and slot in all four ends. Turn the rods to take up the slack canvas. Tighten the nuts.

LEFT SLATE FRAME
1 Bind the canvas to prevent fraying. Mark the centers of each rod and each edge of the canvas. Matching the centers, stitch the canvas to the webbing, working from the center outwards.

2 Fit two locking nuts to the center of each side arm. Fold or roll the canvas to just over half the length of the side arms. Slot the top of the side arms into the holes in the top rod, then the bottom rod. Push the locking nuts towards the rods.

3 Draw the rods along the side arms so the canvas is fully extended. Push the centered nuts close to the rods and apply locking nuts to the end of each side arm. Tighten the nuts on both sides to hold the canvas taut.

4 To stretch the canvas at either side, oversew between the side arms and edges of the canvas using long, slanting stitches. Before finishing the thread, pull on each stitch to tighten it. Secure the thread at each corner of the frame.

GUIDELINES FOR STITCHING A RANGE OF EVENWEAVE CANVASES

Canvas mesh	Available in plastic	Available in interlock	Resulting use	Needle size	Number of wool strands to use	No. of cotton strands to use	No. of silk strands to use	No. of stands of other threads
24			needle painting and shading	24	1 Persian or 1 crewel	3	2	1 Balger fine filament
18		yes	needle painting, shading and Florentine designs	22	1 Persian or 2 crewel	5	4	1 Balger 16
16			Florentine designs	20	Persian not satisfactory 3 crewel	6	5	1 Twilley's Goldfingering 1 Balger 16
14		yes	geometric designs	20	2 Persian 3 crewel	9	7	1 Twilley's Goldfingering 1 Coats soft cotton
12		yes	rugs	18	2 Persian 3 crewel			
10	yes	yes	children's work or quick decorative work	18	3 Persian 4 crewel			2 Twilley's Goldfingering
7	yes		children's work or quick decorative work	16	4 Persian 5 crewel			

Use an extra strand for straight stitches, and when working black strands on a white canvas.
Use a larger size needle when stitching with metallic threads or for pulled thread work.

Frames

Canvaswork is no exception to other forms of needlework: it is better to use a frame. The canvas is easier to see and does not get distorted, which is especially important when working different stitches on one piece, as they all have different stresses. Also the work stays cleaner and the finished piece looks infinitely better. If you choose a frame on a stand, you can use two hands which makes working faster and smoother because of the even pull on the thread.

Other equipment

Paletters are helpful when working in a close color range. Palette shapes or simple rings in wood, plastic or stiff card can be used to give clear ideas of shade ranges and color comparisons.

You will need a large pair of scissors for cutting the canvas and wool, and small sharp-pointed or curved scissors for the needlework. For cutting out, rippers are quick, but great care must be taken to avoid cutting canvas threads. It is easier to cut wools on the back of the canvas where there is more wool to get at. Once the stitches have been cut, a pair of tweezers will help to pull out the strands.

Needles

Tapestry needles are recommended for use in canvaswork, being specially made with blunt points to slip between the canvas threads without splitting them. Choosing the size from a range between sizes 14 and 26 depends on the mesh of the canvas and the thickness of the yarn. The needle must pass through the holes comfortably without dislodging them, and at the same time the yarn must

pass through the eye easily to avoid friction and unravelling. During work, move the yarn to different positions in the needle eye to avoid one section of the yarn going thin. A useful type of needle is a laying needle, which helps to make silks and stranded cottons look smooth.

Needle-threaders are handy and protect the ends of the threads as well as making threading the needle much easier. There are two types. One has a thin wire loop to draw the thread through the eye of the needle. It is good for silks or threading a beading needle but not strong enough for wool; the other, more difficult to find in Britain, is a thin piece of metal with a small hole at either end, and is suitable for wool. If you can obtain one of these it will be a useful addition to your equipment.

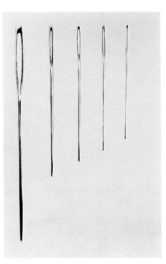

ABOVE *Blunt-pointed tapestry needles of various sizes.*

DESIGN

*M*rs. A. H. Christie in her book *Samplers & Stitches* (1920) states, "In the art of embroidery, the question of design is so interwoven with that of technique that pattern planning, if approached in the right way, grows almost unconsciously out of the study of stitches. It will be found upon experiment that many stitches can introduce new ideas for design. The worker is urged, when thinking over a new piece of work, either simple or complex, to take some characteristic stitches and do what can be done with them, rather than to make a design with pencil and brush and then see what stitches can be adapted to working it out. The former method is fairly certain to result in a true embroidery design; the latter sometimes looks as if it had been stitched with difficulty, and would perhaps have been better if painted with the brush."

Sometimes, however, an embroiderer may particularly wish to copy a picture, or want to reproduce a scene from real life. This approach to design, called 'needle painting', generally includes a naturalistic rendering of the motif, whether it is a flower, an animal or a rural scene. The 'geometric' designs are often based on the contrast between stitches and textures, as well as the colors and patterns in which they are worked. Before choosing the stitches, and the design to suit the stitches, it is worth considering the purpose for the finished item. If it is to be a picture to hang on the wall, then the stitches may be of varying tensions and textures; if, however, it is to be a cushion cover, it probably needs to have more hardwearing stitches. The type of stitches used will influence the design; except in 'pictorial' canvaswork they are the most important aspect of the embroidery.

PICTORIAL These designs are usually worked in tent stitch; a combination of different stitches can be used but if there is also a combination of different colours the finished motif may look overworked.

Variations of stitchery are usually more successful on a 'primitive' or stylist piece. Tent stitch is suitable for detailed, even realistic-looking embroideries, because of its even texture and the small size of these stitches, which allow outlines to look curved and soft.

If you are working from a painting, study the colors and shadows within the colors carefully. It may help to do an outline drawing of the subject, labelling leaves and petals for example, and marking patches of light and shade. Consider adjoining petals or other details, and if their outlines need emphasizing, it may be worth making the appropriate juxtaposing colors stronger or paler. A canvas with a fine mesh allows the outlines of the flowers to be soft and rounded, while the rigid structure of the canvas helps the design to be exactly balanced if desired.

If a floral design is desired, it is worth remembering, when stitching, to complete a flower at a time. In a leaf, the vein should be worked first. Petals, leaves and stems can all be stitched in the direction of their growth, which adds a touch of realism as well as producing a

LEFT *Three sampler cushions worked in wool on canvas, demonstrating different geometric designs worked in a variety of stitches.*

BELOW LEFT *A free interpretation of Florentine stitch worked in string, cord, raffia and strips of leather on rug canvas.*

BELOW RIGHT *A detail from a large floral piece worked in stranded cottons on linen canvas. Only four different colors have been used: cream, yellow, coral and deep coral, but by mixing the strands from the different colored skeins, an extraordinarily wide range of colors has been produced to shade the rose. The area round this flower has been worked in skip tent stitch.*

more interesting result due to the light catching stitches of different directions in different ways. The background, which should be worked last, can be stitched in skip tent, which is a stitch that only covers alternate threads of the canvas, adding a subtle sheen and texture to the canvas without appearing too heavy.

Shading is used to make the subjects look realistic. Having stripped all the yarns, soft color changes can be made by mixing strands of lighter and darker shades in the needle at the same time. Never mix two contrasting colors as the result will be 'tweedy' and obvious.

If you want to make a sampler for a special occasion, you can include the name of the recipient, or dates, or a picture of a house if it has a distinctive outline or features. A picture that hangs on the wall does not receive any wear so surface stitchery and beads can be added for special effects. GEOMETRIC designs are perfect for textural or ornamental stitchery. Often they originate from squares, triangles, hexagons or columns; from patchwork patterns or Edwardian tiled floors. Geometric designs are formed either by the shapes of the stitches, the shapes of areas of stitches or the shapes of areas of color. Where a single color is used, it is important to balance and select the stitches, to create interesting contrasts and complements, and perhaps offset the design with panels of pulled thread. Where brighter colors are used, fewer different stitches are needed.

To learn techniques for this type of embroidery it is best to follow design charts, which allow the beginner to concentrate on the stitchery

without worrying about the shapes of areas. When going on to design, it is important to remember a few basic points. Use small stitches when working a small areas, and larger ones if there is a lot of space. Balance the shape as well as the scale of the stitches: square stitches for square areas, diamond (for example, diamond leaf) for diamond, and corner triangles can have their directional diagonal accentuated by Milanese or Oriental stitches. Textured areas are set off well by a background of diagonal tent. Stitches worked in one color can be interestingly juxtaposed by two-color areas. The whole design, its textures and colors, should look coordinated and balanced within itself.

More sophisticated designs can be found in oriental rugs, although, however complex the designs, rules of scale and stitch are usually followed. Rectangular borders, for example, are often filled with large square stitches, each one surrounded by a row of pulled thread to accentuate the raised texture of the stitch and give a bold edge to the completed piece. Diamond shapes down the center can be filled with diamond-shaped stitches.

Parterres, knot gardens, mazes and potagers (ornamental vegetable gardens) all lend themselves perfectly to canvaswork designs, being beautifully ordered and outlined and filled with contrasting foliage. Stitches to represent the variety of foliage can be used – a neatly clipped yew may be represented in neat cross stitches; the profusion of colors and chaos of shapes and heights in the flower beds may be shown in a combination

RIGHT A Florentine sampler cushion designed to show a variety of patterns that are suitable for all-over designs on belts, bags or other small items. The borders between the different design have been worked in cross corner stitch.

RIGHT *A traditional Florentine design known as 'petit fleur'. Such small repeating designs are often extremely effective for cushion covers and chair seats.*

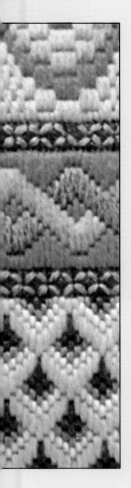

of more textured stitches. The outline of low balustrades and pavilions can be incorporated. FLORENTINE is a general name for a whole range of wave-designs and lozenge-designs with large-scale or small-scale repeats. All Florentine designs use straight stitches placed parallel to the threads of the canvas. Florentine stitch, and variations of it, form the basic Florentine peak-and-valley design. Hungarian, Parisian and brick stitches are other straight stitches which may be used to fill designs.

Because different length stitches, and combinations of lengths, can be used with any spacing rhythm in the rising and falling patterns of the basic Florentine stitch, there is a limitless number of possible designs. Wave designs are formed by peaks and valleys which may result in an even or uneven zigzag, depending on whether the peaks and valleys are of equal or unequal height

and depth, or they may be stitched in a more rounded pattern. Rows of either shading or contrasting colors produce a harmonious or dramatic effect.

Lozenge designs consist of mirrored top and bottom rows, usually repeated, with straight stitches filling the enclosed areas. Four-way designs are produced by working four triangular sections at right-angles to each other, so forming a square block with the pattern worked out from the center. For diagonal Florentine, the canvas is diagonally intersected, and the angle of stitching changed on the intersection.

All Florentine patterns are versatile, and are used in different ways for different purposes. Ribbon patterns are generally worked as a two-color band going across the canvas, suitable for belts or curtain tie-backs. Petites Fleurs is an excellent choice for dining

chairs and all-over cushions, as the stitches within this design are not too long. Pomegranate is a traditional design which repeats well over a large area, making an especially bold design if four are worked at right-angles, using the base of the lowest stitch as the common hole to all four repeats. This is a version of four-way Florentine. This and diagonal Florentine are useful for working over large areas of canvas. Choose the design carefully for the project's finished purpose; patterns that have long stitches will not wear as well as those with short ones. Start stitching in the center of the canvas as this ensures a symmetrical design with the same number of pattern repeats either side.

BELOW *A canvaswork cushion demonstrating a design known as Garden Path. It is worked in stranded cottons and rayons incorporating straight gobelin, Parisian, checker and knitting stitches.*

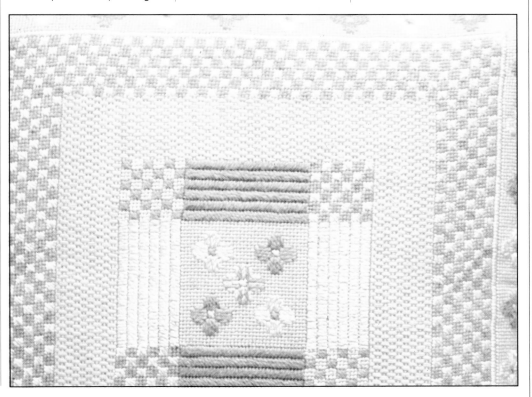

USES OF CANVASWORK

*T*he firm texture of canvaswork makes it suitable for items which need to hold their shape. Cushion covers are an ideal project for beginners, and can be produced in a wide variety of designs. Bags in canvaswork can be beautifully worked, and may be made up professionally or at home. Seat covers for wooden chairs are another project well worth undertaking (see page 223 for instructions). The examples on this page give some idea of the range of uses to which canvaswork can be put.

RIGHT *A canvaswork bag with two simple handles of twisted cord and matching tassels. The same cord has been couched around the entire bag to neaten and finish the edges.*

CENTER RIGHT *Two jewelery rolls, with designs based on traditional Oriental patterns. The one in the foreground is worked in wool on 14 mesh to the inch canvas and the other is worked on finer canvas, 18 mesh to the inch, in mixed threads. The latter also features pulled thread work.*

FAR RIGHT *A modern Florentine cushion worked in wool, with a belt that has been stitched in an adaptation of the same design. The latter is worked in silks, into which fine gold filaments have been twisted. The attractive bell-shaped ends are made from silk.*

BELOW RIGHT *A cross stitch panel for a cushion cover is a simple project for inexperienced stitchers, but a large enough task to provide good practice in following a design and creating neat, regular stitching. The three designs shown here demonstrate very different approaches to the basic square format. A checkerboard design with bold geometric motifs covers the whole panel: a landscape picture in cross stitch is framed by a striped border of satin stitch: an abstract design contrasts vivid stripes with a border of plain color, setting the smooth texture of stranded cotton against heavier stitching in tapestry yarn.*

BELOW *A landscape design using different textures in the thread and stitches so that raised, heavily textured shapes contrast with smooth, flat areas.*

TECHNIQUES

Preparing the canvas

Either bind or sew all the cut edges of the canvas before starting work, using masking tape or by machining a double hem. When mounting the canvas on the frame fix it with drawing pins, which are more satisfactory than staples as they enable you to tighten the canvas from time to time. Always work with the selvage on the left or right side of your work, and mark the top of the canvas so that you do not swing it round by mistake.

Allow plenty of canvas for the piece, and remember you will need at least 2 inches (5 cm) left unworked on all sides for stretching the finished work. Sometimes a more important border than at first planned looks exciting, and it is a shame if there is not enough space to work it. Take pieces of canvas you plan to join from the same roll. In the case of a rug with a number of flowers each worked on a separate panel, for example, which is to be joined when complete, make sure they are from exactly the same piece of canvas, otherwise the joins may not match satisfactorily. If you delay buying matching canvas you may even find the mesh has been discontinued.

Spraying canvas gold or silver can produce interesting results. Use ordinary paint spray sold for Christmas decorations and work on a frame. It is not as yet sure whether this effect will tarnish with time.

Marking the design

As with cross stitch, one of the easiest methods is to work from a charted design on

graph paper. Alternatively, the design can be marked directly on to the canvas with a sharp pencil, a permanent or water solvent marker, fabric paint or basting thread.

If a pencil is used, to avoid the graphite staining light-colored wools during the stitching, rub over the marked canvas well with paper towels before starting work. Suitable markers may be bought from most needlework suppliers. When copying or adapting an original colored picture, for example an oil painting in a museum, it is best to mark only the outlines onto the canvas with the marker and then, working from a postcard or color reproduction, work out your own shading. When marking a piece of pulled thread or work which may finally have a partially bare

canvas background, mark the minimum, using one of the markers that washes out with cold water. Before starting, check all markers carefully on the corner of the actual piece of canvas you intend to use to see that they do not run.

For pictorial designs, enlarge or reduce the chosen design onto paper, or, if the original size is suitable, just outline the details so they are easily visible through the canvas. Mark the center of the design, and the center of the canvas, then draw straight horizontal and vertical lines through the center points. Pin the two centers together to a large board, with the design beneath the canvas, and working first on the weft thread and then the warp, pin the four line-ends to the board. Pinning alternately on opposite sides, attach the canvas and the

design tautly to the board.

If furniture is to be covered by the canvaswork, make a template of the size in paper or calico. On any canvas, allow 2½ inches (6 cm) extra on all sides for turnings.

Stitch key

It is especially useful for canvaswork to work a large token stitch to act as a key. If you are going to work in tent stitch, make a large tent stitch in the upper righthand corner of your canvas. Constant glances back at this key stitch will ensure that subsequent tent stitches all face the same direction. Similarly, a large cross key will help you to cross all your cross stitches in the same way. (Keys should, of course, be removed when the piece is finished.)

STARTING TECHNIQUES

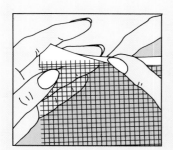

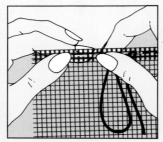

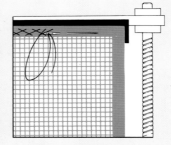

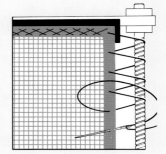

BINDING THE CANVAS
If the canvas has not been stretched onto a frame for working, the edges are liable to fray. This can be prevented by binding the edges with tape.

BASTING THE CANVAS
Alternatively the edges of the canvas can be basted down to prevent fraying. Fold the edges over and stitch them all the way round.

MOUNTING STRAIGHT-SIDED FRAMES
1 It is important to get the canvas evenly stretched before starting the design. Sew the fabric onto the webbing of both rollers.

2 Then fit the rollers into their slots and adjust until the canvas is taut. Use a needle and tough thread to lace the remaining two sides of canvas firmly onto the stand.

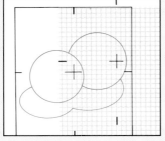

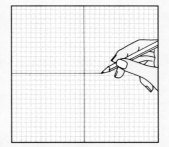

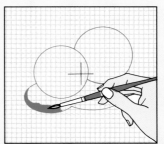

TRANSFERRING A DESIGN ONTO CANVAS OUTLINES
1 First establish the center of the design by drawing a vertical and a horizontal line across it and marking the intersection.

2 Place the canvas over the design, matching up the center points, pin them together and draw the outlines of the designs as they show through the canvas.

COLORED AREAS
1 Find the center on both canvas and design.

2 Match them up and pin the canvas to the design. Paint the design as it shows through with appropriately colored acrylic paints or waterproof inks.

RIGHT *Half-completed piece of canvaswork designed to adorn an antique bell-pull end. Beads, metal thread and silk embroidery are set off by areas of smooth diagonal tent stitch. The outlines of the design have been marked directly on to the canvas with tacking stitches which are covered by the completed work.*

ABOVE FAR LEFT *This contemporary design reverses the usual approach of an elaborate center picture with a simple border: here a detailed border is set around two slightly varied fish motifs upon a bold plain background. The use of color is deceptive; the eye is taken by the dominant color of the background but in fact no less than ten shades of yarn have been used to achieve the overall effect. The cushion is worked in tent stitch throughout.*

STITCHES

*T*he most commonly used canvaswork stitch is tent stitch. It is particularly suitable for pictorial work and shading, producing a very even texture. Diagonal stitches over one mesh can also be formed by half cross stitches, which are less durable than tent stitches and more liable to distort the canvas, but use less thread and may be strengthened by working over a laid thread. There are two types of tent stitch, the preferred being diagonal or basketweave because it is firmer and does not distort. Continental tent stitch should only be used when there is one single line of color to be worked, which may be horizontal, vertical or diagonal.

For a more textured effect, there is a very wide variety of stitches to choose from. The choice partly depends on the size of stitches required by the design and the shape of the area to be filled. It is also worth considering the texture of the stitches; some may be flat but many have particular textures, for example leaf stitches show growth lines in obvious relief.

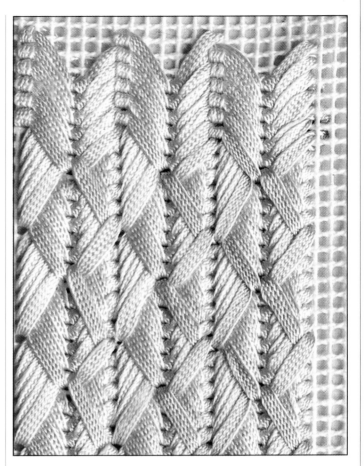

Diagonal stitches, which slant across the threads of the canvas, include tent and half cross stitches. Others are slanted gobelin, and encroaching gobelin, which both create neat textures, the former in rows, the latter uniform over the canvas. The number of canvas threads to work the stitches over is a matter of choice depending on the requirements of the canvaswork. Byzantine stitch forms a jagged, diagonal texture across the canvas. Cushion stitch is worked to form a pattern of square blocks on the canvas, each block consisting of five diagonal stitches. A variation of cushion stitch, producing a more interesting, partly raised texture, is called checker stitch, made by alternating squares of cushion stitch with squares of nine tent stitches. Two more diagonal stitches, Milanese and Oriental, create bold and highly textured triangular units, with the triangle tips running in opposite directions in alternate rows. As a guide, these diagonal stitches need three strands of crewel wool on a 14

mesh canvas for good coverage.

Florentine stitch (which is also called flame stitch) forms the bold zigzag patterns associated with Florentine canvaswork. The stitches are straight, and create the jagged effect by the rows being stepped in peak-and-valley designs. The variations in the length of the stitches and the height of the steps between one stitch and the next, create the degrees of jaggedness. It is important to ensure there is an even amount of thread at the back of the canvas when working peak-and-valley designs. When working up and down across the canvas, short

stitches may result behind the lines ascending the peak and long stitches behind the descent. Over a whole canvas this can result in thick and thin patches which obviously will not wear evenly. The problem can be avoided by starting each line at the alternate end.

Other straight stitches include straight gobelin and

ABOVE *An experimental sample using single canvas and multi-dyed rayon braid. The direction of the stitches and shaded thread give added interest.*

BELOW LEFT *Tent stitch – also known as petit point is a canvas stitch used for fine work. It forms a small diagonal stitch which should always lie in the same direction. Tent stitch creates a flat, fairly smooth surface and combines well with heavier canvas stitches, accentuating their raised appearance.*

RIGHT *It is helpful to work small samples in canvaswork stitches. You should include experiments with both single and double canvas. Vary the scale of the stitches to give an impression of perspective; small stitches for the background and large ones in the foreground. Two or more stitches can be combined in innumerable ways to give other effects – even the angle at which the light falls on the stitches can be exploited.*

In this example rice stitch worked in two colors immediately gives a variety of colors.

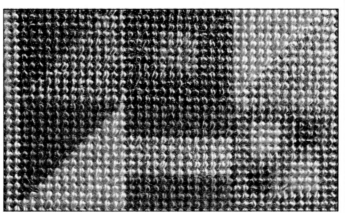

straight encroaching gobelin; brick stitch, which looks much like its name; Hungarian, which produces a pattern of small diamond units; and Parisian, which produces a more complicated texture formed by interlocking rows of long and short straight stitches. All except Hungarian need four strands of crewel yarn on 14 mesh canvas. Hungarian needs only three.

A number of stitches are formed by making crosses of various sizes in various directions.

Of the stitches illustrated in the chapter on Cross stitch, the following are suitable for working on canvas:
Cross stitch
Cross stitch – diagonal
Cross stitch – double
Cross stitch – long armed
Cross stitch – oblong
Cross stitch – oblong with back stitch
Fern stitch

Fishbone stitch
Greek stitch
Herringbone stitch
Herringbone stitch – double
Italian stitch
Knotted stitch
Leviathan stitch
Leviathan stitch – double
Montenegrin stitch
Rice stitch
Rococo stitch
Underlined stitch
Velvet stitch

Fern stitch, fishbone and rococo are further tied stitches. The former two are variations on the basic principle; the latter is different in that the top and bottom holes are the same for each group of four stitches, which cover four canvas threads, and each stitch is tied in the middle with a horizontal back stitch covering one canvas thread. The result is highly textured. All these cross stitches need three plies for adequate coverage over 14 mesh canvas.

The completed Algerian Eye is a square unit, worked by passing eight stitches in a star formation through a central hole. Diamond eyelets are similarly worked but the four extreme top, bottom and side stitches are longer than the other twelve, so forming a diamond unit. Ray stitch is a square unit, with seven stitches worked into one corner. Leaf stitch is a large, particularly individual unit formed with eleven stitches in a fan shape. These stitches need only two or three plies of crewel yarn on a 14 mesh canvas. All these stitches produce highly textured canvases; any of them could be used singly as a small feature within a whole work.

The stitches shown in the following pages are graded

with stars indicating the degree of difficulty, to indicate the amount of skill needed to work the stitch successfully.

BELOW *In this piece of canvaswork, inspired by the multi-color effect of flowers in a border, the central area is worked in rice stitch, the main cross of which is worked in various colors of floss rayon. The crossed corners are all worked in green coton à broder. The cushion stitch border and the double green frame echo the pinks and greens of the center.*

● **Reversed cushion stitch** (Mono canvas) A variation of cushion stitch worked without the framing of tent stitch. It makes a small-scale squared pattern over the canvas and is used for filling shapes and for the background areas. The stitch consists of blocks of graduated diagonal straight stitches worked over squares of three canvas threads. The direction of these stitches is reversed on every alternate block.

An attractive light and shade effect is made by the positioning of the stitches, and this effect can be enhanced by choosing an embroidery thread with a sheen. When used over a large area, reversed cushion stitch can be shaded by the use of several shades of thread.

● **Mosaic stitch** (Mono and Penelope canvas) This makes a tiny, squared pattern and can be used to build up intricate patterns by using many different colors for the tiny squares. Any type of thread can be used for this stitch, providing that it is compatible with the gauge of the canvas selected, but a smooth, non-hairy thread is essential to keep the pattern crisp. The stitch can also be used to work a monochrome area, as the smooth surface makes a good foil for the more raised and textured canvas stitches. It is composed of short and long diagonal straight stitches, and two horizontal journeys are needed to complete a row of squares. When working a complicated design, work all the areas in the main color first, and then go back and fill in the spaces with the other colours.

● **Florentine stitch** also known as bargello stitch, flame stitch and Irish stitch (Mono

canvas) This stitch is used for a type of needlepoint called Florentine work or bargello and makes a characteristic flame-shaped pattern. It should be worked in a hard-wearing thread, such as tapestry yarn. The stitch consists of vertical straight stitches, usually placed over four horizontal canvas threads, worked in a step sequence to form zig-zag rows. The stitches can be arranged in different formations to create curves and pinnacles as well as zig-zags. One row is worked across the canvas, and the following lines of stitches are worked in different colors to fill the canvas above and below the first line, always following its contours. The stitches are the same length on the second and subsequent rows. The stitch is always worked using different colors or different shades of one color and the pattern is created by the use of color.

● **Algerian filling stitch and Algerian filling stitch with bar** (Mono canvas) Worked in vertical blocks of three satin stitches taken over four canvas threads. The blocks are worked diagonally with a half drop from top left to bottom right of the area to be covered. The stitch covers the canvas ground quickly, giving an even, slightly textured effect and is primarily used for background areas.

Algerian filling stitch with bar is a variation of Algerian filling stitch, in which a horizontal satin stitch is worked at the base of each block of vertical stitches. This extra stitch is worked either in the same thread or in a thread of contrasting color or texture.

● **Brick stitch** (Mono canvas) Takes its name from the brickwork pattern that it produces. It is used mainly for

STRAIGHT AND SLANTED STITCHES

Reversed cushion stitch

Mosaic stitch 3

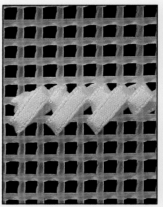
Mosaic stitch 1

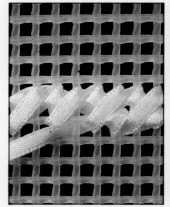
Florentine stitch

Mosaic stitch 2

Algerian filling stitch

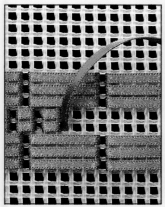

Brick stitch

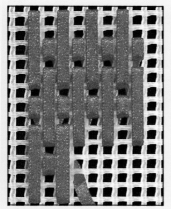

Parisian stitch

Chessboard filling stitch

Double Parisian stitch

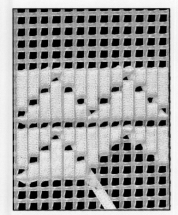

Long stitch

filling background areas. It is a quick and easy stitch to work and looks equally effective worked in yarn or stranded floss, depending on the gauge of the canvas. It consists of blocks of three horizontal straight stitches worked over six vertical threads of the canvas, which run side by side across the canvas. Below this row of blocks are two rows of short horizontal stitches, which are worked over two threads. This stitch looks best when worked in monochrome or in two very close tones of one color; one tone for the blocks and the other for the small stitches.

● **Chessboard filling stitch** (Mono canvas) A canvas stitch adapted from a drawn fabric stitch. It has a regular geometric pattern which fills a large area quickly. Care should be taken when using it, as the pattern produced can be rather dominant unless it is worked on a small scale. It looks most attractive when worked with a lustrous thread, such as stranded floss or silk, as the light and shade effect created by the different directions of the stitches are enhanced by these. Chessboard filling stitch no.2 consists of blocks of horizontal or vertical straight stitches. Each block is composed of three bands of ten straight stitches over three threads of canvas. The blocks are usually worked in diagonal rows, from top left to bottom right of the canvas.

● **Long stitch** (Mono canvas) This makes a triangular pattern and has the appearance of a brocaded fabric when worked in a lustrous embroidery thread. Each horizontal row is worked in two journeys and consists of groups of graduated vertical straight stitches,

arranged in triangles. On the second journey, the triangles are reversed and fill in the spaces left on the first journey. Each journey can be made using a different color and the stitch looks very effective when two shades of the same color are used. Each double row of triangles is worked over five horizontal threads but the stitch can be made deeper by adding extra graduated stitches to each triangular group.

● **Parisian stitch** (Mono canvas) This is quick and easy to work and makes a fairly smooth surface, which is ideal for filling large areas and backgrounds. It is composed of long, vertical straight stitches worked over six horizontal canvas threads and short straight stitches worked over two horizontal threads, alternating across the canvas. Subsequent rows overlap the row immediately preceding them by two horizontal threads. This stitch is very useful where a gradually shaded area is needed, as it can be attractively blended in bands by using very similar shades.

● **Double Parisian stitch** also known as old Parisian stitch (Mono canvas) This simple variation of Parisian stitch (*see above*) has longer stitches arranged in pairs. The long stitches are nine threads high and the short stitches cover three canvas threads. A fairly coarse thread, such as tapestry or Persian yarn, will probably be needed to cover the canvas adequately but a small sample can be stitched first to check if another thread would be suitable. This stitch is used for large areas and backgrounds, which can be shaded in bands, but it gives a less even blend of colors over an area than ordinary Parisian stitch.

● **Fancy brick stitch** also known as fancy bricking (Mono canvas) Fancy brick stitch, as its name implies, is a more complicated version of brick stitch (*see above*) and has a textured appearance. The stitch is constructed in a similar way to brick stitch but the blocks in the first strip are smaller since they are made up of three horizontal straight stitches over three canvas threads. In the next strip, the small straight stitches are interspersed with pairs of vertical stitches. Fancy brick stitch is used for filling shapes and for a background of textured brick pattern.

● **Twill stitch** (Mono canvas) This is quick and easy to work and makes a small woven pattern with a strong diagonal feel. It is used to fill a shape of any size and is ideal for a background area. It is worked in diagonal rows from the top left to the bottom right of the area to be covered. The rows consist of vertical straight stitches worked over three horizontal canvas threads. Wool or cotton embroidery threads are equally well suited to this stitch but a stranded cotton or silk floss enhances the smoothly stitched surface beautifully. The rows can be worked in two colors to give a diagonally striped effect.

● **Tent stitch** also known as needlepoint stitch, petit point, canvas stitch, perlen stitch, continental stitch and reversed tent stitch (Mono and Penelope canvas) It is known to have existed as long ago as the sixteenth century, was probably in use much earlier than that, and appears never to have gone out of fashion, probably due to its versatility.

A small, diagonal stitch, it can be worked in vertical, horizontal or diagonal rows to give a fairly smooth, flat surface; the stitches should all be in the same direction. When filling large areas with this stitch, work the stitch diagonally, as this method is less likely to distort the canvas. The small size of the stitches allows figurative designs to be intricate and full of detail. The designs are often followed from a colored chart, or from a painting on the canvas itself. Commercial needlepoint kits are usually worked in this stitch.

Tent stitch combines well with the heavier, more textured canvas stitches and accentuates their raised appearance. It is used to fill in the gaps of unworked canvas when a larger stitch does not totally cover the shape; in this case a matching thread should be used. It also frames square blocks of stitches, using a contrasting color or weight of thread. Tent stitch can be trammed to make a hard-wearing, slightly ridged surface which, when a durable thread is used, is ideal for covering chair seats. Trammed tent stitch is worked on Penelope canvas, so that the tramming stitch can be worked between the pairs of canvas threads.

Reversed tent stitch gives a slightly more textured surface. It is mainly used for covering a solid colored shape, giving a contrasting area to a textured stitch. It is worked in the same way as tent stitch but in this case the rows are horizontal and the direction of the stitches is reversed on every alternate row.

● **Jacquard stitch** (Mono or Penelope canvas) This is used for covering large shapes and background areas, and has the appearance of a woven or brocaded fabric. It is quick and

STRAIGHT AND SLANTED STITCHES

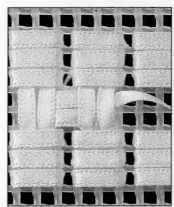
Fancy brick stitch

Tent stitch 2 (back)

Twill stitch

Tent stitch 3 (diagonal)

Tent stitch 1

Jacquard stitch

Knitting stitch 1

Cashmere stitch

Knitting stitch 2

Straight Cashmere stitch

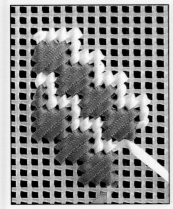

Moorish stitch

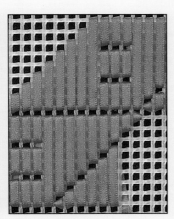

Lozenge satin stitch

easy to work and can be sewn in more than one color and weight of thread, when it makes a diagonal, striped zig-zag pattern. It is worked diagonally from the top left to the bottom right of the area to be covered. Rows of satin stitches, each covering two vertical and two horizontal canvas threads, are arranged in steps of six stitches, as shown. The satin stitch rows alternate with rows of tent stitch.

● **Knitting stitch** also known as tapestry stitch and kelim stitch (Mono canvas) This has a close worked, almost woven, surface and the effect varies depending on the weight of the thread and the gauge of the canvas used. A fine thread on small-gauge canvas gives the stitch the appearance of woven tapestry and the stitch can be used for tiny shapes and fine details. A border effect like that of knitting is made by using a coarse thread, such as tapestry yarn, on a larger gauge of canvas; the stitch can then be used for large shapes and background areas. Each row consists of slanting straight stitches, worked upward first and then downward, with a reverse slant.

● **Moorish stitch** (Penelope canvas) The flat surface produced has an attractive zig-zag pattern, which is usually worked in two colors of thread and can be worked in a combination of wool thread and cotton thread. The stitch is worked diagonally from the top left to the bottom right of the area, in alternate rows. One row consists of groups of four graduated diagonal stitches running in the same direction as those on the preceding row.

● **Cashmere stitch** (Mono canvas) Quick to work and with good covering power, this is useful for stitching large areas of background. It makes a small, neat pattern with a steep slant and consists of a series of groups of three diagonal stitches which form slanting rows. The stitching usually starts in the top left-hand corner of the area and the first row is worked downward to the bottom right-hand corner; the second row is then worked upward, parallel to the first; the third downward, and so on.

● **Straight Cashmere stitch** (Mono canvas) This is used for covering large background areas. It is a relatively easy stitch to work and quickly covers the canvas. A variation of Cashmere stitch (*see above*), it forms neat, rectangular blocks of slanting stitches. The blocks are fairly small and consist of four diagonal straight stitches which fill an area comprising two vertical canvas threads by three horizontal threads. The blocks can be worked in either horizontal or vertical rows to cover the area and, if worked in two colors or shades of thread, will make a tiny chessboard pattern.

● **Lozenge satin stitch** (Mono canvas) Used for filling large shapes and backgrounds. The bold lozenge-shaped pattern is made by arranging ordinary satin stitches in the pattern shown. The vertical stitches are worked in horizontal rows, beginning at the left-hand side of the area to be covered. The central group of three stitches can be left unworked on the first journey, to be filled in later, using a contrasting color of thread. A lustrous thread, such as stranded floss or silk, enhances the smoothly stitched surface of the lozenges but tapestry or Persian yarn is also suitable.

● **Hungarian stitch** (Mono and Penelope canvas) This makes tiny diamond shapes, which can be worked alternately in two colors or used to create a more complex geometric design, using several colors. It also makes a good background stitch in monochrome. When making a complicated pattern, first work all the stitches of one color, then all stitches of the second color, and so on. Each stitch consists of three vertical stitches of different lengths to cover two, four and then two horizontal threads of the canvas.

● **Diamond straight stitch** (Mono canvas) Used for filling large or small shapes and for background areas, this has a small, regular, diamond-shaped pattern. It consists of diamond shapes made of five vertical straight stitches of graduating length, surrounded by small vertical stitches worked over one canvas thread. Work the diamonds in horizontal rows over the area, so that each row fits neatly into the one above. With the same thread, fill the remaining spaces with the small stitches.

● **Diagonal stitch** (Mono canvas) Used for filling large shapes and backgrounds. It makes a flat, patterned surface with the appearance of a woven or brocaded fabric, which can be made more striking by using a lustrous thread such as stranded floss. It is worked in diagonal rows from the top left-hand corner to the bottom right-hand corner of the shape and consists of graduated diagonal stitches. The stitches on each row fit neatly into the stitches on the preceding row and the largest stitches are worked on a line with the smallest stitches so that no gaps are created.

Diagonal stitch can be worked in two or more colors to make a bold, diagonal striped pattern. Work backstitch in a different color between the rows of diagonal stitch to enhance the striped effect.

● **Reversed mosaic stitch** (Mono and Penelope canvas) Like mosaic stitch this makes a tiny squared pattern, although the diagonal stitches run in the opposite direction every alternate square. Each square is completed before moving on to the next one and they are worked in horizontal rows across the shape, and then back again. The light and shade effect created by the slanting stitches is enhanced by the use of a lustrous thread.

● **Linked stitch** (Mono canvas) Extremely quick and simple to work. Suitable for backgrounds, it makes a brickwork pattern of square, barred blocks, worked in horizontal rows. The blocks can be worked in vertical rows with a half drop and the number of vertical stitches in each block can be altered to form a rectangle. Each block consists of five vertical straight stitches worked over six horizontal canvas threads and overstitched by one horizontal straight stitch over six vertical threads.

● **Double twill stitch** (Mono canvas) This simply worked variation of twill stitch has a bold diagonal pattern useful for filling large shapes and background areas. It is worked in diagonal rows, from the top right to the bottom left of the area to be covered. Rows of large vertical straight stitches, worked over four horizontal canvas threads, alternate with rows of shorter vertical straight stitches, worked over two horizontal threads. The rows

STRAIGHT AND SLANTED STITCHES

Hungarian stitch

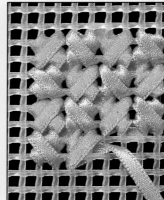
Reversed mosaic stitch

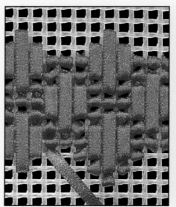
Diamond straight stitch

Linked stitch

Diagonal stitch

Double twill stitch

Byzantine stitch

Gobelin filling stitch 1

Gobelin stitch

Gobelin filling stitch 2

Encroaching Gobelin stitch

can be worked in two contrasting or harmonizing colors to give a diagonally striped effect.

● **Byzantine stitch** (Mono canvas) Useful for large background areas because it is easy to work and covers the canvas rapidly. The regular zig-zag pattern made by this stitch is similar to the formal geometric patterns found in Byzantine art and architecture; hence its name.

Byzantine stitch produces the effect of a woven or brocaded fabric, especially when worked on a small-gauge canvas with a stranded silk or cotton thread. The zig-zag pattern is made by arranging groups of five diagonal straight stitches in equal-sized steps. The rows are worked diagonally, beginning at the top left-hand corner of the area to be covered. Any small spaces at the edge of the shape that are not covered by the diagonal rows are filled in with shorter diagonal stitches, always keeping the pattern correct.

● **Gobelin stitch** (Mono canvas) This makes a smooth surface, which is useful where a flat area of needlepoint is needed to accentuate a more textured stitch. It is very similar to tent stitch in appearance and consists of horizontal rows of small slanting stitches. The rows are worked from the bottom of the area to be covered and run alternately from left to right and from right to left. The stitches are two canvas threads tall and slant diagonally over one thread. It is very important to follow this method closely in order to keep the 'pull' of the stitch correct, otherwise the surface will become uneven.

● **Encroaching Gobelin stitch** This is also known as interlocking Gobelin stitch (Mono canvas). A variation of Gobelin stitch, it makes a flat surface and is an ideal stitch to use if you wish to shade and blend colors over large areas. It is worked in close horizontal rows, starting at the top of the area to be covered, and the rows are worked in alternate directions. The stitches are longer than ordinary Gobelin stitches: they are worked over five horizontal canvas threads and slant diagonally over one thread. The stitches in each row overlap the stitches in each previous row by one horizontal thread, causing the rows to interlock.

● **Gobelin filling stitch** (Mono canvas) Used both for filling shapes and for backgrounds. It makes a fairly flat surface, and it is important to match the weight of the thread to the gauge of the canvas to ensure that the canvas is completely covered by the stitching. A very quick stitch to work, it lends itself very well to shading and blending different colours, as the rows of stitches overlap each other by three canvas threads. To prevent an obvious break between rows, the shades of the colours used should not be dramatically different. The rows are worked horizontally in alternate directions, beginning from the left. Each row consists of spaced, vertical straight stitches worked over six horizontal canvas threads into alternate holes in the canvas. Each row overlaps the preceding row by three canvas threads and fills in the spaces.

● **Square satin stitch** also known as flat square (Mono canvas) Used primarily for filling large shapes and backgrounds. It makes a pattern of diamond shapes, which in turn makes a pattern of large squares when four diamonds are set together. Each diamond shape consists of eleven satin stitches of graduating lengths, with the satin stitches worked either vertically or horizontally. Follow the arrangement of the diamonds and the direction of the stitches shown carefully. This stitch looks extremely attractive when worked on a small scale, using a pearl cotton or stranded floss to accentuate the light and shade effect created by the different directions of the stitches. The diamonds can also be striped in alternating colors: this create a strong bold pattern on the surface if two contrasting colors are used, or a much more subtle effect if two close shades of one color are used.

● **Wide Gobelin stitch** also known as oblique slav stitch (Mono canvas) A larger version of Gobelin stitch, it makes a flat surface, which is useful to contrast with the more textured canvas stitches. It is worked in horizontal rows in the same way as Gobelin stitch but the slanting straight stitches are larger and each cover three horizontal canvas threads. They also have a more angled slant, running across two vertical canvas threads instead of one. Wide Gobelin stitch looks very effective when worked in closely shaded bands.

● **Balloon satin stitch** (Mono canvas) Used for filling large shapes and backgrounds. The pattern of balloon shapes is made with ordinary satin stitches. The horizontal stitches are worked in vertical rows from the top of the shape and the second and subsequent rows interlock closely. A lustrous thread, such as stranded floss or silk, is well suited to this stitch and enhances the smooth, even surface of each balloon shape, but a wool thread can also be used with good results. To add texture to this stitch, an isolated knot stitch can be worked between the balloons.

● **Upright Gobelin stitch** also known as straight Gobelin stitch (Mono canvas) It is simple and very quick to work and makes a close, ridged surface, which lends itself well to working small, intricate shapes, as well as backgrounds. The upright variation of Gobelin stitch, it is worked in horizontal rows, in alternate directions, from the top of the area to be covered. The rows consist of small vertical straight stitches, each worked over two horizontal canvas threads and worked close together, filling every hole along the rows. Upright Gobelin stitch can be trammed to give a hard-wearing surface suitable for upholstery.

● **Linen stitch** (Mono and Penelope canvas) As its name suggests, this stitch creates a neatly woven surface reminiscent of linen fabric. It provides an unusual way of covering large areas and backgrounds and looks equally effective worked in tapestry yarn, matte embroidery cotton or stranded floss. The rows are worked diagonally from bottom left to top right and then back again. A neatly interlocking pattern of straight stitches is made; each vertical and horizontal stitch covers two canvas threads for a stepped effect.

STRAIGHT AND SLANTED STITCHES

Square satin stitch

Upright Gobelin stitch

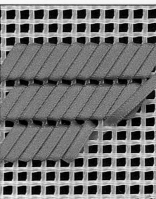
Wide Gobelin stitch

Linen stitch 1

Balloon satin stitch

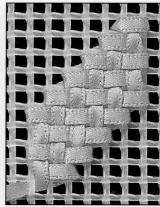
Linen stitch 2

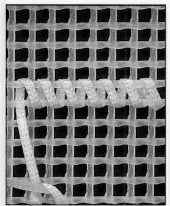
Plaited Gobelin stitch 1

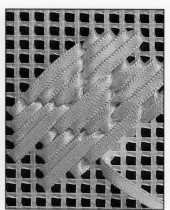
Milanese stitch

Plaited Gobelin stitch 2

Straight Milanese stitch

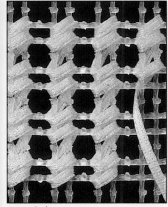
Rep stitch

Oriental stitch

● **Plaited Gobelin stitch** (Penelope canvas) This makes an attractive plaited surface and is used for filling large areas and backgrounds. Quite quick to work, it covers the canvas well. A variation of Gobelin stitch. The stitches are all the same size, covering two double canvas threads and slanting diagonally over one thread. However, the rows are arranged in a different way from Gobelin stitch. They are worked in horizontal rows, from right to left and then back again, starting at the top right-hand corner of the area. The stitches on the first row slant to the left, while those on the second and every alternate row thereafter slant to the right and overlap the stitches on each preceding row by one horizontal double thread.

● **Rep stitch** also known as Aubusson stitch (Penelope canvas) A very small diagonal stitch with a ridged texture, it is used for working finely detailed designs and tiny shapes. This stitch takes its name from the fabric, rep, which it resembles when worked closely, using a heavy thread. Rep stitch should cover the canvas completely, and a small sample should be worked to check the compatibility of the weight of the thread with the gauge of the canvas. It is worked in the same way as tent stitch but in this case the rows are always worked downward and the stitches are less slanted. Each vertical row covers one vertical double thread of the canvas, and the stitches are worked not only in the wider spaces but also between the double threads, giving a very closely stitched appearance.

● **Milanese stitch** (Mono and Penelope canvas) This makes an attractive, triangular pattern, with a brocaded appearance and flat surface, and is excellent for backgrounds.

The triangles consist of four stitches of graduated lengths, arranged so that they point alternately up and down. Instead of working satin stitch blocks, as is usual when producing this type of pattern, Milanese stitch is worked entirely in backstitch. Begin at the top left of the area to be covered and work the rows diagonally up and down the shape, ensuring all the time that the triangular formation is retained.

● **Straight Milanese stitch** (Mono and Penelope canvas) This is a simply worked variation of ordinary Milanese stitch but the triangles are arranged in horizontal rather than diagonal rows. It is worked in backstitch in exactly the same way as Milanese stitch but the rows run alternately from left to right, and from right to left.

● **Oriental stitch** see also Roumanian stitch (Mono and Penelope canvas) This is a variation of Milanese stitch, which makes a larger pattern with a definite zig-zag look to the flat surface. It is quick and easy to work, and is used for large areas and backgrounds. As with Milanese stitch, backstitch is worked in diagonal rows across the shape from the bottom left-hand corner to the top right-hand corner of the shape and back in the opposite direction, keeping the pattern correct.

● **Canvas fern stitch**
(Penelope canvas) This makes a striking ridged surface and is used for filling shapes and for backgrounds. It consists of vertical rows of top-heavy crosses which are worked downward to make ridges. The ridged effect can be accentuated by the use of two or more harmonizing or contrasting colors of thread.

● **Double stitch** also known as alternating cross stitch; see also stepped and threaded running stitch (Mono canvas) This makes a good background stitch as it is quite quick to work and covers the canvas well. It can be worked in two colors by working the different-sized crosses on two journeys instead of one. It looks most attractive when the two threads chosen are close to each other in shade.

Double stitch consists of interlocking horizontal rows of cross stitch alternating with oblong cross stitch. The rows are arranged so that the oblong cross stitches fit neatly under the ordinary cross stitches of the previous row. The oblong cross is worked over two vertical and six horizontal threads, while the ordinary cross stitch covers a square of two threads.

● **Cross stitch plus two** Cross stitch plus two is primarily a canvas stitch used on Mono canvas but it can also be worked successfully on an even-weave fabric. When worked on canvas, this stitch makes a distinctive woven surface and is useful for filling large shapes and background areas since it is quite quick to work. It consists of a large, slightly elongated cross stitch worked over four vertical and six horizontal canvas threads with the addition of a vertical

straight stitch across the center of the cross. A horizontal straight stitch is then worked at the base of the cross. Any type of embroidery thread can be used, but the woven pattern will be most effective if a thick thread such as tapestry wool is used. When working this stitch on an even-weave fabric, it makes a pretty, lacy pattern if a fine cotton perlé or crochet cotton is used.

● **Broad diagonal cross stitch** also known as diagonal broad cross (Mono canvas) Used for filling large shapes and background areas. It makes a raised geometric pattern with a bold, diagonal appearance. Although worked in the same way as broad cross stitch, the blocks are arranged diagonally rather than straight. Each block consists of three straight stitches, slanting from the top right-hand corner to the bottom left-hand corner and crossed by three straight stitches, which slant in the opposite direction. The rows are worked diagonally, from the top left-hand corner to the bottom right-hand corner of the area to be covered and all the rows of blocks interlock as shown.

● **Double Dutch stitch** also known as Dutch double cross stitch (Mono canvas) A variation of Dutch stitch used for filling large areas and for backgrounds. It makes a textured surface with strong vertical lines and is worked downward. This stitch uses oblong cross stitches worked horizontally over four vertical and two horizontal canvas threads. They are worked in vertical rows, and each alternate cross is tied down with a vertical stitch over three canvas threads. Each row is arranged so that the tied

CROSSED STITCHES

Canvas fern stitch 1

Double stitch

Canvas fern stitch 2

Cross stitch plus two 1

Canvas fern stitch 3

Cross stitch plus two 2

Broad diagonal cross stitch

Broad cross stitch

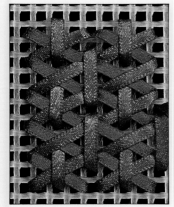

Double Dutch stitch

Canvas herringbone stitch

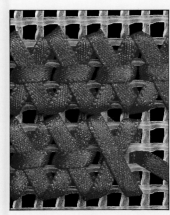

Oblong cross stitch with backstitch

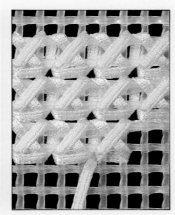

Underlined stitch

crosses line up next to each other. A second journey of stitching is then begun, using either the same thread, or one of a contrasting color and weight. This journey consists of rows of backstitch worked quite large and covering four horizontal threads, placed between the rows of crosses. Double Dutch stitch gives better coverage of the canvas than Dutch stitch.

● **Oblong cross stitch with backstitch and double-tied oblong cross stitch** (Mono canvas) A simply worked variation of oblong cross stitch which can be worked in two colors. It has the same uses as oblong cross stitch and is worked in exactly the same way, over two vertical and four horizontal threads of the canvas. After the required area has been stitched, a row of backstitch is worked over the center of each row of oblong cross stitch. This row can be worked in a contrasting color or a different weight of embroidery thread.

Double-tied oblong cross stitch is similar in appearance to oblong cross stitch with backstitch but the method of working is different and it is worked in one color. Each oblong cross stitch, worked over two vertical and seven horizontal threads, is tied down by two short straight stitches before proceeding to the next cross stitch. This stitch has a more textured appearance than oblong cross stitch or oblong cross stitch with backstitch and has a pronounced ridge running along the center of each row.

● **Broad cross stitch** also known as broad cross (Mono canvas) Used for filling large shapes and background areas. Quite a large stitch, it covers a square of six vertical and six horizontal canvas threads, making a raised geometric pattern, which is bold and striking in appearance. It is very straightforward to work and the blocks consist of three vertical straight stitches, which are then crossed by three horizontal stitches of the same length. It is worked in horizontal rows, beginning at the top left-hand corner of the area to be filled. The blocks in one row fit into the spaces at the bottom of the preceding row.

● **Canvas herringbone stitch** (Mono canvas) Used for filling large shapes and backgrounds. It makes a dense, plaited texture and is worked in exactly the same way as ordinary herringbone stitch. Each crossed diagonal stitch covers four vertical and four horizontal canvas threads and the rows interlock closely. A soft wool thread, such as tapestry or Persian yarn, gives the best coverage of the canvas. Canvas herringbone stitch can be striped in two or more colors to make an attractive chevron pattern.

● **Underlined stitch** (Mono and Penelope canvas) Used to fill a shape or background of any size. A variation of cross stitch, it can also be used on an even-weave fabric, provided that a fairly fine thread is used. It is worked in horizontal rows and each cross stitch is underlined by a horizontal straight stitch before the next cross stitch is formed.

● **Half cross stitch** also known as half stitch (Penelope canvas) A line or filling stitch. It is a small, diagonal stitch, always worked in the same direction, which can be used as a filling stitch to fill shapes with a flat area of stitching, or as a line stitch. As its name suggests, the stitch consists of half an ordinary cross stitch. When worked on canvas, half cross stitch looks identical to tent stitch. However, the method of working the two stitches is different and they should never be used together, as the different stitches created on the back of the work will result in an uneven, distorted surface. Half cross stitch is very easy to work and the rows should run horizontally from the left to the right of the area. When worked on canvas, this stitch can be trammed (*see Glossary*) to give better coverage. Any type of thread can be used on an even-weave fabric but care should be taken when using half cross stitch on canvas to select a thread that will cover the canvas adequately.

● **Oblong cross stitch** also known as long cross stitch, economic long cross and czar stitch (Mono and Penelope canvas) It is used for lines and for filling large areas and backgrounds, since it is extremely quick to work. Each row is worked in two journeys and the stitch has a neat, ridged texture. Almost the same as ordinary cross stitch in construction, the stitches of oblong cross stitch are elongated. One set of diagonals is worked from right to left on the first journey and the crosses are completed on the second journey in the opposite direction. This stitch can be worked over four, or six, or more horizontal canvas

threads but it is usually kept at the width shown.

● **Double cross stitch** also known as double straight cross stitch; see also leviathan stitch (Mono canvas) A very decorative stitch which forms large, raised diamond shapes. The diamonds comprise a row of large, upright cross stitches worked over four vertical and horizontal canvas threads, and then over-stitched by a row of smaller ordinary cross stitch. Follow the sequence of stitches shown and start stitching from the top left-hand corner of the canvas, working the rows first from left to right, and then from right to left.

● **Knotted stitch** also known as Persian cross stitch and Pangolin stitch; see also coral stitch and French knot (Penelope canvas) This has a closely packed ridged appearance and is quick and easy to work, which makes it suitable for backgrounds and large areas. A soft wool thread, such as tapestry or Persian yarn, gives best coverage. The stitch consists of a long, slanting stitch over one vertical and three horizontal double threads of canvas, which is tied down by a short, diagonal crossing stitch. The rows of stitching overlap each other by one horizontal double thread, and a pretty, broken striped pattern is created if alternate rows are worked with a contrasting thread.

● **Leviathan stitch** also known as double cross stitch, Smyrna cross stitch and railway stitch. This consists of an upright cross stitch worked over a basic cross stitch (*see pages,* 74, 138 and 139) and usually covers four horizontal and four vertical canvas threads. Each stitch forms a neat, raised square unit and

CROSSED STITCHES

Half cross stitch

Double cross stitch

Oblong cross stitch 1

Knotted stitch 1

Oblong cross stitch 2

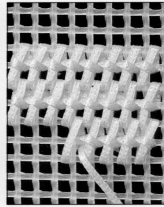

Knotted stitch 2

Leviathan stitch 1

Crossed Gobelin stitch

Leviathan stitch 2

Rice stitch

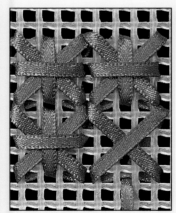
Leviathan stitch 3

Reversed cross stitch

these units can be worked in alternate colors to give a chessboard effect. Leviathan stitch worked in tapestry yarn makes an extremaly hard-wearing surface, suitable for chair seats and pillow covers.

● **Crossed Gobelin stitch** (Mono canvas) A decorative variation of Gobelin filling stitch with a more textured effect. Each row consists of spaced vertical straight stitches worked over six horizontal canvas threads into alternate holes in the canvas. After each stitch is formed an ordinary cross stitch (*see page* 138) is worked over the center. The rows are worked horizontally in alternate directions. Each row overlaps the preceding row by two horizontal threads to fill in the spaces.

● **Rice stitch** also known as cross corners cross stitch and William and Mary stitch (Mono or Penelope canvas). This densely textured stitch covers the canvas ground well and can be used for small areas and for backgrounds. It can be worked in two colors or two thicknesses of thread. Work the large crosses first and then stitch the corner diagonals with a second thread. If using two thicknesses of thread, use a thick thread for the large crosses and a thinner one for the corner stitches. Rice stitch looks very effective when stitched with a combination of tapestry or Persian yarn with pearl cotton for the corner stitches. Interesting shaded effects can be achieved by working an area of large crosses in one color and varying the colors of the second thread.

● **Reversed cross stitch** (Mono canvas) A composite stitch worked usually in two colors. It is a filling stitch worked in three journeys, which can be shaded by choosing graduating colors for the last journey. It has a dense, closely worked texture and is equally useful for filling any size of shape or for backgrounds. Reversed cross stitch is a combination of ordinary cross stitch and upright cross stitch worked in two journeys. These stitches are then repeated in reverse sequence on the third journey and worked over the existing crosses. On the third journey, the stitching is usually completed with a contrasting, finer thread, perhaps metallic. The underneath stitches can be worked in any type of embroidery thread.

● **Ridge stitch** (Mono canvas) This makes a distinctive vertically ridged pattern and is used for filling shapes of any size and for background areas. It is most attractive when worked in a fairly heavy yarn thread, such as tapestry or Persian yarn, as these threads accentuate the ridged appearance of the stitch. This stitch is worked vertically in rows from the top of the area to be covered, beginning at the left-hand side. It consists of an oblique cross stitch worked over four vertical canvas threads. Each vertical row overlaps the preceding row by one canvas thread so that the rows interlock. Ridge stitch can be striped by using two colors in alternate rows.

● **Horizontal fishbone stitch** (Penelope canvas) A variation of fishbone stitch which forms a strong diagonal pattern. These stitches are worked in diagonal rows from the bottom left to the top right of the canvas and the stitches are all set horizontally.

● **Upright rice stitch** (Mono and Penelope canvas) A simply worked variation of ordinary rice stitch which makes a pattern of diamonds on the surface. It is worked exactly like rice stitch but the foundation stitch is an upright cross stitch worked over four vertical and four horizontal threads of the canvas. The corners are then crossed by short vertical and horizontal straight stitches over two canvas threads. Upright rice stitch can be attractively shaded by varying the colors of the short crossing stitches.

● **Dutch stitch** also known as Dutch cross stitch (Mono canvas) This is used for filling large shapes and for background areas, and makes a raised pattern of crosses. It is

worked in two journeys and a contrasting thread can be used for the vertical stitches worked on the second journey. This stitch looks very attractive when tapestry or Persian yarn is used for the first set of stitches and a stranded floss or silk thread is used for the overstitching. The area is first covered by oblong cross stitches worked horizontally over four vertical and two horizontal canvas threads. The crosses fit neatly into each other and are arranged as shown. A second journey is then worked to overstitch the crosses with vertical straight stitches over four horizontal canvas threads.

● **Plaited stitch** see also herringbone stitch (Penelope canvas) This makes an attractive, ridged surface and is used for filling shapes and backgrounds. It consists of overlapping vertical rows of top-heavy crosses, and the method of working is very similar to that of canvas fern stitch. In that stitch the vertical rows are set side by side but in plaited stitch they overlap; each row overlaps the previous row by one vertical double thread of canvas. A soft yarn thread, such as tapestry or Persian yarn, looks best with this stitch and gives good canvas coverage.

● **Fishbone stitch** (Penelope canvas) Used for filling large areas and for backgrounds. It makes an attractive chevron pattern and can be worked in more than one color. It consists of vertical rows of diagonal straight stitches each crossed at the end by a shorter stitch, and is worked alternately up and down over the area. The slant of the diagonal stitches alternates on each row to form the chevrons.

CROSSED STITCHES

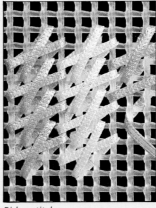

Ridge stitch

Dutch stitch

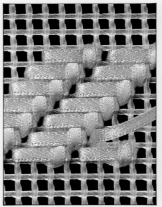

Horizontal fishbone stitch

Plaited stitch 1

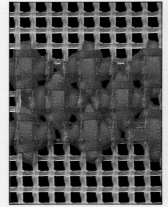

Upright rice stitch

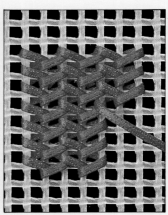

Plaited stitch 2

Fishbone stitch 1

Diagonal fishbone stitch

Fishbone stitch 2

Upright cross stitch

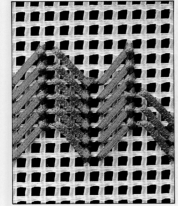

Fishbone stitch 3

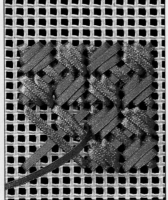

Triple rice stitch and multiple rice stitch

Fishbone stitch makes an attractive pattern when worked in alternate rows with tent stitch. When worked like this, the long diagonal stitches of the fishbone rows should all point in the same direction.

● **Diagonal fishbone stitch** also known as stepped fishbone stitch (Penelope canvas). A variation of fishbone stitch: the stitches are identical but the arrangement over the canvas is different and they make a strongly diagonal pattern on the surface. The stitches are worked in diagonal rows with the stitches set horizontally or vertically in alternate rows. The rows run from the bottom left to the rop right of the canvas. Diagonal fishbone stitch makes a good background stitch as it is fairly quick and easy to work.

● **Upright cross stitch** also known as straight cross stitch (Penelope canvas) This stitch makes a neat, crunchy texture on the surface and it is useful for filling small areas because of the small scale of the stitches. Each stitch is worked over two vertical and two horizontal double threads of the canvas; it is worked diagonally in two journeys, from the bottom right-hand corner to the top left-hand corner of the canvas, and then back again. The vertical stitches are worked first and then crossed by horizontal stitches of the same length.

● **Triple rice stitch and multiple rice stitch** (Mono and Penelope canvas) As the name implies, this stitch is a complex variation of ordinary rice stitch and gives a heavier effect. It can be worked in two contrasting colors but looks equally attractive when worked in one. A lustrous thread, such as stranded floss, enhances the light and shade effect created by the stitch. Each unit consists of six vertical and six horizontal canvas threads, and each corner is overstitched by three graduated diagonal stitches.

The ordinary cross stitch can be made larger, with more diagonal stitches crossing the corners; it is then known as multiple rice stitch. This can be given a pretty striped pattern by working the alternate diagonal stitches in a contrasting color of thread.

209

CANVASWORK

● **Chained cross stitch** (Mono or Penelope canvas) A small stitch worked in rows to make a neat, regular texture and used for filling shapes or background areas. An extremely hard-wearing stitch, it is very suitable for covering chair seats and footstools, provided that a durable thread has been used. It is straightforward to work and covers a square of four vertical and four horizontal canvas threads. A cross stitch is worked across this square, which is then overstitched horizontally with a twisted chain stitch. The loop of the twisted chain stitch is anchored by a tiny diagonal stitch and the rows are worked from left to right of the area to be filled.

Diagonal cross stitch (Mono canvas) Used for filling large shapes and background areas. It is relatively quick to work and covers the canvas well. Worked upward in diagonal rows from the bottom right-hand corner to the top

left-hand corner of the area to be filled, it can be stitched in two or more colors to give a pretty, diagonally striped pattern. Each row consists of upright cross stitches worked over four vertical and four horizontal canvas threads and separated by diagonal straight stitches. Diagonal cross stitch can also be used to fill shapes on an even-weave fabric.

Italian cross stitch also known as two-sided Italian cross stitch, arrowhead cross stitch and Italian stitch (Mono or Penelope canvas) This gives a dense texture and can also be used on even-weave fabrics if the thread is fairly fine. When worked on a very loosely woven, even-weave fabric, the stitches can be pulled together tightly to produce an open-work effect. It consists of a cross stitch which covers a square of three vertical and three horizontal canvas or fabric threads, and four straight stitches arranged in a square around the cross stitch.

CROSSED STITCHES

Chained cross stitch 1

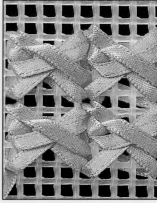
Chained cross stitch 4

Chained cross stitch 2

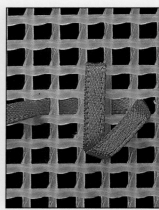
Diagonal cross stitch 1

Chained cross stitch 3

Diagonal cross stitch 2

ABOVE *Canvaswork key tags worked in rice and tent stitch (LEFT) and double Leviathan stitch (RIGHT).*

210

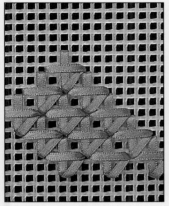

Diagonal cross stitch 3

Italian cross stitch 3

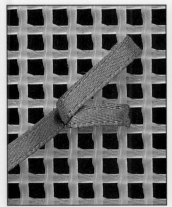

Italian cross stitch 1

Italian cross stitch 4

Italian cross stitch 2

ABOVE AND BELOW *Canvaswork pincushions make delightful gifts. These two examples are worked in cross stitch, one in a 'crazy' design and one in a more traditional block pattern.*

● **Long-armed cross stitch** also known as long-legged cross stitch, plaited slav stitch, Portuguese stitch and twist stitch (Mono and Penelope canvas) This can be used both as a border and as a textured filling when it has a pretty, plaited appearance. It is worked in rows from left to right and consists of long diagonal stitches crossed by short diagonal stitches; the long stitches are worked over twice the number of threads as the short stitches. Long-armed cross stitch is straightforward to work and looks equally effective on fabric or canvas.

● **Woven cross stitch** also known as plaited cross stitch (Mono and Penelope canvas) This stitch forms square blocks that have a textured, woven appearance. It is used for large areas and backgrounds where a geometric stitch is needed. It can be worked in two contrasting or harmonizing colors and the blocks arranged to make a chessboard pattern; another color can be introduced to frame the blocks with a border of backstitch. The blocks consist of a large ordinary cross stitch worked over four vertical and four horizontal canvas threads and overstitched by four diagonal straight stitches. These diagonal stitches are woven over and under each other as they are worked, and the sequence of stitches should be followed carefully. A soft wool thread, such as tapestry or Persian yarn, will accentuate the woven appearance more than a cotton thread.

CROSSED STITCHES

Long-armed cross stitch 1

Woven cross stitch 2

Long-armed cross stitch 2

Double cross 1

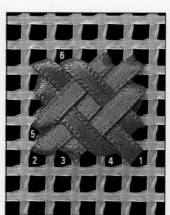

Woven cross stitch 1

Double cross 2

Double cross 3

Plaited Algerian stitch 3

Plaited Algerian stitch 1

Greek stitch 1

Plaited Algerian stitch 2

Greek stitch 2

Double cross (Mono canvas) This makes a heavy, squared pattern of raised blocks, which can be worked in two colors to make a chessboard pattern. Careful choice of thread and gauge of canvas is important, as this stitch looks its best when worked on quite a small scale; otherwise the pattern can be rather dominant. The blocks cover a square of seven canvas threads and each block is worked in two stages. The square is first crossed by two horizontal and two vertical straight stitches to make an upright cross figure. A second cross, made up of four diagonal straight stitches, is then worked: two run from top right to bottom left and two in the opposite direction. To complete the stitch, a tiny upright cross stitch is worked over two vertical and two horizontal canvas threads, where the corners of the blocks meet. Once completed, the blocks can be framed by vertical and horizontal straight stitches.

 Plaited Algerian stitch (Penelope canvas) This is worked in a similar way to closed herringbone stitch, forming neat channels of backstitch on the reverse of the canvas. On the surface, this stitch closely resembles plait stitch but its use of working thread is more economical. Plaited Algerian stitch is most effective when worked on a small-gauge canvas with a smooth thread, such as pearl cotton. It gives a dense, plaited texture and is used for working small areas of color.

 Greek stitch also known as Greek cross stitch (Mono and Penelope canvas) This should always be worked in a fairly thick thread, such as tapestry or Persian yarn. Used for filling large shapes and background areas, it makes a raised, plaited pattern arranged in horizontal bands. It is worked rather like herringbone stitch but the crosses are spaced asymmetrically and are usually two double canvas threads tall. It is worked in horizontal rows with the crosses slanting in the opposite direction on every alternate row.

FAR LEFT *Canvas work badges using cross stitch on plastic canvas.*

RIGHT *A traditional use of canvaswork to cover a chair seat.*

● **Montenegrin stitch** also known as Montenegrin cross stitch and two-sided Montenegrin cross stitch (Mono or Penelope canvas) Similar in appearance to long-armed cross stitch and worked in a similar way, it has additional vertical bars. It is quick to work and can be used for filling large shapes and backgrounds; use a heavy thread so that the canvas is completely covered.

Work Montenegrin stitch upwards in horizontal rows, beginning each row at the left-hand side of the area to be filled. First make an irregular cross, in which the longest stitch is twice the length of the shortest stitch, and then make a vertical stitch. When worked in the correct sequence, this stitch is reversible, as the back builds up a pattern of ordinary cross stitches alternating with vertical stitches. Montenegrin stitch can also be worked on an even-weave fabric, provided that a fairly fine thread is used.

● **Plait stitch** also known as Spanish stitch (Penelope canvas) This makes a dense, slightly raised and plaited surface, which is rather similar in appearance to plaited Algerian stitch but the method of working is different. This stitch should be worked in a fairly heavy thread, such as tapestry or Persian yarn, to accentuate the raised surface and to cover the double threads of the canvas adequately. It can be used for outlines or for filling large areas and backgrounds, and it is quick and easy to work.

The horizontal rows are worked from left to right over two horizontal double threads of the canvas. A series of irregular cross stitches are made; the needle must always

be inserted vertically through the canvas. Every row should begin at the left of the area to be covered and the second and subsequent rows should be worked directly underneath the preceding rows.

● **Rhodes stitch** (Mono canvas) The stitch makes a pattern of raised square blocks and is used for large areas and backgrounds. It can be worked over different sizes of square but is usually worked over six canvas threads.

Each block consists of straight stitches worked across the square, following each other in an anti-clockwise direction, so that they all cross over the same central point. Begin each square by working the first stitch from the bottom left-hand corner to the top right-hand corner and fill every hole around the square. After the block has been covered, work a short vertical stitch in the center over two horizontal threads. This central stitch should be omitted if the stitch is worked over an odd number of threads. When a Rhodes stitch is worked very large, perhaps over ten canvas threads, a neater way of tying it down is to work a straight stitch over each corner, from the mid-point of one side of the square to the mid-point of an adjacent side. The blocks are arranged in horizontal rows, and can be worked in two contrasting colors to give a chessboard effect.

● **Half Rhodes stitch** (Mono canvas) This makes an attractive textured surface, which is used for filling large shapes and background areas. It is a variation of Rhodes stitch. This stitch is worked in diagonal rows from the top left to the bottom right of the area to be covered, and the stitches on

CROSSED STITCHES

Montenegrin stitch 1

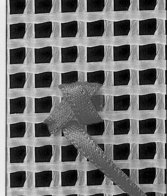

Plait stitch 1

Montenegrin stitch 2

Plait stitch 2

Montenegrin stitch 3

Plait stitch 3

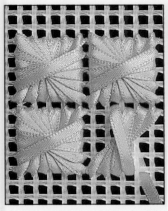

Rhodes stitch

Plaited Rhodes stitch

Half Rhodes stitch 1

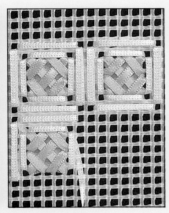

Captive rice stitch

Half Rhodes stitch 2

each row interlock with those on the preceding row. Each stitch consists of a half-worked Rhodes stitch, worked over six vertical and six horizontal canvas threads. Form the first stitch and continue around in an anti-clockwise direction until all the holes at the top and bottom of the square are filled. Any type of embroidery thread can be used, but care should be taken to match the weight of the thread to the gauge of the canvas to make sure the canvas is completely covered by the stitching.

Half Rhodes stitch can also be worked in horizontal rows with the edges of the stitches touching. A series of diamond shapes of canvas are left showing through and these are filled in with a matching thread, using tent stitch.

● **Plaited Rhodes stitch** (Mono canvas) This makes an attractive plaited surface and is a variation of half Rhodes stitch, which is used for filling shapes of any size and for backgrounds. The stitches are worked in horizontal rows and each row interlocks with the preceding row. The direction of the stitches changes on alternate rows from anti-clockwise to clockwise and the size of each plaited Rhodes stitch is quite small, covering four vertical and four horizontal canvas threads. A lustrous thread, such as stranded cotton or silk floss shows it off to better advantage than a hairy woolen thread.

● **Captive rice stitch** (Mono or Penelope canvas) A variation of ordinary rice stitch, this makes a strongly textured geometric pattern and is used for large areas and backgrounds. The stitch consists of a rice stitch surrounded by groups of straight stitches to make a

framed block. The second and third straight stitches are worked into the same holes, making a raised bar, and they cover six canvas threads. The blocks are arranged side by side, and a small area is left where the corners of four blocks meet. This can remain unworked, or a tiny ordinary cross stitch can be worked to fill it. Captive rice stitch looks very effective when the framing straight stitches are worked in a thread of contrasting color to that of the rice stitch.

215

● **Star stitch** see also Algerian eye stitch (Mono canvas) This makes an attractively textured pattern of stars and can be used to fill a shape of any size and for background areas.

Work a grid of large, upright cross stitches over six vertical and six horizontal canvas threads to cover the whole shape. They should be worked in horizontal rows and the four adjoining arms of the crosses should share the same holes in the canvas. Next, work a small cross stitch over two canvas threads over the upright crosses on every other horizontal row. Then overstitch the upright crosses on the remaining rows with a larger cross stitch worked over four canvas threads. The cross stitches can be worked in a contrasting color or weight of thread.

● **Square herringbone stitch** also known as multiplait (Mono canvas) This makes a large, bold, dramatic pattern, which can be rather dominant, and is used for background areas. The stitch makes a plaited diamond shape, which can be altered in size by increasing or decreasing the number of rows worked. It consists of a central ordinary cross stitch enclosed by rows of herringbone stitch. The diamond shapes are worked in horizontal rows, so that the rows interlock. The gaps between the edges of the diamond shapes are filled by two straight stitches of commensurate lengths. A soft wool thread, such as tapestry or Persian yarn, is the most suitable for this stitch.

● **Velvet stitch** also known as rug stitch, tassel stitch, raised stitch, Astrakhan stitch, plush stitch and Berlin plush stitch. Velvet stitch resembles the pile of a carpet and is worked

only on Penelope canvas. It became very popular during the Berlin woolwork craze in Europe and America during the middle to late nineteenth century. It was used to give a three-dimensional quality to animals, birds and flowers, against a flat cross stitch background. When working velvet stitch, use one strand of a thick, soft yarn or several strands of a fine yarn. Cut and trim the loops to length after the stitching has been completed. If the stitches are worked very close together on the canvas and a thick yarn is used, the resulting pile will be dense enough to be sculptured with a sharp pair of scissors.

● **Waffle stitch** also known as Norwich stitch (Mono canvas) This large stitch makes a pattern of square blocks with superimposed raised diamonds, and is used to fill large shapes and background areas. The blocks can be worked in various sizes, but the squares must contain an odd number of canvas threads. The photograph shows a waffle stitch worked over a square of nine threads: eighteen diagonal straight stitches are worked across the square, following the sequence shown. The second and subsequent straight stitches are worked over each preceding stitch until seventeen have been completed. The eighteenth stitch is taken under the last stitch that it crosses, rather than over it. Any type of embroidery thread can be used with waffle stitch, providing that the weight of the thread is compatible with the gauge of the canvas selected.

● **Octagonal Rhodes stitch** (Mono canvas) A variation of Rhodes stitch which makes it a very raised surface of octagonal

CROSSED STITCHES

Star stitch

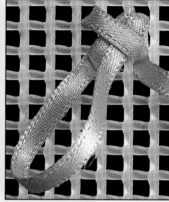

Velvet stitch 2

Square herringbone stitch

Velvet stitch 3

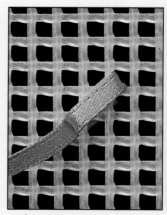

Velvet stitch 1

Velvet stitch 4

Octagonal Rhodes stitch

Criss cross stitch 2

Waffle stitch

Criss cross stitch 1

blocks, and the spaces in between are filled by individual Rhodes stitches; it is used for filling large areas and for backgrounds. It is worked in the same way as Rhodes stitch, with the stitches following each other in an anti-clockwise direction, so that they all cross over the same central point, but the outline shape followed is an octagon rather than a square. Follow the sequence of stitches carefully and arrange the octagons so that they touch at the vertical and horizontal edges. The remaining squares of canvas should be covered with an ordinary Rhodes stitch in a matching thread. Care should be taken when deciding where to use this stitch, as the pattern can be very dominant and may swamp a smaller, more delicate stitch.

● **Criss-cross stitch** (Mono canvas) A complicated stitch to work, it gives a dense, unusual texture. It is used over large areas or backgrounds, as it covers the canvas well. As with other complex canvas stitches, a small sample should be worked to test the compatibility of the thread and canvas: if the thread is too fine, the canvas ground will show through; if it is too heavy, the resulting stitch will be too bulky and distorted to give a pleasing appearance.

Criss-cross stitch consists of five slanting stitches radiating from the bottom left-hand corner and crossed by four slanting stitches from the bottom right-hand corner. They are worked alternately, and make a woven surface. Follow the sequence shown carefully, as accuracy is crucial to the formation of the stitch. The completed stitches are arranged in horizontal rows, and are always worked from left to right of the area to be covered.

ABOVE *Blocks of satin stitch forming a trellis pattern around double Leviathan stitch.*

● **Plaited double cross** (Mono canvas) This is a more complex version of double cross stitch and has the same raised square pattern but with a woven effect. It is worked in a similar way: first the blocks are made in two stages, and then the small upright crosses are worked. The difference lies in the arrangement of the straight stitches that make the square blocks as they are plaited over and under each other. The sequence of stitches shown should be followed very carefully. As with double cross, choice of thread and gauge of canvas is important, as the pattern can be rather dominant when worked on a large scale.

● **Double leviathan stitch** (Mono or Penelope canvas) This is a more complex variation of leviathan stitch and makes a larger, more raised pattern of square blocks. These blocks can be worked in two colors to make a chessboard pattern. A large cross stitch worked over four canvas threads is stitched first, followed by further crossing stitches, and, finally, a large upright cross stitch. Follow the sequence of stitches carefully. The raised, almost crunchy surface of double leviathan stitch looks best when worked in a fairly thick thread, such as tapestry or Persian yarn.

Other canvas stitches

● **Algerian eye stitch** Also known as star stitch and star eyelet stitch. Algerian eye stitch is used in needlepoint and in open-work embroidery on a loosely woven even-weave fabric. It consists of eight stitches, all worked into the same central point, and forms a star within a square. When

used as a canvas stitch, it should be worked on mono canvas with a heavy thread; on an even-weave fabric, the stitches should be pulled quite tight during the stitching to emphasize the holes that form at the center of each eyelet. The eyelets can be spaced alternately to give a chessboard effect or worked as an all-over pattern. Alphabets on early samplers were often worked in Algerian eye stitch.

● **Ray stitch** also known as fan stitch (Mono canvas) This makes a regular pattern of square blocks on the surface and can be worked to give three different effects.

The stitch is normally worked over a square of three canvas threads and is very effective for filling small shapes. The blocks can be made larger by the addition of further stitches and they can be as large as six or eight threads, creating a striking effect for large shapes and backgrounds. When worked over three threads, each square block consists of seven straight stitches radiating from the same hole at the corner of the square and, if the stitches are pulled tightly, a pattern of holes is also made. The blocks are usually arranged so that the direction of the straight stitches is reversed every alternate block. Different effects can be made by working all the stitches in the same direction, or by working diagonal pairs of blocks into the same central hole, which then becomes quite large. A lustrous thread, such as stranded cotton, enhances the light and shade effect created by the positioning of the stitches.

CROSSED STITCHES

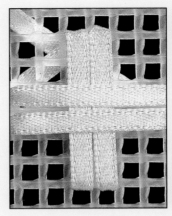

Plaited double cross 1

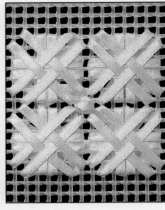

Plaited double cross 4

Plaited double cross 2

Double Leviathan stitch 1

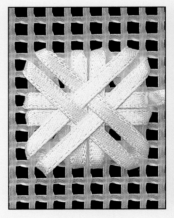

Plaited double cross 3

Double Leviathan stitch 2

Double Leviathan stitch 3

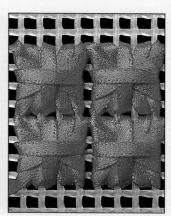

Double Leviathan stitch 6

Double Leviathan stitch 4

Algerian eye-stitch

Double Leviathan stitch 5

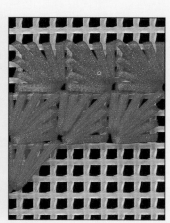

Ray stitch

TOP Leviathan stitch using a variety of shades of green.

ABOVE Leviathan stitch worked in blocks around double Leviathan stitch again using shades of one color.

BORDERS

*D*ecorative borders can be created by using plastic canvas. As the plastic canvas is rigid, you can cut the pieces to shape and there is no need to work on a frame. The edges can be bound with overcast or braided cross stitch for a neat finish.

On the example shown, a border has been made to decorate a plain lampshade. The plastic canvas is cut into four strips, each the length of one side of the lampshade. On each strip, indentations are cut in the lower edge at every alternate group of four threads, to make the geometric design as shown, and the nubs of plastic are trimmed off to give the edging a smooth finish. The strips are then embroidered in cross stitch from the charted design, bound at the top with braided cross stitch and finished at the lower edge with overcast stitch.

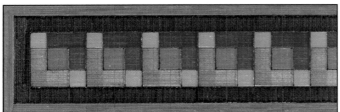

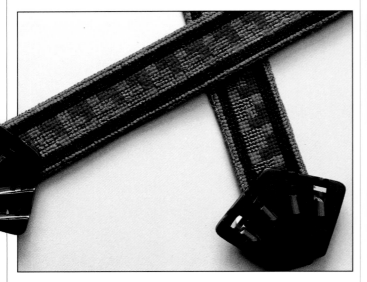

ABOVE *The design for this belt consists of a simple repeat pattern of interlocking L-shapes within a basic square. You can thus make a suitable length by reworking the pattern as many times as is necessary. The blocks are bordered with heavy stripes which are also worked at each end of the belt to finish off the pattern. The colors are close-toned, but the contrast created by setting a warm, bright rust against the clean blues and greens gives a rich, glowing effect.*

ABOVE RIGHT *A plain-colored lampshade is enlivened by an embroidered border, completed on plastic canvas and attached to the lower edge of the shade. As the plastic canvas is rigid you can cut the pieces to shape and there is no need to work on a frame. This border is designed for a lampshade which is square at the lower edge but you can easily adapt the idea for a rounded shade, and change the colors to suit the scheme of your furnishings.*

BRAIDED CROSS STITCH

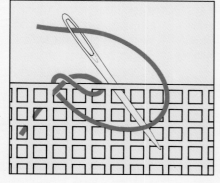

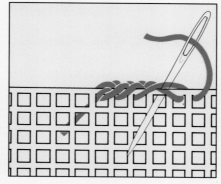

OVERCAST STITCH

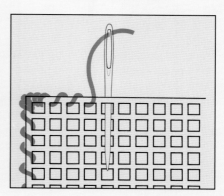

MITERING CORNERS ON CANVAS

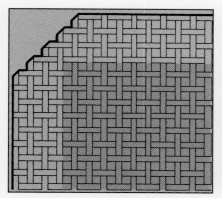

1 Trim the corner of the surplus canvas to avoid excess bulk.

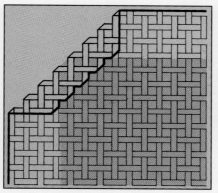

2 Turn over the cut canvas to the corner of the embroidery.

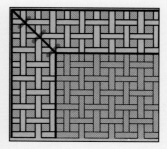

3 Fold in the side edges and stitch down the diagonal join, making sure the corner is square.

LEFT *A canvaswork border inside a card window mount makes an attractive and unusual frame for a photograph or small picture. The photograph and mount are sandwiched together inside a simple clip frame, inexpensive and easy to assemble, and are held in place by pressure from the glass and clips; there is no need to tape the photograph to the mount and you can remove it without damage.*

The border design makes use of a variety of stitches, including French knots, which are worked after completion of the canvas stitches. The design could be adapted to a number of photographs mounted together within a larger clip frame, with separate window mounts cut in the card and edged with narrow borders of stitching.

The sections are backed with strips of felt glued on with a fabric adhesive and, when the glue is dry, joined at the short ends with braided cross stitch. Finally, the border is attached at the lower edge of the lampshade with small running stitches of invisible thread.

Strips of canvas can also be used to make accessories such as belts, chokers or wristbands, or alternatively applied to furnishings — as a pull-cord or upholstery trimming, for example. For these, single-weave canvas will be most suitable, and to avoid distortion

this must be worked on a frame: stretch a larger piece than is required on the frame, and trim it after stitching is finished. A neat finish will be achieved by leaving ½ inch (1.5cm) border of raw canvas around the stitching to turn in. Corners should be mitered. Petersham ribbon or purchased belt stiffening can then be fastened to the wrong side with small stitches along each edge.

Canvaswork borders can also be used to make an attractive and unusual frame for a photograph or small

picture. Again, a larger piece of canvas than is required should be worked on a frame to avoid distortion. After stitching and blocking, the outside edges are trimmed to ½ inch (1.5cm) and the central portion is cut out with a very sharp pair of embroidery scissors, trimming it close to the stitching. A clip frame, which holds together the glass, cardboard mount and canvas border with metal clips, is ideal for this arrangement.

BLOCKING

When the stitching is completed, all canvaswork should be stretched to smoothe out any distortions, however slight. This process is called blocking.

The canvas should be blocked face downwards, unless the stitches used are raised and highly textured, in which case it is blocked face upwards to avoid squashing the stitches. For blocking, you will need a piece of unstained, unpainted wood or blockboard, at least ¾ inch (2cm) thick and a few inches larger than the piece of canvas, covered with polyethylene film; rust-proof tacks; a small hammer; a steel ruler; a sponge or water spray. Dampen the canvas lightly with a spray or wet sponge and place it on the polyethylene-covered board. If the canvas still has a selvage, cut small nicks in it at regular intervals so it will stretch evenly. Lightly hammer a tack into the board through the center of the top strip of unworked canvas. Stretch the work gently downwards, making sure the canvas threads are vertical, and tack at the center of the

bottom strip. Repeat this procedure for the other two sides being careful to keep the canvas threads at right angles to those which run from top to bottom. Ease the canvas into the correct shape, and working outwards from the first four tacks, insert more tacks at ¾ inch (2cm) intervals all the way round. Work carefully, checking the measurements of the canvas with the steel ruler and making adjustments to the tacks where necessary. If the canvas begins to dry out, dampen it again. When you are satisfied that the work is the correct size and shape, hammer the tacks home securely but not so tightly pressed to the board that you will have difficulty removing them later.

BELOW *This canvas has been distorted out of its rectangular shape, probably because it was not worked on a frame. It would be possible to improve the distortion a little by blocking, but the work is too far out of true to be straightened perfectly.*

Once the canvas has been tacked down, sponge or spray the work again. It should be evenly damp, but not saturated. Leave it to dry at room temperature and away from direct sunlight. Canvaswork can take anything up to a week to dry out thoroughly and it is important

not to take it off the board until it is bone dry, or it could become distorted again. If the canvas is still slightly out of shape after removal, repeat the blocking process. This second blocking is often needed for designs which have strong vertical or horizontal features, together them really accurate.

BLOCKING

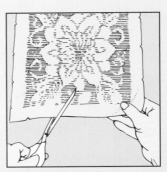

1 *Cover a soft board with polyethylene, and place the finished piece of embroidery face down on it. If the canvas has a selvage, cut a few nicks in it to ensure even stretching.*

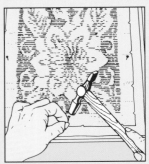

2 *Lightly hammer a tack into the unworked area at the top of the canvas. Stretch the canvas gently downwards, keeping the warp threads vertically aligned, then hammer in a second tack at the center of the bottom edge. Place the third and fourth tacks in the center of the other two sides, ensuring that the canvas is stretched with the warp and weft threads at right-angles to each other.*

3 *On each side of the four sides, work outwards from the center, inserting tacks lightly at 1 inch (2.5cm) intervals and gently stretching the fabric as you go.*

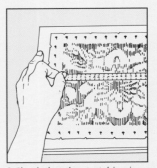

4 *Check that the stretching is even, either by measuring length and width or by checking the right angles at the corners. Adjust the tacks where necessary. Thoroughly dampen the areas that need a lot of stretching. Hammer in the tacks securely when you are satisfied.*

MAKING UP

Many people consider it best to have their work made up professionally; if a great deal of time has been spent on the stitching, it deserves the best finishing. However, if you wish to finish an item yourself, items such as cushions can be made up at home (*see page* 71).

Canvaswork covers for chair seats are always popular, as they are extremely hard-wearing and easy to mount on dining-chair seats or on soft easy chairs.

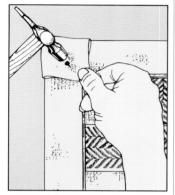

COVERING A CHAIR SEAT
1 Strip any old upholstery from the chair seat, leaving the wood base and foam padding. Cover the foam with lining fabric, securing the lining with tacks on the underside of the seat. Pull the fabric over the corners and tack it.

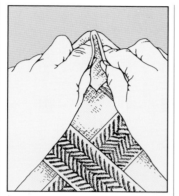

2 Neaten each corner by folding in the fabric at either side. Crease it firmly with your fingers.

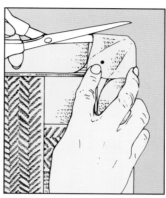

3 Push aside the folds and trim off the triangle of fabric underneath.

4 Put the folded sections back in place and hammer in tacks. If the folds are not neatly creased, press them with a damp cloth before tacking. Neaten all four corners in the same way.

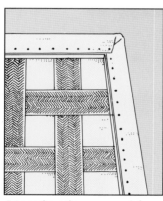

5 Spread out the canvaswork face downwards and place the chair seat on top, also right side down. Center it on the canvas and fold the edges of the canvaswork over the back of the frame. Secure the edges with tacks, working outwards from the center of each edge and stretching the canvas gently into shape. Neaten the corners with folds, in the same way as for the lining fabric.

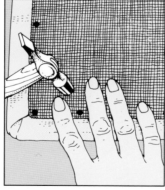

6 To finish off the underside of the seat, tack hessian across the wood frame. Stretch it evenly across the back of the seat and turn under the raw edges and corners neatly.

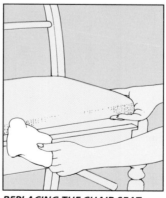

REPLACING THE CHAIR SEAT
The new covering on the chair seat may be difficult to fit at first. Wrap a hammer in clean cloth so you can tap the seat gently into place if necessary without damaging the canvaswork. Fit the back edge first and then ease in the sides and front.

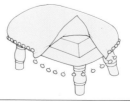

Different types of wood frame chairs are suitably upholstered with canvaswork. Some styles have a panel fitted on seat and back. The canvaswork is stretched directly onto the frame and tacked in place, with decorative braid concealing the raw edges. Canvaswork can be used to cover a small stool, secured at the base with pins. Pucker the edges of the canvas slightly to fit it snugly around the curved shape. Victorian Berlin woolwork for chair seats. The pattern is particularly suited to seat panels with a curving or rounded shape.

CHAPTER 5

QUILTING

INTRODUCTION

Quilting, derived from the Latin word *culcita* meaning a mattress or pillow, involves stitching several layers of fabric together, a method which has been used for warmth over a long period by many cultures. The technique has also been used for protective garments in times of war, on their own or under chainmail or plate armor.

The true quilt is a textile sandwich with a top layer, a bottom layer and a filling which may be added for warmth. A quilt top may be made of patchwork or appliqué or a whole piece of cloth. Quilting is the pattern which holds the three layers together – usually in running stitch. It is the last process in the making of a quilt.

The earliest quiltings seem to have been made in the East, but there is very little documentary evidence of this. A jacket worn by a carved ivory figurine of about 3,400 B.C. which was found in Egypt, appears quilted in a pattern of straight lines which is sometimes used today. The technique was known throughout Asia and spread to the Middle East. By way of the trade routes, it then spread through North Africa to Europe and across to the British Isles where it can be traced back to the thirteenth century. In the seventeenth century, quilting skills were taken to North America by the early colonists.

References to English domestic quilting are very rare, but there are records of quilted

armor from the time of William the Conqueror (c.1028–87), through to the thirteenth century. During the Crusades, men wore quilted jackets under their heavy metal armor to prevent chafing, and the only protection for infantry troops was a thickly padded jacket. The surcoat of Edward, the Black Prince (1330–1376) is in the possession of Canterbury Cathedral; made of red and blue velvet and embroidered with gold, it is quilted lengthways. Soldiers wore quilted clothing for protection even in the seventeenth century. When the English first landed at Jamestown, Virginia,

in 1607, soldiers wore padded jackets in place of armor.

Early bed quilts were purely utilitarian – thick, warm bedcovers and bed hangings were essential in the cold houses of the Middle Ages.

The basic method of creating a padded fabric for

warmth or protection was to insert a soft layer of wadding, originally wool or rags, between two outer layers, which were held in place by working small stitches through the entire sandwich. This is the method which we know today as *wadded* or *English quilting*.

RIGHT *This detail of an eighteenth-century quilted bedcover is filled with the attractive, pastel shades of silks which were by then generally available. Delicately worked in a naturalistic design, the suggested light texture of the petals and leaves contrast with the texture of the basket which is more dense and tightly stitched.*

FAR LEFT, TOP *A plain quilt with a chintz border, from the north of England. A variety of motifs have been incorporated, with particularly attractive designs built up at the corners.*

ABOVE *This contemporary quilt lets the vibrant pattern of the fabric speak for itself. The quilting is minimal and functional.*

LEFT *A coverlet with a pattern of red baskets, worked in New Jersey during the nineteenth century. It is a perfect example of quilting patchwork and appliqué worked into a single and very pleasing bedcover. The white background is made from diamond-shaped blocks quilted with a pineapple design, and the red baskets are formed from small red and white triangles of quilted patchwork with appliqué handles.*

Naturally, quilting soon ceased to be purely utilitarian. The stitching used to attach the layers together, while retaining its function, developed into increasingly elaborate lines. It is characteristic of quilting that the pattern contained within the stitches in a low relief, rather than the stitches themselves, is the key feature, and traditional motifs developed. Irish and Manx quilts often had no padding at all, consisting of only two layers of fabric quilted in what is known as 'waves' – a chevron pattern which covers the entire surface of the work.

By the eighteenth century the making of quilts had become a part of life in many households. In some areas quilting 'bees' or parties were held. American quilting bees have been well publicized in literature and song and similar social events took place in Ulster and the Isle of Man. The program for the bee was much the same wherever it was held. The hostess, who had a bedcover to be quilted, issued invitations to all the experienced needlewomen in the neighborhood who arrived during the afternoon and sewed in relays until supper. In areas where quilting was popular, a girl might be expected to complete six or even a dozen quilts for her dowry.

Wadded quilting has frequently been combined with patchwork and appliqué in making traditional bed quilts; other needlecraft skills such as surface embroidery are also frequently found in combination with quilting.

In addition, more purely ornamental traditions of quilting developed from the functional wadded type.

● **Padding (stuffed) quilting (Trapunto)** has two layers of fabric and the design is outlined by hand or machine stitching in a similar way to wadded quilting. The stitched areas are then stuffed from behind with loose wadding to give a rich, sculptural effect.

● **Corded quilting (Italian)** has two layers of fabric and the design is made by working pairs of narrow parallel lines of stitching in free-style or geometric patterns, either by hand or machine. Cord is then threaded into the resulting channels from behind to give a raised decorative effect.

Examples of corded quilting have survived from the sixteenth century, and from the late seventeenth century there are examples of quilts, hangings and headwear which are closely covered with corded quilting. In the nineteenth century corded quilting was used with whalebone to stiffen the fabric in stays, creating lovely patterns.

● **Shadow quilting** involves stitching together a solid and a semi-transparent top fabric. The design is outlined in a similar way to padded quilting and filled from behind with either colored fabrics, mixed threads, sequins or beads to give the design an unusual effect of diffused colors.

Today, there are few countries in the world where some form of quilting is not worked. Much of it is primarily utilitarian but often decorative at the same time. Although the word 'quilt' brings to mind a bedcover, the technique of quilting can be used on many other items and is particularly suited to clothing: it can also be used as a most attractive technique for such items as wall hangings and cushions.

ABOVE *This contemporary fabric chessboard, made from raw silk patchwork, is lightly wadded and quilted along the seam lines.*

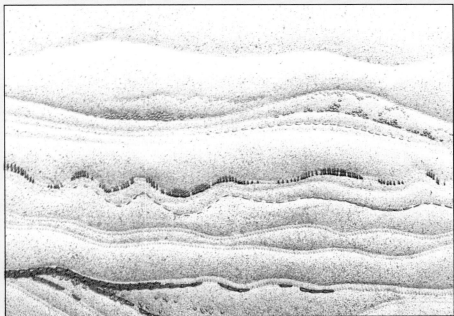

ABOVE *An Irish quilt, loosely based on the design known as Grandmother's Flower Garden. Each 'flower bed' motif is surrounded with white hexagonals, and separated from its neighbors by interlocking red 'paths'. Patchwork made from different configurations of colored hexagon pieces has always been popular, and designing such quilts is the way in which many people first become interested in patchwork.*

FAR LEFT *Simple flower shapes have been quilted in matching threads for this simple but effective bag.*

LEFT *Interesting experimental effects can be achieved by combining several techniques. This piece of spray-dyed firm muslin has been worked in a mixture of hand and machine quilting, with further silk embroidery, to create a delicate landscape.*

MATERIALS AND EQUIPMENT

Fabrics

All kinds of fabrics in plain and mixed colored patterns can be used. However, certain fabrics work better than others.

Generally, smooth, closely woven fabrics such as dressweight cottons, brushed cottons, fine linen, lightweight wool, lawn, poplin, satin, silk or sateen work best. It is better to avoid synthetic, crease-resistant, or very stretchy fabrics as they are more difficult to handle. Preferably fabrics should have a slight sheen to give highlights to the pattern but should not be shiny. The most popular materials today are pure cotton or a polyester/cotton blend. Silk can look beautiful, but it is expensive, difficult to care for, and does not wear well. Heavier damasks, velvets, corduroys, suitings and tweeds combine well together and can be used for bigger machine-sewn projects.

For shadow quilting, a semi-transparent top fabric such as voile, muslin, organza or other sheer silk is used.

Cotton fabrics should be pre-washed and ironed while still damp, to test for color fastness and shrinkage. Avoid using any fabrics where the dyes may run.

With the exception of corded quilting, where an open-weave fabric is used, the backing fabric should be made from the same fiber and of the same quality as the top fabric.

Wadding

The earliest padding used in quilting was rags or wool. With the introduction of cotton, this was utilized as well as wool, although in poorer districts such as South Wales where

wool was too valuable to be used for padding, old blankets, pieces of old clothes, even woollen stockings were used for filling. Quilting still provides a way of using up old blankets as filling, but today several types of manmade fibers are available for padding, making the quilt easy to wash and hardwearing.

Synthetic wadding (batting) is both lightweight and washable and comes in various standard widths and thicknesses. The layers can easily be separated, which means that thinner or thicker waddings (batts) can be made to suit individual needs. The 2 oz (56 g) and 4 oz (112 g) weights are popular for quilting while the thicker 8 oz (224 g) variety is used for tied quilting. Alternative waddings include cotton and wool domettes (woven, fluffy, light-blanket weight), and cotton wadding. Cotton wadding tends to move and separate during washing, which means that it should be closely quilted. It is also more

difficult to sew. All three alternatives give a flatter finish and are heavier than synthetics which is an advantage for hangings.

Loose polyester or cotton fiber is used for padded quilting and three-dimensional quilting.

Quilting cord

This is used for corded quilting and may be unspun soft fleece or white cotton cord. It is available in different thicknesses and can be bought by the yard (metre) from most needlecraft suppliers.

Alternatively, thick loosely spun knitting yarns like Lopi wool, or soft embroidery threads make excellent substitutes. In fact, colored yarns can be combined with a

semi-transparent top fabric to give unusual shadowy effects.

Threads

It is important to choose the thread that will give the best results for your particular needs. Quilting thread is smoother and stronger than ordinary cotton threads and comes in a fairly good selection of colors. Otherwise, No. 50 or No. 60 heavy duty mercerized cotton is an excellent alternative. Cotton/polyester threads and synthetic threads tend to knot and fray and are not generally recommended for hand sewing. However, as with other hand-sewing threads, they can be drawn through a block of beeswax which should

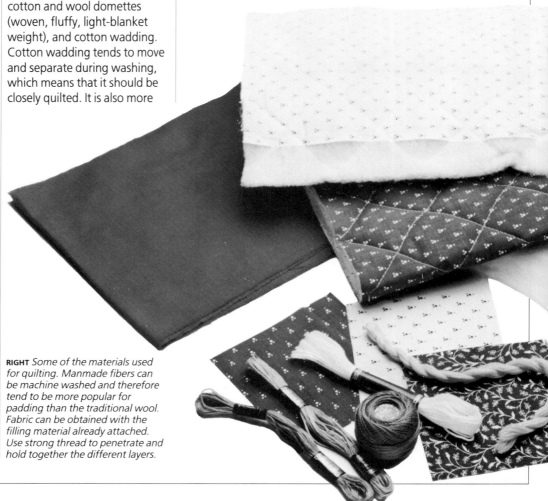

RIGHT *Some of the materials used for quilting. Manmade fibers can be machine washed and therefore tend to be more popular for padding than the traditional wool. Fabric can be obtained with the filling material already attached. Use strong thread to penetrate and hold together the different layers.*

QUILTING ON A FRAME

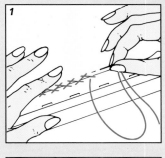

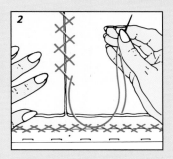

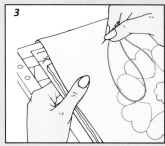

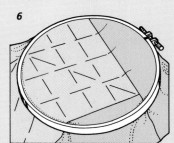

1 Attach backing fabric to runner webbing, wrapping excess round one runner to obtain a convenient size. Secure in frame.
2 Lay padding on top of the backing fabric having trimmed it to the appropriate size. Baste pieces together if necessary, and arrange evenly.
3 Place top fabric over the padding allowing it to hang over unwrapped runner. Baste three layers together at that end and pin them at other end.
4 Use fabric tape to wind zigzag fashion around the side stretchers, and pin these tapes into position on either side through all layers.
5 Quilt stretched area, and then unroll the next section rearranging pinned tapes and securing runner accordingly. Repeat until complete.
6 If you are using a round hoop, extra pieces of fabric stitched to the corners will enable you to quilt into canvas.

strengthen them and prevent twisting.

General sewing equipment

A good selection of pins is needed including fine lace pins for delicate fabrics, dressmaker's stainless pins for general use, and glass-headed pins for pinning together several thicknesses. Being longer than average, the glass-headed pins are much easier on the fingers for pushing through bulky layers of fabric. You will also need a measuring tape and a dressmaker's tracing wheel for transferring designs, using the carbon paper method. Many craftworkers who do not use a thimble for ordinary hand

sewing will find that one, if not two, are essential for quilting. A second thimble is often used on the first finger under the frame to guide the needle back through the fabric. A 2cm (¾in) wide cotton tape is needed for stretching the layers of fabric onto a quilting frame.

Needles

It is as important to practice obtaining the correct size needle and thread to suit your fabric and the way you work, as it is to use the correct needle for the job in hand.

For hand quilting, you will need quilting needles about 1 inch (2.5cm) long or size 8 or 9 betweens, which are slightly longer. For ordinary hand

sewing, a selection of sharps is required and for surface embroidery, crewel needles. For padded and corded quilting, use a large-eyed bodkin and for marking quilting designs, a round-ended tapestry or rug needle.

Scissors

For accurate cutting, use sharp dressmaker's shears, and keep them for cutting only fabrics so as not to blunt the blades. For snipping into corners and curves, when doing padded quilting, and for cutting threads, small embroidery scissors are good. General purpose scissors are needed for cutting paper and cardboard for templates.

Frames and hoops

A frame is an essential piece of equipment for best results in quilting. Some quilters find that a large embroidery hoop is adequate but its use does mean that the work must be very well tacked so that the three layers do not shift when the position of the work on the hoop is changed, and corners need care (see above).

For working large projects such as a full-size quilt, a quilting frame is recommended. On the whole, the advantages of using one outweigh the disadvantages: the work will crease less; less preparatory basting is needed more than one person can

USING A TEMPLATE 1

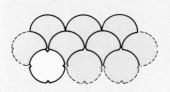

1 Making an all-over shell pattern using a single template.

2 Twisted border showing the template and corner construction.

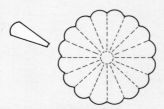

3 Rose motif showing the single template and the central ring, which is always marked.

USING CARBON PAPER

1 Pin the design on the right side of the fabric matching the center lines, and slip the carbon paper between, carbon side down. Avoid pinning through the carbon paper.

USING A TEMPLATE 2

1 Place the template on the right side of the top fabric and lightly draw around the edge with sharpened tailor's chalk or a colored pencil, repeating the marks as needed.

2 Remove the template and fill in the details by hand, or use a smaller template of the correct segment. Always mark the center ring to avoid confusing lines crossing in the middle.

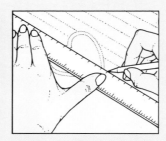

Use a long ruler to mark all background patterns.

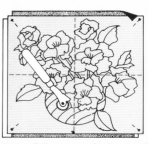

2 Carefully go over the lines with a tracing wheel or an empty ballpoint pen. Try not to press on the surrounding area to prevent transferring unwanted marks.

work at the frame; and you can stitch right up to the edges using both hands. However, the main disadvantage is its size, which means that it cannot be moved around as easily as a smaller frame.

The simplest quilting frame is made from two long pieces of wood known as rails, and two shorter, flat pieces of wood which are known as stretchers. The stretchers fit into slots in the rails and are held in place by pegs. Both rails have a strip of strong material such as braid or upholsterer's webbing nailed to the inner edge. Each end of this type of frame can then rest on the back of a chair and can easily be put

away when quilting has finished for the day.

The top, padding and backing are placed together and basted across one end. This is then sewn to the webbing on one of the rails and wound round until approximately 24 inches (61cm) remain free and can be basted to the webbing on the other rail. The stretchers are then attached and pegged to keep the work taut. After each breadth has been quilted, it is wound on to the front rail and another is unwound from the back.

Templates

Templates are often used for

marking quilting designs on to the fabric. A template can either be a complete motif, such as the outline of a flower or leaf, or a small unit repeated within a larger motif, such as the petals of a flower. They may be bought from craft suppliers, but it is not difficult to make your own by tracing the design on to a suitable material, such as carboard, plastic or metal, and cutting it out.

Where a pattern is to be built up from a repeated unit, notch the edges of the template to show where the shapes meet up.

The template is placed on the quilt top and a yarn needle

RIGHT *In this baby's crib cover a heart-shaped template has been used to repeat a traditional motif over the entire quilt, using a simple square grid in a modern way.*

Interestingly, the grid lines are treated as a feature of the design and contrast well with the quilted texture of the heart motifs. Here, each heart is outlined in purple and filled with a different combination of line patterns in shaded colors, picked up from the binding fabric.

A BABY'S QUILT

or bodkin used to trace round it, leaving a mark on the fabric which is the sewing line. Traditionally, only the outline of the quilting pattern is marked, and the remainder sewn in freehand. On dark materials, very finely sharpened tailor's chalk may be used for marking. It is possible to buy marking pens, the color of which will wash out; lead pencils should never be used for marking as they leave a muddy line which never completely disappears.

Dressmaker's carbon paper

Dressmaker's carbon paper is also used for transferring designs to fabric and gives a fairly long-lasting mark. It is available in several colors including red, yellow, blue, black and white.

This method is relatively quick and reliable and suitable for opaque fabrics. Choose a light colored carbon paper for dark fabrics but, for other colors, a close tone is better. This prevents any excess carbon from staining the fabric and rubbing off on to the quilting threads. Although it will wash off, carbon staining can be an unnecessary irritation. Draw your design on tracing paper.

Sewing machines

A sewing machine is an excellent labor-saving piece of equipment for quick quilting, as well as for stitching very long seams needed in making up items and for many finishing processes.

For best results, choose a machine that will give a good straight stitch, and, if possible, with a reverse stitch for starting and finishing, and a zigzag stitch for quick seaming.

DESIGN

*T*he simplest quilting is based on diagonal lines making squares. Another simple method is to follow the lines of a patterned fabric. In patchwork quilt-making, for example, each geometric shape is outlined either in the seam or just outside, or, alternatively, patches can be filled with contrasting geometric patterns. Appliqué shapes can also be emphasized with several contour lines, as in Hawaiian appliqué work, or freely stitched lines can be repeated at random over an entire surface.

For more intricate designs, templates are used to mark the motifs on the fabric.

Care should be taken in planning the design, which should be suitable in every way for the article which it is to decorate. For instance, if making a bed quilt, the central pattern should fit the top of the bed, and when quilting clothing, the patterns should be central to the figure. When making quilted clothing, the garment should not be cut out until the quilting has been completed, as the quilting pulls in the work slightly making it a little smaller.

While planning the design it is worth remembering that

when natural fibers such as sheep's wool or cotton are used for the filling the lines of quilting should be no more than 2 inches (5cm) apart, in order to prevent shifting, but with manmade fibers, which are usually sold in sheets, the spaces between the lines of stitching can be wider.

Traditional designs are generally more formal and symmetrical and are better for quilts, coverlets and cushions. Contemporary designs tend to depict informal subjects in an asymmetrical way and are more suitable for hangings, pictorial scenes, clothes and accessories.

A traditional design is carefully built up to give a well-

balanced overall effect. Single images are placed around a prominent central motif, linked with background 'filler' patterns and usually bordered with corner motifs.

Spirals, flowers, leaves, lovers' knots and hearts, fans, feathers, shells and chains are all typical traditional motifs.

Many of these have some significance: pineapples, for

ABOVE *A selection of traditional borders showing plain and feathered twists, plaited chains and running feather designs, plus swagged crescents, to be used as a continuous band around a design or combined with corner motifs.*

BELOW *Traditional motifs of circles, flowers, leaves, fans and hearts, used singly or repeated to make composite shapes for central designs, or corner motifs.*

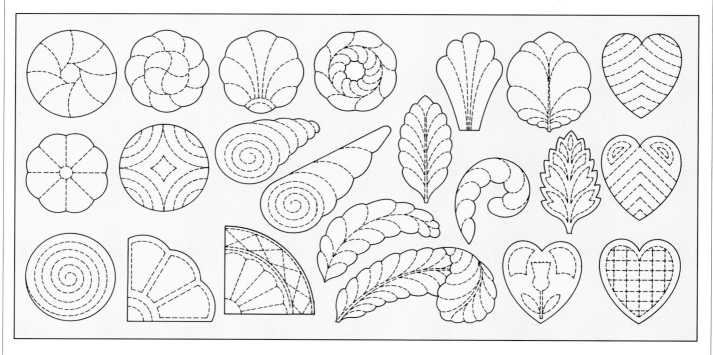

ABOVE *An attractive modern quilt that could be used as a wall hanging. Traditional quilting and patchwork was the inspiration for this piece, but the maker has broken up the design in some sections to achieve a smashed window effect.*

example, were the sign of hospitality, and pomegranates the sign of fruitfulness. The Rose of Sharon used on marriage quilts came from the Song of Solomon, 'I am the Rose of Sharon and the Lily of the Valley'. It was always considered unlucky to sew a heart on any but a bride's quilt.

As well as templates, sheets of traditional designs are available which can either be traced directly on to fabric, or cut up and rearranged to suit your own needs. On most quilting patterns the inner shapes indicated by broken lines are filled in freehand after transferring the outline. The inner lines on stencils are already punched out so that they can easily be filled in.

Background patterns consisting of straight lines can be marked directly on to the fabric using a ruler and colored pencil. Masking tape is also an effective way of marking simple straight lines. Other backgrounds involving units such as the hexagon and shell are best transferred by template or carbon paper.

Borders around a design must be marked accurately and

at right angles to each other. It is a good idea to needle-score two parallel lines to the width of the border as a guide for keeping the patterns straight. Make sure the template size fits evenly into the length of each border, adjusting the corners to it.

Contemporary designs reflecting everyday images often follow a more relaxed style and range from simple contour quilting, through nursery shapes and alphabets, to pictorial landscapes and large figurative or abstract compositions – color and mass being used as an artist would treat a painting.

Working from a photograph, a design can be developed in which quilting is used to give texture and depth to a naturalistic yet formalised picture. The photograph of a family of sheep was used to make line drawings exploring the basic shapes and then translated into an embroidered picture in which the quilting emphasizes the round shapes and curly texture of the sheep and sets them against a background of trees simply outlined.

Hand and machine quilting can be combined to create a variety of texture, as in the flower garden pattern on this the vest (*right*). Here the delicate flowers have been hand quilted at the bottom of the design, and then machine quilting has been employed to form confident, flowing curves giving a further dimension. The contrast between the crowded detail of the flowers and the open, free style machining sets off the effect of both.

ABOVE *This example of chintz appliquéd onto a quilt was worked by Mrs Isabella Wainwright and her daughters in the early 1850s.*

LEFT *This contemporary vest is machine quilted in wavy lines, with hand quilting around the flowers at the bottom.*

SHEEP PROJECT

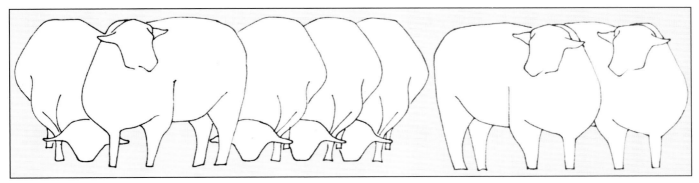

Drawn from a photograph, the traced line drawings make good basic shapes which can be adapted to various needlework techniques exploring the shape, line, tone and texture. The quilted interpretation expresses the rounded forms and soft texture of the animals.

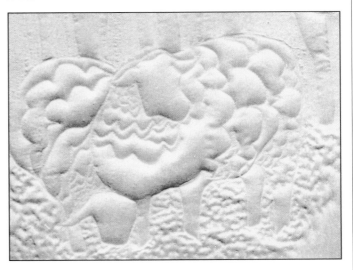

STITCHES

Although small quilting stitches are commendable, the regularity and evenness of the stitches are more important than the actual size.

The stitch most commonly used for traditional quilting is running stitch which gives a pleasing broken line. The traditional quilting stitch is not a stab stitch where the needle goes down then up again in two separate movements, but a true running stitch where several stitches are taken up on the needle before it is pulled through. One hand should be held underneath the work to guide the needle back to the top. At first it may be possible only to take one stitch on the needle at a time, but it is advisable to practise until five or six stitches can be made before drawing through the needle and cotton. The use of a running stitch means that the quilt will be completely reversible.

Where a more pronounced line is required back stitch may be used. Many other embroidery stitches may also be used particularly for wadded quilting. Chain stitch and Portuguese knotted stemstitch are most suitable, but it is worth experimenting with other line stitches for their decorative qualities. The stitch, however, should not be too dominant. Even stitching is more important than tiny stitches, when using running stitch – an approximate guide for length is from ⅛–¼ inch (3.6 mm), depending on the thickness of the wadding used.

Machine quilting

Machine quilting is fast and direct and appeals to many contemporary quilters mainly because they can express their ideas quickly, and, perhaps, more spontaneously. Machine quilting, however, produces a harder line and lacks the beautiful softness of hand quilting.

Careful preparation is the main requirement for success with free machine quilting. Top fabric, padding, and a backing fabric, such as muslin, must be sandwiched and carefully pinned all around the edges. Then, starting from the center, make parallel lines of basting up to the fabric edges to form a grid, and then sew more lines radiating from the center point in star fashion.

Pin and baste the layers together as for hand quilting, and stitch the design, working outwards from the middle. Use a medium length stitch and loosen the tension if the wadding is very thick. You may also need a larger needle.

Any form of free stitching may be used, but simple lines of free running stitch produce good results rapidly. The fabrics may be too thick to frame, in which case the darning foot must be used. During quilting, fabrics tend to 'shrink', so allow extra fabric on all dimensions.

It may require several attempts and specific practice in order to machine a line exactly straight or to follow flowing curves and make perfect circles. Use both hands to feed the fabric under the needle and do not machine faster than you can comfortably control the fabric.

Finish the quilting and neaten the threads by first pulling them through to the back of the work. Thread them into a needle and make a small

HAND QUILTING

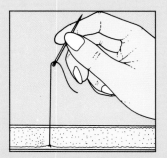

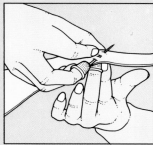

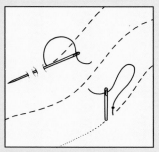

1 Use a fairly short thread, about 20 inches (50cm) long. Wax the thread and knot the cut end to prevent twisting. Bring the needle out and pull the knot through the backing, leaving it caught under wadding.

2 With a thimble on the second finger of the sewing hand, make several stitches. Keep the thumb pressed down on the fabric just ahead of the needle while the other hand below, feels the needle and guides it back through.

3 To finish, make a knot close to last stitch and take thread through to back. Pull knot through catching it under wadding, and cut thread. Working with several needles in a design is easier than stopping and starting new threads.

TIED QUILTING

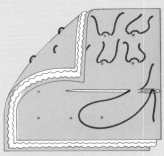

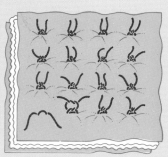

1 Mark generously spaced dots onto the fabric as if for smocking, in the required pattern. Baste all the layers together.

2 Sew the thread or threads through all the layers at each dot. Leave one long end, work a back stitch with the other and tie off with knot or bow.

BUTTON QUILTING

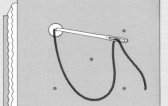

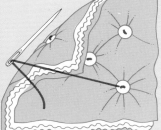

1 Proceed initially as for tied quilting, but sew a button over each dot, with another placed precisely underneath it on the backing.

2 Secure the buttons firmly. They should sink down into the fabric. End off the thread amongst the central padding after every few buttons.

ABOVE LEFT *This charming Album quilt was made for Mrs. Fauset by friends as well as the staff of Warrington College of Art, England where she was a tutor for 20 years. It was to mark her retirement, and the family depicted in the panel at the center of the quilt are Mrs Fauset, her husband and children.*

LEFT *A small purse with a decoration of tied quilting in silk threads.*

back stitch. Pass the needle through the wadding, bring it out a short distance away and cut close to the surface.

A quilting bar can be fitted to the sewing machine and provides an excellent guide for stitching parallel lines. After marking and stitching the first line, adjust the bar so that it rests on the previously stitched line.

Tied quilting and button quilting

As a quick alternative to traditional quilting methods, the layers of fabric may be tied together with knots. This method arose when quilts were stuffed with a lining that was not easy to sew, such as newspapers or even corn cobs; as with stitches, the knots are arranged to create a pattern on

the top layer. Baste the layers of fabric together, mark out the pattern for the knots on the top fabric, and take the thread through all the layers at the point for the knot.

In the same way, button quilting secures each point where the layers are held together with a button instead of a knot. The buttons are stitched tightly to the fabric, without a shank.

WADDED QUILTING

Wadded quilting uses a layer of wadding (batting) between two outer fabrics and, as its name implies, is traditionally made for warmth. The top fabric may be whatever you choose, with a layer of wadding of appropriate thickness and texture; the backing layer should be of the same or slightly firmer weight than the top fabric so that the puffiness is thrown forward. Allow extra fabric and wadding to counteract the 'shrinkage' when quilting. In addition cut the backing fabric larger for attaching to the frame.

Wadded quilting is perfect for all kinds of quilts and throws, jackets, trousers, vests and mitts, as well as a decorative finish for bags and accessories and many household items such as cushion sets and rugs, and egg, tea- and coffee-pot cosies.

Cutting the layers

Following the grainlines, cut the three layers of fabric (top, wadding (batting) and backing) slightly larger than the finished size, as quilting tends to shrink the work. If, on large items, the top and backing fabrics need to be joined from several widths, place a full width in the middle with half widths at each side – in this way a center seam is avoided. Join wadding in the same way, butting the edges together and securing with herringbone stitch to avoid a bulk seam.

Marking the fabric

It is much easier if the top fabric is marked before the layers are assembled together. First lightly press the fabric into quarters to find the center, and make any other divisions helpful for placing or constructing your design. Transfer the design to the right side of the fabric using templates or dressmaker's carbon paper; for marking straight lines, use a colored pencil or round-ended needle and a long, flat ruler. Lines can be overlapped or crossed to make lozenge, diamond or basket patterns.

Assembling the layers

Place the backing layer right side down on a smooth surface, the center wadding on top. Place the top fabric right side up on the wadding. Smooth the fabrics out from the center and pin the layers together. Check that the backing is smooth, and baste the layers together, covering the area with several rows of basting stitches worked across in both directions, first diagonally through the center and then in rows about 2½ inches (6 cm) apart. Avoid knots (which can be difficult to remove from the finished quilting) by working outwards from the center, leaving half the length of thread in the center when basting one half row, and returning to rethread and complete the row in the opposite direction. Smooth out any wrinkles as you stitch outside edges. Attach the work to the frame – a slightly looser tension is needed than that used for embroidery.

If using a hoop, put the hoop in the center of the work and gradually work towards the edges as each area is completed. In order to quilt the edges, pieces of similar fabric should be basted around the work. This extends the area and makes it possible to keep the edges evenly stretched while quilting.

Stitching

Using an up and down movement, commence working from the center of the piece outwards. This enables the work to be kept smooth.

ABOVE *This cushion is quilted in a contrasting shade of coton à broder to emphasize the design, and the edges are piped in a toning contrast.*

BELOW *This enchanting child's horse saddle is thought to have belonged to an Indian prince. It is made completely from tussore silk, and quilted with simple linear patterns.*

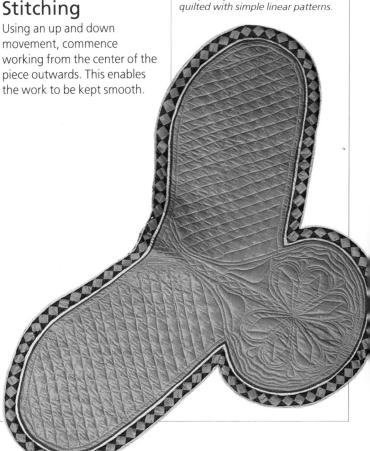

STARTING TO QUILT

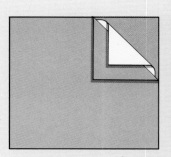

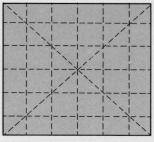

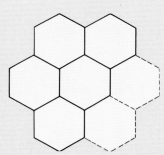

1 Care should be taken to prepare the fabric properly, particularly if a frame is not being used. Arrange the layers on a flat surface.

2 Place the padding on top of the backing fabric and cover both with the top fabric. Baste them down with horizontal, vertical and lastly diagonal lines.

3 and 4 Diamonds and hexagons are simple geometric designs which create an attractive regular effect. A ruler and set-square are needed to mark the diamonds, and a template for the hexagons.

Where the back of the work will not be seen, as in a quilt, begin with a small knot which is pulled through into the wadding. Finish stitching with a tiny backstitch, the needle splitting the last stitch. The end of the thread is run into the wadding before being cut off.

If the back of the work will not be visible, the stitching may be begun and ended with two tiny backstitches, running the thread into the wadding before cutting off.

Modern approaches

Not all traditional quilting need be worked on plain fabric with matching colored thread. Designs can be simplified and interpreted in contemporary fabrics, threads and colors to suit present-day settings. Glamorous silks with beautiful faint watermarking, wild silks with lightly textured surfaces, heavy sateens, slipper satin, several types of upholstery satins and silks, all with soft, lustrous surfaces, can be used together with heavier silk threads or coton à broder in

contrasting or variegated colors for the quilting, and piping, backing fabric or lining picked out in a slightly stronger color. This could be softly patterned (a fabric from an existing interior scheme) in diagonal stripes, pin-head spots, ikat fabric, plain cotton or satin to offset the shape. Cushions worked like this often have greater impact made in sets. Here the designs could be varied but linked by using the same accent colors or vice versa, choosing harmonizing well-balanced colors. Use traditional quilting designs for all sizes of cushions and bolsters, a bedside rug, sofa throw, quilt, and, in carefully worked out proportions, on garment cuffs and yokes. A more experimental approach might be used to design such items as vests, evening jackets or wall hangings.

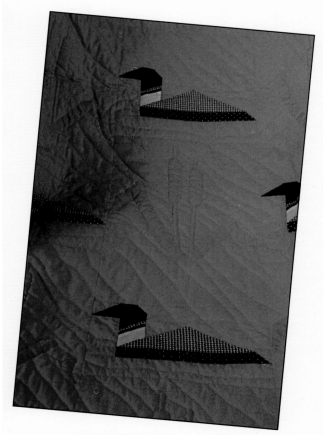

ABOVE *Loon and Rattails quilt. The very brilliant green quilted background, subtle bullrushes and simple well- placed ducks all combine to create an unusual and striking quilt.*

MACHINE QUILTING

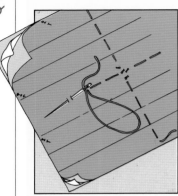

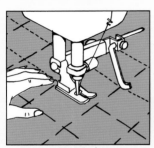

1 Mark the design on the right side of the top layer of fabric with a marking pencil. Sandwich the batting between the two fabric layers and baste them together. Work the basting stitches horizontally and vertically at 4 inch (10cm) intervals across the layers, working from the center outward in each direction. Finish by working two diagonal lines from corner to corner.
2 Loosen the pressure on the machine to allow the basted layers to pass easily beneath the foot. Stitch carefully along the design lines using straight stitch; pay particular attention to curves and corners. Remove the basting stitches when the quilting is completed.

SASHIKO

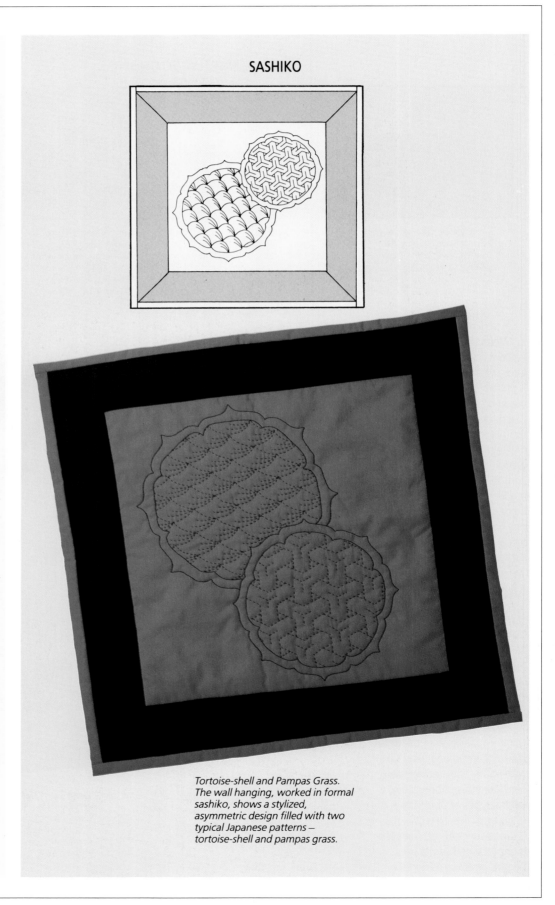

Tortoise-shell and Pampas Grass. The wall hanging, worked in formal sashiko, shows a stylized, asymmetric design filled with two typical Japanese patterns — tortoise-shell and pampas grass.

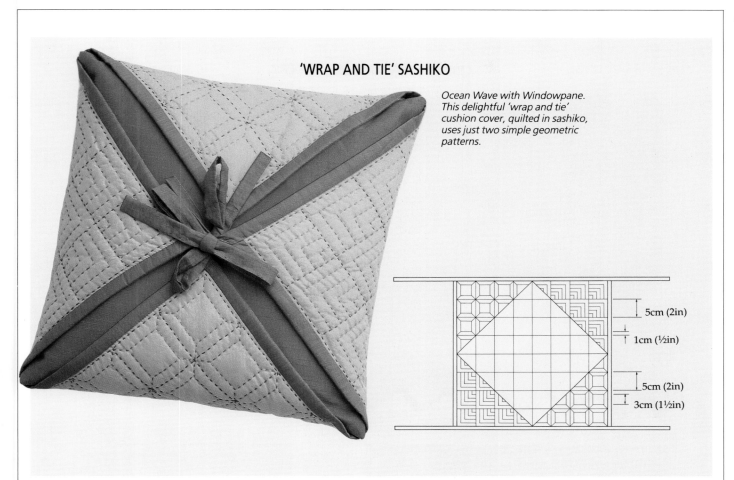

'WRAP AND TIE' SASHIKO

Ocean Wave with Windowpane. This delightful 'wrap and tie' cushion cover, quilted in sashiko, uses just two simple geometric patterns.

5cm (2in)

1cm (½in)

5cm (2in)

3cm (1½in)

Japanese quilting (sashiko)

Japanese quilting, known as *sashiko*, combines stylized motifs and patterns with clear, primary colors to create strikingly simple designs. *Sashiko* originated in rural Japan where the women of fishing and farming communities used it to decorate most of their outer garments. Coats, jackets, aprons, gloves and socks were quilted mainly in white on a dark blue cotton fabric, essentially for warmth. Beautiful, often complex-looking all-over patterns are quilted with running stitch, using a simple grid system. The grid is stitched first and the squares are filled in with designs. One garment may have one or many designs often separated with asymmetric lines. Frequently in more sophisticated *sashiko*, used especially to decorate the traditional *obi,* naturalistic motifs and designs are superimposed on a background of geometric patterns in imitation of elaborate woven silks.

Use *sashiko* quilting either as an all-over pattern or as inset blocks or panels for a jacket, waistcoat, trousers, dressing gown, bag, baby carrier, crib cover or wall hanging.

Cotton is the traditional fabric used in *sashiko*. As in English quilting, traditional motifs and patterns are used in the designs: illustrated here are two patterns known by the delightful names of Tortoise-shell and Pampas grass.

Machined wadded quilting

For geometric designs where the harder line of machine stitching is appropriate, the sewing machine comes into its own.

Mark the design on the right side of the top layer of fabric with a marking pencil. Sandwich the batting between the two fabric layers and baste them together. Work the basting stitches horizontally and vertically at 4 inch (10cm) intervals across the layers, working from the center outward in each direction. Finish by working two diagonal lines from corner to corner.

Loosen the pressure on the machine to allow the basted layers to pass easily beneath the foot. Stitch carefully along the design lines using straight stitch; pay particular attention to curves and corners. Remove the basting stitches when the quilting is completed.

After a little experience of machining straight, geometric patterns, it can be quite stimulating to try a freer approach. Lines of quilting can be purposely made crooked and yet, worked within the confines of a basic idea, can still suggest freedom and spontaneity. Areas of lively textures are created by simply 'taking your machine needle for a walk' and one area contrasted against another to form an all-over pattern. You can 'doodle' with the machine needle like a pencil. Free machining offers fresh scope for interpreting movement and mood in a design.

CREATIVE MACHINE EMBROIDERY

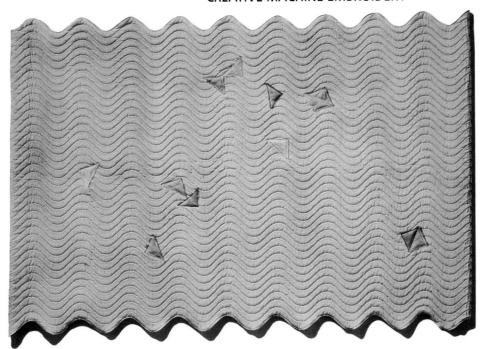

A more formal, symbolic water design is suggested by machining evenly spaced wavy lines over the entire surface. In this delightful quilted wall hanging, pastel colored fragments of fabric are appliquéd on top suggesting flotsam gently moving on the waves.

*Everyday shapes can be a source of inspiration. This drawing of the contents of an old school paintbox (**ABOVE**) sparked off the idea for an elaborately quilted vest. (**RIGHT**). Folded, pleated and crumpled tissue paper was used to assess possible approaches (**LEFT**), before experimenting with fabric.*

'PAINTBOX' WAISTCOAT

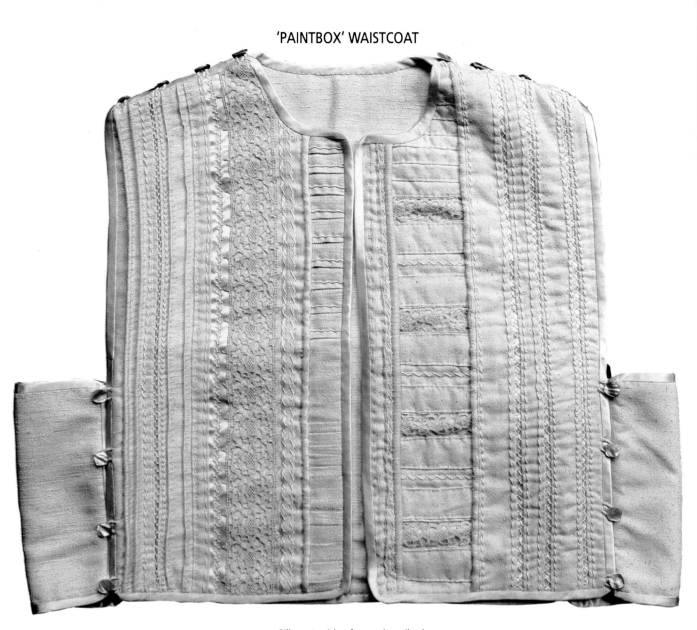

Silk vest, with a free-style quilted design based on an open paint box. The pattern made by the fittings inside the paint box (LEFT) inspired this experiment with free machine quilting.

PADDED QUILTING (TRAPUNTO)

QUILTING

*P*added (stuffed) quilting is a purely decorative technique using two layers of fabric where certain areas of a design are padded from behind, which gives the surface a pleasing, undulating texture.

The depth of the molding can be varied to create shallow relief or highly raised effects for both traditional and contemporary designs. The technique offers great scope for utilizing more unusual top fabrics such as stretchy nylons and knits, velvets, velours and taffetas, as well as the more usual varieties. For the backing, choose a soft, open-weave fabric such as muslin, scrim or voile. When planning your design, each area to be padded must be completely enclosed to make a good shape. Use padding quilting for pillows, bags, and pictures, picture frames and hangings.

Light padding creates a subtle texture, as in the charming eighteenth-century style design on the cushion cover shown here. In this example, corded quilting (*see below*) has been used for the basket, while the fruit shapes are softly padded to create a blistered effect. Note that the shapes in the foreground are slightly more padded than those behind to make full use of three-dimensionalism.

With increased padding, this technique can be used to create all kinds of fabric sculpture, such as the contemporary picture of a doll.

Here the three-dimensional appearance has been wittily increased by making the right hand separately and by painting in shadows with fabric dye.

The method can be taken to extremes to create solid objects of soft sculpture such as the quilted teapot. Here again the fabric has been painted for realism, with the staining inside applied with tannin-colored acrylic paint.

BELOW *Soft sculptured teapot and lid made from quilted cotton and synthetic wadding.*

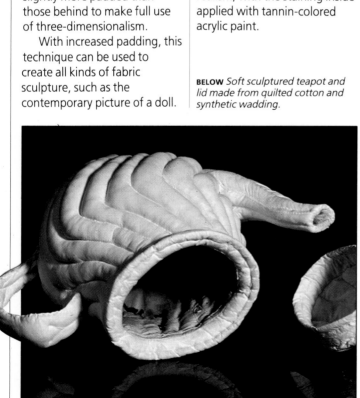

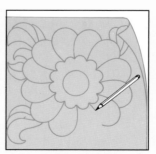 

1 Cut out the main fabric and backing to the same size and transfer the design, in reverse, to the backing fabric, using dressmaker's carbon paper.

2 Place both fabric wrong sides together and, working outwards from the center, baste diagonally and vertically in both directions.

246

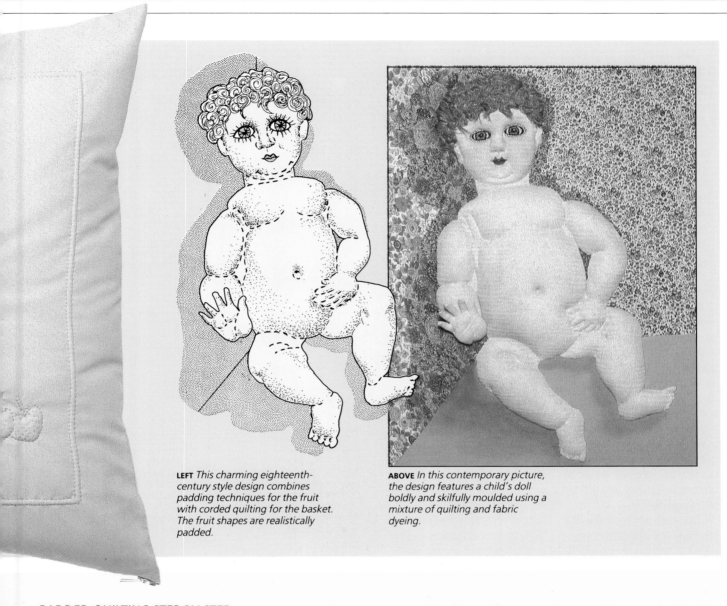

LEFT *This charming eighteenth-century style design combines padding techniques for the fruit with corded quilting for the basket. The fruit shapes are realistically padded.*

ABOVE *In this contemporary picture, the design features a child's doll boldly and skilfully moulded using a mixture of quilting and fabric dyeing.*

PADDED QUILTING STEP BY STEP

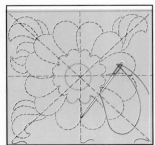

3 Outline the design with small running stitches by hand or machine, taking care to pick up both layers. Work from the center out.

4 Remove the basting threads and then, working from the wrong side, snip the backing in the middle of each area to be padded using small embroidery scissors.

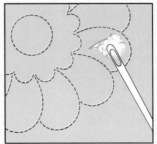

5 Using a round-ended bodkin or a small crochet hook, stuff the shapes with teased-out wadding.

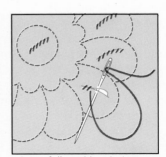

6 Carefully mold each shape, periodically checking the effect on the right side. Finally, slip stitch the openings together, and neaten the finished work with a lining.

CORDED QUILTING (ITALIAN)

Corded quilting uses two layers of fabric and has, as its name suggests, a ridged, linear appearance. The designs are carefully worked out in pairs of parallel lines, which are later filled with cord or quilting wool. The whole effect is of flowing continuous movement. Many traditional designs are based on geometric lines involving intricate tracery and beautiful interlaced patterns, as well as detailed flower arrangements and naturalistic figures in domestic scenes.

Corded quilting can be worked by hand or machine. On many zigzag machines, twin needles can be used to create parallel lines of stitching quickly and efficiently. Follow handbook instructions when using these – if handled improperly, they will break easily and are expensive to replace.

CORDING TECHNIQUES

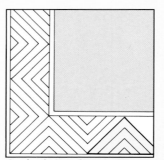

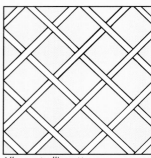

Border design of interlocking triangles, which, when filled with cord, gives a pleasing contrast to the plain center.

All-over trellis pattern constructed with interwoven parallel lines.

1 Transfer your design to the backing fabric and pin the two layers together, right sides outward. From the center, baste diagonally and vertically in both directions, adding more lines of tacking on larger projects.

2 Working on the wrong side, hand sew around the design using small running stitches, being careful to stop and start new channels as suggested by the design. Simple designs can be machine sewn.

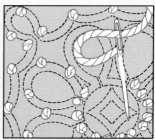

3 With the wrong side facing, separate the backing threads, or snip into the channel, and insert a bodkin threaded with quilted cord. It is best to have a short length of cord in the needle and not to pull the cord too tightly. Pass it through the channel a little at a time, bringing it out at angles and curves.

4 Reinsert the needle into the same hole leaving a small loop of cord on the surface – these will eventually become eased into the channels.

Corded quilting is most suited to a closely woven top fabric and a loosely woven backing, as in padded quilting. Linen and linen scrim are the traditional fabrics used – these are hardwearing and launder well – with a cotton cord or soft yarn for the quilting. Although piping cord now makes a good alternative it gives a slightly harder effect. Incidentally, all cords should be washed first to prevent shrinkage later on.

There are two methods of working. The one-layer method is best suited to stiffer cords. To do this press the fabric and mark the design by the chosen method, on the right side of the fabric. Frame up the fabric.

One hand holds the cord in place under the fabric. The other hand works herringbone stitch across the parallel lines of the design, on the back side of the fabric. This gives the appearance of two lines of back stitch on the right side and holds the cord in place as the work proceeds. Where lines cross each other cut the cord close to the stitching. The finished piece is then usually lined to prevent rubbing and to give a neat finish.

The two-layer method is more versatile and more

generally used. Channels are created with parallel lines through the two layers of fabric and then filled with cord.

An important design consideration, using the two-layer technique, is to carefully plan on paper the exit and entry points for threading the cord. Try to bring out the needle at corners and junctions, to give clear definition to your design.

For a smart, sophisticated look, work the quilting in fabrics such as moiré silk or taffeta for dress panels and accessories, and choose cotton, linen or cotton/wool mixes for coverlets, cushions and pillows.

Worked closely over an entire surface area, corded quilting gives a very pleasing blistered effect. Designs can be worked with different thicknesses of cord to raise certain parts of a design higher than others, and to suggest an illusion of perspective, as shown in the pillow.

Fabrics with a matt surface, such as linen, firm cotton, fine wool and brushed cottons, are best for this type of design. Slightly narrower channels are used in the quatrefoil to give it the appearance of being behind the circle. Instead of

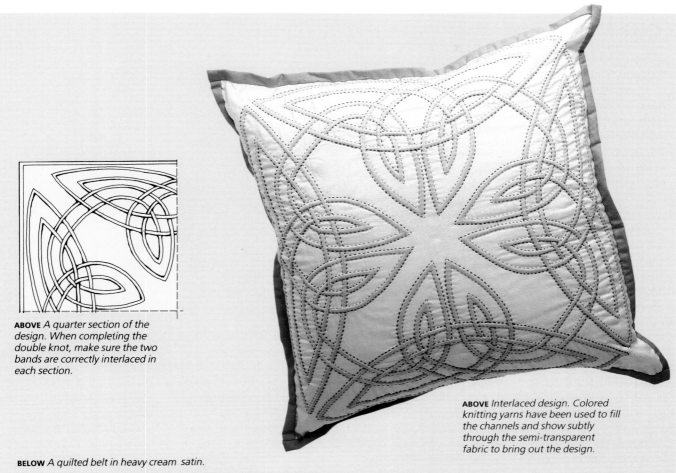

ABOVE *A quarter section of the design. When completing the double knot, make sure the two bands are correctly interlaced in each section.*

ABOVE *Interlaced design. Colored knitting yarns have been used to fill the channels and show subtly through the semi-transparent fabric to bring out the design.*

BELOW *A quilted belt in heavy cream satin.*

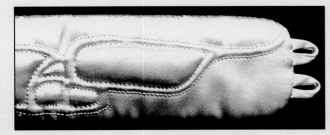

To cord quilt the basket handle in the 'Fruit Basket' design on page 246, use a single strand of quilting yarn and insert the needle through the backing fabric, from right to left. Pull through and reinsert it in the next channel from left to right. Continue in this way, leaving a small loop at each end. Do not pull tightly, otherwise the twisted cane handle effect will be lost.

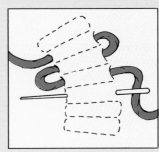

quilting cord, use stranded embroidery cotton, pearl threads or coton à broder for more intricate shaping. With a lightweight fabric, colored cord is often used to show subtly through the top layer with a pleasant shadowy effect.

Interlacing designs are traditional favorites for corded quilting techniques, ranging from simple trellis patterns to more complex knot formations.

Certain interlacing designs can be puzzling to work. To avoid unnecessary complications, it is important when stitching the channels to make sure that they follow an 'under and over' sequence throughout.

Though it is rather exacting work and time-consuming, corded quilting gives very satisfying results. Use it on small, precious pieces such as a set of scatter cushions, pot-

pourri or lavender sachets — with an open-weave backing to allow the perfume to escape — or as a center motif on a baby-carriage or crib cover.

Machine corded quilting

Mark the design on to the right side of the top layer of fabric with a marking pencil. Baste the two layers together as for

padded quilting, with the wrong sides facing.

Stitch along the design lines using a widely spaced twin needle and straight stitch. If your machine will not take a twin needle, work the two rows of stitching separately with a single needle.

Remove the basting stitches and thread pre-shrunk, fine filler cord through the channels using a tapestry needle.

SHADOW QUILTING

Shadow quilting is a variation of padded quilting using two layers of fabric with colored insertions under the semi-transparent top layer to give the design fascinating effects in soft, muted colors.

Transparent fabrics of all kinds can be used for the top layer. Traditional voile, muslin and organdie will give a crisp finish while modern synthetic sheers, being much softer and more pliable, are perhaps better for this kind of shadow quilting. Some of the knitted sheers available may be too stretchy, which is a point to bear in mind when buying.

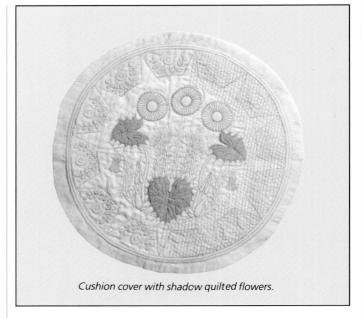

Cushion cover with shadow quilted flowers.

Muslin or scrim can be used for the backing, and a variety of bright, even vibrant colored fabrics or threads for the filling. As colors become subdued (shadowy) under the top fabric, subtle and delicate effects can be achieved, or quite shocking contrasts can be used and will still be interestingly muted. Fascinating effects can be achieved by inserting sequins, glitter fabrics and threads, even beads, under the sheer fabric of the top layer.

Designing for shadow quilting has the same basic limitations as padded quilting. Individual shapes are enclosed with stitching, either by hand or machine, and padded from behind in exactly the same way.

Use shadow quilting for spot motifs on garments, for bags, cushion sets, pictures and pieced-quilt blocks – even for mock jewellery.

This is the perfect technique in which a beginner can experiment by making small and beautiful pieces such as the pincushion shown. Here a synthetic sheer top layer over a light-colored cotton backing features nine triangular pockets containing a selection of mixed-colored sewing threads and bright red star-shaped sequins.

More ambitiously, the large floral cushion combines contemporary shadow work techniques with wadded and padded quilting and surface embroidery in an innovative design.

In this delightful cushion, the outlines of summer flowers are stitched through a synthetic sheer placed over a printed curtain fabric. The flower centers are padded from behind with mixed-fiber threads and sequins, and outlined on the right side with tufts of colored threads worked in knot stitch. Certain petals are padded with slivers of toning fabrics before the sheer is placed on top.

The entire surface is freely stitched, picking out areas of flowers and foliage to balance the design, as the particular print dictates. French knots are scattered over petals and running stitch is worked along the veins of leaves. The finished shadowy effect gently diffuses the printed design with subtle colors.

Use such shadowy flower designs for extra special quilts, covers and cushions.

LEFT *A repeat pattern of trees, in shadow quilting. Some shapes are filled with flat pieces of colored felt, inserted from the back, others are stuffed with colored fabrics to give a more rounded surface.*

RIGHT *Shadow-quilted triangular pincushion.*

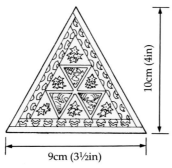

ABOVE *A 1930s cushion cover in shadow quilting. White organdie is laid over brightly colored fabrics, giving the effect of muted pastel shades and a 'quilted' surface.*

LEFT *Measurement diagram for the pincushion pattern.*

10cm (4in)

9cm (3½in)

FINISHING

There are several ways of finishing the edges on quilted work depending on the function of the particular item. Quilts and coverlets, for example, can be self-neatened (making the edge reversible) – bound, bordered or piped – whereas garments and accessories usually need to be cut out from the quilted fabric and finished as instructed in the pattern.

Remove the work from the frame, take out all the basting threads, and finish the edges using one of the following methods.

Reversible edge

Trim the wadding back to the finished size, and, if needed, trim the top and backing to within ½ inch (1.5cm) of the wadding. Turn both the fabric edges to the inside, lapping one edge over the wadding. Press and pin the edges together and then stitch round the quilt as close to the edge as possible, catching in the wadding. Stitch a second line ¼–½ inch (6–15mm) further in.

This is the traditional method of finishing a quilt in Britain, using two rows of running stitch, ⅛ inch (3mm) apart. Some early American quilts were finished in this way, but in others the bordered method was used.

Bordered

For this type of finish the backing fabric is cut a little bigger than the top, taken over to the right side, turned under and neatly hemmed down.

Binding

As fabrics became more plentiful it became customary to bind the edge either with a self color or a contrast.

Use either commercial binding, which is available in different fabrics and widths, or cut your own bias strips from the fabric used. For large items such as quilts, long strips are needed and should be made following the instructions given on the opposite page. You will need fabric at least 20 inches (50cm) wide.

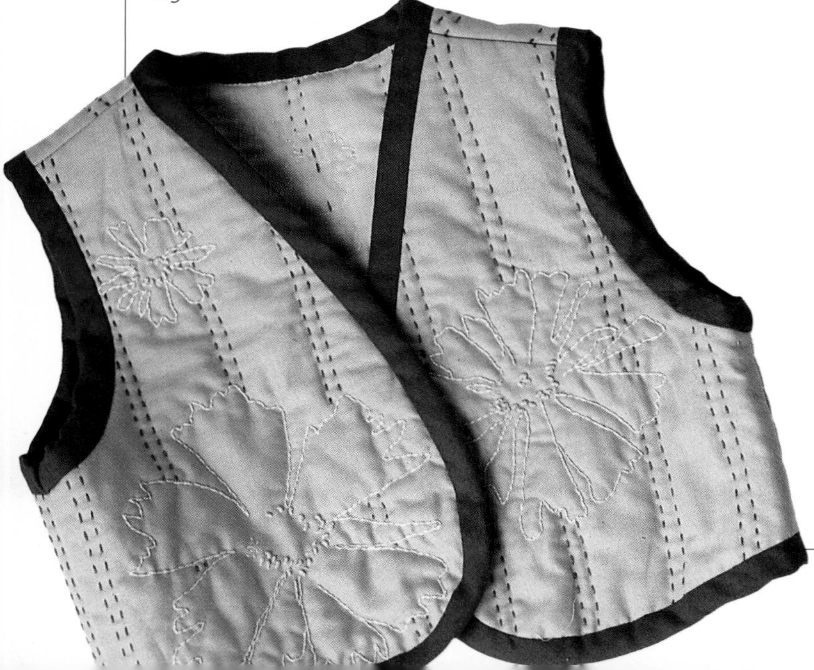

BELOW *Quilted vest with bound edges.*

BINDING

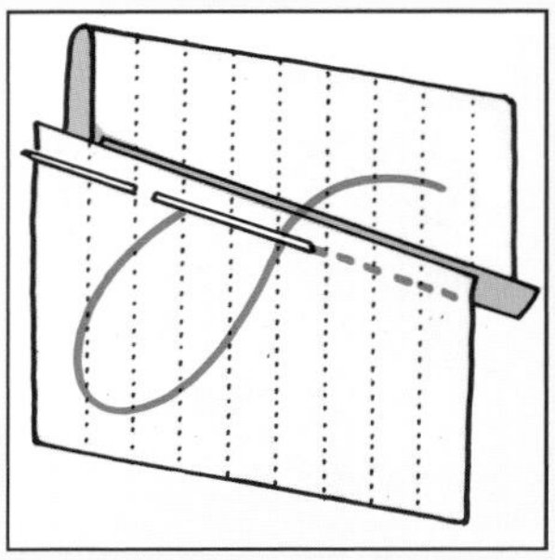

__1__ On the wrong side, mark the fabric with diagonal lines 2-3 inches (5-8cm) apart and trim off the corners. With right sides together, fold the fabric in half on the straight grain and stitch with one strip extending beyond the seam at each side.

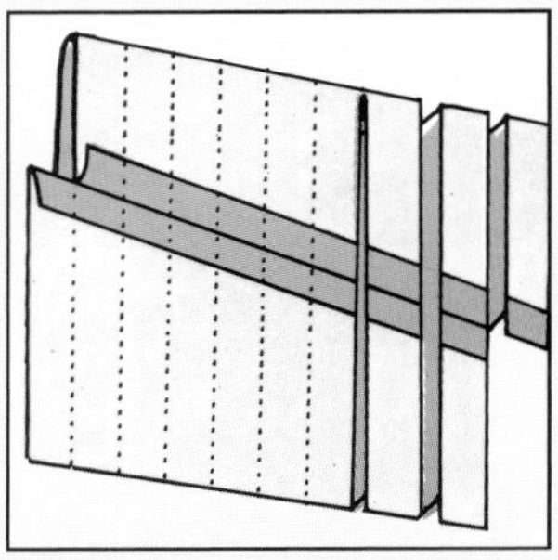

__2__ Press the seam open. Begin at one end and cut around the tube of fabric on the marked line to give a long, continuous bias strip with already finished seams.

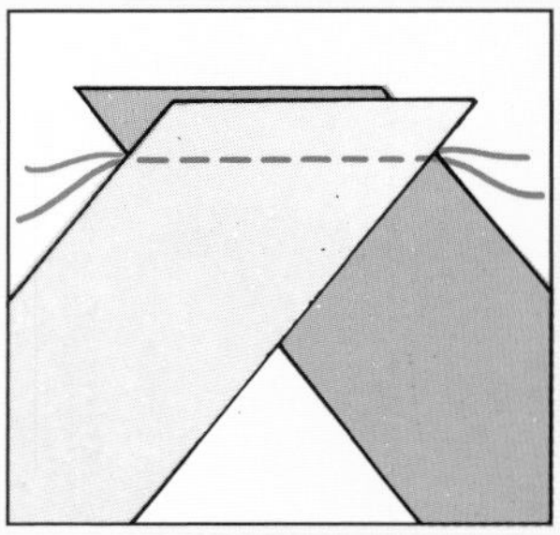

__3__ Calculate the length of binding needed and cut to size allowing extra for all seams. Join the ends together, and any intermediary seams, as shown and press the seams open.

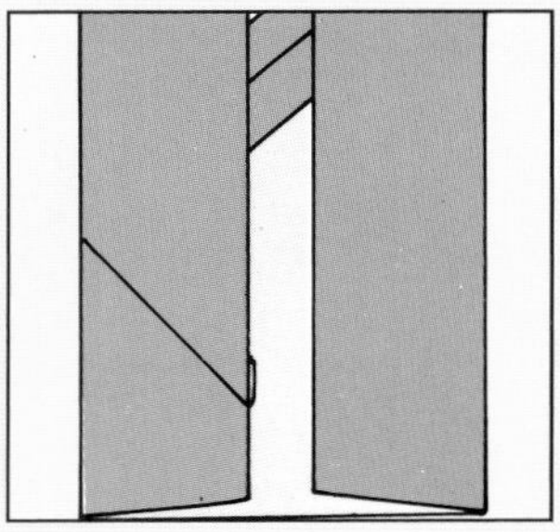

__4__ Press the edges towards the middle with the right side outside.

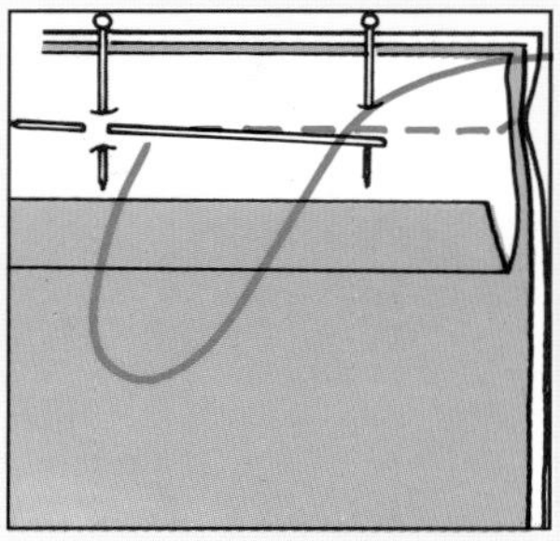

__5__ With edges even and right sides together, pin the binding to the quilted item. Using matching colored thread machine stitch or hand sew along the foldline through all layers.

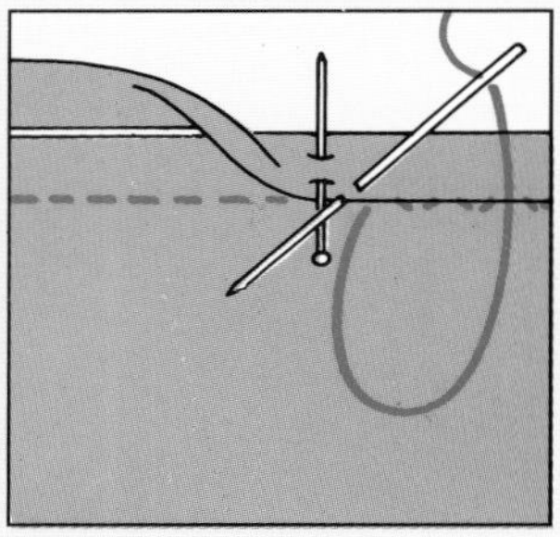

__6__ Turn the binding to the wrong side and pin to hold. Using a matching colored thread, slip stitch over the previous stitching.

BORDERED AND PIPED EDGES

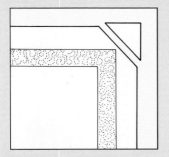

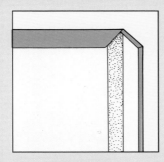

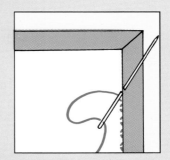

BORDERED 1 *Trim the excess backing to twice the width of the border required ½ inch (1.5cm) for turning. Cut the wadding back to the finished width of the border, and cut off the corners, as shown.*

2 Turn under the raw edge and press, and then fold the border over the wadding to the front and pin in place. Miter the corners, as shown.

3 Stitch either by machine or hand, taking care to hand sew neatly and securely across the mitered corners.

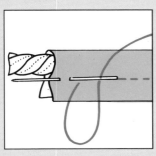

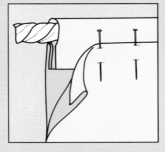

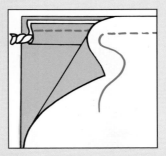

PIPED 1 *Cut the required length of bias strip by the circumference of the cord plus 1¼ inches (3cm) for seam allowances. Place the cord inside the strip right side outside, and stitch across close to the cord either by hand or machine using a piping foot.*

2 For quilts, baste piping to quilt right sides together and raw edges even. Stitch close to previous stitching and press seams to the wrong side. Turn in edges of backing, pin over stitchline and slip stitch in place.

3 For cushions, baste the piping in place with right sides and raw edges even. Ease piping around corners clipping into edge. Cover with second layer of fabric, baste and stitch through.

Piping

An extension of the simple binding technique is to insert a piping cord. Piping gives a professional finish to a quilt edge, where it is inserted between the top and backing fabrics. It is also an attractive trim for cushions and garments, for example, when it is stitched into the seams as they are made up.

You will need matching or contrasting fabric and piping cord of a suitable thickness.

REVERSIBLE EDGE FINISHING

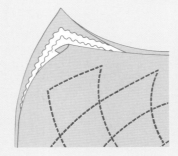

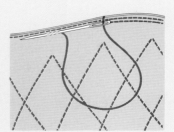

CHAPTER 6

PATCHWORK

INTRODUCTION

Patchwork, or piecework as it is sometimes called, is a technique of cutting materials into different shapes and sizes and stitching them together to create a whole new fabric. It is the making of an entirely new fabric that sets patchwork apart from any other textile craft.

Traditional construction methods can generally be divided into all-over mosaic designs or 'block' patterns. A block is a complete pattern and a number of blocks are stitched together to make the finished work. Patterns can be extended or reduced to fit any size requirements. Borders can be added, lattice strips (borders) inserted between blocks, fabrics pinched and pleated, painted, frayed, folded and embroidered before and after being stitched together and fashioned into all kinds of objects from patchwork quilts to floor rugs.

Like quilting, patchwork is an ancient technique which began as a functional practice and developed along increasingly decorative lines. Almost certainly it originated as a method of salvaging usable scraps from worn-out garments and furnishings. It was a natural development to arrange such scraps into pleasing patterns, and as fabric became more plentiful, the scope for increasingly elaborate patterns grew. Today we no longer need to make patchwork for reasons of economy and it has become a purely ornamental technique, making use of the many beautiful designs evolved during its long practical history.

Although patchwork is a needlecraft technique in its own right, for many people, the terms 'quilting' and 'patchwork' are synonymous with 'patchwork quilt' because of the long association of the two skills. The evolution of patchwork techniques has been very closely linked with the development of the quilt. When, during the 1700s, settlers moving out to the New World took these skills to America, the shortage of fabrics and the need for warm coverlets helped patchwork to come into its own as a quick and thrifty means of providing whole fabric for much-needed bedcovers — and thus began the great American patchwork tradition. In order to speed up piecing, the block and set were devised whereby plain strips of fabric were set between pieced blocks. This provided a new design element and a grid on which hundreds of patchwork patterns have since been based.

As patchwork developed and spread across to the West Coast, a dazzling selection of new patterns and variations was created, each one with its own fascinating name such as Rocky Road to Kansas, Lincoln's Platform and Slave's Chains — many of them of immediate topical interest reflecting the political and social changes that took place. In both England and America, quilting parties or 'bees' became important social events, particularly for women, when neighbors would meet to share in quilting the patchwork tops.

Traditions grew up of making patchwork quilts for particular occasions. Dowry quilts were prepared by unmarried girls in some areas,

particularly in the United States, where a girl aimed to have twelve patchwork quilts in her hope chest at the time of her marriage, possibly even thirteen, the thirteenth being the grandest – her bride's quilt.

In nineteenth-century America, and less frequently in the British Isles, Album quilts were often made for a special purpose or occasion, the blocks illustrating landmarks in the area or historical events which had some meaning for the residents, or incorporating motifs relevant to the recipient. The quilt was a cooperative effort; each of the many blocks was made by a different person or group of people who usually signed and dated their work. Freedom quilts, another type of Album quilt, were made for young men on reaching the age of 21, album quilts were often

presented to a bride with hearts included in the design. Friendship quilts, where a group of girls each made and signed a block to make up the whole, were also popular.

Fashions change, patchwork, which was for many years a country craft, has once more become an art-form. Patchwork motifs are used today for decoration on many other items as well as quilts.

ABOVE *A patchwork quilt made in Maryland, U.S.A., in the 1840s to the well-known Grandmother's Flower Garden design. The border is made from chintz, and the hexagonal motifs from English furnishing fabrics. Some groups of three hexagons have been cut in one piece.*

LEFT *An enchanting coverlet made for Mrs Waterbury by her friends in 1853. The blocks range from the purely decorative to the religiously or historically significant.*

TYPES OF PATCHWORK

*A*lthough there are several styles of patchwork, the sewing methods used fall generally into two categories – pieced patchwork, where either single patches are pieced together, as in hexagon or shell designs, or blocks of patches are built up, and applied patchwork, where the patches are applied to a backing fabric, as in Log Cabin or Folded patchwork.

Pieced patchwork was traditionally hand-sewn, although today the sewing machine may be used for certain forms. There are essentially two sub-divisions of this technique, the English and the American methods. The English method uses backing papers to make the patches – mostly of small geometric shapes such as hexagons and diamonds – which are sewn together by hand. The American block method is much quicker and tends to use larger units to make the block, which is secured with running stitch or machine stitch. Frequently the blocks are joined with lattice strips between. These are 2 inch (5cm) wide borders set around a 12 inch (30cm) block, for example – a method devised by pioneer American quiltmakers to speed up the piecing process.

● **Applied patchwork** can be sub-divided into Log Cabin, Strip (sometimes called Random), Crazy and Folded patchwork, including Folded star and Mayflower, where each style is applied to the backing in a completely different way. Certain strip patchwork is also called the 'pressed' block method.

● **Strip patchwork** falls somewhere between the two – being pieced in strips rather than blocks.

● **Pleated patchwork** is another variation where fabric is pinched and tucked before being pieced together.

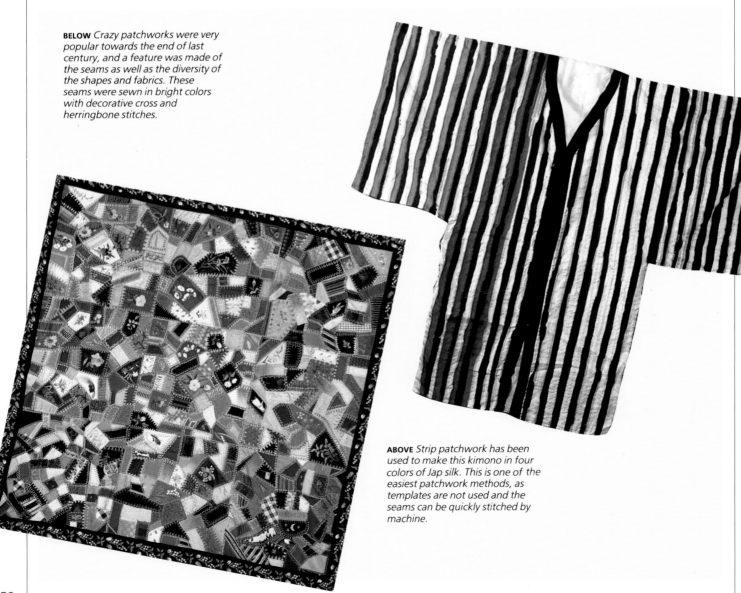

BELOW *Crazy patchworks were very popular towards the end of last century, and a feature was made of the seams as well as the diversity of the shapes and fabrics. These seams were sewn in bright colors with decorative cross and herringbone stitches.*

ABOVE *Strip patchwork has been used to make this kimono in four colors of Jap silk. This is one of the easiest patchwork methods, as templates are not used and the seams can be quickly stitched by machine.*

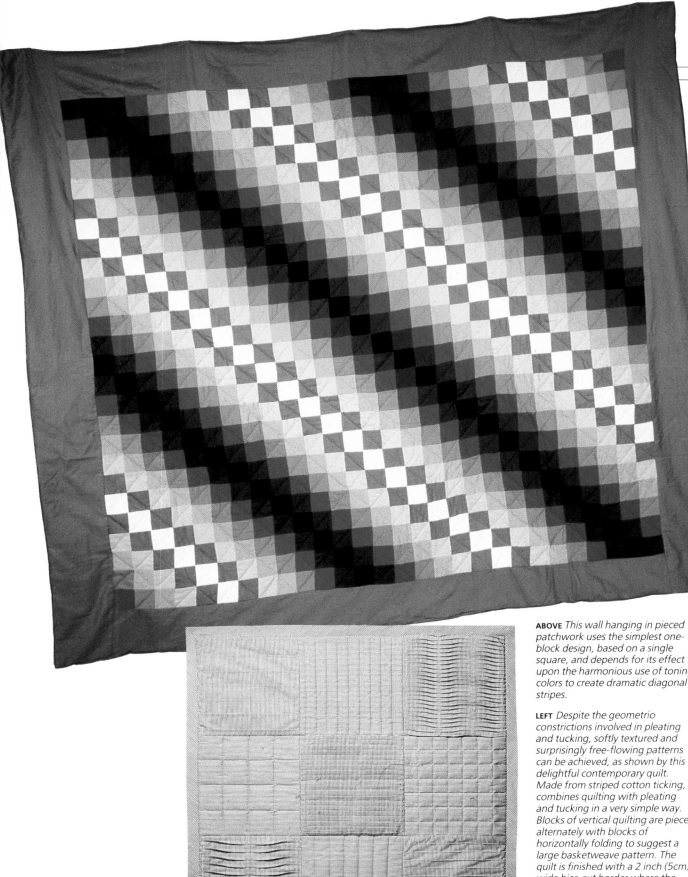

ABOVE *This wall hanging in pieced patchwork uses the simplest one-block design, based on a single square, and depends for its effect upon the harmonious use of toning colors to create dramatic diagonal stripes.*

LEFT *Despite the geometrio constrictions involved in pleating and tucking, softly textured and surprisingly free-flowing patterns can be achieved, as shown by this delightful contemporary quilt. Made from striped cotton ticking, it combines quilting with pleating and tucking in a very simple way. Blocks of vertical quilting are pieced alternately with blocks of horizontally folding to suggest a large basketweave pattern. The quilt is finished with a 2 inch (5cm) wide bias-cut border where the diagonal stripes of the ticking make an interesting contrast.*

MATERIALS AND EQUIPMENT

*M*aking patchwork is very simple and no special equip-equip is required. There are, however, a few rules which should always be observed.

The fabrics should be firm and, if possible, fairly new. Brand-new fabrics should be laundered before use to prevent shrinkage of the work. It is inadvisable to mix fabrics of different types and weights in the same piece of work because different types of material may need different treatment and suit different purposes, and mixed weights pull out of shape most unattractively. Synthetics and certain kinds of knits are really too springy and stretchy to make good patchwork shapes, and they should be kept for more decorative, experimental work.

Care should also be taken in choosing colors and prints, and solid colors should blend. For practical items, dress-weight cottons, ginghams, lawn, linens, corduroys, tweeds, velvets and silks are all well-tried favorites.

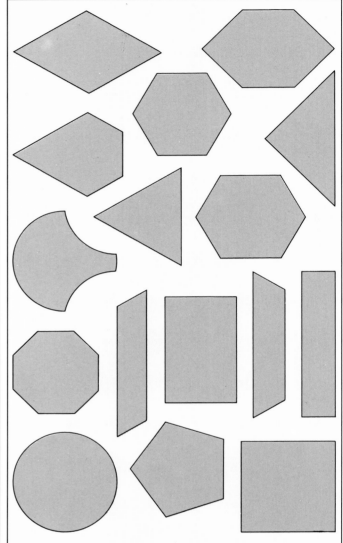

Equipment

As with other needlecrafts, a good sharp pair of scissors is needed. A good selection of pins, sharp needles and appropriate threads will be required. For hand- or machine-sewn patchwork, No. 60 cotton thread is best.

Templates

Metal or plastic templates can be bought in several shapes and sizes, usually in pairs – a

ABOVE *A selection of straight-sided and curved geometric templates. Note that the shapes are not all interchangeable.*

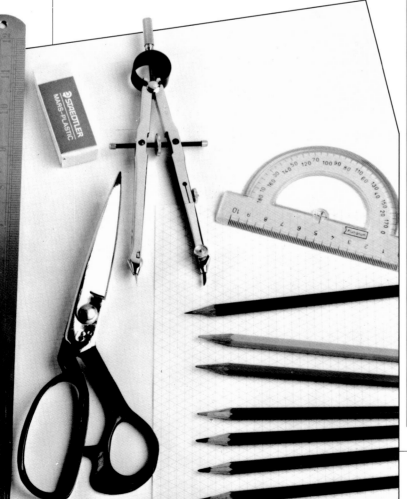

smaller solid template is used for cutting back papers and a larger window template for cutting the fabric. The latter is also useful for judging patterned patches and includes a ¼ inch (6mm) seam allowance.

If you cannot buy the correct size template for your design, then you will need to make your own. It is essential that these be accurately cut and firm, made preferably of metal or plastic. Cardboard templates easily fray at the edges, resulting in inaccurate shapes of fabric, and ill-fitting corners. Where possible, use graph paper for making precise measurements. Isometric graph paper is ideal for constructing hexagons, equilateral triangles and the lozenge. Incidentally, as these shapes share a common angle, they will interlock and mix well together.

Templates for machine sewing should include ¼ inch (6mm) seam allowances for fine to medium fabrics and ⅜ inch (9mm) allowances for heavier fabrics.

CHOOSING A DESIGN

The purpose to which the patchwork will be put and the weight of the fabric should be considered before deciding on the size and shape of the individual pieces. If possible, all patches should be cut with the grain of the fabric running in the same direction. Before actually cutting the cloth, it is often helpful to draw out the design on graph paper and to color the shapes in different combinations until a satisfactory arrangement has been achieved.

The most important consideration when choosing a design is that it should relate to the item you plan to make in size, style and color. Bear in mind that a small piece of patchwork is more effective made with small patches, but not so small as to make sewing difficult. Consider the patchwork style and its suitability – a Log Cabin design made from rough tweeds and shirtings may not be the ideal choice for a nursery, for example, whereas pretty cottons in a hexagon design might be. If you are designing a major piece of patchwork to fit in with an existing color scheme, there are several considerations to make. Look first at all the colors in the room beginning with the actual color of the wood in furniture, floors and woodwork. Notice the wide difference in local colors such as buff-colored pine and dark red mahogany. Then check the walls, carpets, curtains and upholstery. Your choice of color can serve either as an accent to a colorful scheme by choosing one or two of the main colors and using similar tones, or it can highlight a restrained color scheme by choosing more striking colors to make a strong focal point.

BELOW *This delightful patchwork camel cover from Uzbekistan, Russia, has openwork bands decorated with sawtooth edgings, and uses an amazing variety of fabrics including cotton, velvet, felt, embroidered braids, and woven ikat.*

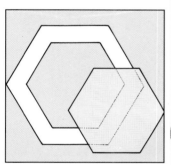

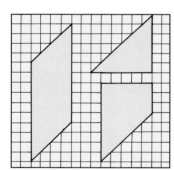

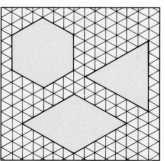

Plastic window and metal templates. Templates drawn on graph paper and templates drawn on isometric graph paper.

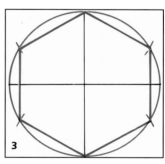

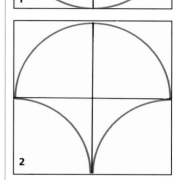

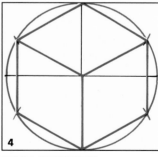

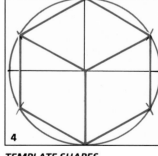

TEMPLATE SHAPES
1 *Paper templates must be accurate. Use a sharp pencil, ruler and compass to draw the shapes.*
2 Shell shape *Use a compass to draw a semicircle. Lightly draw in two diameters, and keeping the same radius, mark in the two quadrants.*
3 Hexagon *Draw a circle and keeping the same radius, mark off six arcs on the circumference. Join up these dots to form the hexagon.*
4 Baby block *Draw out the hexagon as described, and then draw in two radii from alternate corners into the center as shown.*

The scope for design is limited only by your imagination. There are literally hundreds of traditional designs ranging from the rigidly geometric pieced blocks via the soft curves of Clamshells and the unusual puffed texture of Suffolk Puffs to the completely random. You need not be bound by tradition, either, but can experiment freely with any combination of fabrics and arrangements, varying the texture with applications of, for example, beads, embroidery or cords.

ABOVE *A Star of Bethlehem quilt of the type that was extremely popular in the last century and at the beginning of this century. The central star is mimicked by the four peripheral stars, with their identical red centers and tips. The border has a somewhat improvised feel to it, in contrast to the impeccably matched stars.*

RIGHT *A Feathered Star patterned quilt worked towards the end of the last century. Some of the triangular pieces are minute, and the quilt has been beautifully and very finely sewn throughout.*

BELOW *Diamonds in light, medium and dark tones form this all-over 'Tumbling Blocks' design.*

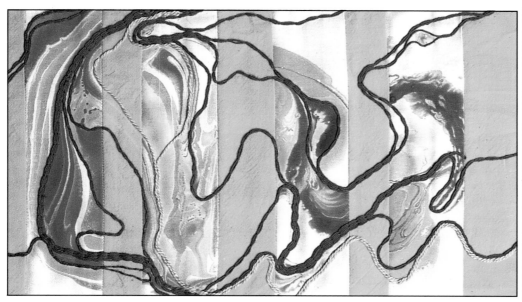

LEFT *Simple contemporary stripwork in which strips of plain yellow alternate with strips of a marbled design. The patchwork has been decorated with flowing lines of couched threads worked across to reinstate the marbled patterns.*

BELOW LEFT *This detail of a twentieth century Turkoman tent-hanging from Afganistan shows a patchwork of richly colored and textured fabrics. Some of the pieces are of ikat-dyed silk, where the pattern is made by dyeing the warp threads before the fabric is woven. Other fabrics used include felt, velvet and strips of patterned braid.*

BELOW *Contemporary patchwork quilt using blocks made up of squares and triangles, broken up by a contrasting quilted pattern running diagonally through the blocks.*

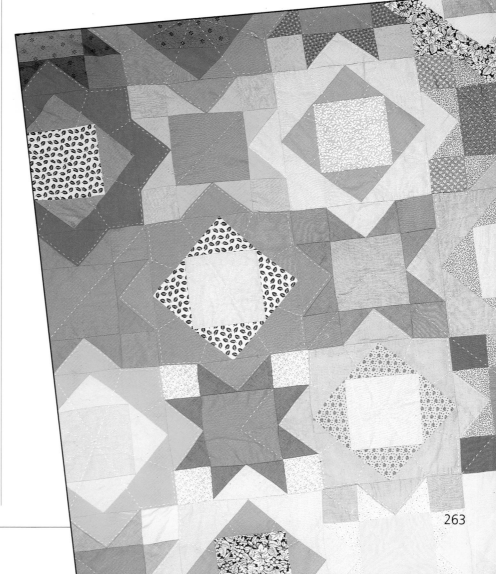

TECHNIQUE

Construction

Although the traditional methods of joining patches and blocks into over-all repeat patterns are often the easiest, many contemporary designers, while still using standard geometric shapes, are creating new ways of putting them together – perhaps radiating from a base point, or asymmetrically – most certainly with great mathematical dexterity.

The simplest way to work is the one patch, or single unit, repeated in an all-over design. Most traditional pieced blocks are based on the four-, five-, seven- or nine-patch grid systems. Each grid has the same basic number of units which can be sub-divided in any number of ways. Pieced blocks can be joined edge to edge in an all-over repeat pattern, but, if the effect is too 'busy', they can be alternated with plain blocks of fabric or have lattice strips (borders) stitched between. These borders tend to give a design strength and unity. Another way to position the patches is to alternate plain and patterned blocks diagonally with half blocks at the edges. Whatever your choice, it is important to plan a scaled design on graph paper using colors to indicate the patches. Keep this by you as a guide for estimating fabric and piecing together the finished work.

Estimating fabric quantity

This is not always easy, especially if oddments are included, but an approximate calculation can be made once you have cut the templates to size and counted how many different patches are needed.

Using a fabric width of 36 inches (90cm) and a 4 inch (10cm) square template, for example, calculate how many

PATCHWORK CONSTRUCTION

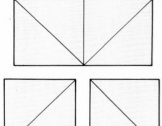

A block is pieced by first joining the smaller units such as triangles to make squares, and then joining the squares to form larger blocks.

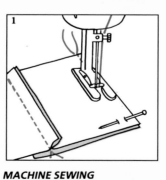

MACHINE SEWING
1 Place the patches right sides together and stitch on the marked seamline or use the inside width of the presser foot as a guide, stitching ¼ inch (6mm) in from the edge. Reverse stitch at both ends. If your presser foot is narrower than ¼ inch (6mm), and the plate below is not marked, use a strip of masking tape as a guide.

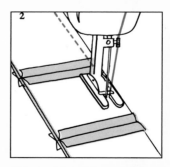

2 Having joined the small units together, press the seams open, or to one side, whichever you prefer. Then join the rows together accurately matching the seams. It is a good idea to pin through the two seams to hold them firmly in place while stitching.

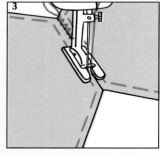

3 Hexagons and other more complicated shapes can be joined very quickly. Simply butt the edges together and join on the right side with zigzag stitching. Use a stitch width of 1½-2 and a medium stitch length.

using an appropriately colored pencil. Make sure you place the templates on the straight grain of the fabric, avoiding the bias grain. Reverse asymmetric shapes, such as the trapezoid, so that they appear the correct way round when stitched together. Cut out the patches separately using very sharp scissors.

Machine sewing

Although curves and some complicated geometric shapes are better stitched by hand, most patterns involving simple triangles, squares and rectangles can be pieced quite successfully by machine.

Hand sewing

Many traditional forms of patchwork are sewn by hand. The stitches form an integral part of the work so there is no need for them to be invisible, but they should not be obvious. Details of particular stitches are given with the different patchwork techniques. For example, English pieced patchwork is oversewn (whipped), while American pieced work uses running stitch.

Size of block

This need not be a random guess. In order to calculate the size, measure the overall area you plan to cover. For a wall hanging, measure the wall space, and, for a quilt, drape a sheet over the bed to get the right effect and then divide the total measurement into smaller units.

Blocks of 12–15 inches (30–38cm) are popular for large quilts and 6 inches (15cm) for cot quilts. For a cushion, use one large block or four smaller

blocks. Plain or patterned borders can be invaluable for increasing overall dimensions. Patchwork for clothes is generally best pieces together and treated as any other fabric – positioning the paper pattern according to the cutting layout.

Sewing pieced blocks together

Before sewing, lay out your patches to check the overall design. Certain hand-sewn patterns may vary slightly, but in general it is good practice first to join small units, such as triangles, to form squares and then join the squares progressively into bigger blocks, and so on. Finally,

assemble the larger units to form rows and stitch the rows together. Add strips or borders as needed. Once you have established the sequence for making a block, continue with it for all the blocks.

1 One-patch block, A Thousand Pyramids; 2 Four-patch block, Crosses and Losses; 3 Nine-patch block, Variable Star; 4 Lattice strips.

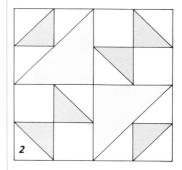

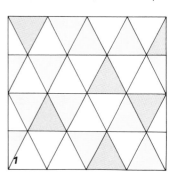

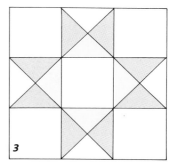

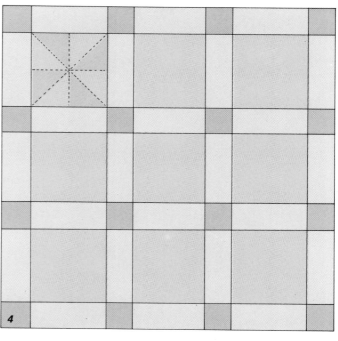

shapes can be cut from one width (36 ÷ 4 = 9). If you require 80 blocks, for example, calculate the length needed by dividing this number by the number of times the template fits across the fabric and multiply the figure by the depth of the template (80 ÷ 9 = 9 [rounded up] × 4 inches = 36 inches). You will need 36 inches (90cm) of 36 inch (90cm) wide fabric. Bear in mind that certain templates can be more economically placed than others. Calculate border strips in the same way.

Marking and cutting fabric

Position the templates and lightly mark all cutting lines on the wrong side of the fabric,

PIECED PATCHWORK

Pieced patchwork is the most basic and perhaps the most versatile patchwork technique. The fabric shapes are cut out using a template and are sewn together by hand or machine.

English method

In what is generally known as English patchwork, paper shapes are cut round the template from good quality paper or thin cardboard – one shape for each patch. These must be very accurate or the patchwork will not lie flat and corners may not meet. The papers are placed on the reverse side of the material and cut round, leaving a seam allowance of about ¼ inch (6mm). The turning is folded over the paper and basted, taking care not to catch the paper. Two patches are placed right sides together and oversewn (whipped) along one side. Other patches are made in the same way until the required motif has been assembled. Once a patch has been completely surrounded on all facets, the papers can be carefully removed. For a neat outline and accurate angles, it is advisable to make hexagons and octagons by the English method.

Hexagons are one of the most characteristic shapes used in English patchwork. A popular traditional pattern made up of hexagons is that known as Grandmother's Flower Garden, in which one hexagon is surrounded by six others and sometimes a further circle is added. When sufficient motifs have been made, they are joined together, with a band of neutral colored hexagons between. Traditionally, the flower garden is made with a central yellow patch followed by two rows in either pinks, blues or yellows in mixed prints, and surrounded by a row of toning green hexagons to represent foliage, with a linking border of white patches to form the path between the flower beds. However, this can be varied to suit smaller projects and more restricted color schemes.

Smooth, dressweight cottons or lightweight furnishing (curtain) fabrics are best for hand sewing patches with backing papers. Hexagon patchwork is ideal for large or small items from crib and baby carriage covers to cushions, quilts, curtains, and bags.

American method

In American patchwork, no backing paper is used and the pieces are joined with running stitch: the patches are set together as blocks, which are then joined, either directly or with lattice strips. This method is best suited to geometric shapes such as squares and triangles.

The template is placed on the wrong side of the fabric and a pencil line drawn round it. Each shape is cut out, leaving a suitable seam allowance. The shapes are arranged with the right sides facing and sewn together along the pencil lines with a running stitch. The seams are then trimmed to about ⅛ inch (3mm) and pressed to one side. If possible, press towards the darker material so that the seam will

SQUARES
Hit and miss
Castellated pattern
Framed squares
Checkerboard
Going down stairs
Strip pattern

RECTANGLES
Checks
Brick wall
Zigzag bricks
Turned rectangles
Up and down
Roman squares

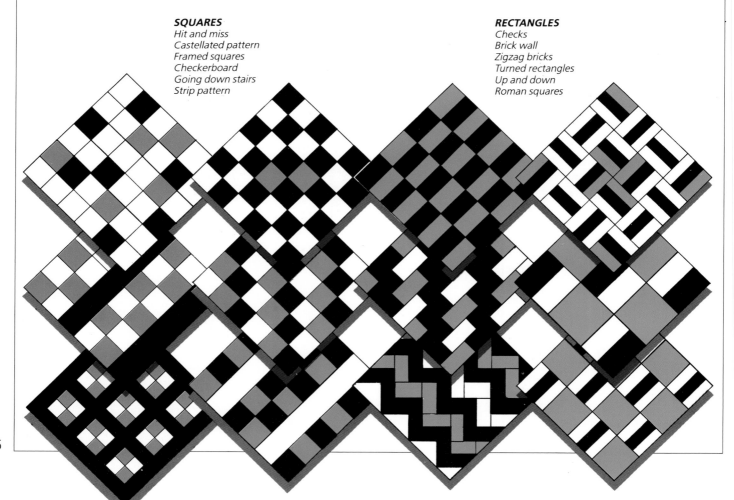

METHOD

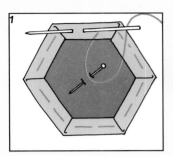

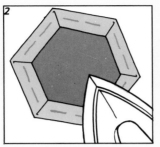

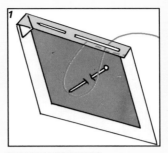

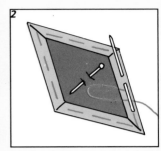

BACKING THE PATCHES
1 For hand sewn patchwork, pin paper template to wrong side of patch. Fold edge over and secure with pieces of masking tape. baste around edges.

2 Remove tape, press folded edges with toe of iron – this makes sewing the patches together much easier.

FOLDING CORNERS
1 Pin paper template to wrong side of fabric, fold over and the first baste side of diamond.

2 Before folding over second side, fold point of first turning onto second side. Fold and second baste side.
3 Baste side three as for stage two and then baste side four.

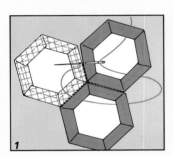

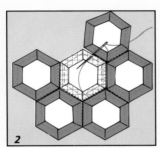

HEXAGONS INTO ROSETTES
1 Join two hexagons together with neat overstitching. Then join a third hexagon to both of the original ones as shown.
2 One of the first hexagons must be considered the center of the rosette, and six others sewn round its sides. This rosette is the basis for many designs.

not show through. It is always helpful to build up the patches in such a way that they make larger blocks which can be joined with long straight seams rather than many short seams.

Squares are simple to sew. A four-patch block consists of four squares, two each of two contrasting materials, sewn together to make a larger square. A nine-patch block consists of five squares of one fabric alternating with four squares of a contrast. All block patterns can be made into many designs according to the way in which the blocks are joined together. Triangles and diamonds can be joined to make stars and flower shapes, and used in conjunction with squares to make up the block.

Patterns

Each of the many traditional patterns has a name, and these names have varied and fascinating origins. Dresden Plate and Churn Dash are taken from domestic objects; Whig Rose, Burgoyne Surrounded and Queen Charlotte's Crown from history; Turkey Tracks, Pineapple, Rose, Lily and Dahlia have obvious domestic origins. Other designs are named after star patterns, and people and places from the Bible or Bunyan's *Pilgrim's Progress*. Some refer to the environment, such as Bear's Paw, Fence Rail, Windmill and The Rocky Road to California. Names for patterns vary from region to region.

Some of the patterns are illustrated here and overleaf.

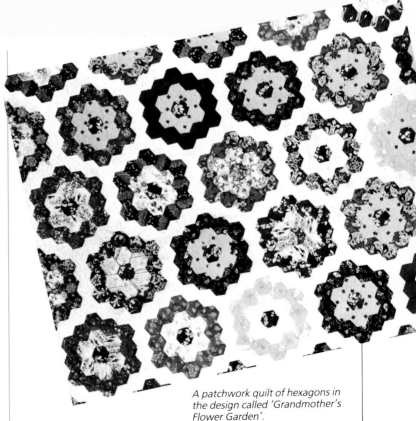

A patchwork quilt of hexagons in the design called 'Grandmother's Flower Garden'.

TRIANGLES
High noon
Railroad crossing
Cotton reel
Birds in air

TRIANGLES AND SQUARES
Jacob's ladder
Water wheel
Winged square
Ohio star

Shark's tooth square
Double T
Handy Andy
Boxed square

TRIANGLES AND SQUARES
Rising star
Eight hand round
Lemoyne star
54-40

Greek cross block
Flying Dutchman
Tall pine tree
Weather vane

Red cross
Goose in the pond
Sherman's march
Rolling stone

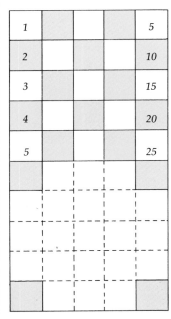

1				5
2				10
3				15
4				20
5				25

ABOVE *Five-patch block (**TOP**) and appliqué block (**ABOVE**) making up pattern for Double Irish chain (**BELOW**).*

Within the formats of the traditional block patterns, an immense variety of effects can be achieved, as the quilts shown here demonstrate.

The contemporary Sugar Bowl quilt shows how a complex effect can be built up from the use of only two template shapes in a simple four-patch block.

The Sugar Bowl design is a favorite old American pattern, and one of many variations each with its own evocative name such as Drunkard's Path, Fool's Puzzle, Falling Timbers and Wonder of the World. This is a four-patch pattern where each patch is made up of two units: a small square with a quarter circle set in one corner – the curved seam being best hand sewn. The patches are pieced together so that the four corners form a circle within a larger square block.

Traditionally, two colors

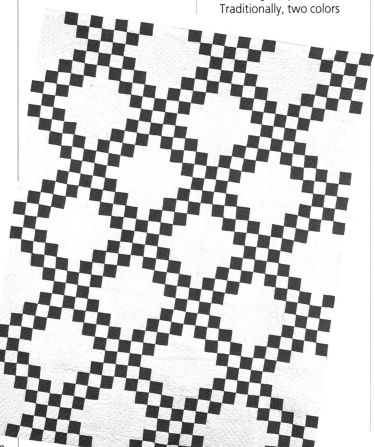

are used but mixed colors arranged as in this contemporary quilt can be very attractive – an excellent scrap-bag design. Here pretty prints salvaged from discarded dresses have been cleverly designed and pieced into a large symmetrical pattern with a random effect. Similar designs could be planned with mixed colors but using fewer prints; spots with sprig prints and plain colors; stripes with spots and plaids; plaids with tiny checks and plain colors would all give interesting results. This kind of imposed restriction often helps in planning a design.

The late nineteenth-century quilt worked in a popular American pattern known as Double Irish chain uses only one template shape, a square, and two colors to form a large repeat pattern.

The design uses two blocks – a five-patch block, and a plain block with a small square cleverly appliquéd to each corner. When pieced together, this gives a most intricate effect. The pieced blocks (the 'chain') can be arranged diagonally, as shown, or in a square repeat, and either machine or hand sewn. Traditionally, the plain blocks are quilted all over following the lines of the pieced square to give the over-all effect of a solidly pieced quilt.

ABOVE *Sugar Bowl. A fascinating scrap-bag design showing mixed prints arranged in a random way. Make up each of the two units before assembling them into a four-patch block as shown.*

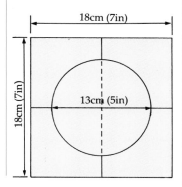

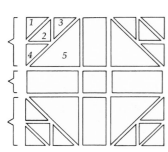

There are several ways of piecing this block for Grandmother's Choice. The simplest is to sew the small units first and join them into three horizontal rows. Then stitch the rows together to form one block.

Amish quilts are famous for their use of powerful geometric designs. The Amish, or Plain People, who belong to the Mennonite church, do not believe in decoration and, although their patchwork is essentially plain and simple, the results are dramatic in their use of shapes and colors. The example shown here was made in Milton, Iowa, in the 1920s and is a striking example of an old American pattern called Grandmother's Choice. Here, rather sombre colours are boldly contrasted with black to give an overall effect of a twinkling, faceted pattern.

The design uses two blocks – a pieced four-patch block, and a plain block – stitched alternately together in a diagonal repeat pattern. As the blocks are set diagonally, the edges are filled in with half plain blocks and quarter blocks in the corners. The pattern forms a fairly large repeat and is ideal for beginners working by hand or machine. It is most suitable for coverlets, and quilts and larger soft furnishing items. Single pieced blocks are good for cushion sets and groups of four or more for floor cushions.

In contrast the modern wall

hanging (opposite) based on triangular pieced blocks gives a deceptive appearance of simplicity with what is in fact a far more complex pattern than it seems. The design, worked in silk, uses a single triangular block throughout, which is repeated in several color combinations and joined together diagonally and vertically by narrow bands of grey to form larger diamonds. These grey bands along with

black not only form the background but give the optical effect of space. Half triangles are used at the top and bottom to complete the rectangle and the finished work is quilted in such a way as to further emphasize the depth of each triangle.

ABOVE *Amish quilt based on the 'Grandmother's Choice' pattern. Names for patterns vary considerably between different regions – for example, the American 'Orange Peel' is called 'Robbing Peter to Pay Paul' in Somerset. 'Grandmother's Choice' is sometimes considered a variation of 'Ohio Star' or 'Shoo-fly'. It is wise not to be too dogmatic about patchwork pattern names.*

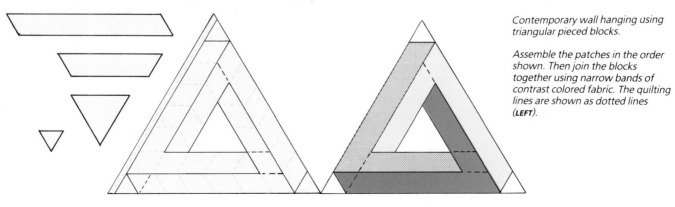

Contemporary wall hanging using triangular pieced blocks.

Assemble the patches in the order shown. Then join the blocks together using narrow bands of contrast colored fabric. The quilting lines are shown as dotted lines (**LEFT**).

A vivid kaleidoscope effect is achieved by this contemporary quilt, using just four template shapes for two pieced blocks.

The visual impact of such a design relies on skilful use of color. Here colors are cleverly chosen and expertly arranged to give the brilliant sunburst effect. Basically, two complementary colors (in this case, orange and turquoise blue) form the lighter area, and other closely related colors with deeper tonal values make the surrounding border.

The two blocks, each simply divided into squares and triangles, are repeated alternately on a square grid. One block is based on a star (the old American Saw Tooth), and the second has the same basic units but the corner squares are sub-divided into triangles and others reversed, so that, when they are repeated together, large diamonds are created. The finished work is quilted diagonally through the patterns to give the appearance of a superimposed texture.

An entirely different approach is illustrated by the modern Bicentennial friendship quilt made by the staff of the American Museum in Britain in 1976. Here each block has been made by a different individual in the form of a picture, using patchwork, appliqué and embroidery techniques. Each participant chose the design for the block she was working, and some of these designs represent objects from the Museum's collection. The crossed flags at the center of the quilt stand for the friendship of England and America. The quilt has been backed with green and white printed cotton, the green matching the banding.

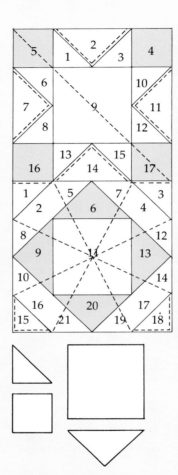

ABOVE *The diagram shows the templates used and the order in which the blocks are assembled for the 'Sunburst' quilt (**FAR RIGHT**). Dotted lines show the quilting pattern.*

This design demonstrates how a complex pattern can be built up from simple template shapes. A many-pieced block like this depends upon a coherent color pattern to avoid disintegrating into a visual muddle. This type of design needs to be worked out accurately on graph paper first – you will find dressmaker's pattern paper, with its larger squares, easier for planning a large-scale work.

Bicentennial friendship quilt.

ABOVE *'Sunburst', a modern quilt making dazzling use of interlocking shapes and shaded colors.*

SHELL PATCHWORK

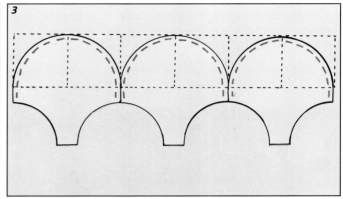

3 To join the patches, lay them out to check the pattern. Place the top right side up on a soft surface – an ironing board or clear floor space is ideal – and pin through. Make sure the top edges are level and the edges touching. The bottom edges can be overcast with one or two stitches, if preferred.

The shell (or clamshell) is one of the oldest motifs used in quilting and patchwork. This single shape forms a classic, all-over repeating pattern known in many countries as Fishscale or simply as Fish.

The technique involves hand sewing rows of overlapping shells in a pattern or in a random way, either with or without a foundation fabric. Each shell is carefully cut out using a template and made with a backing paper to ensure a perfectly curved outline. As the patches are stitched from the right side, it is crucial that the edges are accurately curved since there is no other seaming to help disguise any imperfections. If you have a sewing machine with a swing needle, you may prefer to experiment by zigzag stitching the patches together.

Smooth-textured, fine cottons in patterned or plain colors are best for making the patches. You will need contrasting colors for designs such as chevrons, diagonal stripes and diamonds; mixed plain and patterned prints for random placing; graduated toning fabrics for shaded effects.

Shell patchwork works particularly well on small items like tea- and coffee-pot cosies, bags, bolsters and cushions, as well as on larger quilts and coverlets. Larger items should be lined and tied to keep the layers together.

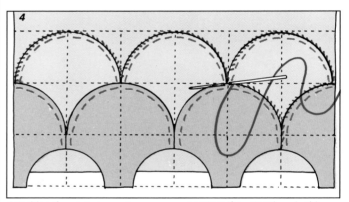

4 Position the next row on top overlapping the bottom half of the shells, and tack in place. Hem around the curves joining the two rows together. Continue in this way to finish the patchwork. Work half shells at the side edges on every other row.

How to make shell patches

Metal templates are available in pairs: the smaller one is used for cutting the paper backing and the larger one for cutting the fabric which includes the seam allowance. To make your own template, see the diagrams, which show how the patches are made and joined. As an alternative to the traditional method of using a backing paper inside each patch, the technique uses one slightly stiffer backing paper for making many patches.

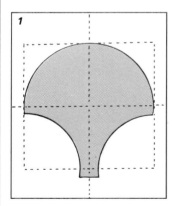

SHELL PATCHES
1 To make the template, draw a circle on heavy paper or thin cardboard using a pair of compasses, and mark the center both ways. Then draw two arcs at each side of the bottom section just inside the center line. Cut out the template as shown in the diagram.

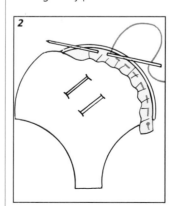

2 Cut out the fabric patches, adding ¼ inch (6mm) seam allowances all round. Pin the template to the right side of the fabric. Snip into the curved edge and fold it to the wrong side. Baste through the fabric only, easing the fullness around the curve. Remove the template ready to make the next patch.

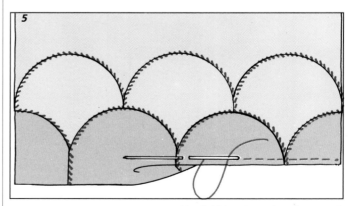

5 On the last row, trim the bottom half of the shells and turn under the seam allowance. Tack across ready for finishing the project. Remove all visible tacking stitches.

SUFFOLK PUFFS

Suffolk Puffs are gathered circular patches which are handsewn together with the edges touching and leaving small spaces in between. The most effective fabrics to use are fine ones such as silk, soft cotton voile or organdie. The gathered side of the circle is the right side and the central hole creates a decorative, textural effect.

This open, lacy type of patchwork is purely ornamental and not very strong; it can be used to create unusual textures for wall hangings or cushion covers.

How to make Suffolk Puffs

Begin by cutting circles of fabric about twice the diameter of the finished patch. Fold over a ¼ inch (6mm) seam allowance to wrong side, and using a strong thread secured firmly, run even gathering stitches around the edge. Pull up the gathering thread tightly. Flatten the shape so that the gathered edge is in the middle and fasten off thread. The puffs are then joined together with a few small stitches.

This simple technique can be varied in several ways: the puffs may be stitched to each other for a closely textured effect, or widely spaced as in the photograph. The puffs may be lightly padded with wadding before they are gathered. You may combine puffs of different sizes in one project or place a decorative filling in transparent puffs. The gathering thread need not be pulled tight, thus showing the inside of the patch, which could be padded or filled with a contrasting color, or stitched varying the length of the connecting stitches. Since hard wear is not to be expected, you can experiment freely.

SUFFOLK PUFFS

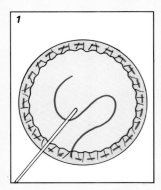 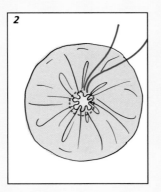

1 Begin by cutting circles of fabric about twice the diameter of the finished patch. Fold over a ¼ inch (6mm) turning to wrong side, and using a strong thread secured firmly, run even gathering stitches around the edge.

2 Pull up the gathering thread tightly. Flatten the shape so that the gathered edge is in the middle and fasten off thread.

This charming example of Suffolk puffs shows a number of variations on the basic technique. A soft, semi-transparent fabric is used; the long ends of the silk gathering threads add delicacy to the piece. The puffs are stitched closely together in rows, which are then joined again with longer thread covered with small shiny beads.

CRAZY PATCHWORK

Crazy patchwork (or Puzzle patchwork) was a favorite pastime devised by the Victorians as a means of using small scraps of the rich and beautiful fabrics then in fashion – from silks, satins, velvets and brocades to many brightly colored and inexpensive printed cottons and chintzes.

The patchwork was made with an all-over design where irregular fabric shapes were overlapped and stitched to a foundation fabric. A crazy quilt might be totally irregular in design, simply using any color, size or shape of scrap that the maker could lay hands on, or some unity might be brought to the design by working in blocks with one recurrent motif like the fan pattern in the example shown.

Crazy quilts were renowned for the richness and variety of their designs. Typical colors included many dark reds and blues, bright golden yellows and black. The raw edges were then lavishly embroidered with herringbone or feather stitches in a twisted thread, usually in the same rich, golden yellow. Quite frequently, the patches were also elaborately embroidered, or embellished with ribbons, appliqué, metallic thread, beads and sequins. Throws, pelmets, cushions and cosies were made, and the edges scalloped, satin frilled, fringed or corded to give a colorful and energetic form of Victorian over-decoration. The work was always lined and tied randomly.

This is the perfect technique for indulging sentiment. If, for example, you have a collection of old fabrics, oddments of real lace, embroidered motifs, ribbons, mottoes, woven labels, even pretty buttons and braids, they can all be worked into a keepsake patchwork, in true Victorian style. Alternatively, much contemporary patchwork is made with the sewing machine, using zigzag stitch to cover the edges or straight stitch for turned-in edges.

A colorful variation with a stained-glass window quality can be made by covering the seams with ½ inch (1.5 cm) wide black tape (or any other dark color). In crazy patchwork, color and pattern play a very important part, so be selective when choosing and positioning the patches.

Although at first it may not be apparent, a good kaleidoscopic effect needs careful planning. The use of a predominant color randomly interspersed helps to strengthen and unify a design.

For making larger patchwork, you may find it easier to make blocks first and then piece them together, either herringbone stitching over the seams or top stitching. Patched and plain blocks can be alternated to give a less 'busy' effect and the seams machine-zigzag stitched instead of hand embroidered.

Plain and printed fabrics – silks, cottons, lightweight wools and velvets, leather and suede – can all be used but, when planning a project, bear in mind their cleaning requirements. Mixed fabric patchwork, wool, silk or leather, for example, will need dry cleaning, but all cotton may be hand laundered.

Crazy patchwork is most effective for covers of all kinds – crib, baby carriage, duvet, car blanket, sofa throw, cushions – for garments and curtains, for abstract 'painting with fabric' pictures or hangings.

Hand sewing

Crazy patchwork does not use a template. For a small item, mark the required shape on the backing fabric (firm cotton or sheeting). For a larger item it will be easier to work in blocks, so cut the backing fabric into squares the size of the intended block, plus ½ inch (1cm) seam allowances on all sides.

Starting in one corner, lay the fabric scraps on to the backing fabric and baste down each patch slightly overlapping the preceding one. It is only necessary to turn in a hem on edges which will not be covered by other patches. When the foundation has been completely covered, the edges of all patches should be embroidered with a feather stitch, herringbone or another fancy stitch in a variety of colors. The blocks are then joined together and the joins also embroidered over. Crazy patchwork is backed but not usually quilted. Instead the top and backing are 'tied'. This involves taking two small back stitches over each other at unobtrusive places, and tying off the ends on the back of the work.

Machine sewing

Begin placing the patches at one corner of the backing fabric, starting with a right-angled patch. Gradually build up the design by placing the patches in turn on the backing so that they overlap the edges of the already positioned patches.

LEFT *Crazy patchwork is the original form of patchwork. It is assembled rather like a jigsaw from randomly shaped patches which are pinned, basted, and then stitched to a firm backing fabric.*

RIGHT *This late nineteenth-century American quilt is a typical example of crazy patchwork. A rich variety of fabrics has been used, further embellished by the use of surface stitches to embroider small motifs, and the ornamentation of the seams of the pieced fabric by a variety of stitches, including variations of feather, herringbone, and buttonhole. The quilt is made up of a series of square blocks of crazy patchwork, joined together and surrounded by a striking decorative border.*

The design can be worked in sections, by pinning and basting one area before moving on to the next, or all the patches can be laid out before they are pinned.

When all the patches are basted in place, work either close zigzag stitch or satin stitch over the edges for a plain finish or make narrow seam allowances on the patches and secure with straight stitch. If your sewing machine also does a variety of embroidery stitches, you could simply sew them down with a pretty stitch in a complementary color.

Use a clear plastic zigzag foot on the machine and take care to follow the outlines accurately.

HAND SEWING

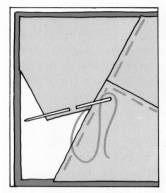
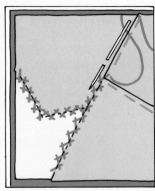

1 *Beginning in one corner, arrange the unfinished patches on the foundation fabric overlapping the edges, and secure with small running stitches.*

2 *Complete all the patches in this way, and then cover the edges with either herringbone, double or triple feather, blanket stitch, or couching.*

LOG CABIN PATCHWORK

*P*erhaps one of the best-known patterns is Log Cabin. It is built up of contrasting light and darker strips of fabric, which are supposed to represent the logs of the roof of a cabin round a central square representing the chimney, the strips on two sides being of dark colors and the strips on the other two sides of light colors. Traditionally, the central square of material should be red to denote the fire; the dark part of the square represents the shadow and the light part the firelight. If the square is yellow it represents the lantern put in the window to light the traveller on his way. Another version of this pattern, called Courthouse steps, has a black central square, symbolizing the judge's robes. The name Log Cabin must have been given to this pattern once it reached the United States, as in the north of England it is called Log Wood, in the Isle of Man Roof pattern, and in Ireland a Folded quilt. It was at one time thought that the Log Cabin pattern had come to Ireland from America, but research has shown that it was used in Scotland during the eighteenth century and subsequently crossed the sea to Ireland. Because the narrow 'logs' were often made from ribbon this is sometimes known as Ribbon patchwork.

ABOVE *Contemporary quilt showing a typical striped pattern using strips varying in width, ½-6 inches (1.5-15cm), in strong contrasting colors, with just one lively print.*

RIGHT *A nineteenth-century quilt designed in the Straight Furrow pattern, a commonplace variation of the Log Cabin design. The blocks are very large in this particular quilt, and the stripes or furrows are worked in a fiery combination of yellow and earthy browns and red.*

The advantage of this design is that all kinds of leftover scraps can be put to good use. Originally, it must surely have been devised as the most economical means of using up oddments of fabric too small and narrow to be useful for anything else. Traditionally, dress and shirt cottons, wool, worsted and tweeds were used. Later, the Victorians used shiny silk and satin ribbons transforming the finished effect from a homespun textile born of thrift and ingenuity into a smart, multi-colored fabric. While all cottons are easy to handle and thoroughly reliable for patchwork, other contemporary fabrics offer a fantastic range of textures and finishes to experiment with, including novelty synthetics, sheer metallic fabrics and a vast choice of ribbons. Plaids, spots, checks, flecks, stripes and many other patterns may all be used to give new optical effects.

Using the basic square, an amazing variety of patterns can be constructed, depending on how the light and dark sections are arranged within the block, and on how the blocks are finally put together. In America each pattern has its own name; Log Cabin, Courthouse steps and Pineapple, for example, are three variations of the individual block while Straight furrow, Stepping stones, Flight of stairs, Barn raising and Checkerboard are names of the arrangements.

The patchwork is not usually bordered but it should be lined and top stitched between the seams of the blocks. A 12 inch square (30cm) block is a popular size for making quilts and 6 inch (15cm) square for cushions or smaller projects. The strips are usually 1 inch (2.5cm) wide plus ¼ inch (6mm) seam allowances, but, on fine fabrics, they may be cut twice the width and used double. You will need equal amounts of light and dark fabrics for the patchwork, plus foundation and lining fabric the size of the project, excluding seam allowances.

Log Cabin is eminently suitable for cushions, using one large or four smaller blocks, crib covers with 12 smaller blocks, cot quilts, full-size quilts and wall hangings.

Method of working

In Log Cabin patchwork, templates can sometimes be used but they are not essential.

MAKING THE BLOCK

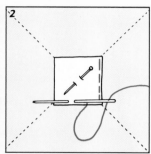

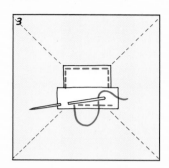

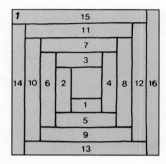

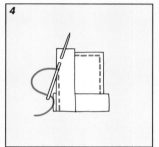

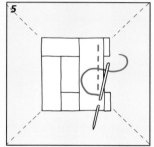

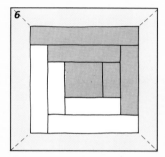

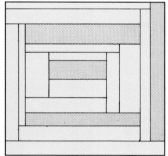

1 Cut a square of backing fabric to size plus ½ inch (15mm) seam allowances all round. Mark it diagonally both ways either by tacking (basting) stitches or with a light pencil line.

2 Pin a 2 inch (5cm) square in the middle and secure with small running stitches, or by machine.

3 Cut a light strip ¼ inch (6mm) longer at each end than the central square by 2½ inch (6.5cm) wide, and fold lengthways in half. With right sides together, place the fold over the edge of the central square and stitch across.

4 Press the strip back to the right side. Apply a second light strip ¼ inch (6mm) longer at each end than the length of the central square and strip, stitch and press back.

5 Apply dark strips in the same way working around the square stitching and pressing them back to the right side.

6 Repeat the sequence adding light and dark strips to complete the block.

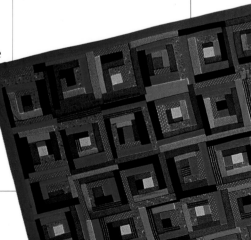

ABOVE *A typical example of a Crazy Log Cabin block.*

RIGHT *Crazy Log. The lively, haphazard effect of the quilt is emphasized by an imaginative choice of colors, including strong primaries, and clear greens and purples.*

The foundation block of the required size, with ½ inch (1cm) all round for seams, should be creased diagonally in both directions, the resulting creases being the lines at which the rows of 'logs' cross. Pin the central square, representing the chimney, to the center of the foundation, then assemble five different fabrics in light shades and five in dark shades, and decide how wide the strips of fabric for the logs should be. Cut two strips of light material and two of dark about 2 inches (5cm) longer than the central square. With right sides facing and using a running stitch, sew the first light strip to the central square ¼ inch (6mm) in from the edge, taking the stitches through the foundation block. Press the strip away from the center. Sew the second light strip to the second side of the square in the same way, followed by dark strips to the remaining two sides. Continue in this way with the other fabrics, making the strips longer on each row and keeping light and dark fabrics always at the same side until the foundation has been covered. When the required number of blocks have been made they can be sewn together in many different ways. Lay out the blocks and move them around to see which pattern is the most effective.

Some designers prefer to make blocks without the foundation fabric, stitching directly to the central square.

By varying the proportions of the strips and losing the diagonal dividing lines, a contemporary Crazy Log pattern is achieved.

STRIP PATCHWORK

*L*ike Log Cabin, strip patchwork involves stitching to-gether long strips of fabric in pattern. This is one of the easiest methods of making patchwork. Templates are not used and the whole patchwork can be quickly stitched by machine without a foundation fabric. Strips of fabric are cut or torn across the width of the chosen fabrics. The strips may be stitched to a backing, or to each other, to produce an area of fabric of the required size. Press each seam before sewing the next.

Simple designs can be adapted quite imaginatively for floor rugs, sleeping bags, crib or cot covers and play mats. Made up and quilted without a wadded interlining, the patch-work would make stunning duvet and pillow covers – team-ing the colors but varying the stripes. Any fabric can be used from wool, tweeds and suitings (for rugs) to silks, satins, cottons, cotton/wool mixes, velvets and corduroys.

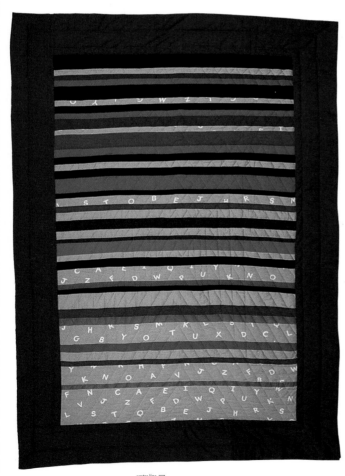

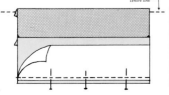

Starting in the middle of the quilt, apply the strips for the first half as shown. Turn the work round and complete the second half working in the same way, taking care to place any motifs or letters the correct way up.

Before starting, always make a full-scale plan. (Many people attracted to the unpredictable effect of random placing are not always aware that most successful designs are invariably worked out beforehand with such a full-scale plan. Tear or cut the strips across the width of the fabric. Make them up to the width of your design and arrange them in pattern.

If working on a backing fabric, use a lightweight cotton or cotton/polyester. Place the first strip right side up across the center of the backing fabric. Place a second strip, raw edges and right sides together, and stitch taking a ¼ inch (6mm) seam. Turn the second strip over, and press.

Repeat these two stages until that side is complete, then repeat for the other half.

Strips can either be joined and quilted at the same time, or joined and then quilted by the usual wadded quilting method.

This type of patchwork can be made up by the block method. When using this method, work on all the blocks in sequence, so that any new fabric that needs to be introduced appears in every block in some way.

The strips can be applied vertically, horizontally, or diagonally. Take great care while stitching strips on the diagonal, as they may easily pucker. A layer of wadding can be placed on the backing fabric, and the strips stitched in place through both fabrics.

A variety of fabrics can be used, contrasting matt with shiny, textured with smooth. The width of the strips can also be varied.

Contemporary strip patchwork has made exciting use of random strips. In the cushion shown, irregular strips are used to make up an abstract landscape. Printed cotton fabrics are used to suggest foliage and some are overlaid with colored gauze to soften the effect. The whole panel is machine stitched on to a backing fabric, surrounded with a log cabin border.

In the search to find new ways of expressing abstract themes such as rhythm and movement modern designers are exploring random patchwork more and more.

Strip patchwork lends itself well to this kind of exploration. In the contemporary wall hanging shown, mixed colored strips have been joined together, cut into random shapes, and restitched again into several random-shaped borders to surround the three central images. The multi-colored background fabric has been painted with lively strokes to give continuity of movement and color. Patchwork created in this way, using all kinds of cotton sateens and poplin, develops a lively, jolly character most suitable for younger members of a family.

BELOW *In this contemporary cushion, random strip patches create an abstract landscape. The diagram demonstrates the tapering strips used.*

LEFT *Fabric and paint are used in this contemporary wall hanging to create a unique patchwork effect.*

RIGHT *Strips of plain and patterned cotton, silks and satins are pieced together to make this attractive quilted hanging. The strips, which vary greatly in length, are combined with lengths of pieced fabric, resembling lines of small squares or triangles. Lengths of covered piping cord are inserted into some of the seams to enrich the surface.*

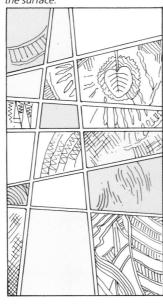
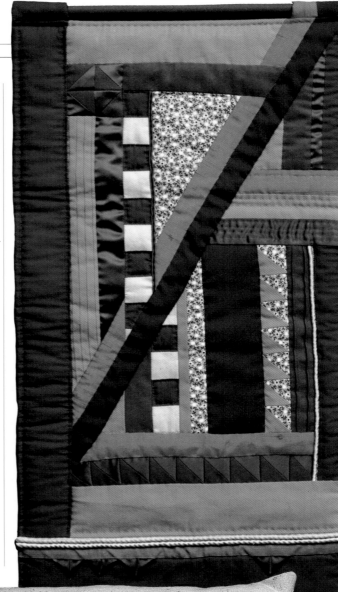
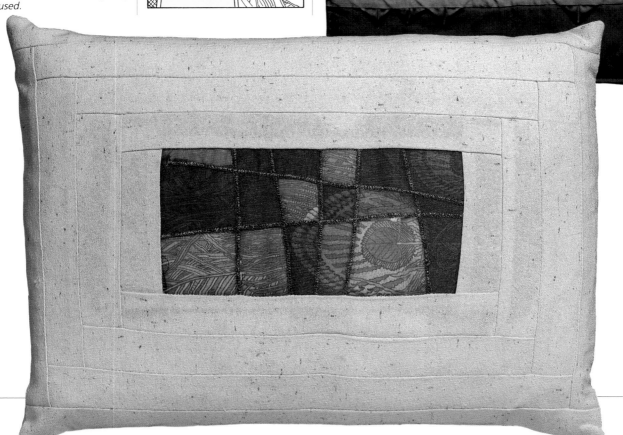

283

SEMINOLE PATCHWORK

*T*his form of strip patchwork developed by the Seminole Indians uses thin strips of colored fabrics which are first stitched together, cut up and then rearranged into brilliant colored patterns – often with tiny mosaic-like patches much smaller in size than in ordinary patchwork. The technique is sometimes called Cut and Stagger patchwork from this method of working. It can produce some of the most complex-looking patterns in patchwork. The full range can be quite amazing – from tiny multi-colored zigzags and plaids to ingenious pieces of op art.

The development of this simple, yet ingenious method of creating complex-looking designs was directly influenced by the introduction of the sewing machine. Closely-woven cottons or silks in plain, primary or subtle colors work well but patterned fabrics should be chosen with care. Certain patterns do not always give the right amount of contrast and the finished effect may be disappointing. Also, since there are so many seams involved, heavier fabrics are best avoided. These would be bulky and unattractive. Although the width of the strips can be varied, more intricate effects are achieved with narrower strips, but they should not be less than ¾ inch

BELOW *Straight-cut strips.*

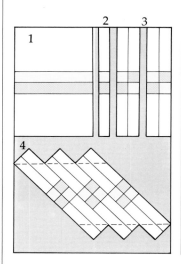

(2cm), including seams.

The small-scale effect of the patchwork makes it ideal for children's clothes – inserted dress panels and borders, for example; shirt yokes, pockets, bags, cushions and wall hangings.

In the contemporary cushion shown, strips of different colored and plain cottons are first pieced into bands of chevron and stripes. The final pieced fabric is cut and staggered into radiating diagonal shapes to create a pattern of broken borders.

Dazzling, eye-catching designs are a special feature of Seminole patchwork. Many geometric patterns designed to create optical illusions translate well into this type of patchwork. Several colors can be used for more complex effects, or just two strongly contrasting tones, as in the dramatic Op Art quilt illustrated. Here blocks of black and white checks are cut and repositioned to create a third illusory dimension of swirling movement. Fine- to lightweight cotton or cotton mixtures are excellent for designs where so many seams are involved. In order to fully appreciate the effect, optical designs usually require a fairly large expanse, such as quilts, covers, duvets and rugs. However, four blocks would make a handsome floor

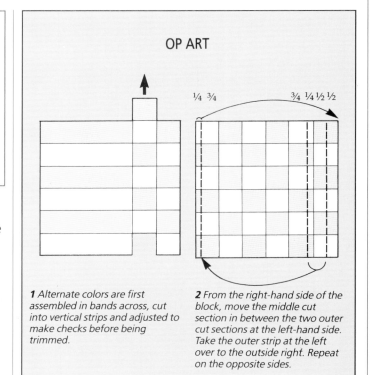

OP ART

¼ ¾   ¾ ¼ ½ ½

1 Alternate colors are first assembled in bands across, cut into vertical strips and adjusted to make checks before being trimmed.

2 From the right-hand side of the block, move the middle cut section in between the two outer cut sections at the left-hand side. Take the outer strip at the left over to the outside right. Repeat on the opposite sides.

cushion or bolster, or a smaller wall hanging.

The eye-catching effects of Seminole work are achieved by careful planning. To avoid a muddled effect, either make a scaled plan of your design, or, if you are not sure how your

shapes will work out, experiment, using fabric oddments, by cutting and stitching several different strip patterns to find the most pleasing arrangements, and then plan your design on paper.

BELOW *Seminole work.*

Contemporary interpretation of Seminole work to create an Op Art design.

FOLDED STAR PATCHWORK

*F*olded star patchwork (sometimes called Quill patch-work) is made by attaching folded triangles of fabric (quills) to a ground fabric. The present technique, which was developed in Canada, is traditionally worked in patterns based on an eight-pointed star – one of the most popular motifs in American pieced patchwork.

Light- to mediumweight cottons fold and crease well and are preferable to synthetics or silks which are too springy and slippery. Fabric oddments can be used mixing patterns where necessary to give the correct tone rather than pattern. Small-scale prints, including flower sprigs, spots, checks, stripes and strong contrast plain colors, help to define the star motif. You will also need a foundation fabric which should not be too difficult to sew through – unbleached firm cotton is ideal.

The star pattern is built up by working outwards from the middle overlapping triangles around a central point, and increasing the number in the rows as the patchwork is enlarged to the size required. The work naturally forms a circle but a design can easily be extended into a square. Each

triangle needs a 2 inch (5cm) square of fabric, so, to get a rough idea of the overall amount needed, first make several practice triangles from fabric oddments or paper. Arrange them in patterns following the instructions, and then calculate the number of rows needed and the amounts of different fabrics for your planned design.

The finished patchwork block is the perfect shape for making cushion sets, or for piecing with alternate plain blocks, for example, into larger patchwork – and for lining the lids of laundry or sewing baskets. For a neat finish, borders and piped edges can be added, picking up the same or contrast colors, with a plain backing.

BELOW *Folded star patchwork has a very attractive tactile quality. Flower prints, spots and plain cottons in strong contrasting colors have been used to make this pretty cushion cover.*

METHOD

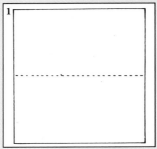

1 Cut out the correct number of 2 inch (5cm) squares from your chosen fabric. Fold in half.

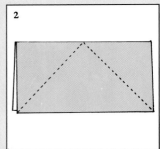

2 Press flat. Make a triangle by folding the top corners to the center of the base.

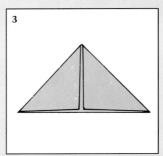

3 Make three more triangles in the same color. Press the edges flat.

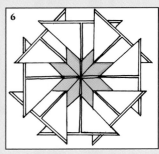

4 Mark the foundation fabric both ways through straight and diagonal centers. Pin the first triangle in place, and secure with a short straight stitch, as shown.

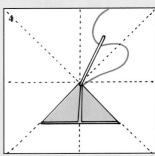

5 Attach three more triangles catching the center points, and then secure the outer edges with running stitch through all layers ½ inch (5mm) from the edge.

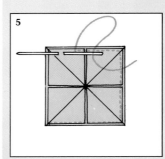

6 Add eight triangles in color sequence placing the points about ½ inch (1cm) from the center, overlapping the corners. Sew as before. Add eight more triangles on the next row placing the points between those of the last row, and continue in this way adding 16 on subsequent rows as the size increases, and so on, to finish your planned design.

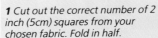

MAYFLOWER PATCHWORK

Mayflower or Cathedral window patchwork combines simple appliqué with folded patchwork. This ingenious technique is thought to have originated on the *Mayflower* carrying pilgrims to America, where the women used flour sacking to make the folded foundation blocks on which they stitched their precious pieces of printed and colored fabrics in such a way as to be sparing (without making hems) and yet give a bright overall effect of colorful patchwork.

Essentially, the work involves folding and refolding squares of the foundation fabric so that the finished patchwork is several layers thick and makes a light, warm covering suitable for throws. Also, as the outer edges are self-finishing, additional borders are not needed.

The method of preparing the foundation reduces the size of the original square by just over half, so allow about two and a quarter times the finished size for the foundation fabric. 6 inches (15cm) is a popular size; a square this size will need a contrast square patch of about 2 inches (5cm).

Mediumweight cottons such as calico and poplin work well for the foundation and dressweight cottons for the patches. Plain fabrics inset with multi-colored patches can look quite stunning and give dramatic cathedral window effects. Alternatively, multi-colored backgrounds with plain patches can be equally attractive, reversing the effect to give a series of four-petalled flowers on a mixed ground.

Mayflower patchwork adapts well for cushions, bags, quilts, and wall hangings.

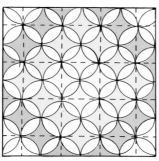

ABOVE AND BELOW *Mayflower patchwork traditionally uses contrasting plain and patterned fabrics. In this cushion toning fabrics are used, and the contrast is between textures – a cream colored satin for the folded foundation and a darker velvet for the centers. The shiny texture of the satin catches the light.*

METHOD

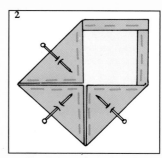

1 *Cut out sufficient squares from the foundation fabric. Make single ¼ inch (6mm) turnings all round, baste and press flat.*

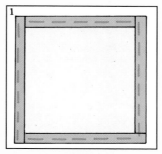

2 *Fold the four corners to the middle, pin each one down and press the edges to give a good sharp crease.*

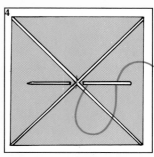

3 *Repeat, folding the corners of the smaller square to the middle and pressing the edges flat, as before.*

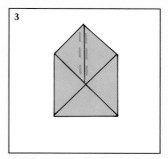

4 *Secure the points in the middle with one or two small cross stitches through all layers.*

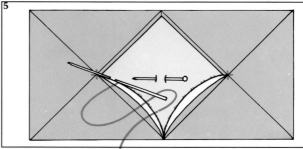

5 *Complete all the foundation squares and then join them together first to form rows across. Begin by placing two squares wrong sides together and then oversewing the edges. Cut out sufficient small squares ¼ inch (6mm) smaller than the diamond formed between the two squares. Pin a small contrast patch over the seam between the joined squares. Turn the folded edges of the squares over the raw edges of the patch to form gently curved lines, and hem in place through the layers.*

6 *Repeat, and continue in this way to complete all the rows across. Then join the rows together in the same way. The remaining triangles left at the edges can either be left plain or filled with triangular patches, turning in the outer edge and hemming in the usual way.*

PLEATED PATCHWORK

As its name suggests, pleated patchwork involves joining together blocks of pleated fabric arranged to give interesting textural and optical effects. This purely decorative patchwork, in which the surface texture of the fabric is deliberately altered before the blocks are joined, offers great scope for innovation.

Regularly formed pleats are machine stitched and can either be stitched down at each side of a block, following the direction of the folds to give a softly ridged surface, or additional lines may also be stitched diagonally across, or at right angles to the first set of folds. This alters the surface tension, and, in this way, the play of light creates quite amazing effects of movement reminiscent of drifting sand dunes.

Pin tucks can also be used. These are usually stitched quite near the folded edge of the fabric, although the depth can be varied as needed. They can be stitched in sequence either vertically or horizontally, or in both directions to form a checkered pattern. The same stitching can be used throughout, or in different sequences of straight stitch and satin stitch worked over the edge in matching, contrast or variegated colored threads. Pin tucks combined with pleating and 'movement stitching' offer a whole new range of visual effects. Despite the geometric constrictions involved in pleating and tucking, softly textured and surprisingly free-flowing patterns can be achieved.

The prepared fabric is cut into the correct size blocks and arranged to suit the design. Rectangular blocks can be joined together either following a simple square grid, in vertical or horizontal bands across, or cut into block-size geometric shapes such as triangles, parallelograms and diamonds, for example, before being stitched in pattern.

As most of the interest in pleated patchwork relies on the undulating surfaces created and the way in which the blocks are put together, plain, pastel colored fabrics will give best results. All cottons and other light- to mediumweight fabrics that keep their creases well are perfect for pleating and tucking projects, preferably in plain or pale, colored stripes so that the full effect of the shadowy textures can be seen. Voile, cotton, cotton/polyester,

gingham, fine velvet, chiffon, lace and certain nets, as well as mediumweight silks with matt rather than shiny surfaces, are ideal. However, simple, spotted, striped and shaded fabrics might also be exploited. By obscuring and distorting the design with pleats and tucks, areas of solid color, or increased density of pattern, can be produced and used in imaginative piecing.

A 12 inch (30cm) square block is an average size for a quilt and other larger works such as rugs and wall hangings. Single blocks will make handsome cushions, and four blocks are ideal for jumbo-size floor cushions, but the size can easily be adapted to fit other geometric designs.

Pleats

Pleating and tucking reduces the fabric depending on the

PLEATS AND TUCKS

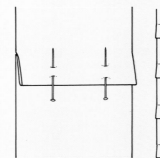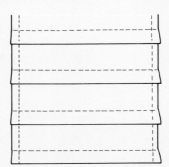

PLEATS
1 Decide the depth of the pleat — ½ inch (15mm) is a popular size. Working on the right side, and along the straight grain of the fabric, pin the first fold across and press.

2 For the next and subsequent pleats, release the first fold, measure the depth and the distance between and then, using pins, mark the foldlines and positioning lines along both edges. Complete each pleat stitching ½ inch (15mm) in from the edge. Press and stitch the pleats down each side in the direction of the folds.

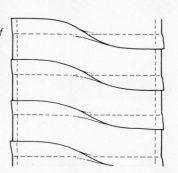

FOR 'MOVEMENT STITCHING'
Either machine the outer edges of a block with the folds in opposite directions, or repeat over the entire surface stitching the folds up and down, or diagonally, in alternate directions. Hold the fabric with both hands as you feed it through the machine, using pins as a guideline for stitching.

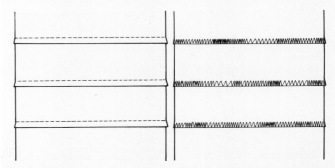

TUCKS
1 To make simple tucks, fold the fabric along the straight grain and, using matching or contrast colored threads, machine between ⅛-¼ inch (3-6mm) in from the edge. Press the tuck to one side and repeat as needed. Accurate straight stitching is essential.

2 Alternatively, zigzag stitch the edges, using a variegated thread.

depth of the folds used. For full pleating, allow at least three times the finished size.

As an alternative to using regularly spaced pleats of an equal size throughout a patchwork, you can ring the changes by mixing areas of both deep and shallower pleats in a design. This will give a more undulating and sculptural effect to the surface, which can also be further emphasized by stitching with shaded threads. Take extra care when estimating the amount of fabric needed.

Tucks

For a combined effect of tucks and pleats stitch the pleats as far as setting the folds, as previously described, and then stitch the creased lines as described for tucks. Use matching or contrast colors, changing them to emphasize the effects of movement.

Being much finer than pleats, tucks can be stitched quite close together over an entire area in regular or random designs, to give a gently ridged surface. They can also be spaced apart and worked in both directions to produce checks, and with a little more effort, checks can be varied to create a tartan effect. As with pleats, take care in estimating the amount of fabric needed, remembering with tartan-type designs, to calculate both directions accurately.

Use of colour

Striped fabrics, with slightly wider stripes than ticking, provide the opportunity to introduce subtle color tones to pleating and folding with some fascinating results.

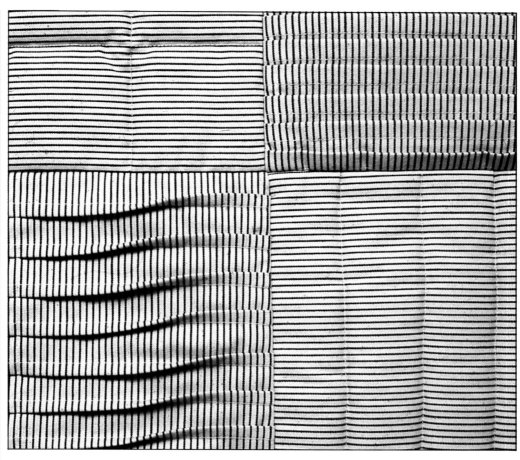

Simple two-color stripes can be folded so that the two colors are made to fall on either side of the crease line, and, when pressed flat, each fold effectively blocks out the color underneath.

Pastel colored dressweights and sheeting will give good effects. It is a good plan to experiment with different striped fabrics before embarking on the major project. This may lead to making a series of samples, which could be framed as a collection of pleated pictures. To recreate this particular effect, the depth of the fold should be exactly the same as the distance between.

ABOVE *This detail shows pleats with 'movement' stitching and contrasting quilted patterns worked on striped ticking.*

BELOW *This detail shows clearly the different colors created by applying the pleated bands of striped fabric in opposite directions.*

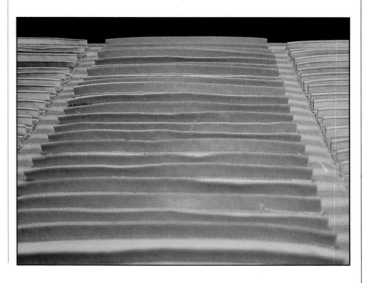

FINISHING

All patchwork should be well finished. Ideally, the way a piece of patchwork is finished should be an integral part of the overall design and be considered at the beginning. Items such as garments, cushions and other soft furnishings will have their raw edges neatened in the making-up process whereas the edges of quilts and wall hangings are treated individually. Plain colored borders in varying depths with either mitered or square corners can be added, or a decorative border as shown in the diagram. Piped edges can be very effective; choose one of the fabrics used in the patchwork itself to provide continuity of color. Binding or self-neatening the edges are also effective. Refer to the quilting section for instructions.

With a 'busy' patchwork design, often a plain border will serve best. A contrasting fabric may set off your patchwork pattern, or a toning shade may bring a feeling of harmony to the whole. A double border, for example a narrow light-coloured border framed by a second wider and darker one, can give an effective frame effect. It may be best to complete the patchwork before deciding which kind of border will be most appropriate.

The width of the border may depend upon the size you have in mind for the finished article, or upon the aesthetic effect that a wide or narrow edging will have in relation to the main pattern.

Folded star patches can make an effective edge for garments and wall hangings. Tabs, fringes and tassels can be used to decorate the edges of hangings, quilts and cushions. Notice that styles such as Mayflower and Shell patchwork have their own built-in edges.

The finished patchwork (with or without interlining) should be lined to neaten and strengthen the seams, and large pieces quilted to hold the layers together.

For added strength, you may prefer to back some cushions and other soft furnishings and unquilted wall hangings with a stiff bonded interfacing before lining.

As lining and finishing the edges are worked in exactly the same way as for quilted items, refer to the quilting section for full instructions.

BELOW *Straight-edged patterns like Log Cabin can be treated as self-finishing, with no need for a border. Here, four Log Cabin blocks have been used for a cushion cover. Although a border has not been felt necessary, the edges have been piped to give a neat finish.*

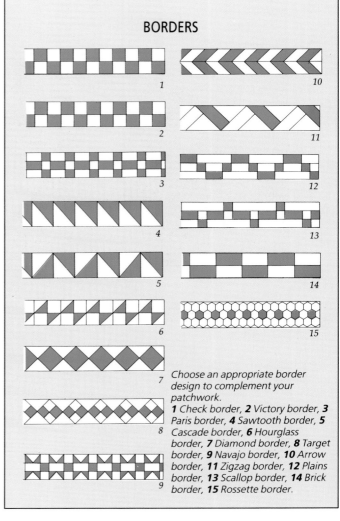

BORDERS

Choose an appropriate border design to complement your patchwork.
1 Check border, **2** Victory border, **3** Paris border, **4** Sawtooth border, **5** Cascade border, **6** Hourglass border, **7** Diamond border, **8** Target border, **9** Navajo border, **10** Arrow border, **11** Zigzag border, **12** Plains border, **13** Scallop border, **14** Brick border, **15** Rossette border.

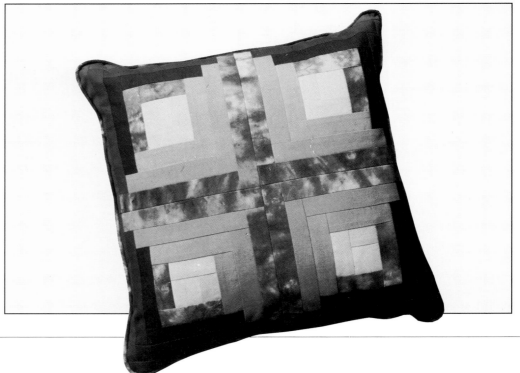

PRESSING PATCHWORK

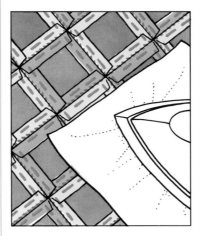

1 Working on a padded surface, place the patchwork right side down and pin through the patches on each side.

2 Press under a cloth to prevent glazing the fabric, first on the wrong side and then on the right side, having previously removed all tacking threads to avoid marking.

3 Remove the backing papers — these can be used again if they are not damaged. Add any half patches to straighten the edges before making up the finished item.

FINISHING CORNERS

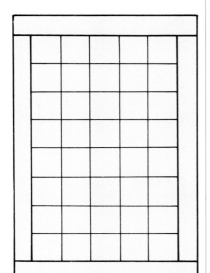

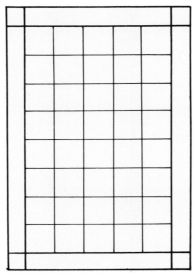

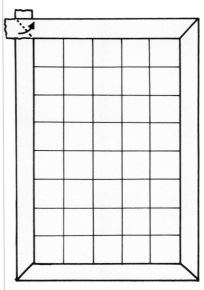

STRAIGHT CORNERS
Apply the two long sides of the border cut to the length of the patchwork. Cut the two shorter sides to include the patchwork and the width of the two borders, as shown, plus seam allowances, and stitch in place. Hand stitch the outer corner seam.

BLOCK CORNERS
Apply the two long sides as for straight borders. Cut out the four corners to size or piece block to fit, and then join each corner to its respective border to form two long strips. Stitch the top and bottom borders in place, finishing the outer corner seams as for straight borders.

MITERED CORNERS
Cut all four borders the required width and depth. Position them on the patchwork with the corners overlapping, and fold back the fabric diagonally across each corner. Use the creases as a guide for stitching.

CHAPTER 7

APPLIQUÉ

INTRODUCTION

Appliqué is the process of attaching cut-out fabric shapes to a foundation fabric by means of stitching, which may itself be plain or colorful and decorative. Essentially, appliqué is a two-dimensional technique which may be strictly functional, such as a knee patch on dungarees, or purely decorative such as a satin motif on a négligé. However, in picture making and more experimental work, it can be a vital art form in which personal statements are expressed. The play of light on surfaces, stitching, subtle modelling of fabric may all be exploited to create work with immensely tactile qualities.

Appliqué is one of the oldest forms of needlework. Initially used to cover or strengthen worn cloth, it developed into the practice of applying definite shapes and colors in individual designs for esthetic reasons. Applying patterned fabric to a plain background takes less time than embroidery, and plain areas of fabric applied to a sumptuous brocade stand out in a bold design. It is an economic use of precious scraps of cloth, silks or velvets with either curved or rigid edges, and has proved to be a handsome and unusually decorative form of needlework. The stitches can be worked unobtrusively or more boldly.

The earliest appliqué work that survives today, dating back to several centuries B.C., uses bold designs of cut-out figures with details added in simple embroidery. Felt, bark-cloth and leather appliqué work was used in ancient times for religious and ceremonial purposes as well as purely for decoration. Early man also used skins and furs for elaborate applied and inlaid work, and this tradition still persists in cold climates in northern countries.

For many centuries appliqué was used to dramatic effect for heraldic banners, altar frontals and wall hangings, often from the most precious fabrics.

Appliqué was used on the flags and banners of the Middle Ages which were carried into battle. Simple designs were applied to surcoats and jupons for the recognition of men wearing armour. At the start, only lords and knights carried devices, but later all their followers also wore heraldic symbols. It became a technical language of its own.

The technique remains particularly appropriate in cases where the work has to be seen from a distance (as in church and ceremonial work) as its patterns can be readable as far away as its colors can be distinguished.

Crusaders returned to France and Britain from the Holy Wars with sumptuous silks, velvets and brocades which encouraged appliqué work. The reflective qualities of these different surfaces made these fabrics stimulating to look at.

With the coming of the Industrial Age, the new availability of cheap printed cottons made appliqué practicable at a more popular level, and it became a common method of decorating quilts and coverlets, both in England and in the United States.

Today, apart from its widespread use to decorate clothing and accessories, appliqué is often used to create large and striking murals. The wide range of fabrics now available and the development of protective fabric sprays offer many advantages to the designer of hangings and panels incorporating appliqué. In domestic use, it can be used for cushions and covers in styles ranging from the subtle to the dramatic, or for creating pictures.

There are several distinct styles of appliqué to choose from involving a number of techniques. The technique is often determined by the final use of the work; if it is for hard wear, or has to be washed often, it is essential that the method of attaching the patch can stand up to this treatment. On any fabric which frays, the edges must be turned under; when working with felt or leather the edges can be sewn invisibly to the base fabric, or the stitching can be made a feature of the design. The raw edges of a patch can also be finished with close stitching, couching a cord over the join, or by machine satin stitch. Features from printed fabrics can be cut out and applied to a background fabric.

STANDARD APPLIQUÉ (ONLAY) has plain or patterned fabric shapes cut out and stitched to a ground fabric, as in traditional English and American quilt designs.

APPLIQUÉ PERSE has printed birds, flowers and animals, for example, originally cut from whole cloth and applied to a ground fabric.

REVERSE APPLIQUÉ (INLAY) has designs of two or more colors cut out to form a counterchange pattern, or has several layers cut through – a technique adopted by the Cuna Indians of Panama and Colombia to make their famous molas (blouses) and headbands.

FOLDED APPLIQUÉ is a simple method of designing whereby whole fabric is folded into eighths and the pattern cut out – much like paper snowflakes are made – before being applied to a contrast colored background.

SHADOW APPLIQUÉ uses sheer and semi-transparent fabrics overlapped on either the right or wrong side to give subtle changes of color density. Combined with free machine stitching, and fabrics and threads rich in texture and color, it offers wide scope for experiment.

PICTURE APPLIQUÉ — where the choice of subject is wide open for innovation – combines manipulating fabric, shape, texture and technique to create unique effects.

LACE APPLIQUÉ uses all kinds of lace, net, sheet and fine fabrics and trims and applies these in individually shaped motifs, doilies, edgings and whole cloth to a ground fabric in order to produce very delicate, lacy effects. The ground fabric may be cut away from behind the finished motif.

PADDED APPLIQUÉ involves stuffing certain areas of the appliqué with either whole or loose wadding to give the surface a softly sculptured effect. To take padding slightly further, and make fully stuffed shapes, a whole new area of three dimensions is possible.

ABOVE *The Country Wife, a three-dimensional mural commisioned for the Festival of Britain, and designed by Constance Howard in 1951. The panel is worked to five-eighths life-size, and a wide variety of crafts and activities have been represented.*

LEFT *A detail from the beautifully worked New Forest Embroidery commissioned by the New Forest Association, England to commemorate 900 years of Forest life. Designed and organised by Belinda Montague, and worked by more than 60 volunteers, it measures 25 × 2 feet (7.7 × .7m) and depicts New Forest birds, animals and flowers, and historical scenes such as the one shown.*

MATERIALS AND EQUIPMENT

Fabrics

Almost any material can be used in appliqué, and, like patchwork, a varied selection is often a stimulating source of design inspiration. Your ultimate choice should be governed by what you plan to make, bearing cleaning requirements in mind. For practical items, the fabric needs to be easy to handle and either washable or suitable for dry cleaning. While felt and lace scraps, for example, are excellent for picture-making, they would not wear well on a child's dungarees that have to be regularly laundered.

A firm but pliable fabric is most suitable for the background. A collection of any plain, patterned or textured materials can be applied, but it is best, although not always practical, to be consistent in using cotton on cotton and wool on wool. The applied fabrics should not be heavier in weight than the ground fabric, although a second (finer) supportive layer can be added to the background, if needed. Clear plastic bags keep selection of different colored pieces separate and easy to view.

Leather and felt are easy to apply on decorative articles,

BELOW *This Swedish bag, dated 1868, is a simple rectangle made from white leather and decorated on the front with a red and green appliquéd design. The border and applied motifs are cut from felted wool cloth, and these are sewn down with silk threads using back, straight and satin stitches. Some small white buttons are added for further decoration. The back of the bag is left plain and cut higher than the front showing the lining of patterned cotton. A braid shoulder strap is sewn on the top edge at either side.*

and materials like Viyella and cotton make appliqué work more straightforward at the beginning. Many manmade textiles have a springy nature and are difficult to handle, as are loosely woven or bulky fabrics, although this may be overcome by experience. Materials such as Thai silk are exciting to use when placed to catch the light on reverse weave. Shot silk can also be used to great effect; similarly, unusually visual results can be made from silk organzas and nets. Felt has an ancient history of use for appliqué in Middle Eastern countries and continues to be popular today. It is made by kneading or trampling moistened goat's or sheep's wool together, which is then flattened and laid out to dry. As it is a non-fraying fabric, felt lends itself well to appliqué work.

With delicate fabrics and those that fray easily, such as some silks and satins, a lightweight iron-on interfacing is recommended for extra support. Designs are transferred (in reverse) to the interfacing, either before or after ironing it to the wrong side of the fabric.

One of the main features of appliqué is making fabric 'work' not just in color and shape but in pattern and texture. Patterned fabric, for example, can be used to suggest all kinds of images and textures such as stripes for ploughed fields, flower sprigs for gardens, pile surfaces for animal fur and checks for brickwork.

Thread

As a general rule, the color and character of the thread should be similar to the

material used. For cottons and materials of a similar weight, use an all-purpose (size 50) sewing thread. Never force a thread through a fabric as immediate puckering and distortion occurs. Use colored threads for particular effects, and silk or metal threads for further decoration when the basic appliqué is completed. Remember dark basting threads may leave marks on a pale material.

Equipment

Sharp scissors and fine sharp pins are essential. Crewel, sharps or between needles should be used. You may also need gloving needles for leather appliqué.

If complete accuracy is desired, then work should be performed using a frame. The background fabric mounted into the frame needs to be slightly slack while tacking the pieces into place, then tightened for final sewing to prevent puckering. (Some would argue that all rules are meant to be broken; even puckered shapes can be used to create part of the design.) The shape and size of the frame depend on the type of work: a square frame is needed for large work, a narrow bordered, circular frame for machine work.

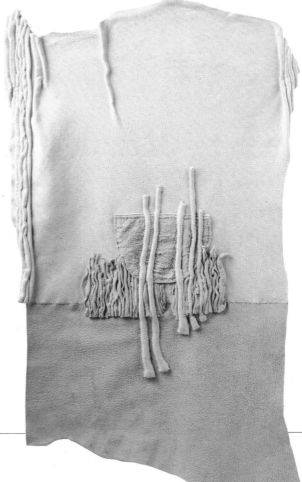

TOP This detail of a Meo hilltribe baby carrier from Thailand shows a design of small yellow squares outlined with corners of red cross stitch. Pink squares are superimposed onto the evenweave fabric. Bands of cotton strips hae been folded at the corners and machined around the rectangle to form a border. The lining and the panel are held together by pompons formed from loops of pink cotton thread stitched to the work in a tight circle forming a tuft. The loops are then cut.

ABOVE Lisu hilltribe embroidery. Onto a narrow strip of cotton a second strip is sewn, right sides and edges together; it is turned down, leaving a slight ridge. More strips are added in the same fashion. The triangles are made from rectangles of fabric with the long side turned under the folded in half.

RIGHT A contemporary wall hanging in chamois leather, using the same color and fabric for both background and appliqué.

DESIGN

*T*here are two essentially different approaches to appliqué design. One is to plan a design on paper and work from tracings or templates, and the other is to work spontaneously with fabric, scissors and stitches, applying the design directly to the ground fabric without pre-planning.

Inspiration for designs may come from widely different sources – traditional quilt patterns, Hawaiian appliqué, family photographs, landscape painting, a child's drawing, or simply from a colorful arrangement of fabrics. Before deciding, it is important that your design should suit the item you plan to make in both a practical and artistic sense.

For the beginner, it is best to start with a design clearly worked out on paper. Pencil several ideas roughly on paper. Simple, bold shapes are necessary for this type of embroidery. Tribal art is often simplified and a useful source. Outline shapes of leaves, petal, fruit and letters will initiate a free design, which can be added to as the work progresses. Compositions are more complex, and need detailed planning.

Consider the juxtaposition of colors in the intended design. Using colors next to one another in the spectrum, with small areas of opposing color, may be a guideline. Also, light against dark colors, and warm against cold, can create interesting contrasts. Particular care must be taken for work to be used in a church or on a dark wall.

To plan the design, colored paper cut into shapes, or designs or shapes taken from magazines, wallpaper or photographs, can be moved around until a pleasing arrangement is achieved. These shapes can be fitted with glue, tape or pins to a background sheet. It may be easier to create the whole design from one piece of wallpaper or from a picture. Either way, these designs can be transferred to the background fabric by using tracing paper, or by copying, preferably in sections.

Transferring designs

Whatever approach you decide, it is best to put your idea down on paper. If you prefer to work spontaneously, the drawing will be an invaluable guide as you cut and stitch through the different appliqué stages.

To work from a plan, you will need to make a full-scale drawing, preferably with colors and textures indicated, and sections that are to overlap noted. This makes sewing easier if awkward angles can be avoided. If the original design is too small, enlarge it, following the diagram opposite. Wash the ground fabric and press it flat. Then trace off the finished design and, using dressmaker's carbon paper, transfer it to the right side of the prepared ground fabric, following the straight grain.

A more direct method of transferring the design is to trace around templates onto the background fabric using a dressmaker's pencil or a hard lead pencil. Templates may be freely drawn, traced or copied onto a piece of stiff cardboard and cut out, or they may be shapes cut straight from magazines or wallpaper.

If a shape is repeated in the whole design, it is sensible to have a paper shape cut from the template for each repeat, to maintain accuracy.

Preparing to appliqué

Before cutting the pieces to be applied, it is important to match the grain of the background and the applied materials exactly, as the two materials then move together and will not pucker. (A pulled thread will define the directions of warp and weft threads in the fabric.) Some patterned materials, which demand a specific placement in the design, can be applied with iron-on interfacing. This can be used to prevent puckering, but will immediately change the character of the material. Test a scrap first, in case the iron-on interfacing alters the surface.

Felt and leather need no preparation before being applied but other appliqué fabrics may need to be backed with an interfacing to prevent fraying or to give extra body. Velvets and wools can also be backed with lightweight materials, and silks, cottons or linens with muslin.

Fine or lightweight fabrics may not need backing, but their edges can be turned under, ready for hemming to the article. First, mark the motif on the appliqué fabric. Cut ¼ inch (6mm) extra all round to allow for turning the edges under. Edges of curved outlines and corners may need to be clipped or notched so they can be turned under neatly. Finger-press the turned edges. It is best only to iron the edges if they are otherwise

BASIC APPLIQUE

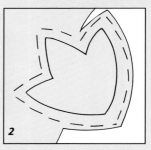

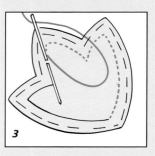

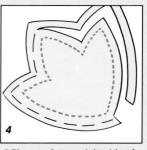

1 Pin template to right side of fabric and draw around the outline with a sharpened colored pencil. Mark a ¼ inch (6mm) seam allowance outside the drawn line.
2 Cut out the motif outside the two lines.
3 Stay stitch just outside the turning line.
4 Trim fabric to outer marked line.

PREPARING TO APPLIQUE

Templates numbered in order of application.

1 Position the template on the right side of the correct fabric and draw around the outline with a sharpened colored pencil. Mark a cutting line ¼ inch (6mm) outside the line.
2 Cut out the shape leaving a little extra fabric – about ¼ inch (6mm) all round, in case of fraying while handling and working the next stage.
3 Work stay stitch by hand or machine, just outside the fold line. This helps to make turning easier and gives a sharper edge to the patch.
4 Trim back the fabric to the outer marked line being careful not to cut into the stay stitching.

---

unmanageable, because this leaves a hem mark and destroys the slight puffiness of the two-dimensional edge.

Having transferred the whole design to the background fabric, lightly pin on the pieces using fine sharp pins horizontally and vertically, then tack them in the same way, never around the outside edge. If pin or needle holes mar the surface of the fabric, the woven threads can be gently coaxed back into line with a blunt-ended needle.

Leather must not be pinned, as the holes will always show. Work long stitches across the shapes in both directions to hold it firmly in place.

Neatening curves and corners

This helps to give a really neat finish to your appliqué shapes.

Seam allowances may vary

from ¼ inch to ¾ inch (6mm to 2cm) depending on the type of fabric used and the purpose required. Straight seams can be neatened in several ways, but where a seam curves or where you need to eliminate excess bulk, the resulting seam allowance must be trimmed either by clipping or notching. This helps to give a really neat finish to your appliqué shapes.

BELOW This Rajasthani bridegroom's bag for carrying sweetmeats has a fine red cotton base, with bands and shapes of white cotton applied with running and blind stitch. It is bordered with bands of yellow and faded blue with zigzag points.

CURVES AND CORNERS

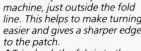 

On inner curves clip into the seam allowance as far as the stay stitching.

On outer curves cut out notches to prevent bulky folds forming underneath.

 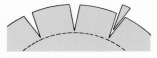

On outside corners trim the point back to reduce the amount of fabric in the mitered corner.

On inner corners clip into the point as far as the stay stitching.

METHOD 1

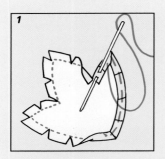

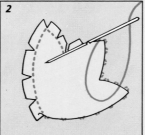

1 Clip into curves and corners. Fold seam allowances to wrong side and finger press. Baste allowances in place.
2 Pin patch to main fabric and if needed, secure with vertical basting stitches to prevent fabrics from wrinkling. Slipstitch in place along folded edge.
3 Take out basting threads.

METHOD 2

1 Clip into edges of patch and pin in place on main fabric without turning in raw edges. Secure with vertical basting stitches if needed. Avoid basting into seam allowance.
2 Using point of needle to turn raw edge under, slipstitch in place.

STRAIGHT STITCH

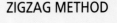
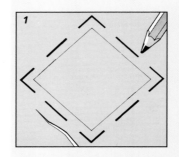

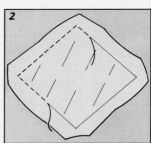

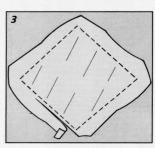

1 Place the template on the fabric and draw round it. Mark a second line ¼ inch (6mm) outside the first. Cut out leaving a margin.
2 Stay stitch round the outline. Trim to second line, cut and notch the fabric at curved sections, fold over and tack.
3 Place the shape on the background fabric, and tack it lightly into position.
4 Machine stitch the shape on round the edges using a medium stitch. End off threads securely on the wrong side.

ZIGZAG METHOD

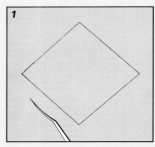

1 Place the template on the fabric and draw round it. Cut out the shape leaving a generous margin.
2 Place the shape on the background and tack into position. Machine stitch on exactly over the drawn outline.
3 Use a sharp pair of scissors to trim off the excess fabric close to the machine stitches as possible.
4 Set the machine on a fairly close zigzag stitch, and sew round the outline over the straight stitches and the raw edge. End off securely.

STITCHES

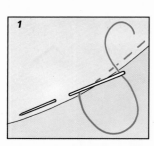

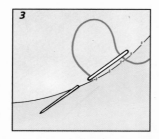

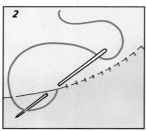

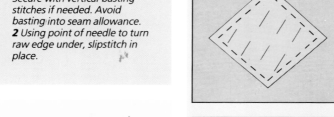

1 Running stitch. Take several evenly spaced stitches on needle before pulling through.
2 Slip hemming. Bring out needle through seam fold of patch and take a small stitch in ground fabric below. Insert needle directly above, next stitch through fold and repeat.
3 Stab stitch. Bring needle through just outside patch. Reinsert it above close to edge and repeat.

LEFT *The beautifully designed Monarchy embroidery worked by Audrey Walker in 1973, and displayed in the Pump Rooms at Bath. The piece is largely appliqué work, with additional embroidery for details and lettering. Most remarkable is the fashion in which the designer has contrived to make the different eras flow into one another along the central pictorial section.*

Hand sewing

There are several ways of stitching appliqué by hand, the choice depending mainly on the fabric used and the effect needed. Some methods are meant to be concealed, as in plain handstitching, while others are decorative, being embroidered or couched, or they can be both.

On fabrics that fray, where seam allowances are recommended, secure the patches with slip hemming, or running stitch.

On non-fraying fabrics, such as felt and leather, cut patches without seam allowances and apply them unobtrusively with stab stitch or small running stitches, using a colored thread to match the appliqué. The edges can, of course, be decorated afterwards.

Instead of basting or pinning, which would make permanent holes, these materials can be held in place by applying a small amount of fabric adhesive.

Machine sewing

Motifs can be attached by machine if the stitching does not need to be invisible. Machine-sewn appliqué has the advantage of being hardwearing, most suitable for practical items, and generally time saving. It is a faster, and probably more durable method of stitching. Straight stitching a motif to the background involves turning the edges of the motif under and hemming them, before attaching it by stitching beside the folded edge. A zigzagging method involves basting the appliqué material to the background in the shape of the designed motif, trimming the material to the basting line in the precise shape of the mofit, and zigzagging over the raw edges.

This is also one of the areas in appliqué where new ideas can be quickly expressed. A combination of appliqué – superimposing different layers of fabric and printed motifs, for example – with free machining can produce unconventional effects. In experimental work, the contrast between raw edges, straight stitching, and the firm lines of zigzag and satin stitch offers a wide choice of linear expression. Braids, ribbons and strips of fabric can be applied by free machine techniques.

Stitches

Many different stitches may be used in appliqué, including running stitch, chain stitch, overcast and back stitch, depending on the desired effect. Buttonhole, herringbone, feather and cretan stitches are ideal for decorative edges, adding another dimension or color to the shape. Stitches made to overlap outwards onto the background fabric lose the hard edge of the appliqué and are rewarding to use with freely designed work. Slip stitch is useful for applying motifs invisibly, if they have a seam allowance. If the allowance need to be basted to hold them in place before stitching the motif to the background, there are two steps. The motif may be more quickly applied by tucking the seam allowance under at the same time as attaching the motif, leaving out the basting stage. For slip stitch, bring the needle up through the background fabric directly under the folded edge and take a small stitch through and along the folded edge, then down through to the back, keeping the tension consistent.

Stab stitching may be used for leather and fabrics which do not fray. With this stitch, it is important to bring the needle up through the background fabric by the edge of the shape, and then stab vertically down into the shape. Continue the stitch around the edge of the shape.

Of the many different types of stitches that can be used for edging a motif, blanket stitch is a popular choice especially for non-fraying woven fabrics, and should be worked fairly close together over the edge of the motif. On non-woven fabrics such as leather or felt, stitches such as chain stitch and couching can be worked just inside the edge. For a more decorative finish, work fly stitch over the edge, adding French knots or seeding between to soften the outline.

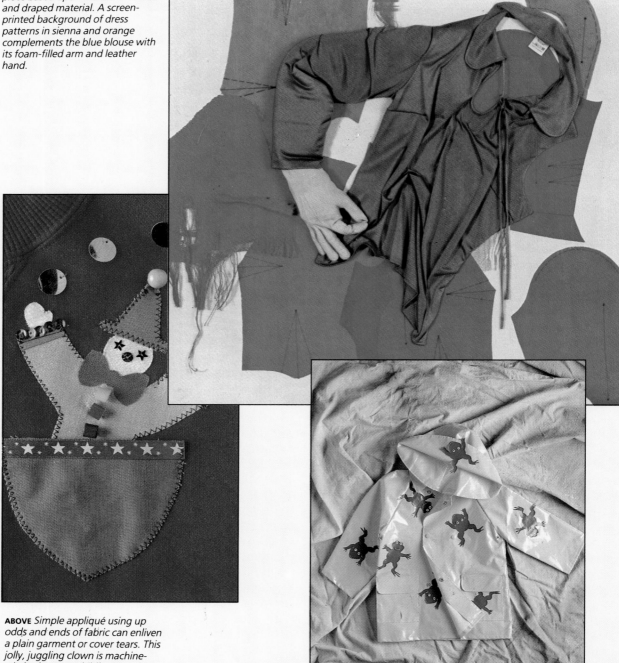

RIGHT *A contemporary appliqué piece based upon the use of folded and draped material. A screen-printed background of dress patterns in sienna and orange complements the blue blouse with its foam-filled arm and leather hand.*

ABOVE *Simple appliqué using up odds and ends of fabric can enliven a plain garment or cover tears. This jolly, juggling clown is machine-stitched on to a child's sweatshirt to provide a decorative pocket, with sequins and beads sewn on to finish.*

LEFT *A bold contemporary use of appliqué to decorate a jacket. The letters, the flowers and their black background are cut from felt, which gives a clean, sharp edge to shapes so long as a sharp knife is used. Stamens and the petal edges of the white flowers are embroidered after the appliqué motif is completed.*

LEFT *Here a child's PVC raincoat is decorated with appliqué frogs cut out of scraps of PVC and glued on to the garment. This idea is not only decorative, but can be used to camouflage small holes, rips or marks.*

RIGHT *Contemporary shadow appliqué design using white cotton organdie over a strongly colored cotton poplin.*

STANDARD APPLIQUÉ (ONLAY)

*S*tandard appliqué, using the methods described above, is perhaps the easiest and most versatile appliqué technique. The traditional formal designs of eighteenth and nineteenth century quilts are easily copied. Like patchwork, the motifs are worked in blocks to make them more manageable.

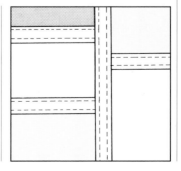

ABOVE *Contemporary abstract 'Cube' with tape covering the seams. There are several ways of applying the tape but the simplest is to tack and stitch in place all the horizontal pieces first, and then the vertical pieces on top, making sure they are accurately positioned, and all raw edges neatly covered.*

Cut the motifs, with the correct number of blocks for your design. Fold each block diagonally in both directions, and lightly press with a warm iron to mark the central guideline. Apply the shapes, positioning them centrally on the block in the order indicated by numbers in the diagram. Using matching thread and slip hemming neatly secure the appliqué in place. The blocks are then ready to be joined.

The sources of inspiration for contemporary appliqué design can differ widely. It may come from stained glass windows, aerial photographs of fields, primitive art, television graphics, or modern painting.

In the colorful abstract 'painting' shown, commercial tape (which requires no turning under) was used not only to cover the seams but also to provide an integral part of the design – using it as a line to link one unit to another – by being applied directly to the background. Such a technique makes this type of appliqué easy for beginners.

The patches are tacked into position on the background fabric before the tape is pinned over the raw edges, with the short ends turned under or tucked under adjacent edges. The tape is then stitched in place along both edges.

Mixed fabrics – silks, cotton, tweeds and velvets – can be combined for pictures and wall hangings of all shapes and sizes, but fabric for practical items should have similar cleaning requirements. Larger appliqué shapes may tend to pucker slightly without extra stitching or quilting, but this can be helped by backing the appliqué fabric with bonded interfacing ironed on before cutting out.

ABOVE *A nineteenth-century American quilt known as the Garden Wreath. The quilt top is divided into a number of blocks and shows appliquéd spray and wreath patterns combined with patchwork maple leaves. Many of the American quilts of this period were made in a similar way by a combination of patchwork and appliqué.*

Picture appliqué

Many contemporary designers are rediscovering picture appliqué to record simple daily activities in fresh, appealing styles. The subjects, as in this charming picture, frequently show lively characters in bright, colorful felt – simply stitched and unadorned.

Apart from the individual clothes of the children, and the chintz curtains at the door, the rest of the picture is cut from a range of different colored felt. The children's clothes are cut from printed striped and patterned fabrics, corduroy, denim and cotton. Their limbs and heads are also cut from felt and have hand-stitched features.

Hand-embroidered details are used to suggest the two bay tree tubs and the wall behind. The brickwork is embroidered with chain stitch to make the bonding pattern, and lines of chain stitch are worked down the tubs.

Essentially, the whole picture is very simply constructed and would not be too difficult for a beginner to tackle. An ideal size would be about 9 × 12 inches (23 × 30cm).

The picture's attractive nursery rhyme quality, with its colorful and easily recognizable figures, makes it the perfect present for a small child.

Make a full-scale drawing, and then choose the appropriate fabrics and felt, including a firm cotton backing fabric slightly bigger in size to allow for stretching in an embroidery frame, or, later, in a picture frame.

Following the instructions in Appliqué techniques, cut out the shapes from the fabrics suggested and apply them to the backing fabric in the correct order – stretching the backing in a frame, if preferred. Tack or apply a little fabric adhesive to hold the appliqué shapes. Using matching colored threads, neatly stab stitch the shapes in place, and add the features. Stretch and frame the finished picture as required.

Colored photographs can be used as a starting point for appliqué pictures. First make a preliminary drawing from the photograph, to simplify the images into color areas, textures and tone. Select fabrics and threads with an eye to texture as well as color. In the 'Sea Bathing' picture overleaf, for example, the beach huts are suggested with rough tweeds and corduroys, the sky with smooth cotton, the sea with sheer net, shingle with knobbly linen, trees and shrubs with velvet and felt, and so on. In the 'Wedding Party' picture on the same page, felt is used for a major part of the picture, including the trees, grass, gravestones, figures, wedding cars, and all the decorative ragwork on the church and window details. In contrast, slub linen is used for the church, velvet for the roof and windows, hessian (burlap) for the path, tweed for the road and wall, and cotton for the sky. Both pictures are built up on a hessian backing.

A sense of perspective is created partly by the use of color tone and partly by the care with which the layers are built up in the correct order.

Details are best added with surface embroidery when all the shapes have been attached. Six-stranded embroidery thread gives a well-raised effect. To keep a good shape around the edges of shapes that are

decoratively cut, attach them with running stitch rather than stab stitch. Formal shapes, such as the church roof and clock in the 'Wedding Party' picture, may be outlined with couching to give a smooth line.

Other techniques that may be brought into use for variety of texture are quilting and light padding of appropriate areas.

The drawings of a scene can also provide a starting point. Here, a cherry tree was sketched as seen through a kitchen window. The drawing was explored via a paper collage which simplified shapes, colors and tones, and finally the design for an appliqué picture was developed.

LEFT AND ABOVE *Ring O'Roses. Using the main picture as a guide, first select the different fabrics for the appliqué shapes, and then number your drawing in the order of application.*

TOP *Picture appliqué has a long history. This lovely hanging from Hardwick Hall depicts Patience. She is one of the Virtues on a series of large hangings, that could have been made out of cut up vestments.*

ABOVE *Seabathing.*

RIGHT *Wedding Party. Much of the charm of this picture is its subject, which is quite realistically portrayed in a wide range of textured fabrics – all cleverly cut and embellished with embroidery stitches to show many fascinating and well-observed details.*

APPLIQUÉ PERSE

This technique differs from standard appliqué only in that the motifs are cut complete from a printed fabric instead of being made up of pieces. The practice arose as a method of salvaging motifs from worn out chintzes; as fabrics became less expensive quilt makers continued to cut out motifs, but now from new material, and cotton manufacturers responded to the fashion by printing bolts with motifs designed to be cut out and stitched on to a plain background.

Between about 1800 and 1815, cotton manufacturers were printing cotton panels with topical scenes often commemorating some notable happening: a royal occasion, a battle or perhaps a well-known political event. A panel such as this was often used to form the center of a quilt top, borders being pierced and built up around it until the required size had been reached. These panels were again popular towards the end of the nineteenth century when many were printed to mark the centennial of the American Declaration of Independence (1876) and to honour Queen Victoria on her 1887 Jubilee. Today, quilts made in this way, are called Framed quilts or Medallion quilts.

The technique can still be used effectively today. Motifs cut from contemporary furnishing fabrics can be used to create most enchanting designs as shown here in the three cushions.

Each cushion is individually designed, taking as a starting point the cut-out motifs from printed chintz, and rearranging them in a pleasing way on a plain or patterned background. In this way, an interior scheme can be perfectly co-ordinated by appliquéing motifs from the same fabric used for the soft-furnishings – which is also an ideal way of utilizing leftover oddments. Floral, rather than formal, motifs are much easier to build up into free-flowing designs, although stylized and geometric patterns can be included. These may be used quite graphically – perhaps as a patterned background or a flower vase, or as a trellis behind a trailing plant, for example.

Surface stitching is another important element in the design. Here, the main outlines are machined using a wide satin stitch in darker and lighter tones picked out from the printed fabric. Straight stitching is used to fill the flower centers with radiating lines, the outlines of veins, shadows under petals, and the swirling tendrils and stalks that link leaves and flowers together. Alternative uses for perse motifs include the edges of table cloths and napkins, bed linen and duvet or down quilt covers: a quick and effective decoration is to break into the edge with just one or two motifs zigzag stitched around and trimmed.

Select your motifs from firm furnishing fabrics, such as glazed chintz, and arrange them on a plain background in a pleasing design. Decide which of the flowers (or leaves) should be 'in front' and tuck the others underneath trying them in different directions until you have an interesting composition. Add contrast fabrics between the motifs to form part of the background, as in the blue and pink designs.

Place a thin layer of wadding backed with tissue paper underneath the work and then, following the instructions in appliqué techniques for machine stitching, pin and tack the motifs in place.

To prevent puckering on large flowers, stitch the centers with radiating straight lines before covering the raw edges with wide satin stitch. Using matching or contrast threads, work the leaves in a similar way, stitching the veins before the outlines. Remove the tissue paper and make up the cushion cover.

Iron-on interfacing helps with this method as difficulties may not be found cutting out shapes which do not match the background fabric grain.

ABOVE *The diagram shows the basic outline of cut-out printed flowers arranged on a striped fabric appliquéd to a plain ground.*

BELOW *These cushions use glazed chintz for both the appliqué and the ground fabric.*

RIGHT *Here, the art of cutting a motif from a patterned fabric, as opposed to an already printed motif, is demonstrated in these lively animal shapes and flower stalks. Suitably patchy fabrics in realistic colors are used for the salamanders and the frog. Large printed flowers are appliquéd and the centers and stamen added separately, while the stalks are suggested with leafy fabrics applied to a basic earthy color.*

REVERSE APPLIQUÉ

*T*his method is the reverse of the usual appliqué method, involving the removal of fabric to form a design. Layers of different colored lightweight cottons may be used; non-fraying materials are best because of the intricate cutting. All the layers should have a matched fabric grain.

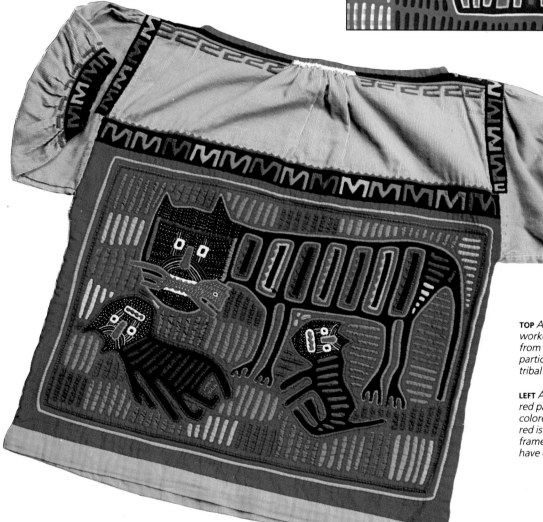

TOP *A brilliantly colored hanging worked in Indian reverse appliqué, from Panama. The technique is particularly suited to this type of tribal design.*

LEFT *A Mola blouse built up from a red panel with layers of fabric and colored patches. The last layer of red is cut and sewn to produce frames, slits and cat shapes which have embroidered faces.*

REVERSE AND INLAID APPLIQUE

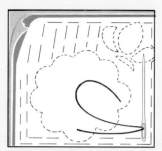

REVERSE APPLIQUÉ
1 Place the collected fabrics on top of each other, align the edges if possible and tack them all together. Mark the design on the top layer.

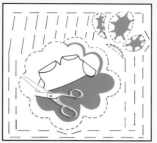

2 Cut out the pattern from the top layer of fabric leaving a margin of ¼ inch (6mm) beyond the marked line for turning under. Do not cut the second layer inadvertently.

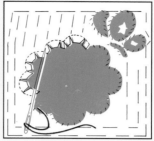

3 Clip and notch the margin at curved sections and turn it under with the point of the needle back as far as the marked line. Sew edge to next layer neatly.

4 Continue to cut, tuck in and sew back each layer until the desired overall design has been realized. Work some stitches through all the layers if possible.

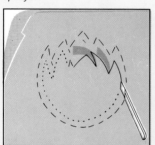

INLAID
1 Mark the design on one piece of fabric, lay it over another in a contrasting color and baste the two together outside the marked line. Cut through along the line.

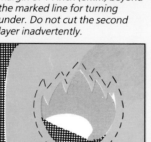

2 Baste one of the pieces of fabric onto some backing material, and drop the shape or motif in the contrasting color into the hole. It should fit exactly.

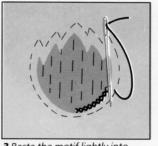

3 Baste the motif lightly into place in its hole with vertical basting stitches. Then sew the two edges neatly together with herringbone stitch. Remove basting.

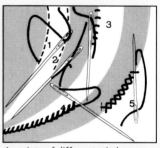

A variety of different stitches can be used for appliqué work: blind stitch **1**, running stitch **2**, overcast stitch **3**, blanket stitch **4**, and cross stitch **5**.

There are two methods: the traditional San Blas method and the recently adapted cut-through method, the difference between them being the order in which the layers are cut and stitched. The more intricate results of the traditional method involve working from the bottom layer up, with more improvising, and the adding of patches and layers both inside and outside the motif.

Cut-through appliqué is achieved by stab-tacking up five layers together, then cutting away shapes to expose the layers below. The first 'hole' must be large enough to accommodate the whole motif.

The bottom layer acts as a lining and is never cut. Having turned back the edges, and clipped or notched them if necessary, each layer is slip stitched to keep the area firm. Two layers cut at once can expose a color out of sequence.

Designing reverse appliqué may seem puzzling, but experimental arrangements of colored paper or tracings on top of each other can help. Either use tissue paper for the pattern, and stab tack it onto the fabric with small stitches, starting from the center to prevent puckering, or trace or copy the design onto the fabric layer by layer.

The simplest method of reverse appliqué is *appliqué découpé*, which uses just two layers of fabrics. The top layer is cut away in a pattern to show a contrasting fabric underneath. Interesting patterns can be made by using embroidery in contrasting tones on both layers, to finish features in the design, or to decorate. Alternatively, contrast patches can be sewn to the back as needed. This technique has been perfected by craftworkers in India, Pakistan, Thailand, Laos, and the Cuna Indians of Panama, who are famous for their distinctive designs particularly the multi-layered Mola work.

Inlaid appliqué

or *Persian resht* is a form of reverse appliqué in which shapes are cut from the ground fabric, and patches added which fit exactly into the negative shapes created. The fabrics to be used are placed one on top of the other, and the shape required cut through both. The first layer is placed on a background fabric mounted in a frame; the vacant space is filled by the piece from the second layer, and the edges are finally oversewn.

It is almost impossible with materials which fray unless backed with iron-on interfacing.

PADDED APPLIQUÉ

Beautiful relief surfaces can be made by padding certain areas or individual appliqué shapes. There are two very simple methods.

In the first, the appliqué is attached in the usual way, either by machine or hand sewing using slip hemming – this stitch giving a nicely rounded edge to the padding – but an opening is left in which loose wadding cut to the same size as the appliqué patch (less turning allowances) and the two layers applied as one.

Motifs in relief

A more complicated way to pad appliqué shapes can provide amusement in a piece of work because the edges of motifs are not completely attached to the ground fabric – flowers and leaves, for example, treated in this way give a very pretty effect.

Pin two layers of appliqué fabric together with a layer of interfacing between to give body. Trace the motif on top, zigzag stitch around the outline and trim back the edges to the stitching. Make a small slit in the back and pad with loose wadding to give a pleasing shape. Over sew the slit. Position the motif on the ground fabric and secure either through the middle by hand or partially zigzag stitch to the ground fabric.

MOTIFS

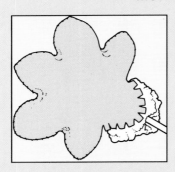

Padded appliqué. Use a fine knitting needle to ease the wadding into the corners of a motif to give a nicely rounded surface.

Motifs in relief. After stitching around, cut out the motif close to the stitching.

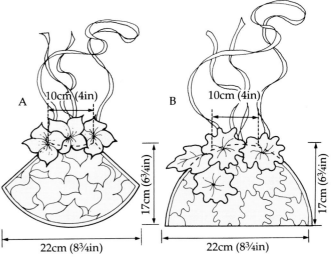

A 10cm (4in)
B 10cm (4in)
17cm (6¾in)
17cm (6¾in)
22cm (8¾in)
22cm (8¾in)

ABOVE *The front of each of these evening bags is appliquéd with a cluster of separately padded flowers and leaves which are spray-dyed and embroidered in softly shaded colors to match the dyed and quilted background. In each case, an interesting feature is made of the quilting where the outline of the individual appliqué motifs is overlapped and repeated as an all-over pattern. As a finishing touch, tiny silvery beads are dotted over the surface to highlight the design.*

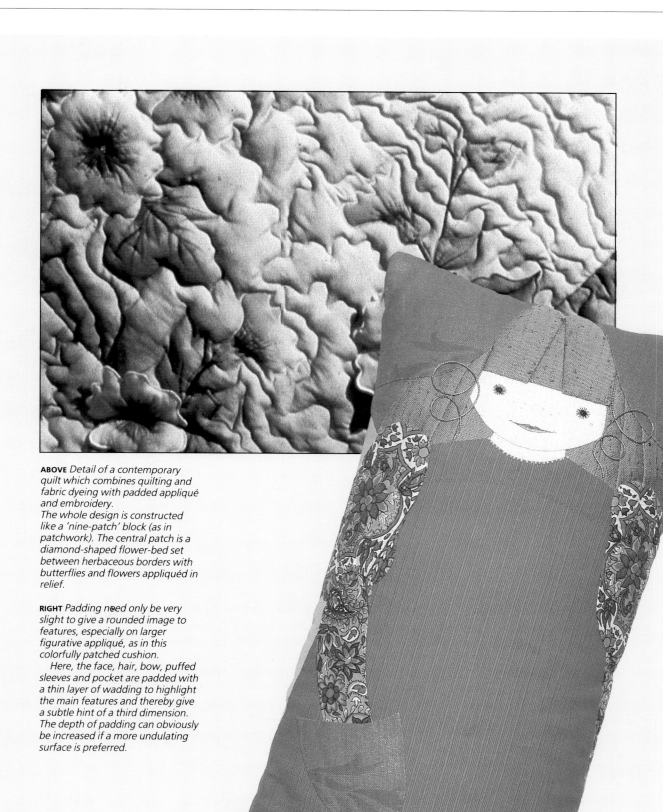

ABOVE *Detail of a contemporary quilt which combines quilting and fabric dyeing with padded appliqué and embroidery.*
The whole design is constructed like a 'nine-patch' block (as in patchwork). The central patch is a diamond-shaped flower-bed set between herbaceous borders with butterflies and flowers appliquéd in relief.

RIGHT *Padding need only be very slight to give a rounded image to features, especially on larger figurative appliqué, as in this colorfully patched cushion.*
Here, the face, hair, bow, puffed sleeves and pocket are padded with a thin layer of wadding to highlight the main features and thereby give a subtle hint of a third dimension. The depth of padding can obviously be increased if a more undulating surface is preferred.

315

Stumpwork

Padded appliqué was taken to extremes in the seventeenth century in the technique known as stumpwork.

Stumpwork developed from the raised and detached Elizabethan embroidery with the addition of padded shapes and applied motifs used to build up elaborate pictures. It was chiefly worked by the ladies of the great Stuart houses; often the finished embroideries were subsequently sent to be made up into cabinet or mirror frames by professional workmen. Some pieces were framed to stand as pictures on small portable easels. Others formed the panels on 'caskets' or miniature chests.

The subjects of the embroideries were usually scenes from the Bible or mythology. The figures were lavishly dressed in Stuart costume and set in elaborate landscapes. Trees, castles, animals, insects, flowers and fruits were added in profusion, with total disregard for scale. Occasionally fishponds would be included, complete with fish and a mermaid holding a tiny mirror which reflected her face.

A typical stumpwork piece of this period would include a king and queen (perhaps under a canopy and sometimes resembling Charles I and his queen), a castle or house, a stag, a unicorn, a lion, birds, butterflies, fruit and flowers, all set in a stylized rural setting. Religious themes – Esther and Ahasuerus or Solomon and Sheba – were also common, as were figures depicting the virtues or the seasons. Many of the scenes are alike enough to suggest designs might have been taken from drawings

originating from professional workshops. Stumpwork was clearly a development of the high-relief ecclesiastical embroideries, but other influences are not hard to find. The excellent printed designs seen by travellers to Italy, Spain and Germany provided one source of material. Illustrated herbals, copies of needlework pictures and tapestries, bestiaries and pattern books were widely available from the beginning of the seventeenth century. *A Schole House for the Needle* by Richard Shorleyker was published at the same time, and this, too, had an influence on needlework methods.

During this period, white satin with a traditional blue-green selvage, embroidery silks and gimp cord (a firm central core bound with fine silk) were imported from Italy. Milan and Venice produced metal threads and Florence specialized in plain woven silks.

The white satin, or sometimes silk, with a design sketched in ink, was backed with firm muslin or linen and mounted on a large frame, ready for the high-relief pieces; these were worked separately on stretched linen held in a small hand frame.

Colored wools, silks, metal threads, chenille, ribbons, spangles, beads and small pieces of mica were all used in the embroidery. Motifs, known as slips, were worked on fine canvas or linen, then carefully cut out and applied to the silk background.

Figures and animals, usually 2½–3 inches (5.5cm–7.5cm) high, were padded in life-like shapes with horsehair or lambswool and cut out, leaving surplus material to be tucked under and stuck onto a firm

paper shape. The completed figure was then sewn onto the sketched satin ground. The attaching stitches were cleverly concealed by a couched fine gimp cord or linear stitches.

Faces were made of modelled wax, simple padded silk or embroidered satin stretched and glued over minute carved pieces of boxwood. Hands and legs were made in the same way, or formed of silk thread over twisted wire. The legs were often covered with tiny needlelace (fine buttonhole) stitches to suggest stockings. Shoes with red heels and bows or long boots with spurs were also added, all executed in immense detail. Hair and bunched ringlets were made from looped stitches, or real hair held in place with a lattice of threads. Embroidered fashionable gowns in bright colored silk needlelace were neatly pleated and draped onto the figures; sometimes fine petticoats were also added. The draperies of the canopy could often be closed.

The background trees and sprigs of flowers were often worked in flat embroidery on the satin ground using floss silks. Leaves and petals were worked in frames of fine wire filled in with needlepoint lace stitches. These were attached only in one place, giving a three-dimensional look, sometimes with the addition of an embroidered shadow. Spring-like coiled purl was often used to give realistic foliage effects. Small pears and apples of carved wood, covered in minute lace stitches, were hung in clusters from the trees, often showing a childish lack of proportion. The landscape also included fountains and rock gardens tufted with velvet

stitch and coiled wire. Talc or mica was used for the windows of the house.

Plumules of peacock feathers were used to decorate birds, insects and sometimes the necklines of dresses. Seed pearls added touches of grandeur to necklages and crowns. Spangles, small circles of silver wire beaten flat, were sewn on to suggest snow-storms in some earlier works. A good example of the use of spangles occurs in the earliest known piece of American stumpwork, dated 1644, by Rebeker Wheeler.

Although stumpwork travelled to the North American continent with the establishment of colonies there, this type of embroidery, together with raised embroidery generally, went into a decline by the end of the seventeenth century. Later examples show these techniques taken to excess, which may have contributed to their fall from favor. Another factor in the disappearance of raised work was the arrival of Indian and Chinese goods and the resultant fashion for Chinoiserie. Today, many surviving examples have lost the colorful character they once undoubtedly possessed, but the dexterity of the work is still impressive and can only be fully appreciated if one tries to copy a piece. Modern embroiderers have adapted and used many of the techniques of raised work in murals and needlework pictures, often to vivid and striking effect.

LEFT *A detail from an example of stumpwork depicting David and Bathsheba. This particular type of embroidery flourished towards the end of the seventeenth century, most themes being Biblical or historical.*

ABOVE *This panel, called Esther and Ahasuerus and dated 1686, is a typical example of raised work, with figures in contemporary costume surrounded by a profusion of animals, birds, insects, trees, flowers and fruit. In the center the king sits under a canopy, holding a scepter and orb; his hands are shaped from covered wire. The castle in the background has windows of mica; a large lion sits outside, showing a total disregard for scale.*

ABOVE *The Paget family twentieth-century stumpwork worked between 1901 and 1927. The Paget family of Somerset, England, own a stumpwork picture worked by an ancestor Mary Ruddock who was married to John Paget. This inspired Sir Richard Paget to draw and design a picture of his family on the terrace of Cranmore Hall. The faces and hands were carved in wax from which plaster casts were made and later painted. Each lady of the family designed and embroidered her own costume and that of her husband, child or brother. The magnificent foliage and family arms were worked by Sir Richard Paget's mother. Sir Richard Paget holds a stick of fused silica, a newly developed process on which he was working at the time.*

Stumpwork has a charm of its own, but distance lends enchantment, and if slavishly copied now it would look too cluttered and fussy. However, by limiting the number of techniques in any one piece, and by using modern materials it can be attractive, interesting and fun to do. The designs should be kept simple and the color schemes worked out carefully.

● **Materials and equipment**

FABRIC AND THREAD Traditionally, white satin has been employed as a background fabric, with linen or firm muslin used for the raised work. Paddings for the raised figures of the past might have been sheep's wool, hair or cotton tow. For modern three-dimensional work, stretching materials can be used because they mold easily around paddings, and other materials will stretch on the diagonal weave or if slightly moistened. Modern paddings include cotton wool, polyester wadding for rounded shapes, and cardboard or balsa wood for crisp shapes. Twisted, colored silk threads are needed for working the raised motifs, and silks for flt embroidery. Figures and objects can be further decorated with metal threads, spangles, small glass beads and pearls. Small flakes of mica or talc can be incorporated for window glass; faces, hands and occasional bare limbs may be made from carved box-wood, modelling clay, shaped wire or plaster cast from wax molds.

NEEDLES Pointed crewel needles of varying sizes are needed for laying foundation stitches and for embroidering. Tapestry needles with blunt points are useful for working needlelace stitches, which may be made to stand out from figures, so imitating clothes.

● **Techniques** It is important to

plan raised work carefully, and it can be helpful to have drawings or photographs of the subjects from different angles. It is worth experimenting with paper to solve the problems of designing sizes and shapes before cutting into the material.

SLIPS ON FIRM MUSLIN Draw the outline of a motif on fine firm muslin, and frame the muslin to hold it taut. Place the shaped areas of padding on the fabric, and hold them in place with long retaining stitches.

Next, work needlelace stitches over the padding. The stitches depend for their size and type on the intended motif. If specifically made shapes are not used, a woman's face, neck and arms, for example, may be executed in split stitch and her hair in bullion stitches. Dress may be indicated by miniature embroidered garments. Strips of lace may be applied for collar and cuffs, and pearls may illustrate a necklace.

When the motif is complete, cut the fine muslin about ¼ inch (6mm) outside the edge of the motif, then cut small notches to accommodate the curves. Tuck the surplus under, stick onto the cardboard shape and slip stitch to the background. It is possible to add stitches after the motif has been applied to the background, but this can stretch the fabric. Gimp cord may be used to outline the motifs when they are in place.

Alternatively, the appliqué form may be applied directly to the ground fabric and the padding inserted at this stage. The shape to be applied should be cut slightly larger than the required finished size. Turn under the raw edges and secure in place with tiny slip stitches. Leave a small opening and push in the wadding using a stiletto or knitting needle.

CANVASWORK SLIPS Motifs can be worked on canvas with crewel yarn or silk thread, keeping to simple stitches such as tent, Hungarian, and Gobelin. When the motif is complete, cut it out leaving a small border all round. Tuck this under and stitch the slip in position on the background using small stitches.

PADDING WITH FELT Cut out the shape required, then another slightly smaller and a third smaller again. Begin by sewing the smallest shape in position with tiny stab stitches. Apply the next size over the top and then the third and largest over the two. Always bring the needle up through the background fabric and down through the felt; this will prevent the felt tearing. A final layer of fabric or fine kid can be applied or the shape can be covered with detached buttonhole stitch.

RAISED SHAPES OVER WIRE By using wire as a framework motifs can be made which stand free of the background, attached only in one place. Fine craft wire or florist's wire is the most suitable. Cut the required length of wire and wrap it closely and tightly with a soft thread, not wool or a springy silk. Knot the thread around the wire before winding it, and secure it at the other end when the wire is covered. Twist the wire into the desired shape. Tie another thread on, and begin filling in the shape with detached buttonhole stitch. When it is finished, sew the shape in place on the background, tucking the ends through the fabric with the help of a stiletto or a large tapestry needle. Secure with tiny stitches.

ABOVE This modern example shows the use of slips. The trees in the foreground are stitched with French knots on firm muslin; those behind show canvaswork stitches on fine canvas.

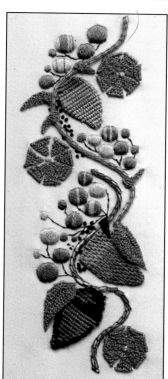

LEFT A modern example, worked in silk threads on a silk background fabric. The main stem is raised by couching a bundle of linen threads close together; rows of stem stitch are worked over this foundation to cover the core. The flowers and some of the leaves are worked in detached buttonhole stitch; other leaves are canvaswork slips. The small berries are embroidered in satin stitch over shapes cut from thick bonded interfacing.

BELOW Borders make ideal subjects for using simple repeat motifs which can be padded. Shells, flowers, foliage and fruit, and many natural forms, can be raised with layered padding and stitched with shiny threads to great effect. This embroidered mirror frame is worked in silks and stranded cottons on a background of silk fabric.

FOLDED APPLIQUÉ

*T*his method of designing is popular in many countries including India, Pakistan, Hungary and Hawaii.

Using two squares of different colored fabrics (the lower one cut slightly bigger to include seam allowances), press and then fold the layers separately first in half, then in quarters and finally in eighths. Pin the layers of the appliqué fabric together and transfer your design to the top section. Cut out very carefully and unfold. Position the design centrally on the ground fabric matching the fold lines. Pin and baste the appliqué in place, working from the middle out.

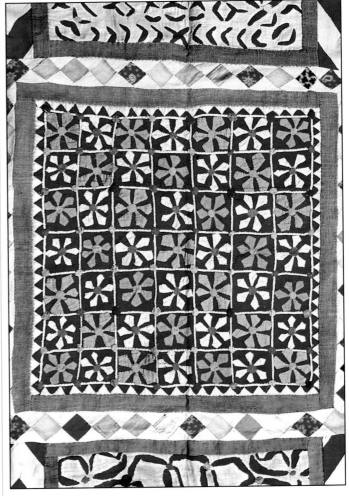

The technique is clearly shown in the Hawaiian *kapa lau* quilt.

This striking example of a folded quilt typifies the brilliant color and bold, formalized design of Hawaiian appliqué. The design, which is intricately cut from cotton whole cloth using the folded technique, shows traditional motifs of Hawaiian flowers and foliage on a grand scale. The appliqué is first hand stitched to a colored background, interlined, and then quilted and the motifs outlined and filled with contour quilting so that the entire surface is covered.

Designing appliqué with ordinary paper cut-outs is amazingly simple, and it was this technique that the women quiltmakers of Hawaii were first shown by American missionaries, which they quickly developed into their own individual style.

Interestingly, the small snowflake-type design taken by the missionaries soon grew in size to the proportions of the local vegetation which the islanders used as inspiration for their magnificent designs – the Bread-fruit tree and the Pineapple being the most famous. These cut-out patterns, *kapa lau*, are often so enormous that they cover a full-size quilt. Other favorite motifs, also taken from nature, include ferns, figs, paw paws, waterfalls and turtles.

In India, large hangings, carriage cloths and flags are decorated with colored cotton cloth, often with counterchange designs. The squares which decorate the Indian quilts and ceiling covers are large pieces of cotton cloth, folded and folded again, cut into a pattern, spread out on white firm muslin and then applied. The stitching for ceiling decoration, often hemstitching, may be quite crude, since it is to be viewed from a distance. This method (though with very fine stitching) was also used by German and British colonists in eighteenth- and nineteenth-century America on quilts, where the appliqué technique was often combined with patchwork.

Traditional color combinations are vividly striking. They are usually limited to just two or three colors such as white on a brilliant red or green background, or vice versa, or schemes such as red, green and orange, or scarlet and white on yellow. Alternatively, a printed cotton could be appliquéd to white, or a pastel color superimposed on a pretty print. For best results, choose fine, closely woven cotton or lawn fabrics.

ABOVE *A detail of a Jain wedding ceiling canopy (Shamiana) from Rajasthan, India. The canopy is made up of nine large squares, eight of which are folded and cut from white cotton fabric which is applied to red cotton. They are joined together with bands of patchwork diamonds and triangles.*

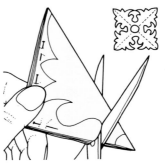

ABOVE *Folded patterns. Holding the folded fabric firmly, cut out the design keeping the scissors at right angles to the fabric.*

KAPA LAU

Transfer the design to the top section, pin and hold the eight layers securely before cutting through.

LEFT *This is a fine example of Meo hilltribe appliqué. Regular symmetrical patterns are made by first folding a square of fine cotton in half, folding in half again and then folding diagonally in half. On the final triangle a curved or linear design can be drawn and partly cut through – unfolded, the design will be an eight-fold repeat. The square is basted centrally to the ground fabric, the edges turned under with the point of the needle, and stitched to the base. Red patches have been inserted under the corners and in the center. The tiny running stitches in the remaining spaces are worked from the back of the work. The yellow circles are worked in blanket stitch.*

SHADOW APPLIQUÉ

Shadow appliqué, like shadow quilting, uses semi-transparent fabrics such as gauze, organdie, lace, net, muslin and voile through which stitches or fabric shapes can be seen to form a shadow effect, giving variety of tone.

A form of shadow appliqué appeared in the eighteenth century, worked on muslin and combined with surface embroidery. In this instance the shadow effect was achieved by applying fabric shapes either behind or to the front of the muslin. The Victoria and Albert Museum, in London, possesses some aprons incorporating this technique, which also reflect the oriental influence on design at this period. These muslin aprons formed part of the fashionable woman's dress and were not intended for practical use.

In the first half of the twentieth century, some very dainty work was produced, but it was often poor in design and lacking in imagination. Shadow work enjoyed a vogue during the 1920s and 1930s and was much used for mats, tablecoths, dressing table sets, collars, blouses, handkerchiefs and delicate lingerie. For these purposes fine cotton lawn, silk or crêpe de chine were used as well as organdie; babies' gowns, pillowslips and cot covers were worked on robing muslin. The background fabric was usually white, and it was sometimes worked in white, but often brightly colored threads were used, which on the right side of the work gave the appearance of pastel tints outlined in a brighter color. For the designs, sprays of leaves and flowers were much in favor. Sometimes colored shapes – leaves, petals or geometric shapes – were applied at the back of the work

with pin stitching (also called lace stitch or three-sided stitch) which gave an openwork decorative edge to the shape.

Since the Second World War embroiderers have used shadow work methods more freely, with some interesting results. Man-made fibers have brought the introduction of new fabrics. Painting, spraying and dyeing can be combined with stitchery and stitches themselves are sometimes reversed, so that in parts of the work the threads are seen on the right side of the fabric and in others they are seen through it. Parts of a design may also be cut away to reveal what lies behind. Colors are bolder for both fabric and threads and black can be particularly effective.

Contemporary shadow appliqué often makes apparently bold use of colored sheer fabrics to create illusions of space, color and form, as in the landscape picture, 'Elm Tree Lane'. The design uses a simple collection of sheer fabrics and machine stitching to express a wide spectrum of tonal densities, where in certain areas, such as the trees, several layers have been built up to give the impression of form. Here, as in more experimental picture-making, frayed edges are exploited and play an important part in the atmosphere and overall effect.

The whole landscape with its softly feathered edges is outlined with a fine, machine-stitched line in a slightly darker tone. The fineness and

apparent random placing of the lines are key elements in the composition – an effect which may need a little preliminary practice to recreate.

This technique is best suited to experimental picture-making. It is helpful to work a small sample piece to get the feel of working in this way with sheers, before embarking on a project. Experiment with the feel of different fabrics. You may find silk organzas and other slippery sheers difficult to control whereas matt fabrics are easier to handle in layers.

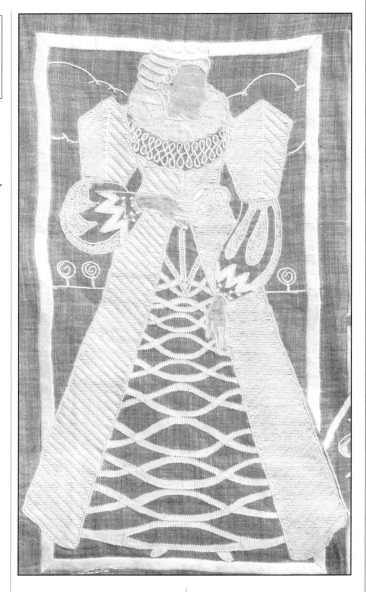

ABOVE *A detail from a twentieth-century whitework organdie runner illustrating the history of costume. There is a great variety of stitches, and in places double or treble pieces of organdie are applied to give a contrast of tone.*

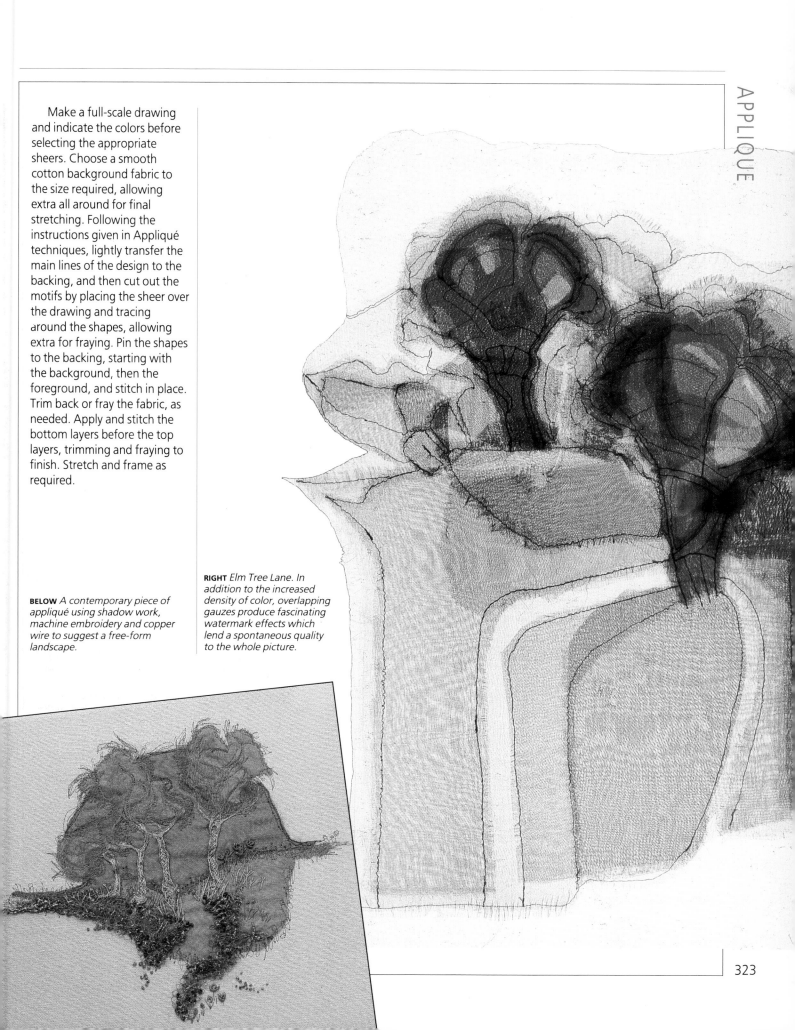

Make a full-scale drawing and indicate the colors before selecting the appropriate sheers. Choose a smooth cotton background fabric to the size required, allowing extra all around for final stretching. Following the instructions given in Appliqué techniques, lightly transfer the main lines of the design to the backing, and then cut out the motifs by placing the sheer over the drawing and tracing around the shapes, allowing extra for fraying. Pin the shapes to the backing, starting with the background, then the foreground, and stitch in place. Trim back or fray the fabric, as needed. Apply and stitch the bottom layers before the top layers, trimming and fraying to finish. Stretch and frame as required.

BELOW *A contemporary piece of appliqué using shadow work, machine embroidery and copper wire to suggest a free-form landscape.*

RIGHT *Elm Tree Lane. In addition to the increased density of color, overlapping gauzes produce fascinating watermark effects which lend a spontaneous quality to the whole picture.*

323

LACE APPLIQUÉ

Some of the daintiest effects in appliqué can be achieved by this technique in which richly textured and highly decorative lace fabrics and trims are used, as in this prettily frilled pillow cover.

The design shows a large central diamond (with butterflies) and corner motifs cut from white cotton curtain lace and appliquéd onto a creamy cotton ground fabric. Straight-sided insertion lace is used to cover the edges of the motifs and the central border is further trimmed with gold piping and narrow satin ribbon tied in decorative bows. To complete the romantic effect, the pillow is surrounded by a deep double frill of cream cotton and scalloped lace.

Although designed to fit a large 24 inch (60cm) square pillow, the appliqué design can easily be adapted to suit other shapes and sizes. A selection of mixed shapes combined with simple design variations would make a very attractive set of bedroom cushions.

As alternatives to lace curtaining, wedding lace, pieces of antique lace, filet net, edgings, doilies and crochet can be used for the appliqué with some stunning results. Other suitable ground fabrics include light- to medium-weight silk, satin, cotton and polyester.

To make the pillow cover you will need sufficient main fabric for the pillow front plus a generous double frill about 4 inches (10cm) deep – for the length, allow roughly one and a half times the measurement around the pillow. Allow extra for the back, if you prefer a pocket opening, and for all seam allowances.

From lace, cut out the diamond motif and corner sections to size. Position the diamond centrally on the ground fabric, and tack to secure. Pipe the edges of 2 inch (5cm) wide insertion and machine stitch it over the raw edges. Pipe separate squares for each corner of the diamond and stitch on top. Stitch lengths of ribbon close to the insertion leaving the ends free for tying. When sewing, pin them away from the edge to prevent them from getting caught in the seam.

Position the corner sections with the outer edges in the seam allowance. Tack in place and cover the diagonal edges with 1¼ inch (3cm) wide insertion.

Large expanses of lace appliqué such as the central diamond, may need to be supported by catching it to the ground fabric with a few tiny stitches judiciously placed within the pattern.

Attach separate butterfly motifs stitching through both layers.

Finally make the frill by running a gathering thread around stitching through both layers ½ inch (1cm) from the raw edge. Attach a similar length of 2 inch (5cm) wide scalloped lace just below the stitching. Pull up the gathers to fit around the pillow, tack it to the top section and make up the cover, as preferred.

The second design shown is for a fragrant herb pillow, with a handful of sweet-smelling herbs, rose petals or *pot pourri* placed inside the pad before it is made up. This delightful rose-scented pillow uses the prettiest appliqué combining écru lace trim with a contrast ribbon and hand-embroidered flowers. The design is worked on a wadded ground in matching cotton and shows a center panel filled with rows of hand quilting. This is surrounded by a lace border, edged with narrow ribbon and a daintily pleated frill.

A scalloped edging 2 inches (5cm) wide is used for both the lace border and the frill, where the border is simply appliquéd with mitered corners and decorated with embroidered roses and French knots. More tiny flowers and knots are embroidered on the ribbon edging to complement perfectly the rose perfume and give an extra delicate finish to the pillow.

A size of about 12 inch (30cm) square is ideal for the design, which is very easy to work either in the hand or an embroidery hoop.

When making a herb pillow, allow the perfume to escape by choosing a main frabric that has a slight open weave, such as unbleached firm muslin. Cut out two sections to size and back the top with wadding and muslin and prepare them as for wadded quilting. Pin and tack ½ inch (1.5cm) wide ribbon 2 inches (5cm) in from the edge, mitering the corners and turning in the raw edges at one corner. Pin the lace border in position, mitring the corners and placing the straight edge just over the ribbon, and, with matching thread, slip stitch neatly in place. Then, mark parallel lines diagonally through the center about 6 inches (15cm) apart and quilt using pale green coton à broder.

Following the diagram given far right, work the embroidery in bullion knots and French knots, as shown, in rose pink and green coton à broder. For the frill, allow one and a half times the measurement around the edge. Pin over the edge of the ribbon in even pleats, making sure that a pleat falls on each corner. Hide the joining under a pleat and neatly hand stitch through all layers. Make up the cover and add perfume, as preferred.

The delicacy of lace appliqué makes it appropriate only for items which will not be expected to stand hard wear. However, this technique can be used to create all manner of decorative items. In fact, lace appliqué can often be utilized as an alternative to traditional whitework methods.

Uses might include formal baby clothes such as a christening gown and bonnet, a child's party frock, decoration for an evening blouse, or ornamental borders for bed linen. Herb pillows are another appropriate item for this form of ornamentation.

One charming idea is to make 'sweet bags', small sachets of muslin filled with fragrant dried herbs such as lavender, basil, bergamot, hyssop or rosemary, to lay amongst one's clothing. A lace appliqué cover will permit the scent to permeate through into the surrounding garments.

For more striking effects, colored net and nylon lace are now widely available. This will be most attractive used with some restraint to avoid the blend of colors and textures giving a fussy and even discordant result.

BEDROOM PILLOWS

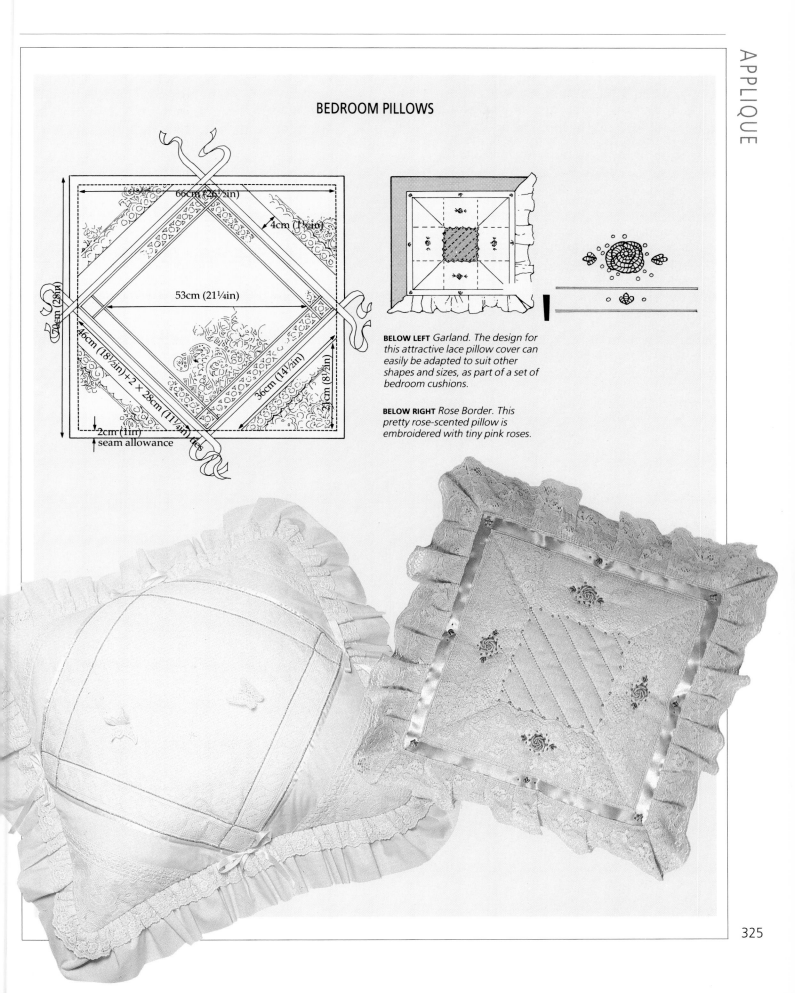

66cm (26½in)

4cm (1½in)

53cm (21¼in)

70cm (28in)

46cm (18½in) + 2 × 28cm (11¼in) tie

36cm (14½in)

21cm (8½in)

2cm (1in)
seam allowance

BELOW LEFT *Garland. The design for this attractive lace pillow cover can easily be adapted to suit other shapes and sizes, as part of a set of bedroom cushions.*

BELOW RIGHT *Rose Border. This pretty rose-scented pillow is embroidered with tiny pink roses.*

FINISHING

When all the appliqué is finished, and any further decoration added, take out the basting threads – using tweezers to hold stubborn ends – and remove the work from the frame, if used. Press on the right side, using a cloth. Avoid over-pressing so as not to flatten the appliqué.

Many people prefer to remove the backing fabric from under the appliqué patches, cutting to within ¼ inch (6mm) of the stitching. This usually allows the work to hang better, and dark-colored ground fabrics are prevented from showing through lighter appliqué, although a light, iron-on interfacing will also prevent this happening. However, wall hangings do benefit from retaining the ground fabric, and any other extra backing you may have added, intact, as they provide support for the finished weight.

Finish your appliqué as required. Add a fabric casing along the top edge of a hanging to take a dowel rod. Pictures should be stretched and then tacked over a firm wooden stretcher before being framed, without or under non-reflecting glass, as preferred. Refer to the Quilting and Patchwork sections for quilting, adding borders, finishing edges and lining. Instructions are given here for making a simple cushion cover.

Cushion cover

To back a cushion cover you will need fabric the same size as the top section, which should be pressed. Before cutting the fabric, check the size of the cushion pad and make the cover 1 inch (2.5cm) smaller, to give a well-plumped shape. Cut out the back section to size adding ½ inch (1.5cm) all round for seam allowances. Pin the right sides of the sections together, machine stitch around ½ inch (1.5cm) from

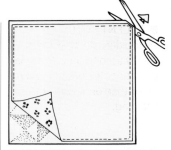

Finishing. Trim the corners across fairly close to the stitching to prevent unsightly lumps appearing on the right side.

the edge, leaving an opening for turning through. Trim the corners. Neaten the seams by overcasting by hand or machine zigzag stitching, turn the cover right side out, and press. Insert the pad and slipstitch the opening to close.

Tassels

For a finishing touch, you may like to add tassels to the corners of a cushion. Any fiber or yarn is suitable, so long as it consorts well with the fabrics of the cushion cover. Colors and textures can be mixed for added contrast. Bold tassels can be made from generous bundles of wool, rolled-up pleated fabrics or fringed leather. Long tassels need to be made from fibers that hang well. Although silk is an old favorite it is nowadays quite expensive, but rayon cord makes a good substitute.

Small, fluffy tassels can be made from wool or chenille, and tiny ones from embroidery threads or unravelled yarn from the ground fabric. Use plenty of material or the result will look insignificant. On the other hand, a tassel should not be too heavy for the fabric into which it is sewn or it will drag it out of shape.

SIMPLE TASSEL WITH BUTTONHOLE TOP

1 Make the tassel on card. Thread yarn onto needle and make a loop around threads in centre.

2 Pad tassel with a small ball of cotton wool. Secure with looped thread underneath. Slip needle through head to top.

3 Leave threads to be used for attaching tassel. Work detached buttonhole stitch around the head beginning with stitches worked close together.

GLOSSARY

● **ACCENT STITCH** An embroidery stitch which is chiefly used to provide a splash of color or texture to enliven a monotone or flat area of stitching.

● **AMERICAN CREWELWORK** Eighteenth-century crewelwork in America developed characteristics distinct from similar work in Europe. Due to a scarcity of threads, designs were worked more sparsely; the background was often left unstitched and the motifs became specifically American – for example, describing indigenous fruit and flowers.

● **APPLIQUÉ OR APPLIED WORK** A technique in which shapes of different fabrics are placed on the ground fabric to form a design. The edges are secured by tiny stitches which are hardly seen, or by a decorative embroidery stitch.

● **ASSISI WORK** A type of counted thread embroidery originating in Assisi, Northern Italy. The patterns or motifs are outlined before the background is filled in using cross stitch or long-armed cross-stitch, leaving the motifs unstitched.

● **AWL** A sharp pointed instrument used for making holes in fabric.

● **AYRSHIRE WHITEWORK** A form of whitework characterized by intricate floral designs and hence sometimes called 'The Flowering'. This nineteenth century Scottish cottage industry is still practiced today.

● **BASTING (TACKING)** A basic stitch used either for tracing out a shape or for holding two or more layers of fabric together ready for permanent stitching. It is simply a large running stitch worked in and out of the fabric. Begin with a knot and work a back stitch at the end to hold. *Basting* can also be worked unevenly or diagonally.

● **BAND SAMPLER** A sampler with a typically long and narrow shape. The designs were carefully arranged in horizontal bands and the stitching was sometimes worked from both ends.

● **BEAD COUCHING** A method of stitching beads to fabric by threading the beads and couching the thread to the fabric with a small stitch between each bead.

● **BEADWORK** A decorative technique particularly popular in the seventeenth and eighteenth centuries, when beads were applied to fabric either to make a complete design or to highlight a stitched motif.

● **BEESWAX** A small, solid block of wax used for both strengthening and smoothing sewing thread. Used extensively in beadwork and metal thread work.

● **BERLIN WOOLWORK** A technique of working designs in colored wools on canvas, following a chart in which the design is shown in grid form, each square representing one stitch. The wools and chart were originally produced in Germany, but the method became very popular throughout Europe and the United States in the nineteenth century.

● **BIAS** Any slating or oblique line in relation to the warp and weft threads of a fabric. The true bias is formed when the selvage is folded at a right angle across the fabric parallel to the weft and runs exactly at 45 degrees to the straight grain.

● **BIAS BINDING** Strips of material cut on the diagonal frame of the fabric and used to bind raw fabric edges or to cover piping cord. They can be bought ready made or can be cut from fabric as follows. Fold the selvage at right angles across the fabric parallel to the weft. The bias will run at 45° to the fabric grain. Cut the strips along the bias.

● **BINCA CANVAS** A multiple-thread embroidery canvas woven with squares formed by the warp and weft threads. It is suitable for all kinds of coarse embroidery. It is not necessary to fill the ground completely.

● **BLACKWORK** This technique, used on clothing and household linen, was most popular in the sixteenth century. It consists of outline and filling stitches worked in black thread on line, to create geometric designs, often including motifs of flowers and fruit.

● **BLOCK** A group of patchwork pieces stitched together to form a pattern. Several blocks are pieced together and then joined to make up a large patchwork.

● **BLOCKING** The process of smoothing and squaring a finished piece of embroidery by damping it with water and pinning it into shape on a flat surface, where it is left until thoroughly dry.

● **BODKIN** A long blunt-edged needle with a large eye, used for threading tape, cord or elastic through a channel or casing.

● **BORDER STITCH** A wide embroidery stitch which is always used in a straight line and makes a very attractive border. Multiple rows can be worked to make a more complex decorative border.

● **BOXER** A motif popular in seventeenth century embroidery, originally showing a small figure nude except for a fig leaf. Clothed figures also gradually became common. The description 'Boxer' may have derived from the figure's stiff pose, suggesting an aggressive attitude.

● **BOXES** Panels embroidered at both sides of the yoke on the traditional rural smock, often featuring motifs of the wearer's home county and occupation.

● **CANVAS** A ground material for embroidery in which vertical and horizontal threads are woven together to produce precisely-spaced holes between the threads. The fabric has a regular grid-like structure and is available in different weights and thicknesses.

● **CANVASWORK** A general term for embroidery worked on canvas. Typically, the entire surface of the canvas is covered with stitching and a wide range of stitches can be used. Canvaswork is also commonly known as needlepoint.

● **CARRICKMACROSS** An extremely fine form of whitework resembling lace. This nineteenth century Irish cottage industry is still practiced today.

● **CASING** A channel formed by a row of stitching a certain distance from a folded or seamed edge or by working two parallel rows of stitching. Used to house elastic, hanging poles, etc.

● **CHENILLE NEEDLE** A long, thick needle with a sharp point and a large eye.

● **CLOSED FINISH** The term used when an embroidery stitch is compressed in order to cover the ground fabric completely.

● **COMMON-WEAVE (PLAIN-WEAVE) FABRIC** A fabric in which the warp and weft threads are not woven regularly enough to provide a grid for embroidery by counted thread techniques.

● **COTON À BRODER** A tightly twisted, pearlized thread. It is similar to pearl cotton, but with a less lustrous finish.

● **COTTON PERLÉ** (see Pearl Cotton)

● **COUCHING** A method of tying down one or more threads laid on a ground fabric, by stitching over them at regular intervals with another thread, to form an outline or solid area of stitching. It is particularly suitable for textured and metallic threads that are not easily drawn through the fabric.

● **COUNTED THREAD WORK** A term that refers to several

different embroidery techniques, the common factor being that the scale and placing of the stitches is determined by counting the warp and weft threads of the ground fabric over which each stitch is worked.

● **CRAZY PATCHWORK** A technique in which irregularly shaped pieces of fabric are sewn at random on a ground fabric. The raw edges where the pieces join are secured by decorative stitching.

● **CREWEL NEEDLE** A needle of medium length and thickness, with a sharp point and a large eye.

● **CREWEL YARN** A fine 2-ply yarn for delicate canvaswork or free embroidery.

● **CREWELWORK** Embroidery stitched with crewel yarns on a linen background, using a variety of stitches to create freely worked designs. In traditional crewelwork the motifs were often represented naturalistically and were usually plants and animals rather than geometric designs.

● **CUTWORK** A technique in which motifs of patterns are outlined with close buttonhole stitching and the ground fabric is cut away in various sections of the design.

● **DARNED NET** A pattern formed in the squares of net fabric with closely-worked darning stitches. This type of work has been popular all over Europe from the Middle Ages to the present day, originally using hand-made net and later machine-made fabrics.

● **DART** Method of disposing

of fullness in fabric by matching up two points on the outer edge and graduating the stitching from the matched points into a center point.

● **DETACHED STITCH** An embroidery stitch which is anchored to the ground fabric at the edges only, with the main part of the stitching remaining free.

● **DIAPER PATTERN** Fabric woven with a small geometrical design. Sometimes applies to staggered rows which give the effect of diagonal lines, called bird's eye diaper. The same pattern is used in gold couching.

● **DRAWN THREAD WORK** A type of embroidery in which threads are drawn from the ground fabric and the spaces left are then filled or edged with different stitches. There are many forms of this technique, including Hardanger embroidery and needle weaving.

● **DRESDEN WORK** Type of drawn thread work on muslin made popular in the eighteenth century in Dresden, Hanover. It was made as a substitute for expensive bobbin lace.

● **DRESSING** A stiffening agent of starch gum, china clay or size found in new fabrics. Sometimes hides poor quality fabric but can also be an integral part of the fabric, as in glazed chintz.

● **DRESSMAKER'S CARBON PAPER** A type of carbon paper used to transfer an embroidery design on to fabric. It is available in several colors.

● **EDGING STITCH** An

embroidery stitch used to finish a raw edge to prevent the fabric from fraying, or to decorate a plain hemmed edge.

● **ENCROACHING STITCHES** A term used to describe the overlap of one row of stitching with the preceding row.

● **EVEN-WEAVE FABRIC** A fabric with warp and weft threads of identical thicknesses, which provide the same number of threads over a given area, enabling the threads to be counted to keep the stitching even.

● **EYELET EMBROIDERY** A type of cutwork embroidery which evolved from Ayrshire embroidey *circa* 1850, and became very popular as a decoration on children's garments and ladies' underclothes. The formalized designs consist of a series of tiny round and oval holes.

● **FABRIC PAINTING** A method of coloring plain-weave fabric with specially prepared dyes, paints or crayons, all of which must be fixed to make the color permanent. The fabric is stretched on a frame while it is painted.

● **FACING** A piece of fabric stitched to a raw edge to neaten.

● **FILLING STITCH** An embroidery stitch which is used to fill a shape on the ground fabric. Filling stitches can be light and delicate with a lacy appearance, or they can completely cover the ground fabric.

● **FINE CROCHET COTTON** A tightly twisted pearlized thread similar to pearl cotton but with a less lustrous finish.

● **FLOUNCE** A skirt of fabric, which can be plain, gathered or pleated, around a valance, bedspread, divan cover, etc.

● **FLOWER THREADS** Single strand cotton embroidery threads sold in skeins, and produced in an excellent range of colors.

● **FOOT** A sewing machine attachment through which the needle passes. Most machines have a variety of feet suitable for different stitching techniques.

● **FOUNDATION GRID** The regular arrangement of threads laid across a shape to provide a framework for an embroidery stitch.

● **FOUNDATION ROW** A row of stitching which provides the basis for a composite stitch. This terms is also used to describe the stitched outline which anchors a detached filling stitch to the ground fabric.

● **FRAME** A square or rectangular wooden frame used to keep fabric taut during stitching.

● **FROGGING** A decorative fastening made from spirals of cord or braid.

● **GAUGE** The number of threads which can be stitched in an inch (2.5cm) of canvas. Also the number of threads or woven blocks which can be stitched in an inch of even-weave fabric.

● **GOLD EMBROIDERY** Stitching with threads made of

gilt, or gold strands wound around silk, used in a variety of embroidery techniques including couching. The technique was most widely used during the Middle Ages and Renaissance, particularly for ecclesiastical garments.

● **GRADING** A technique for avoiding bulky seam allowances where several thicknesses of fabric are joined, by trimming each layer back to a different level.

● **GRAIN** The line of the warp in woven textiles. To cut horizontally, along the weft, is called cutting across or against the grain.

● **GRAPH PAPER** Paper printed with a grid of equidistant vertical and horizontal lines.

● **GROUND FABRIC** Any fabric on which embroidery is worked. See canvas, even-weave fabric, plain-weave fabric.

● **GROUNDING STITCH** A term used in needlepoint to describe a stitch that is suitable for covering large areas of background.

● **HARDANGER EMBROIDERY** A drawn thread technique that originated in Norway and was used particularly on household items. It is worked on open-weave, double-thread linen with thick linen or cotton threads.

● **HEDEBO** A Danish form of whitework featuring cutwork fillings and characteristic interwoven buttonhole edgings.

● **HOOP** A round frame for stretching the ground fabric while the embroidery stitches are worked.

● **INTERFACING** A layer of fabric placed between the top fabric and lining to add body and permanent shape and reinforce the fabric. It is available in different weights and in either iron-on or sew-on varieties.

● **INTERLOCK SINGLE CANVAS** Canvas with a 'locked' construction, formed by vertical threads made up of two thin threads twisted around each other, and round a single, thicker, horizontal thread. It is more stable than single canvas.

● **ISOLATED STITCH** An embroidery stitch which is worked individually and can be used alone or massed together to fill a shape.

● **JACOBEAN EMBROIDERY** A type of free embroidery worked on linen, popular during seventeenth and eighteenth centuries.

● **KLOSTER BLOCKS** Blocks of geometrical satin stitches worked over an even number of threads to cover the cut edges in Hardanger embroidery.

● **LAID-WORK** An embroidery technique used to fill a shape. Long threads are laid across the shape and anchored to the fabric by a second thread to create a pattern.

● **LINE STITCH** Any embroidery stitch which forms a line during the working.

● **MITER** The diagonal line

formed at 45 degrees to the edges of fabric joined to form a 90 degree angle, or when two hems meet at a square corner. Makes a strong, neat corner.

● **MONO CANVAS** Canvas in which the weave is formed by the intersection of single vertical and horizontal threads.

● **MOTIF** Part of a design that can be isolated as a single unit. Often geometric or stylized in form, it may be featured singly, or repeated to form a border or allover pattern.

● **MOTIF STITCH** An embroidery stitch which is worked individually, with each stitch making a distinctive shape, such as a star or triangle.

● **MOUNTMELLICK** A distinctively strongly textured and rather heavy form of whitework. This nineteenth century Irish cottage industry is still practiced today.

● **NAP** Soft, downy raised surface given to some woven fabrics by a finishing process. If the raised nap looks a different shade from opposite angle, it may lie in one direction, as in a pile surface.

● **NEEDLEPOINT** A general term for embroidery on canvas. The entire surface of the canvas is covered with stitching and a wide range of stitches is used.

● **NEEDLE WEAVING** A form of drawn thread work popular in Eastern Europe and Scandinavia, in which colored threads are darned or woven into a pattern to take the place of threads that have been removed from the ground fabric.

● **NOTCH** A small nick made in the seam allowance to ease a curve.

● **OPUS ANGLICANUM** A form of ecclesiastical embroidery practiced in England in the thirteenth and fourteenth centuries, characterized by the rich use of precious metal threads and colored silks.

● **OYA EDGING** Traditional Turkish form of embroidery used to decorate women's head squares. The colorful motifs, usually in the form of fruit and flowers, are worked in the finest cotton, linen or silk thread, using buttonhole stitch and tiny beads.

● **PAILLETTE** A large sequin with two holes for stitching.

● **PASSING** Metal threads, including pure gold and silver, made with a solid core. These threads are usually couched on to the surface of the fabric with decorative stitching.

● **PATCHWORK** The art of joining small shaped pieces of fabric together to gain a larger piece while producing an attractive design.

● **PATTERN BOOK** A book of designs printed specially for the use of embroiderers or lacemakers.

● **PATTERN DARNING** A development of darning into an embroidery technique, with parallel rows of straight stitches worked regularly on an evenweave fabric, often densely.

● **PEARL COTTON (COTTON PERLÉ)** A twisted two-ply thread with a lustrous sheen. It cannot be divided into separate strands but it is available in three different weights.

● **PEARL PURL** (or bead purl) Hollow metal threads made from convex shaped wire that look like a string of tiny beads. Used for outlining.

● **PENELOPE CANVAS** Canvas in which the weave is formed by the intersection of pairs of vertical and horizontal threads. It is also known as Double canvas.

● **PERSIAN YARN** A loosely twisted three-ply wool which can be divided into separate strands.

● **PICOT** A small loop of twisted thread forming a decorative edging on lace or embroidery.

● **PICTORIAL SAMPLER** A sampler in which the stitches are worked into a pictorial image, rather than as rows of patterns or single motifs.

● **PINTUCKS** A series of very narrow tucks stitched on the right side of the fabric and used as decoration.

● **PIPING** A strip of bias-cut fabric folded lengthways to enclose a thin cord. It is inserted into a plain seam to give a decorative finish.

● **PLATE** A broad, flat metallic thread, usually gilt, with a very bright, shiny surface. Can be crimped to give texture.

● **POUNCING** A method of transferring a design to fabric. A series of pinholes are made outlining a design drawn up on paper, then a fine powder (pounce) such as charcoal is shaken through the pinholes onto the fabric beneath.

● **POWDERING** A light filling for a shape made by scattering an isolated stitch over an area of ground fabric.

● **PULLED FABRIC WORK** A technique in which stitches are pulled tight so that the threads of the ground fabric are bound together and the design is created both by the stitching and by the holes in between.

● **PURL** Made up of finely drawn metallic wire coiled tightly round into a spring-like spiral. It is made in lengths of about 39 inches (1 metre) which are then cut into lengths as needed. Purls are threaded on to a needle and stitched in place like beads.

● **QUILTING** The method used to join two layers of fabric with a wadded center together in a decorative way.

● **RAISED WORK** Any type of embroidery that is made three-dimensional by the use of some form of padding – for example, cardboard, felt, cotton or wool.

● **RENAISSANCE EMBROIDERY** A form of cutwork in which the design is outlined in buttonhole stitch before the ground fabric is cut away. Parts of the design are strengthened by buttonhole bars.

● **RETICELLA** An early form of cutwork which consisted of withdrawing threads from the fabric and working patterns in buttonhole stitch over the remaining threads.

● **RICHELIEU EMBROIDERY** A form of cutwork similar to Renaissance embroidery; the main difference is the addition of picots to the buttonhole bars which join parts of the design.

● **ROCAILLES** Trade names for transparent beads used in embroidery. They are divided into three groups: round rocailles, or seed beads, are round with round holes; toscas are square rocailles with square holes but are rounded outside; charlottes are faceted on the outside.

● **ROULEAU** A thin fabric tube made by stitching together the long edges of a strip of material and turning it inside out to conceal the raw edges. Used, for example, for button loops.

● **SAMPLER** A piece of embroidery originally worked by an adult needlewoman as a directory of stitches, patterns and motifs, used as technical reference. Samplers later became needlework exercises carried out by school children for practice in different stitching techniques.

● **SEEDING** Small embroidery stitches worked in a random, all-over way to fill an area, or worked gradually to soften an edge.

● **SELVAGE** The non-fray tightly-woven edge of fabric that runs down each side parallel with the warp.

● **SEQUIN** Small flat shiny disc used to add brilliance and glitter to fabrics or embroidery, and available in various metallic finishes and colors. The usual type is round with a central hole for stitching; other commonly found shapes include stars, leaves, flowers and ovals.

● **SHADOW EMBROIDERY** A type of embroidery worked on a semi-transparent fabric.

● **SHISHA EMBROIDERY** A traditonal embroidery technique using tiny mirrors, which originated in India.

● **SLATE FRAME** A wooden frame consisting of two rollers with webbing attached and two side pieces with slots at the ends to take the rollers. The side pieces have a series of holes in which pegs or screws can be inserted and adjusted to give the right amount of tension to the fabric.

● **SLIPS** Traditionally, an embroidered motif showing a flower with stem and foliage and with a small piece of root attached. Ready worked slips can be cut out and applied separately to a ground fabric.

● **SMOCKING** Evenly spaced gathers in a piece of fabric which are held in place by ornamental stitching.

● **SOFT EMBROIDERY COTTON** A tightly twisted 5-ply thread, fairly thick and with a matt finish, used as a single thread.

● **SPANGLE** See **SEQUIN**

● **SPOT SAMPLER** A sampler exhibiting motifs placed haphazardly over the fabric, simply to show off a wide range of stitches and techniques.

● **STILETTO** A very sharp pointed tool used in embroidery for making eyelets in broderie anglaise, cutwork and eyelet embroidery. It may also be used in metal thread work of making holes in the ground fabric through which the ends of heavy threads are taken to the back.

● **STRANDED COTTON** A loosely twisted, slightly shiny, six-strand cotton thread. For fine embroidery, the threads can be separated and used in twos or threes.

● **STRANDED SILK** A pure silk thread similar to stranded floss but with a more lustrous finish.

● **STRETCHER** A wood frame of fixed proportions on which a ground fabric is stretched while the embroidery is worked. It can also be used as the framework for mounting a finished embroidery.

● **STUMPWORK** A highly raised and padded form of appliqué popular in the seventeenth century, which has the appearance of a low relief carving.

● **TAILOR'S CHALK** Chalk used to mark stitching lines on fabric, which brushes out without leaving a mark.

● **TAILOR'S TACKS (BASTES)** Loose stitches used to mark a titching line and removed once the sewing is completed.

● **TAMBOUR WORK** Type of embroidery worked in a frame with a tambour hook. The designs are worked in continuous lines of chain stitch. It is often associated with whitework embroidery.

● **TAPESTRY NEEDLE** A long thick needle with a blunt tip and a large eye.

● **TAPESTRY YARN** A twisted four-ply wool with hard-wearing properties, mainly used in needlepoint.

● **TENSION** The tightness or slackness of a stitch. On a sewing machine it is important to keep the tension between the upper and lower threads balanced so that the stitching lies flat.

● **TOPSTITCHING** A row of straight stitching worked on the right side of the fabric.

● **TRAMMING** The preparation of double thread canvas, before the decorative stitching is begun, to make the stitched surface hard-wearing. Horizontal straight stitches are worked between the double canvas threads, using colors that match the design. Tramming fills out the stitch that is worked over it and also helps to cover the canvas ground.

● **VANISHING MUSLIN** Stiffened, treated muslin used as a backing or support for some hand and machine embroidery. The stitching is done through both layers and the surplus muslin vanishes when pressed with a warm iron.

● **VOIDING** Part of the design where the unworked areas define the pattern and the background fabric shows through. The technique is, in effect, similar to stencilling.

● **WADDING** A padding made from cotton, wool or synthetic fibers. Usually 3 feet (90cm) wide, it comes in these thicknesses and is used in quilting, upholstery etc.

● **WARP** The threads in a woven fabric that run lengthwise on the weaving loom.

● **WAXED THREAD** A thread which has been strengthened by rubbing it against a block of beeswax.

● **WEFT** The threads running across the width of a woven fabric that are interwoven with the warp threads.

● **WHIPPING** A term used in embroidery to describe the method of passing a second thread over and under a simple line stitch to give a raised effect.

● **WHITEWORK** A term referring to all types of embroidery which may be worked in white threads on white fabric. They include cutwork, drawn thread work, pulled fabric work.

● **WINDOW TEMPLATE** A patchwork template with the centre cut out so that the outer edge gives the shape for cutting the fabric piece and the inner edge provides the shape for the backing paper.

A

abstract themes, 283, *283*, 284, 285
 see also modern design
Afghan patchwork, *263*
Aida fabric, 128
Album quilt, *239*
Algerian eye stitch, 195, 218
Algerian filling stitch, 196, *196*
alphabets *see* lettering
altering:
  paper patterns, 13
alternate cross stitch, *136, 139*, 204, *204*
American embroidery, *96*
American patchwork, 256–7, *257*
American patchwork techniques, 258, 266–7
American quilting, 227, 228, 271, 274, *274*, 305
  Amish, 272
American samplers, *9, 73, 127*, 160, 162, 163
American stumpwork, 317
Amish quilts, 272
amorini, 160
  see also motifs
applied patchwork, 258
appliqué, 8, 228, 294, 295–305, *296*, 298–9, 301, *304*, 306–7, *307–8*, 310, *310–5*, 312–13, 316–20, *317–23*, 322–4, *325–6*, 326
  cut-through method, 313
  finishing, 326, *326*
  folded, 294, 320, *320–1*
  Indian, *321*
  inlaid, 313, *313*
  lace, 294, *324, 325*
  machine, 301
  padded, 8, *117*, 294, 314, *314–5*, 319
  perse, 294, 310, *310*
  picture, 294, 306–7, *307–8*
  reverse, 294, 312–13, *312–13*
  San Blas, *313*
  shadow, 294, 322–3, *322–3*
  standard, 294, 304
  stumpwork, 8, 316–19, *317–19*
  Thai, *297*
appliqué blocks, 304
appliqué design, 298, 304, 306, 310, 316–17, 320, 322–3
appliqué fabrics, 294, 296, 304, 312, 316, 318, 322, 324
appliqué motifs, 294, 310, *311*, 314, *314, 315*, 316, 320
appliqué perse, 294, 310, *310*
appliqué pictures, 320, *322*
appliqué quilts, 305, 310, *315*
  framed, 310
appliqué stitches, *300*, 301
appliqué techniques, 298–9, *298–300*, 301, 313, *313*, 316–17, 318–19, 320, 322, 324
  canvaswork slips, 319, *319*
  felt padding, 319
  kapa lau, 320, *321*
  wired shapes, 319
appliqué templates, 298, *298*
appliqué threads, 296
architectural forms, *132*, 177, *177*
  see also shapes and forms
Assisi work, *73*
Astrakhan stitch *see* velvet stitch
attachments:
  for sewing machines, 18
Aubusson stitch *see* rep stitch
automatic sewing machines, 15
automatic stitches, 122
Ayrshire embroidery, 104, *105*

B

backstitch, 20, *20*, 72, 82–3, *82, 140, 143*, 238
bags, *190, 296, 312, 314*
  quilted, 40, *40*, 229
balance wheels, 17, *17*
  see also sewing machines
balloon satin stitch, 202, *202*
ballpoint pins, 12
banners *see* flags and banners
bar tacks, 22, *22*
bars, 108
  overcast, *106*
  woven, *106*
basic stitches, 72–5, *72–5*
basic zigzag sewing machines, 14, 120
basket stitch, *136, 138*
basketweave *see* diagonal tent stitch
basketwork, *118*
  see also metal thread embroidery
basting 20, *20*, 134, *135*
Bayeux Tapestry, *90*, 91
beading needles, 60
bed covers, *7, 226, 227, 232, 259, 262*
  see also quilts
bed hangings, *36, 91, 93*, 133
belts, *220, 249*
Berlin plush stitch *see* velvet stitch
Berlin woolwork, *126, 180, 181*
betweens, 12
  see also needles
bias binding *see* binding
biblical motifs, 316, *317*
Bicentennial friendship quilt, 274, *274*
Binca fabric, 128
binding, 13, 40–1, *40–1*, 252, *252*
  bias strips, 40, *40*
  double, 40–1, *40–1*
  flat finish, 41, *41*
  single, 40, *40*, 41
  temporary, 64
  see also finishing
binding feet, 18
binding, 13, 40–1, *40–1*, 252, *252*
  see also sewing machines
blackwork, 98, *89–103*, 101–2
  see also embroidery
blackwork design, 98, 101, *101*
blackwork stitches, 102, *102*
blanket stitch, 21, 21, 72–3, *72*, 301
blind stitch, 22, *22*
blind-stitched hems, 38, *38*
block corners, 291
block shading, 94, 97
blocking, 222, *222*
blouses, *312*
bobbin cases, 17
  see also sewing machines
bobblin lace, *7*
bobbin winders, 17, *17*
  see also sewing machines
bobbins, 17
  see also sewing machines
bodkins, 13
  see also needles
Bokhara couching, 82, *82*
bonnets, 104, *105*
  see also clothing
bordered edges, 252, *253*
  see also finishing
borders, 130–2, *131*, 160, 165–6, *165–6*, 220–1, *220–1, 234*, 235–6, 290, *290, 319*
Bouclé wool, 56
bound buttonholes, 44, 45–6, *45–6*
bound openings, 51, *51*
Bourdon cord, 56
box pleats, 37, *37*
boxers, 160, 161
  see also motifs
braided cross stitch, *221*
brick stitch, 196–7, *197*, 198, *198*

brides quilts *see* marriage quilts
broad chain stitch, 79, *79*
broad cross stitch, 205, *205*
broad diagonal cross stitch, 204, *205*
broderie anglaise, 104, *107*
bullion knots, 80, *80*, 108
button loops, 44, 46, *46*
  see also fastenings
button quilting, 239, *239*
buttoned openings, 44–7, *44–7*
  see also fastenings
buttonhole insertion stitch, *30*
buttonhole stitch, 21, *21*, 73, *73*
buttonhole twist, 12
  see also threads
buttonholes, 44–6, *44–6*
  bound, 44, 45–6, *45–6*
  hand-worked, 44, 45, *45*
  horizontal, 44
  machine-worked, 44, 45, *45*
  vertical, 44
buttons, 44, 46–7
  Dorset wheel, *47*
  see also fastenings
Byzantine stitch, 194, 201, *201*

C

cable stitch, 115
canvas, *126, 128, 138*, 182, *183*, 185
  see also fabrics
canvas fern stitch, 204, *204*
canvas gauges, 182
canvas herringbone stitch, 204, *204*
canvas stretcher, *184*
canvaswork, 8, 126, 180, *189–5*, 182–3, 185–7, *187–90*, 189–90, 192, *192–223*, 194–210, 212–18, 220–3
  see also embroidery
canvaswork design, 186–7, *187–9*, 189
canvaswork samplers, 187, *187*, 188
canvaswork slips, 319, *319*
  see also appliqué techniques
canvaswork stitches, 194–210, *194–219*, 212–18
canvaswork techniques, 192, *193*
captive rice stitch, 215, *215*
carbon paper, 13, 134, *232, 233*
Carrickmacross work , 104, *104*
Cashmere stitch, 199, *199*
cathedral window patchwork *see* Mayflower patchwork
centering, 64, 84
  see also techniques
chain stitch, 74, *74*
chained cross stitch, 210, *210*
chained stitches, 78–9, *79*, 301
chairs, *181, 223*
chalk pencils, 13
channel seams, 29, *29*
charts, 134–5, 163
  see also design
chenille needles, 60, 92, *92*, 128
checker stitch, 194
chessboard filling stitch, 197, *197*
chevron stitch, 78, *78*, 114, *114*, 115
children's clothing, *6, 302, 303*, 324
Chinese embroidery, *54, 75*, 126
Chinoiserie, 317
Christie, A H, 186
circular couching stitch, *118*
circular hems, 39, *39*
clamshell patchwork *see* shell patchwork
Clay, Mary, *105*
clipping:
  seams, 33, *33*
closed herringbone stitch, *145, 147*
clothing, *105*, 294
  blouses, *312*
  bonnets, 104, *105*
  children's, *6, 302, 303*, 324
  cuffs, *51*

dresses, 98
dungarees, *6*
ecclesiastical, 116, *116*, 117
folk costumes, 47, *47*
hats, *119*
jackets, *49, 115, 303*
mittens, *54*
necklines, 50, *50, 51*
personal touches, *6, 168–70, 170*
quilted, 234
shirts, *9, 98, 131*
sleeves, *99*
smocks, 112, *113*, 115
uniforms, *119*
waistbands, 13
waistcoats, *104, 236*, 224–5, 252
cloud filling stitch, 81, *81*
coil filling stitch, 111
Colby, Averil, 160
colors, *180*, 187
  choice of, 163, 241
  of fabrics, 58, 128, *129*, 182
  of patchwork, 271, 274, 281, 289
  of wools, 183
commercially produced designs, 84
common-weave fabrics 128, *138*
composite stitches, 82–3, *82–3*
computerized sewing machines, 16, 17
concealed zippers, 42, 43, *43*
contemporary design *see* modern design
continental tent stitch, 194
contour darts, 34, *34*
  see also shaping techniques
controls:
  sewing machines, 16–17, *16–17*
coral stitch, 81, *81*
corded quilting, 8, 248–9, *248–9*
corded seams, 32, *32*
Cordonnet threads, 56
cords, 47, *47*, 56
  Bourdon, 56
  quilting, 230
  rat tail, 56
corner seams, 27–8, *27–8*
corners:
  appliqué, 299, *299*
  block, 291
  in designs, 86, 165, 166
  machine stitching, 19
  mitered, 39, *39*, 221, *221*, 291
  on hems, 39, *39*
  patchwork, 267, 291
  straight, 291
  see also curves
coton à broder, 56, 128, *128*
  see also threads
coton perlé threads, *see* pearl cotton
cotton canvas *see* canvas
cotton drill, *113*
cotton fabrics, *24, 113, 128, 128*
cotton-wrapped polyester threads, 12, 16
  see also threads
couched filling stitch, 82, *82*, 319
couching stitches, 82–3, *82–3, 97, 107, 118*, 119, *119*, 301
counted thread embroidery, 98, 128
Country Wife appliqué, 195
craft work, *297, 299, 312*, 313, 320, *320–1*
Crazy Log patchwork, 281, *281*
crazy patchwork, 258, *258*, 278–9, *279*
Cretan stitch, 77, *77*, 108, *114*
crewel embroidery, *7*, 90–4, 91–4, 96–7, 97
crewel embroidery design, 93, *93*
crewel needles, 60, 92, *92*, 128
crewel stitches, 94, 94, 97, 97
crewel wool, 56, 92, *92*, 182–3, *182*
criss-cross stitch, 217, *217*
Crompton, Rebecca, *123*
cross stitch design, 126–7, *126–7*, 130–2, *130–3*
cross stitch embroidery, 126–32,

126–55, 134–7, *157–9*
cross stitch plus two, 204, *204*
cross stitches, *73, 74*, 74, 136–7, *136–43, 152, 154*, 180, 194, 195, 204–10, *204–18*, 212–18, 221
crossed Gobelin stitch, 207, *207*
crossed seams, 26, *26*
Cube appliqué, *304*
cuffs, *51*
curved darts, 34, *34*
  see also shaping techniques
curved designs, 86, *86*
curved seams, 27, *27*
curves:
  appliqué, 298, 299, *299*
  machine stitching, 19, *19*
  see also corners
cushion stitch, 194
cushions, 30, *71, 71, 181, 187–90*, *240, 243*, 250–1, 253, 286, 310, *310*
  zipped openings, 44, *44*, 71
  see also soft furnishings
cut-through method, 313
  see also appliqué
cutwork, 104, 108, *109*
  machine, *108*
  Renaissance, 108
  reticella, *106*, 108
  Richelieu, 108, *109*
  see also embroidery
cutwork stitches, 108
cutwork techniques, 108
czar stitch *see* oblong cross stitch

D

darning stitch, *9*
darts, 34, *34*
  see also shaping techniques
decoration *see* design
  personal touches
decorative seams, 29–30, *29–30*
deep darts, 34, *34*
  see also shaping techniques
design, 6
  and photographs, 88, *88, 236*, 306
  appliqué, 298, 304, 306, 310, 316–17, 320, 322–3
  architectural forms, *132*, 177, *177*
  blackwork, 98, 101, *101*
  canvaswork, 186–7, *187–9*, 189
  charts, 134–5, 163
  commercial, 84
  corners in, 86, 165, 166
  crewel, 93, *93*
  cross stitch, 126–7, *126–7*, 130–2, *130–3*
  curved, 86, *86*
  drawn thread, 104, 110, *110*
  Eastern, *91, 91, 119, 240, 321*
  enlarging, 86, *86*, 134
  floral, 186–7, *187*
  Florentine, *188, 189, 190*
  geometric, *188, 189, 190*
  graphs, 134–5, 163
  interlaced, 249, *249*
  lozenge, 189
  mistakes in, 65
  William Morris, 93
  numerals, 160, 166
  patchwork, 261–2, *261–3*, 278, 282–3, 284
  petit fleur, 188
  pictorial, 186–7, *247*
  Pomegranate, 189
  pricking and pouncing, 85
  quilting, 234–6, *234–7*, 244–5, 246, 248
  reducing, 86, *86*, 134
  ribbon, 189
  samplers, 160, *160*, 162–3, *162–4*
  shapes and forms, 86, *87*, 88, *132*, 177, *177*
  transfers, 84, *85*, 134–5, *134*, 192,